THE MODERN SIOUX

The Modern Sioux

Social Systems and Reservation Culture

Edited by

ETHEL NURGE

UNIVERSITY OF NEBRASKA PRESS · LINCOLN

Publishers on the Plains
UNP

Manufactured in the United States of America

Contents

Preface

THIS BOOK HAD its origin at a meeting of the Central States Anthropological Association in Detroit early in 1963, when Professor Ruth Hill Useem and I talked of the many anthropologists who had worked on the Teton Dakota reservations but who had, for various reasons, never published their data. We discussed the possibility of determining the kinds of field notes and manuscripts extant and the possibilities of collecting them in a volume dedicated to and focused on the Teton Dakotas. Since we wished to do more than merely compile existing pieces, we also considered an integrative theme around which we might organize the material. Early in 1964, Mrs. Useem and I sent questionnaires to thirty-one people who we knew or had reason to believe had carried out field work on the Rosebud or Pine Ridge reservations. Informing them that if the available materials justified it, we were interested in compiling a book of essays on the Teton Dakota reservation culture, we asked about the nature of their work and the kind and amount of material they had in field notes, and requested a list of their articles or books in print.

In November, 1964, at the American Anthropological Association meeting in Detroit, Dr. Useem presided at a symposium on reservation culture. The material presented was mainly on the Teton Dakotas—not by coincidence, but by a plan worked out by Dr. Useem and me, and with the cooperation of the participants, Gordon Macgregor, Robert Thomas, and Rosalie and Murray Wax. James A. Clifton, James Officer, Philleo Nash, Alice Kehoe, and John Provinse were discussants. Attendance at this session was particularly good and the discussion was spirited.

Meanwhile, the responses to our questionnaires were arriving, and they showed that there was indeed reason to believe that a volume with a fresh perspective on the Dakotas was possible. Thus encouraged, in December, 1964, Mrs. Useem and I submitted a proposal to the Wenner-Gren Foundation for Anthropological Research, requesting funds to bring together a number of people who had had field experience among the Dakotas. By airing our various and divergent viewpoints, we hoped to develop a framework within which to discuss the status of the present-day Dakotas in their several locations, on reservations and in cities. The hypotheses to be developed centered on the nature of a derived culture—that culture which has emerged as a result of the meeting and commingling of the native Americans, the Dakotas, with the contact group, the European immigrants. Considered in the light of a century of interaction, first in war and later in "peace," the hypotheses would be suitable for testing in other cases in the United States as well as more broadly elsewhere. We anticipated that our method of study and findings would have relevance to many other studies in culture change, the dynamics of societal interrelations, community development, and programs such as the war on poverty, or whatever the current name for similar societal evolution may be.

Financial support was granted, and in March, 1965, in Chicago, we held a Conference to Explore a Theoretical Framework for the Study of the Modern Dakota. The official participants in the conference included Miss Ella Deloria, Professor William O. Farber, Mrs. Beatrice Medicine Garner, Dr. Alice Kehoe, Mr. Luis Kemnitzer, Dr. Gordon Macgregor, Professor Ernest Schusky, Professor Murray Wax, Father Robert A. White, S.J., Mrs. Useem, and myself. Also attending were Professor Sol Tax, who welcomed the group and participated in several sessions; Mr. Stephen Feraca; Dr. Thomas Kehoe, who was present at several sessions; and four students: Robert Daniels, Paul DeVore, and Raymond DeMallie, from the University of Chicago, and Gordon Northrup, from Michigan State University.

The aim of the conference was only partially realized. Although we did not devise a theoretical framework, we found many concepts and issues stimulating and provocative, and we did contribute the writings which are the substance of this book. Most of the papers which are presented here were prepared for the conference, and only one—that by W. K. Powers—is not by a conferee. Some of the papers have been revised; more were not. All have been edited by me and reviewed by the author after editing. Although the original plan was that Mrs.

Useem and I should jointly prepare the volume for publication, the pressure of her duties was such that she could not undertake this additional work, and I accordingly assumed full editorial responsibility. I wish to express my debt to Mrs. Useem. It was her vigor, warmth, and enthusiasm that sparked the conference and inspired the conferees to the fruitful discussion we enjoyed. Preparation of the papers for publication took two years. It is perhaps not surprising that a major collection of this nature should have been so long in appearing, but let us hope that it is only the first in a series.

The writings included here are valuable in several respects. To my knowledge, this is the first volume containing contributions from many authors to be devoted to a single tribe or Indian group, the Dakotas, or Sioux. Indeed, initially we had thought to confine our study to two reservations, Pine Ridge and Rosebud, but some excellent materials on other groups (Schusky on the Brules and Alice Kehoe on the Saskatchewan Dakotas) were suggested and found to be illuminating. Furthermore, while these studies are largely focused on the Dakotas, their import is much more far-reaching. Much of the Sioux experience is characteristic of other American Indian groups as well. The problems which have arisen and the solutions which have been attempted at Pine Ridge, Rosebud, Lower Brule, or Yankton have been repeated on many reservations. The question arises whether we may not legitimately speak of a reservation culture. Is there not a concatenation of thought, orientation, action, and behavior which is the result of reservation influences? Thus, many of the selections in this book deal with what may validly be called reservation culture, while others deal with the effects of reservation culture on those who leave the reservation and migrate to the cities.

Part I, "Social Systems and Reservation Culture," opens with Ruth Hill Useem and Carl K. Eicher's "Rosebud Reservation Economy," which provides background and baseline data, particularly with reference to the economy. My "Dakota Diet: Traditional and Contemporary" contains detailed information about the precontact diet and tells what changes have come about in food procurement and consumption. "Changing Society: The Teton Dakotas," by Gordon Macgregor, illuminates the relations among various governmental agencies and local Indian communities; and Ernest L. Schusky, in "Culture Change and Continuity in the Lower Brule Community," demonstrates how culture change may ensure continuity. The complexity of political organization and especially the difficulty of inaugurating representative government is treated in further detail by William O. Farber in "Representative Government: Application to the Sioux." Certain similarities in the organization and effect of missionaries and the Bureau of Indian Affairs are noted by Schusky in "Political and Religious Systems in Dakota Culture." Alice B. Kehoe's "The Dakotas in Saskatchewan" provides us with a rare opportunity to compare the Dakotas as they have fared under a different cultural system in Canada.

In "The Lower-Class 'Culture of Excitement' Among the Contemporary Sioux," the first selection of Part II, Robert A. White, S.J., makes the point that reservation culture is giving way to a Dakota Indian version of the American culture of the lower class. Robert E. Daniels explores the complexities of self-identification in "Cultural Identities among the Oglala Sioux," and a related focus but a different approach is given to a study of the same phenomenon by Luis S. Kemnitzer in "Familial and Extra-familial Socialization in Urban Dakota Adolescents." In William K. Powers's "Contemporary Oglala Music and Dance: Pan-Indianism versus Pan-Tetonism," a discussion of the traits and behavior associated with music and dance illuminates changes.

Three maps supplement the essays. The first, titled "Sioux Territory, 1680–1963," is adapted by permission of the author, Royal B. Hassrick, and the University of Oklahoma Press from *The Sioux: Life and Customs of a Warrior Society* (1964). While the present volume contains little material on the Dakotas before 1940, there are nonetheless many references to Sioux locations, migrations, neighbors, allies, and enemies; and Hassrick's map should help the reader in locating places and people. The second map shows Sioux and neighboring reservations in the United States and Canada. Designed to orient the reader and the interested traveler, it includes state and province boundaries and interstate highways. The third map presents schematically the population of the Sioux reserves and reservations in 1962. Further information on the sources and compilation of the maps appears in Appendix I.

Appendix II contains information about materials which are difficult to find and whose existence is all too often known only to a few: unpublished source materials. This appendix was derived from letters and responses to a questionnaire sent to people who had worked among the Dakotas and from correspondence with officials of the Bureau of Indian Affairs. Appendix III, which grew out of the search for unpublished material, stands alone because of its length and substance. It includes manuscripts relating to the Sioux which can be found in the archives of many institutions.

The present study is not an attempt at ethnography; the selections do not give a description of the traditional divisions of society such as is found in standard ethnographical monographs. There is no straightforward listing of subsistence, housing, diet, political organization, religion, and social change. Yet all of these customary aspects of social organization are touched upon by some of the authors, and indeed these papers contain source material on matters of time-honored interest such as those listed above and also on some contemporary and emergent interests, such as personality formation, social adaptation, and cultural identity.

There remain many areas where additional research into the nature of reservation culture will be helpful. To begin with, much can be learned from the geography of reservations: their location, topography, soil, mineral content, flora, and fauna. I have recently been introduced into the wonders of stereoscopic analysis of aerial photographs and believe that comparative stereoscopic analyses of many reservations would yield sound generalizations about the ecological limitations on reservation inhabitants. That special kind of analysis aside, I wish that the present volume had a study delineating the relationships among land base, natural resources, subsistence techniques, and man. Again, I suspect that the generalizations we would be able to make for the Sioux would hold true for many other reservation Indians as well. A good demographic study would also be useful. As the reader will see upon referring to Appendix I, we lack even the wherewithal to compile accurate population figures. The problems of determining who is an "Indian" and how the census takers may collect ethnic data while protecting the privacy of citizens are vexing. Not only population figures but also birth statistics and rates of morbidity and mortality should be collected and published.

Alcohol and drug addiction are not touched upon herein except in passing, and with our current interest in these problems and developing techniques to tackle them, a study of them would be welcome. Clothing as protection from the elements and as an indicator of social status is yet another subject on which we could use more data. Strikingly absent from the present volume is a kinship study—a study on the family per se as it functions today. These, then, are some of the areas of challenge and opportunity for further field work among and description of the Dakotas.

In discussions, correspondence, and the writing and editing of the essays in this book, a continuing problem has been how to designate the people we are talking about. "Sioux" is the term most commonly used; "Dakota" is preferred by some. The Indians traditionally and the anthropologists earlier have referred to the tribe as a whole as the Dakotas. Within the tribe there are subdivisions which reflect both linguistic and cultural differences, and they give rise to other designations which will concern us later. The majority of readers know the tribe as "Sioux," but this designation is resented by some Dakotas, for there are sophisticates among them who know that etymologically the term "Sioux" is derived from the Ojibwa language and means "snakes" or "enemies." A further complication comes with the term "Siouan," which is the linguistic stock to which the Dakota language belongs, but which is sometimes incorrectly used as an adjectival form of "Sioux." In this book, my policy has been to abide by the author's usage, avoiding only the barbarism "Siouan." "Sioux" is too well established to be wished away by purists or by those with the best of intentions. In this book, also, I abide by the wish of the University of Nebraska Press to pluralize tribal names by adding an *s*.

The Dakota, or Sioux, peoples originated east of where they are now found. When they first came in contact with the white man in the seventeenth century, the Dakotas were west of the Great Lakes in territory which is now the southern two-thirds of the state of Minnesota with adjoining areas in present-day Iowa and Wisconsin. Hunting, fishing, collecting, and the harvesting of wild rice were supplemented by limited slash-and-burn horticulture. With the acquisition and increasing use of the horse, and because of the pressure of enemies (Ojibwas and other Indians, and whites), as well as for other reasons of lesser import, the various bands which were the Sioux moved slowly westward. By 1750 the westernmost groups had begun to cross the Missouri and to filter into the Black Hills of present western South Dakota. Readers interested in some detail about the origin and early migrations of the Dakota should see Howard (1960 and 1966).

While the Dakotas were in their more easterly homeland, they were divided into the following seven bands, or council fires:

1) *Mdewakantonwan*, "Spirit Lake People" (referring to Mille Lacs Lake in Minnesota)
2) *Wahpekute*, "Shooters among the Leaves"
3) *Sisitonwan*, or Sisseton, "People of the Ridged Fish Scales(?)"

4) *Wahpetonwan*, or Wahpeton, "Dwellers among the Leaves"
5) *Ihanktonwan*, or Yankton, "Dwellers at the End (Village)"
6) *Ihanktonwana*, or Yanktonai, "Little Dwellers at the End"
7) *Titonwan*, or Teton, "Dwellers on the Plains"
     (Howard 1966, p. 3, and personal communication)

As the bands moved westward and settlement and land-use patterns began to stabilize, dialectical differences developed and the tribe split into three recognizable divisions. The first four bands listed above came to be known as the Santee division, or Eastern Dakotas; the fifth and sixth as the Middle Dakotas; and the last, the Tetons, as the Western Dakotas (Howard 1966, p. 3). Dakota is the name of the dialect spoken by the Santee, or Eastern, division, while the Middle bands speak Nakota. The dialect of the Tetons is Lakota.

Formerly the Santees more closely resembled the Central Algonquian tribes in several particulars such as being less reliant on bison and having adopted corn cultivation early (Howard 1966, pp. 4–5). Although the Santees consider themselves the oldest or original Dakotas, only a few still reside in the ancestral region of Minnesota and the eastern Dakotas. A strike at the settlers in 1862, known as the Minnesota Uprising, brought retaliation from United States forces. When the troops had quelled the trouble, some Santees sought refuge in Canada; others were placed on reservations. Today they are found in Minnesota, Nebraska, Montana, Manitoba, and Saskatchewan. Howard (1966, p. 10, and personal communication) locates them as follows:

Mdewakantonwan or Mdewakanton (Spirit Lake Village). On the Lower Sioux Reservation, near Morton, Minnesota; Upper Sioux Indian Commission, near Granite Falls, Minnesota; Prairie Island Settlement, near Red Wing, Minnesota, and Prior Lake Reservation, Minnesota; Flandreau Reservation, South Dakota; Santee Reservation, Nebraska; and in Canada on the Oak River Reserve No. 58, near Griswold, Manitoba.

Wahpekute (Shooters among the Leaves). Santee Reservation, Nebraska; Fort Peck Reservation, Montana; in Canada on Oak River Reserve, No. 58, Manitoba; Oak Lake Reserve, No. 59, near Pipestone, Manitoba; Wahpeton Reserve, No. 94a, Carlton Agency, near Prince Albert, Saskatchewan.

Wahpetonwan or Wahpeton (Dwellers among the Leaves). Devils Lake (Fort Totten) Reservation, North Dakota; Flandreau Reservation, South Dakota; Sisseton (Lake Traverse) Reservation, South Dakota. In Canada on Bird Tail Reserve, No. 57, Birtle Agency, near Russell, Manitoba; Oak River Reserve, No. 58, Manitoba; Portage La Prairie (Sioux Village), No. 8a, near Portage La Prairie, Manitoba (*Wiyakotidan Wahpeton*); Oak Lake

Reserve, No. 59, Manitoba; Standing Buffalo Reserve, No. 78, Qu'appelle Agency, near Ft. Qu'appelle, Saskatchewan; and Wahpeton Reserve, No. 94a, Saskatchewan.

Sisitonwan or Sisseton (People of the Ridged Fish Scales). Sisseton Reservation, South Dakota; Devils Lake Reservation, North Dakota; Upper Sioux Indian Commission, Minnesota. In Canada on Oak River Reserve, No. 58, Manitoba; Moose Woods Reserve, No. 94, Duck Lake Agency, near Dundurn, Saskatchewan (*Cankute* Sisseton); Standing Buffalo Reserve, No. 78, Saskatchewan; and Wahpeton Reserve, No. 94a, Saskatchewan.

The Middle Dakotas (Yankton and Yanktonai) were noted in the Mankato area of the Minnesota River in the late 1700s. As they moved west they adopted traits from Missouri River peoples such as the Mandans, Hidatsas, Arikaras, and Poncas, and "by the beginning of the reservation era both Yankton and Yanktonai bands had approximated many of the cultural patterns of the riverine tribes to a remarkable degree" (Howard 1966, p. 1). At present the Yanktons are living on the Yankton Reservation in South Dakota and also in the surrounding white communities. The Yanktonais are more widely dispersed. Howard writes (1966, p. 9):

> The Ihanktonwana proper or Upper Yanktonai are located on the Standing Rock Reservation, North and South Dakota, North Dakota portion; Devil's Lake Reservation, North Dakota (*Pabaksa* or Cut-heads sub-band). In Canada a few are found on the Oak Lake Reserve, No. 59, near Pipestone, Manitoba. The *Hunkpatina* or Lower Yanktonai (Campers-at-the-horn, or End of Camping Circle) are found on the Crow Creek Reservation, South Dakota, and on the Fort Peck Reservation, Montana.

The Teton, or Western, Dakotas were originally a single band, or council fire, but after their migration onto the High Plains their population became greater than that of all the other bands combined. Their adaptation to the High Plains was exceptionally successful and their history is the most dramatic of all of the Dakotas, including as it does Crazy Horse, Sitting Bull, and the Custer battle. At present the seven Teton sub-bands are located as follows:

> *Hunkpapa* (Campers-at-the-Horn or End of the Camp Circle). Standing Rock Reservation, North and South Dakota, both portions; also a few on the Fort Peck Reservation, Montana; in Canada on the Wood Mountain Reserve, No. 160, Saskatchewan (also called Moose Jaw Sioux).

> *Minneconjou* (Planters-beside-the-Water). Cheyenne River Reservation, South Dakota.

Sihasapa or Blackfoot. Cheyenne River Reservation, South Dakota; Standing Rock Reservation, North and South Dakota, both portions.

Oohenonpa or Two-Kettle. Cheyenne River Reservation, South Dakota.

Brule (Burnt-Thighs). a) Highland people or Upper Brule: Rosebud Reservation, South Dakota; also several families on Pine Ridge Reservation, South Dakota. b) Lowland people or Lower Brule: Lower Brule Reservation, South Dakota.

Sansarcs (Those-without-Bows). Cheyenne River Reservation, South Dakota.

Oglala (They-Scatter-Their-Own). Pine Ridge Reservation, South Dakota; also a few in Milk's Camp Community, Rosebud Reservation, South Dakota.

(Adapted from Howard 1966, p. 6).

These, then, are the Dakotas, or Sioux. Let us proceed to some contemporary views of their problems and accomplishments. I hope that something of the excitement of the conference and the spirit of the discussions has carried through to quicken the reader's interest, and that he will find the essays informative and stimulating. Reactions, criticisms, and suggestions are invited.

ETHEL NURGE

REFERENCES

HOWARD, JAMES H. 1960. The cultural position of the Dakota: A reassessment. In *Essays in the science of culture*, ed. G. E. Dole and R. L. Carneiro. New York: Thomas Y. Crowell Co.
———. 1966. The Dakota or Sioux Indians. Part III: The Teton or Western Dakota. University of South Dakota *Museum News* 27, nos. 9–10: 1–6.

Part I

Social Systems and Reservation Culture

Rosebud Reservation Economy

Ruth Hill Useem and Carl K. Eicher

Introduction

Studies of culture contact, acculturation, and third-culture phenomena are of importance in an increasingly interdependent world characterized by the meetings of peoples with different loyalties, languages, cultural traditions, and political aspirations. Among other people in culture contact, the Teton Dakotas stand out in that they have been and continue to be one of the most documented ethnic groups in the history of social sciences. However, if one is of the persuasion that documentary knowledge, in addition to having value for its own sake, should have some positive contribution to make to the quality of life, either immediate or long-term, then one can only conclude that the mountains of scholarship have produced a molehill of improvement.

Periodically, sectors of the American public discover what the American Indian has intimately lived and experienced for decades: that American Indians, particularly reservation Indians, are poor. No matter what value system is invoked to assess reservation conditions, the picture is not a pretty one. The personal and social demoralization expressed in unemployment, apathy, violence, drunkenness, hostility, dependency, illness, and factionalism are painfully apparent to the Indians themselves. With each rediscovery by outsiders, fresh starts are made in the forms of legislation, programs, action projects, and calls

3

for research to "solve the Indian problem." New goals are set; time, money, and energy are enlisted for reaching them. These efforts have not been without effects, but the results, *in terms of goals*, have been embarrassingly short-lived and relatively sterile.

The most recent rediscovery of the circumstances of the reservation Indian has been in connection with the discovery of the "new poor" in the affluent America of the sixties. Whether the new flurry of activity which has been initiated will be the hoped-for "breakthrough" to bring dignity and meaning to these American citizens, or just another frustrating "happening" leading to even greater bitterness and distrust of whites, is problematical.

To gain some understanding of this complicated process, we should like to present some facts derived largely from two studies of the Rosebud Reservation of South Dakota, one made twenty years later than the first (Useem 1947; Eicher 1960). We shall let the facts speak for themselves and for the Indians, but we also shall try to conceptualize them in the framework of third-culture theory.

The First Culture—A Preliterate Society

The flowering of Teton Dakota Plains culture has been well documented elsewhere (Ewers 1938). Suffice it to say that in the early part of the nineteenth century, it was the Dakota man's work to hunt buffalo. Although prestige was given the successful hunter, the route to high status among males was the performance of brave deeds in warfare. The Dakotas went to war for any number of reasons—to gain territory, to protect hunting lands, to capture women, to steal horses. As Ewers has pointed out (1938, p. 46):

> The fact that glory was to be won in battle was itself a great encouragement and little further cause was necessary to send the Teton into battle against any wandering parties of the Pawnee, Crow or Shoshoni which they might meet.

But a society cannot be maintained by warfare; it must have logistical support, replacement of its warriors, ways of meeting its day-to-day problems. It was woman's work to convert the buffalo into their multiple uses; gather and preserve foodstuffs other than buffalo; erect, take down, and transport the tipi; care for the household articles; carry the water; bear and care for the young of both sexes; socialize the girls into adulthood; complement the male roles of hunting and fighting; and, one suspects, compliment the males.

Life was harsh but it had meaning for its members and there was a feeling that the hardships were challenges which could be met by individual and group acts of bravery and discipline. The first members of the second culture, the Western world, who came into contact with the Tetons were male fur traders. These westerners were easily incorporated and further added to the exciting life of the Tetons. As Howard has summarized this period (1966, p. 5):

> From the time the Teton entered the High Plains region until the closing decades of the 19th century they were rich in horses, buffalo robes, and trade goods. They had a tremendous *esprit de corps* and a flair for doing things in the grand manner. Poorer groups, such as the Middle Dakota, and especially the Santee, were scorned by the Teton, who often showed their contempt by bestowing costly gifts on their less-well-to-do tribesmen. Clearly, Teton culture of nineteenth century was a burgeoning thing. Even today, after several generations of squalid reservation life, the Teton possess an *hauteur* and at the same time an openness of character which distinguishes them from both the Middle and Eastern division of the tribe.

The memories of this golden-age past not only still linger in the minds of the Tetons but also have captured the imagination of generations of European and American men, women, and children. Scarcely recalled, however, is the price paid for such grand living—the squandering of the natural resource which was the basis of the society, the buffalo; and the ambivalent admiration and fear of other Indian groups and whites who do not fully trust them to this day.

Into this man-woman-land-buffalo-outsiders adjustment came, in the late 1840s, the immigrant trains of the westward-trekking whites. Their entrance upon the scene seriously threatened the buffalo herds, which had already been decimated by the fur trade. It is small wonder that a people who would fight just for the glory of fighting should fight cleverly and fiercely when their very existence was at stake. The Teton Dakotas were feared, and understandably so, by the whites attempting to cross or settle in the Teton area.

But the tide of white expansion could not be stopped by the Indians. No matter how many battles were won, more whites kept coming. Finally the United States troops were called out to protect white migrants and to lay claim to Teton territory. The fight for control over the area west of the Missouri River was on; intermittent and bitter warfare ensued. Although eventual defeat of the Dakotas was predictable, hunger accomplished expeditiously what the superior technology and larger numbers of the whites could not. As the buffalo dwindled down to nothing, hunger drove the Indian warriors into a humiliating capitulation and into a series of treaties with the United States government—treaties which were never completely understood because defeat itself and loss of a gratifying way of life were too painful to be comprehensible. Memories of this ignominious end to which a proud people came live on in the minds of the Tetons and are basic to an understanding of the Indian descendants' reaction to the children, grandchildren, and great-grandchildren of whites. Nor have the whites forgotten. For example, an economist and a clinical psychologist (Hagen and Schaw 1960, pp. 1–2) explicitly enunciated this living memory, which lies behind many of the programs set up to "solve the Indian problem," as the rationale for their recommendations in the following way: "We believe that the American government and the American public, *out of a sense of obligation to the people whose lands we have occupied, and out of a sense of our own dignity,* should foster the conditions which . . ." (italics ours).

These and other memories which underlie and tend to structure relationships between the direct descendants of members who carried the disparate cultures rest uneasily on the descendants of both groups, the mixed-bloods, who belong to both—and neither. But we are getting ahead of our story.

THE THIRD CULTURES

In 1868, the Tetons agreed to relinquish all claim to territory east of the Missouri River in return for the establishment of the Great Sioux Reservation, which included all of what is now western South Dakota. However, when gold was discovered in the Black Hills, the Indians' treaty rights to the lands were violated. Miners and prospectors rushed in after the Sioux had refused to grant rights of entrance. A series of further battles followed, with the Tetons ceding the Black Hills in 1876 (the white version; the Indian version differs more than slightly) and becoming "reservation" Indians. Mekeel (1943, p. 194) has summed up the purposes of this settlement as follows:

> The idea of the United States government in locating the Indians on reservations was to keep them under control in a restricted area. It was also hoped that the Indians could become civilized by enforcing the education of the children, by encouraging missionaries to Christianize them, by teaching them to farm and become self-supporting, by forcing white man's dress, and by consistently damning native institutions.

Since the initiation of reservation life, the federal government and the Teton Dakotas have been interlocked in an administrator-administered relationship characterized by policies which have appeared necessary, rational, and even humanitarian to the administrators but which have seemed vacillating, capricious, and deleterious to the administered. The prevailing policies can be used to distinguish various periods of interaction between the Dakotas and the dominant society, although in actuality periods merge imperceptibly. Although the policy gives a distinctive stamp to the overall relationship of a particular period, in no era are all spheres of interaction equally affected by the policy nor are all reactions to the policy homogeneous. There are varied reactions on the reservation and in the dominant society. These accumulate and are the subject of argument and hearings and then a new policy is precipitated. As policies change, each leaves a historical legacy to be dealt with in subsequent periods, just as the memories of the war relationship between independent nations are still alive. The "dead hand of history" operates through the hands and minds of the living descendants of the conquerors and the conquered as they act in terms of passed-on memories; make decisions within or against agreements, laws, and social structures which are the precipitates of previous periods; and attempt to construct their futures out of the conditions of the here and now.

The ultimate goals of both reservation Indians and the dominant population have been nearly identical from the beginning: 1) sufficient food, protection from the elements, and medical care to keep the individuals alive and producing viable offspring; 2) the proper distribution of power (economic, social, and political) so that both Indians and whites can survive together in the future; and 3) dignity and meaning to life. With respect to the substantive content of the goals and the means for achieving them among both whites and Indians, there have been wide disparities, open and covert conflict, frustration and hostility, misunderstanding and understanding, rejection and cooperation.

The first period of the continuum between the conquerors and the conquered was characterized by extensive rationing and free disbursement of food, clothing, and shelter. This was in line with the terms of the 1876 treaty and was in keeping with the needs which had led the Indians to capitulate—hunger, particularly the hunger of women and children. It took place in land areas of the Great Sioux Reservation where whites were denied entrance. Except for wars of extermination, every period of hostilities is followed by a period in which the victorious army of occupation has to meet the daily exigencies of the bodily needs of the survivors. By 1888, the federal government decided that extensive rationing was itself a factor in pauperizing the Indians and in retarding their adjustment to the dominant conception of life of that period, that each family should be self-supporting from the land; and rations were drastically curtailed.

In 1889, the Great Sioux Reservation was broken up and the Teton Dakotas settled on six smaller reservations—Standing Rock, Cheyenne River, Crow Creek, Lower Brule, Pine Ridge, and Rosebud. On Rosebud were placed the Sicangu Brules and some Two-Kettles. Settlement on these reservations followed the Dawes Allotment Act, which became law in 1887. It is not surprising that a dominant society which was largely agricultural in perspective should presume that "land hunger" could be satisfied in only one way, a self-subsistence, family-owned farm. Land in severalty instead of tribal ownership of common lands became the policy of the government for the Indians. During the allotment period, which extended up until the Indian Reorganization Act of 1934, much of the land assigned to the Dakotas on these smaller reservations was alienated and large portions became fractionalized holdings due to the operation of inheritance laws when Indians died intestate and land was divided equally among heirs. Individual ownership of land not only did not lead to self-dependence in emulation of the dominant population—the rationale of the Dawes Act—but actually became a major factor in preventing the establishment of a range economy, the only type of economy suitable for the area. It also contributed to the establishment of a landless mixed-blood grouping on the reservation.

The Indians were deprived, economically, socially, and culturally, and they became more dependent. Their former social organization, which centered around hunting and fighting, was impossible. Enforced social change, indirectly because of the loss of the buffalo and the hunting lands and directly by policies of the administrator, led to the partial loss of some traditions, the redefinition of traditional prereservation patterns, and the incorporation of some patterns of life of the dominant society, which altogether added up to the establishment of a new way of life indigenous to neither culture—a reservation culture, a colonial "third culture."

In 1928, the Meriam Report called attention to Indian conditions and set the stage for a change of policy. The new policy was implemented nationally during the depression when the United States found a third of a nation to be ill-housed, ill-clothed, and ill-fed. This third included all the Indian reservations. The national ideology was implemented for the Indian population by the Wheeler-Howard Act, commonly known as the Indian Reorganization Act (IRA) which was passed in 1934. It was an attempt to reverse fifty-year-old policies and bring a "new deal" to the reservation Indian. The main functions were 1) to restore to the Indian management of his individual assets (mostly land), and to the Indians collectively, management of tribal assets (mostly land); 2) to prevent further depletion of the reservation resources; 3) to build up a sound economic foundation for the reservation population; and 4) to return local self-government to Indian people on a tribal basis. The Bureau of Indian Affairs pursued the objectives with full vigor from 1934 to the beginning of World War II. Its manifest aim of strengthening tribalism and tribal control was more suitable to the Southwest, where factionalism between mixed-bloods and full-bloods had not proceeded as far as it had on Rosebud Reservation. On Rosebud, its impact was three-pronged: it strengthened the dependency way of life for full-bloods and furthered their isolation on the reservation; it pushed further the modernization of the mixed-bloods and precipitated their entrance into the larger society; it initiated change in the status of the reservation Indian from that of personal ward of the government to that of special citizen.

The breach brought about by the IRA in the all-encompassing colonial-like third culture through which all relationships between the groups had been funneled, through the Office of Indian Affairs, subsequently was widened by World War II, when off-reservation employment opportunities opened up and when many of the young men served in the armed forces. The pathways and connections between the reservation and the outside world were increasing. The multiplication of connections was made into a policy in 1953 when Congress passed House Concurrent Resolution 108 (83rd Congress, First Session), which set assimilation of Indians into the larger non-Indian society as an urgent and immediate goal. This new statement of policy called for speeding up the transfer of federal services from the Bureau of Indian Affairs to other federal agencies, to the state, and to tribal governments. Furthermore, Resolution 108 threatened complete termination of federal services to reservation Indians. In contrast to controlling the person, it aimed at Indian self-dependency, which, in the opinion of many, would come if social overhead services in the form of roads, schools, and other programs were implemented, the benefits from which could be activated by the Indians themselves. During this period, the full-bloods and mixed-bloods reacted differently to the social services rendered by the various agencies and institutions. One effect was the drawing off of a number of mixed-bloods into more or less permanent off-reservation residence, and some full-bloods experienced off-reservation living either directly or indirectly.

Some of those who have moved off are participating in a new social identity which has been called pan-Indianism. As tribals moved into centers of population and met members from other tribes, there was a heightened awareness of their having shared a common history of relationships with the dominant whites. At the same time, there has been a heightened sense of tribal identity as each group's unique history on one reservation confronts the unique history of other reservations. An additional factor is that maintaining an enrolled status on particular reservations entitles tribals to some special rights, either actual or potential, growing out of old treaties and in social services. Furthermore, the reservation has become not only a geographical symbol for social and cultural identity but also an actual base to which to return periodically and, in some cases, permanently.

The Rosebud "Indian problem" now has two dimensions: the Rosebuds who have moved off the reservation and are merging into an Indian-American ethnic group in the cities, and those who are resident on the reservation. The Indians are dispersed in a number of areas. If they are in metropolitan areas, their difficulties go largely unnoticed by the dominant population; their problems are similar to those but their numbers vastly overshadowed by those of the Negroes. Hence when Indians were rediscovered in the general "war on poverty," it was on the reservation that they were "found." Once again the Bureau of Indian Affairs was asked to draw up programs, reservation by reservation, to take advantage of the Office of Economic Opportunity's programs. But the nature of the relationship between the Bureau of Indian Affairs and the reservation is no longer the old one of the pre-1934 days. They cannot put a program directly into operation—negotiations are much more complex, power much more dispersed, and the structures of relationships between the various segments much more intricate. This is the broad outline of the relationship between the dominant population and the Rosebud reservation, which we would now like to spell out in detail.

THE RESERVATION ECONOMY: THE LABOR MARKET

To offset imperfections in the functioning of the reservation labor market, the Bureau of Indian Affairs and the State of South Dakota have provided five special services: extension service, industrial development, Employment Security Service, a relocation program, and adult vocational training service. The five kinds of services are subsumed under three broad classifications of employment thus:

1) Permanent reservation employment
   a) Extension service
   b) Industrial development
2) Seasonal employment on and off the reservation
   a) Employment Security Service
3) Permanent off-reservation employment available by out-migration
   a) Relocation program
   b) Adult Vocational Training Service

We shall isolate the imperfections and constraints, and analyze the effectiveness, of these services over the period 1940 to 1960.

Many Rosebud people place a premium on reservation living and employment despite the fact that permanent reservation job opportunities are very much restricted by the ecological and climatic conditions of a cattle economy. To aid such people the Bureau of Indian Affairs had established two special services in an effort to increase permanent reservation job opportunities. The first, an agricultural managerial training program, was carried on by BIA extension agents until 1954, with the primary aim being to train Indian people through intensive managerial assistance to cattle operators, and through home demonstration aid to women and 4-H clubs for children. After 1955, the South Dakota State Extension Service continued to render extension assistance at Rosebud. The second service to increase permanent reservation employment is the Bureau's Industrial Development Program, established on a national scale in 1955. The aim was to encourage industrial or commercial firms to locate plants on or adjacent to Indian reservations.

Another employment opportunity open to Rosebud people who want to live on the reservation is seasonal work on and near the reservation. A special job placement service was offered by the State Employment Securities Branch to Rosebud people from 1954 to 1958. It was designed to improve the flow of information about permanent jobs too, but in reality only seasonal job information was given.

The third possibility is off-reservation employment. Since the United States does not have a positive migration policy, our economy has relied on individual choice to seek better jobs. It is explicitly assumed that the normal operation of the market forces will equilibrate local and regional income differentials. Accordingly, researchers have hypothesized that the persistent long-term out-migration from regions of low income will accomplish three main objectives: 1) reduce income inequality between regions, 2) increase incomes in agriculture relative to incomes in other occupations, and 3) enable a recombination of resources to provide a solution to our agricultural problems.

A growing body of literature offers evidence that population adjustments are slow, unpredictable, and painful, with repercussions both in the sending and in the receiving areas of migrants. It has been suggested that the federal government should aid in reducing some of the major obstacles to internal migration by investment in human development through improved education, vocational training, and health services, and through investment in physical facilities such as rural transportation, as well as in improved job information. The BIA facilitates Indian migration to urban areas for permanent employment by its subsidized relocation and vocational training programs.

Now let us turn to the first division of the discussion of the labor market, an analysis of permanent reservation employment and the two services, extension managerial training and industrial development, which are designed to mitigate the necessity to leave the reservation.

PERMANENT RESERVATION EMPLOYMENT

The employment status of Rosebud people in 1942 will provide a bench mark for comparing reservation employment today. In 1942, the status of the estimated two thousand fully and partially employable males was as follows: 33 percent were unemployed for the whole year, 33 percent were employed on government relief programs, 15 percent worked part-time with the BIA at Rosebud Agency, 10 percent operated farms or ranches, and 9 percent were employed as farm laborers.

These data reveal that in a period of growing prosperity in the nation and the Northern Plains, two-thirds of the employable males at Rosebud were unemployed or dependent on government relief work. Seventy percent of the employable males had worked on some form of relief program during the nine years of July, 1933, to December, 1941. The Indian Division of the Civilian Conservation Corps (CCC-ID) was the most important relief work employer. It differed from the usual CCC program in that both married men living at home and single men were employed. In reality, the CCC-ID functioned more like the WPA than the regular CCC. During the nine-year period, a total of 1,573 different Rosebud workers were employed by the CCC-ID. The average worker was enrolled on the program a total of thirty and one-third months and was paid an average monthly salary of $45.

The rate of employment of the Rosebud people in 1942 varied according to their degree of Indian blood. Almost half (45.8 percent) of the full-bloods were unemployed in that year, compared to 26 percent and 10 percent, respectively, of the half- and quarter-bloods. Moreover, a total of 63 percent of the Indian males over fourteen were in the labor force compared to 83 percent of the white males in the three counties of Todd, Mellette, and Tripp within the reservation. Of those in the labor market, almost twice as many whites were gainfully employed in jobs other than relief work.

Rosebud farmers proved unable to cope with drought and economic instabilities in the thirties, for one out of two failed from 1930 to 1940, compared to one in four white farmers in the three-county area within the reservation. The average size of the 287 Indian farms in 1940 was 571 acres, compared to 939 acres for the white farmers. Likewise, the average value of land and buildings of Indian farms was $2,863, compared to $4,808 for non-Indians in 1940.

In 1956 the percentage of permanent unemployment of the employable labor force remained about the same—one-third—as in 1942, although accurate data are not available for all degrees of employability of Indians. After the adult women and temporarily unemployable males between the ages of eighteen and sixty-five are excluded, the BIA figures show at least one-third of fully employable males were unemployed at the time of the survey in the summer of 1956. We estimated on the basis of a 25 percent sample that in 1942 at least one-third of all males of all degrees of employability were permanently unemployed. Thus a conservative estimate is that the same percentage of permanent unemployment existed in 1956 as in 1942. In addition, a considerable portion of the two-thirds who held some employment were greatly underemployed in the winter months. Ranching is a dwindling occupation for Indian people; the number of entrepreneurs in ranching and farming fell from 287 in 1940 to 129 in 1959.

Except as self-employed ranchers, the Rosebud Indians have not been able to enter the permanent labor force beyond government and tribal employment. A report from the South Dakota Employment Security

Office states that service occupations in the stores and shops of the larger prairie communities with large non-Indian populations were generally closed to Indians. The Employment Security Officer stated that Indian youth were in competition with the white high school graduates; and since only about one-third of the Rosebud students complete high school, educational disadvantage was another barrier to obtaining jobs. Hence, Rosebud teenagers without a high school diploma found little more than seasonal employment when marketing their limited skills in the non-Indian prairie communities.

Rosebud and other Indian people are given preference over equally qualified non-Indians in obtaining Bureau employment. In 1960, a total of 58 Rosebud adults received their major source of income from regular federal employment on the reservation in the Bureau and Public Health Service. Tribal employment provided the primary means of livelihood for twenty Rosebud people in 1960. The tribal turnover rate is high, since clerical employees usually change when new officers are elected. The mixed-bloods hold proportionately more of the federal and tribal jobs than do the full-bloods; in 1960, mixed-bloods held 64 of the 78 such jobs.

Arts and craft work provided employment for a few families in 1960. Some critics of Bureau policy contend that this source of employment could be greatly expanded if Bureau policies provided more credit and educational assistance. Let us turn to the facts. An arts and crafts center was established at Rosebud in 1937 with the aid of a $7,200 government rehabilitation grant. A sum of $750 was used to purchase raw materials. The BIA arts and crafts teacher for the reservation schools acted as shop manager and supervised production of bead and leather work. A tribal board, of which the BIA superintendent was a member, managed the operation. The tribal council suggested in 1944 that the arts and crafts center be abolished. Tribal management problems arose, and the tribe delegated all administrative authority to the superintendent until 1953.

During the 1948–53 period, the average gross income for the center was $8,000, with an estimated $2,500 net income. After the BIA abolished the two Rosebud arts and crafts positions in the early 1950s, the administration of the center was turned over in 1953 to an arts and crafts board of directors, which consisted of five elected tribal craft producers and a hired manager. The tribal officers offered little support to the crafts program, and the federal government no longer aided it financially. An Indian arts and crafts representative from Rapid City visited the reservation several times a month and purchased items for the Sioux Exhibit and Crafts Center in Rapid City and advised the local manager.

In 1959, the Rosebud Arts and Crafts Association had thirty members, but a total of eighty-nine craftsmen sold their products through the association during the fiscal year. Gross sales for 1959 were $8,700. The estimated $3,000 to $4,000 annual net income distributed among the twenty to thirty key craftsmen provided a few hundred dollars per year per producer. The token craft net income added little economic assistance to the people. Genuine Indian craftwork is expensive; moccasions cost $13 to $18, a price beyond the reach of trinket-seeking tourists.

After some field work was completed, tribal attention was directed to tourist development. Following the national spurt in tourist development on other reservations in recent years, the Rosebud tribal council passed Resolution 6019 on March 21, 1960, which authorized the resources committee to expend $10,000 from any tribal funds and to borrow another $10,000 from any bank in order to develop the reservation tourist industry. A tribal spokesman said they hope to attract "thousands of tourists" to witness authentic Indian dances, horseback riding, camping, etc.

Two special services—extension managerial training and industrial development—are designed to ensure permanent reservation employment.

Extension Service

The forerunners of extension agents were known as head farmers in the 1880s, and later boss farmers, who established homes and offices in the remote areas of the reservation. The head or boss farmers were an integral part of the Indian Service. One function of the early boss farmer was to disperse the Dakotas over the land and instill in them a will to farm like all other American settlers. The *Nineteenth Annual Report of the Board of Indian Commissioners* (1887) described this procedure:

> One camp of Indians adjacent to the Rosebud Agency, where no farming has been done, has been broken up and divided into three camps and removed, respectively, 60, 25, and 10 miles, and all are now doing comparatively good work at land cultivation. They were told they must break up and go or they would be forcibly removed, and they decided to go and did go peaceably.

During the early thirties, the reservation cattle economy collapsed under the drought in the Plains. As part of the New Deal or IRA policy, boss farmers played a major role in promoting the various rehabilitation programs which emphasized subsistence farming on irrigation projects, gardens, cattle pools, cattle marketing, yard and home improvement, and food preservation. The extension staff at Rosebud in 1939 included both extension and credit personnel; it consisted of an agricultural and a home demonstration agent, four boss farmers, a rehabilitation project manager, a credit agent, and two farm aides. The shortcomings of the boss farmers are well known. Many lacked formal schooling in colleges of agriculture. Also, many spent most of their time administering Indian Bureau loans.

A concerted congressional drive was made in the late 1940s to transfer extension responsibility to the states. By 1952, the number of extension supervisors and farm aids at Rosebud had been cut to one-half the number in 1932. Rosebud agency officials warned in 1952 about the impending reluctance of the State of South Dakota to provide the necessary services for Rosebud Indians (Rosebud Agency "Withdrawal Report," 1952):

> County Agricultural Extension people do not want the low-income Indian any more than they want his white counterpart. . . . They know they are criticized for not working with similar white people and politics being what it is, they are not compelled to do so.

Nevertheless, the transfer proceeded with dispatch.[1] A state pilot project was started on the Pine Ridge Reservation in 1954, and the contract between the BIA and South Dakota State College was broadened in 1955 to include all Indian reservations. South Dakota State College Extension Service received $96,500 annually from 1955 to 1959 for the employment of approximately seventeen extension agents to assist South Dakota Indians.

Since World War II, state extension has served a commercial farmer audience,[2] while the BIA extension efforts have provided intensive and

[1] During the 1950–59 period, the responsibility for providing extension assistance was transferred from the BIA to sixteen of the eighteen states where the Bureau had carried on extension programs for a number of years. For an account of this transfer, see Pennsoneau (1957).

[2] Public support of agricultural research was established in 1887 when Congress passed the Hatch Act, which provided for state experiment stations. The next step was to set up a communications agency whereby the technological innovations from

sometimes unsolicited advice and assistance to Indian livestock loan clients and a subsistence Indian clientele. Thus, each agency served polar ends of a continuum: the BIA directed most emphasis to low-income people and the state served a high-income audience. A number of adjustments have to take place before a state can successfully meet the needs of both groups.

In 1955, three state extension agents were allotted to the two western counties of the reservation where 83 percent of the Rosebud population resides. A county agent and a home demonstration agent were based at Mission and served both Indians and non-Indians in Todd County. Another agent in White River served both Indians and non-Indians in Mellette County. Approximately $22,500 of the state total of $96,510 received from the BIA was used for wages and travel expenses for these three extension agents on the Rosebud Reservation. Local counties provided office space, secretarial help, and supplies. The dual clientele served by the three agents added a dimension of misunderstanding and confusion, for the agents received office space and other assistance from Todd and Mellette County funds, reported to Todd and Mellette County extension boards composed of a non-Indian membership, devoted about half of their time to non-Indians, and received their salary and travel expenses from the Johnson-O'Malley funds paid by the BIA to South Dakota State College. In addition, the 1960 BIA–South Dakota State College extension contract is vague; it stated, "To the extent that it may be practical to do so, all of the extension agents so employed shall devote their time to providing extension services to the Indians." Extension agents did not seem to know how much of their time should be spent with Indians. Furthermore, the contract stated: "The extension director shall . . . determine with the cooperation of the Area Director and representative Indians, the needs and desires of the Indian people in their respective communities and for advice and assistance."

---

land grant college experiment stations could be introduced to farm families at the county level in each state. The cooperative extension service was organized in 1914 under the provisions of the Smith-Lever Act.

Experiment stations and extension services were decentralized on a state basis when they were established in order, theoretically, to provide equal educational service to rural people throughout the country. Theodore Schultz (1956) reports, however, that two major agricultural regions found themselves in a relatively disadvantaged position in providing research and extension services from the beginning. The first was the South because it was poor, and the second, the Great Plains because it was sparsely populated. Indians in South Dakota suffer from this handicap today.

The confusion, however, is deeper than the dilemma of the state extension agents. The tribal council, new to decision-making and lacking in the knowledge by which wise decisions could be made, was slow in defining its extension needs. They emphasized gardening and requested the county extension agent in Todd County to visit Indian families and encourage garden exhibits at the annual Indian fair, although few successful gardens are raised in South Dakota's broiling summers. Rosebud tribal officers turned back to the subsistence days of the 1930s, the only pattern they knew, instead of concentrating on a specialized cattle economy.

On the one hand, Rosebud people seem to view extension programs with universal apathy and a lack of understanding about their aims, purposes, and priorities. On the other hand, the BIA extension officer in Washington observed (Pennsoneau 1957):

> In the beginning, some of our Bureau personnel were not in favor of the transfer of extension services to the States. It has been interesting and heartening to observe these same people, after a determination was made, to fall in line and do everything possible to make the transfer a success. They have been good soldiers in this respect.

The "good soldiers" of the BIA have fallen into line and cooperated, but some of these soldiers in South Dakota felt that the quality of service provided by South Dakota extension agents was lagging behind the minimum needs of the Indian. Further, they pointed out that little effective leadership was coming from the special Indian extension program division in the federal extension service.

The average salary of the state extension workers on the Indian extension program was $5,000 per year for the 1955–59 period. The state extension director noted that a $200-per-year salary increase was given to each extension worker on the Indian program from state appropriations in 1958 because of lack of BIA funds. The state had to furnish insofar as it was possible the seventeen agents required in the contract; they could not use the funds to hire ten extension agents at $8,000 per year instead of seventeen in order to solicit better-trained agents. Sixteen agents were employed in the three years 1956 through 1958.

The same ratio of extension agents to Indians was adopted by the state as used by the BIA prior to 1955. This ratio has been a matter of disagreement between field BIA workers and the Washington administrators. For example, as early as 1952, Benjamin Reifel commented on the transfer of extension to the states and stated unequivocally the need for considerable *increase* in staff instead of transferring the responsibility to the states and keeping the same level of services:

> The Indian Extension Service gives much more individual attention to the family than the White Extension Service. More individual attention is given than will be found true of the Farmers' Home Administration for its clients. Under the old Farm Security Administration an attempt was made to help some of the Indian families but with discouraging results because it was not equipped to deal adequately with the special problems it had to meet. . . . Most public services will require considerable increase in staff and methods to meet Indian needs. [Reifel 1952, pp. 351–52]

In practice, the BIA provided funds to states for the same number of extension workers as the number of boss farmers formerly provided by the BIA to the reservation Indians. This ratio is clearly based on assumptions about the adequacy of past BIA extension services. But past inadequate services are a poor guide to follow in allocating funds. An economist contends that low-income instead of high-income farmers need more intensive educational help from extension in the future:

> If there are any clear directions for increasing total welfare through farm techniques alone, education should emphasize low-income farms. . . . relatively more emphasis must be placed on low-income farmers in any county. This is in contrast to the general pattern where states and counties that have farmers with the highest income also have the largest number of extension specialists and county personnel. [Heady 1957, p. 116]

Reference to the amount of moneys devoted to agricultural extension work and experiment stations in South Dakota and other states sharpened the dilemma facing Indian families, the BIA, and the extension services in South Dakota. For example, although the theoretical intention of providing research and extension activities on a state basis ensured local and state participation and direction, the failure of sparsely populated states to provide adequate moneys for these activities is well known. South Dakota, North Dakota, and Nebraska ranked first, second, and third of all states in the percentage of total personal income payments derived from agriculture in 1954. South Dakota, with $256 million of its state income derived from agriculture, had less than one-sixth as much money for extension and experiment station activities as New York, which received $315 million of its state income from agriculture. South Dakota spent $600,000 for agricultural research in 1954, while New York spent almost $5 million on research.

Moreover, the prospects are dim for expanded research in South Dakota as reflected in the following recommendation by the Agricultural Research Subcommittee of the South Dakota Legislature in 1958 (*Report of the Agricultural and Conservation Committee*, 1958):

> It is natural for administrators of this program to think in terms of expansion, both in numbers and scope of projects. The Committee appreciates this ambition. . . . The Committee recommends that the efforts of agricultural research programs on South Dakota be concentrated on strengthening the research staff and facilities to do the most competent job within the limits of available funds, rather than on expansion in number and scope of projects.

Freedom of administrators to determine the scope and direction of research endeavor is also restricted by the committee's recommendation that "continuous and periodic review be undertaken by a committee composed of members of the Legislature of all agricultural research projects, to the end of determining what projects are essential to the needs of the primary industry of the state."

Further, little economic research on cattle ranching in western South Dakota was published by Brookings State College economists in the 1950s, and a Nebraska economist reported that the most recent economic research study of cattle ranching in the sandhills area of northwestern Nebraska (contiguous to Rosebud Reservation) was completed in 1929.

In summary, the transfer of extension responsibility from the BIA to the South Dakota Extension Service has met with universal frustration. All actors in the social system, the BIA, South Dakota, and Indian officials are dissatisfied. Progress reports mask this dissatisfaction. Cooperation between the two administrative bodies—the BIA and state extension—is stressed rather than the obstacles and problems of the Indian people and extension agents. The following excerpt from the 1959 South Dakota extension director's progress report emphasizes this friendly spirit: "We work very well with the Indian Bureau. They attend our meetings and we attend theirs and in that way we work out many things together."

The Merriam Report of 1928 noted that the Bureau extension agents were underpaid and poorly trained.

> Teachers to train adults of a retarded race in agriculture and other industry cannot be secured for wages which are little if anything above those paid for the least skilled laborers in those fields. The Indian Service requires, if anything, better teachers than are needed for the white race because they are confronted by a far more difficult task. [P. 437]

Thirty years later we see the extension agents of South Dakota State College in the same dilemma, with low salaries and short tenure, and facing confusing obligations, in addition. The transfer of extension work from the BIA to the state ensured administrative convenience for the BIA but few tangible results for the Indian people. Managerial training for the Indian cattle economy has not been carried out by the state extension agents. If extension aid continues to focus on the subsistence philosophy of a garden economy of the past rather than on current economic organization for survival and expansion of ranches, the Indian cattle economy is likely to deteriorate further.

Industrial Development

The second service designed to ensure employment for Indians who want to live on or near their reservation is the BIA's industrial development program, initiated in 1955. Its purpose was to encourage the establishment of small plants on or near reservations for the employment of Indian people. In addition, the Industrial Development Branch seeks established manufacturers who will hire Indians at the going wage rate while the Bureau subsidizes the employer at the rate of twenty dollars per Indian worker per week for a thirteen-week training period.

No new plants were lured to South Dakota by the program during the 1955–59 period. One on-the-job training contract was negotiated with a house-trailer plant, New Moon Homes, Inc., which was established in Rapid City, South Dakota, in March, 1957. This plant is a branch of the parent organization of Alma, Michigan. The BIA made a forecast in 1957 that from seventy-five to a hundred Sioux Indians would be employed at this plant in Rapid City. The average Indian labor force of this one-hundred-man plant has been around eight or ten workers, or ten percent of the work force. The BIA and the employer signed an on-the-job training contract and Indians entered employment and training in 1957. In the fiscal year 1958, twenty-seven Indians entered training and fourteen of them completed their thirteen-week program. Four were still on the job as of January 16, 1959. In the fiscal year 1959, the Bureau subsidized the same employer $4,000 for hiring an equivalent of fifteen Indian workers under the training program.

National publicity is given to the BIA's industrial development program. Various Bureau spokesmen point to the thirteen on-the-job training contracts which had been negotiated up to January, 1959. For instance, a BIA report states, "Many of these trainees are continuing in employment with the various firms with whom training contracts have been negotiated" (Bureau of Indian Affairs, "Progress Report, July 1, 1952–January 1, 1959," p. 12). However, only a few Rosebud Sioux and perhaps several dozen other Sioux have benefited from the industrial development program in South Dakota over the 1955–60 period.

The Rosebud tribal council made three abortive attempts to lure industry to the reservation in a ten-year period. The first was a 1950 proposal to the BIA for a $500,000 loan to convert the BIA boarding school facilities into a leather-processing business. The recommendation came from observing that the area had a livestock base and that hides could be obtained from cattle-slaughtering plants in nearby states. If this project were not feasible, they proposed to establish a sugar beet-growing and -processing activity at the boarding school. They planned to use the irrigation network established by the BIA in the late thirties to produce the beets, and the physical facilities of the boarding school to convert the beets into sugar. On June 30, 1953, Acting Commissioner Greenwood, in a letter to the Rosebud tribal council, reported that Bureau representatives:

> emphasized the need for hard, business thinking on commercial enterprises and suggested that the tribe contact the University of South Dakota concerning the possibility of having an economic development survey made. . . . It was also observed that the State has a development commission that may be in a position to be of assistance to the tribe.

Tribal council officers met with the commissioner on July 14, 1956, and stated that they were developing a sugar beet project with the aid of state extension agents. They reported that the tribe had contributed $1,000 worth of seed to reservation families in 1956 and that beets could be hauled 170 miles to Scottsbluff, Nebraska, for processing. No further action was taken by the tribe.

The tribal council endorsed the Area Development Bill in 1957 which would have provided technical assistance and loans to depressed areas of the United States, including Indian reservations. The tribal council president stated before a hearing that

> the Indians in our two states, Nebraska and South Dakota, are very much in need of the technical assistance and loan grants that are available under the bill before us today. . . . The only thing that we lack is funds with which we can develop our land and resources to the point where we can get water

industry in. . . . I am talking about industry in this case as canning factories that would be utilized if we could have our land developed. [U.S. Congress 1957, pp. 806–7]

On June 12, 1959, Congressman E. Y. Berry from South Dakota introduced a bill (HR7701) called "Operation Bootstrap, Indian-Style," which was modeled after the Puerto Rican program of tax exemptions that would encourage firms to locate plants in Puerto Rico. Berry proposed essentially the same plan to authorize Indian tribes to set up corporations empowered to construct plants to sell or lease to an industrial firm on a long-term basis. Industries moving onto reservations would receive exemption from all federal, state, and local taxes for ten years, along with other privileges. No action was taken by Congress. Subsequently, however, a number of measures have been taken by the federal government to give incentives for industrial development. A plant has been in operation on a neighboring reservation, but none has been established on Rosebud.

A third industrialization attempt was made by tribal officers and the Rosebud superintendent in the summer of 1959 when they tried to buy the patent for a plastic sponge cleaner. Close examination of the patent rights revealed that the patent ownership was not in the hands of the seller. This closed the door on the industrialization attempts of the council and Bureau in the 1950s. Prospects for industrialization to solve reservation problems are dim. Many factors, such as lack of raw materials, high transportation costs, an unskilled labor force, and so on, dampen hopes for this development.

Our first major conclusion is that under the pressure of the rapidly expanding farm size, at least the present rate of unemployment and underemployment will continue and the prospects are dim for the presently unemployed people on the reservation as well as for their offspring who will be entering the labor force.

SEASONAL EMPLOYMENT ON AND OFF THE RESERVATION

The second source of employment—seasonal wage work—has provided opportunities for Rosebud people during the May–October period for many years. There have been jobs for general farm and ranch hands, and in specialties such as sugar beet thinning and blocking, plus the grain and potato harvest opportunities. Seasonal wage work occupied the highest number of Rosebud people at the time of the BIA survey in the summer of 1956, whereas government relief work had provided the major source of employment in 1940. Curtailment of the relief work programs on the reservation in December, 1941, shifted these workers into nearby defense employment and after the war into the ranks of seasonal workers.

Ranch and farm hands received an average of $1.50 per day in 1942. The average length of·employment was three and one-half months, and few jobs were available in the winter months. In 1959 ranch and farm hands received an average of $5.00 per day. This represented little actual change in the purchasing power of this group.

Prior to World War II, a few Sioux had worked in the beet fields, but migrant whites, Japanese, and Mexicans performed most of the beet thinning in northwest South Dakota, Colorado, and Wyoming. The general labor shortage and the restriction of Japanese workers brought a sudden call for the Sioux to block and thin beets. It was a new experience for most of them. The Rosebud Sioux were recruited by the BIA and the State Employment Security Service. Many of the undesirable workers were unloaded on the beet operators. Payment was made on a group basis to those who lived and worked together on the same farm. The marginal workers and chronic alcoholics caused dissension among the able Sioux and dissatisfaction among the employers, whose cultural values of steady and aggressive work habits conflicted with the Indian patterns of high absenteeism. (Further, beet employers had had previous contact with the speedy and tenacious Mexicans.) The recruiters of the Employment Security Service had little knowledge of Indian patterns and were unequipped to offer practical advice about how to select Indian workers who would be temporarily suited to beet work. In 1958, a total of 462 field hands worked in the sugar beet area in northwestern South Dakota. After Indian workers were informed that they had priority over foreign workers, it was still necessary to import 276 Mexican nationals for weeding and thinning. The Employment Security Service stated: "Indians are unsuited for this type of field work and have very little interest in it" (South Dakota Farm Placement Service 1958, p. 5). Thus, while Mexicans are imported, a labor surplus on the reservation remains untapped.

Several hundred families were picking potatoes in nearby states in 1942. An average worker earned $3.50 per day, while a family was able to accumulate up to $150 during the six-week work period. Since Rosebud people had been picking potatoes since the end of World War I, a satisfactory relationship had been established between many individual families and their employers. Generally, employers had learned to make allowances for Sioux behavior patterns; for example, some adopted payment on demand in order to reduce absenteeism which had occurred with the end of the weekly pay period. Indian families often returned to work for the same employer for many years. In more recent years, a dwindling number of Rosebud people have left the reservation to pick potatoes, because mechanical potato harvesters are doing their old job, and because school officials are encouraging families not to take their children out of school for the normal six-week fall harvest. Consequently, school administrators are pleased, but Indian people have lost another source of income.

There is no clear reason why Indians failed as beet workers but prospered as potato pickers. The continuous work record of all members of the family as potato pickers for several generations and the special allowances and personalized attention granted them by their employers contributed to their proficiency and satisfaction. On the other hand, the sudden wartime call for a new type of work experience, faulty recruiting and payment techniques, and impersonal treatment might explain their poor performance as beet workers.

The pattern of reduced seasonal jobs for Rosebud people follows the trend in the region. The total quantity of hired and family labor has been reduced dramatically, mainly through substitution of capital in the form of labor-saving machinery. This entails a dwindling number of migrant jobs for the Rosebud.

In summary, seasonal employment in 1959 provided the same low wages and high insecurity of twenty years earlier. A South Dakota Employment Security official wrote in 1959 that "farm and non-farm employers in and adjacent to Rosebud reservation have, in many cases, expressed a preference for non-Indian labor" because of the "lack of confidence in the Indian as a reliable worker." The "lack of confidence" is based on high absenteeism and on lack of training in the operation of farm machinery. He adds: "The majority are capable enough but lack the qualities of aggressiveness and dependability necessary to secure and retain steady employment" (letter from C. F. Daum, 1959).

Improved job information has been suggested as a measure to ensure more seasonal employment for Indian and non-Indian people. The Employment Security Service offers basically the same assistance to both. Its main functions are seasonal and permanent job placement, employment counseling, occupational testing, and administering unemployment insurance. To help Rosebud people, the State Employment Security Service assigned a full-time interviewer to the reservation on June 1, 1954. Two different people held this job for two-year tenures. The employment officer was housed in the BIA office at Rosebud along with the relocation officer. He tried to place Indians in off-reservation work with emphasis on agricultural employment in South Dakota, Nebraska, Colorado, and Wyoming. Few Indians used this information service. The program fitted into the Bureau administrative orientation but not into the scope and responsibility of the tribal council. The service was discontinued in 1958 when the work load justification formulas of the Employment Security Service revealed that there was "insufficient activity" to warrant a full-time worker. Now the employment office in the prairie town of Winner, 55 miles from the heart of the reservation, serves both Rosebud and non-Indian people. Thus Rosebud people travel up to 120 miles to use this service.

One is more impressed by the limitations of the Employment Security Service for Rosebud people than with opportunities for the future. Job placement includes neither the creation of new employment opportunities nor an increase in the capacities of the Rosebud labor force. By furnishing information and by using mass, depersonalized techniques for job placement, the service merely ensures the harvesting of employers' crops. These same limitations are reported in other states.

MORE PERMANENT OFF-RESERVATION EMPLOYMENT

The third alternative is for Rosebud people to seek off-reservation employment and residence. The high rate of non-Indian out-migration during the "colonial" period, and especially during the thirties, forced the non-Indian people to adjust to low income in the reservation area and an overpopulated agriculture. Our objective in this section is to appraise the net rate of Indian migration between about 1940 and 1959.

Rural areas regret and oppose the loss of migrating adults because of the investment in the rearing, training, and educating of these individuals. However, in the Rosebud case, since the federal government paid for a substantial portion of the health, education, and welfare of the people, this resistance was not operative; and, furthermore, since the policies of the 1950s were to encourage assimilation, out-migration developed.

In the spring of 1942, Useem, Macgregor, and Useem studied (published 1943) the employment status and job histories of employable people on the reservation. The study was particularly enlightening because this was a time of labor shortage in war industries and in agriculture. Interviews with a sample of 250 of the estimated 1,000 employable males on the reservation revealed that:

1) Seventy-five percent of the employable male group said they would accept work off the reservation at even less than prevailing wages off the reservation. Nevertheless, only 20 percent of the Rosebud male population had gone to off-reservation work centers.
2) The chief obstacle to obtaining off-reservation work was the lack of finances for travel, clothes, board, and room until the first pay check.
3) Two out of three who had worked in a city returned in less than one year.

In interviews with Rosebud workers off the reservation, it was found that:

1) The chief obstacle to city life was adjustment to their residential neighborhoods and to white people rather than to their job.
2) Chronic drinking was a major problem in city adjustment.
3) Many of those making a successful city adjustment had formerly been employed on the reservation in the Civilian Conservation Corps.

Relocation Program

Now let us turn to the subsidized labor transfer process of the 1950s. The BIA established a national relocation program for Indians in 1951. This was an outgrowth of a job placement service provided to Navaho workers since 1948. The first relocation office was opened in Chicago in 1951. By 1960, there were ten city offices.

The primary objective of the BIA's relocation program is to overcome barriers to Indian migration to urban areas for permanent employment by subsidizing the cost of transportation, shipping household goods, subsistence en route to the relocation centers, and subsistence for relocatees and their families during the first few weeks in their new environment. In early 1952 the first relocatees left the reservations.

The relocation program over the 1952–59 fiscal-year period brought about the subsidized transfer of 753 Rosebud people: 438, or 58 percent, had returned to the reservation by 1959. The Rosebud data were obtained from exhaustive checks in contrast to the national estimates used by the commissioner to support his claim that 70 percent became self-supporting. Thus it is likely that fewer than four out of every ten family heads were permanently relocated.

TABLE 1

NUMBER OF UNITS AND PERSONS RELOCATED FROM ROSEBUD RESERVATION AND NUMBER REMAINING IN RELOCATION CITIES, FISCAL YEARS 1952-59

RELOCATION CITY	UNITS		PERSONS	
	Relocated	Remained in City	Relocated	Remained in City
Los Angeles	46	22	151	86
Oakland	18	10	68	34
San Francisco	17	6	51	21
San Jose	2	1	6	3
Chicago	79	25	270	74
Cincinnati	6	3	20	6
Cleveland	2	2	11	11
Dallas	9	5	27	16
Denver	13	7	54	26
St. Louis	5	3	12	4
Other Cities	25	10	83	35
Total	222	94	753	316

Table 1 shows the number of family units and persons who left the reservation and remained in their relocation destination during the fiscal years 1952–59. The 753 relocatees were classified into 222 units. A unit is defined by the Bureau as a breadwinner with or without his dependents. The two main receiving areas were Chicago and the four California cities. Information on these two areas is consolidated in Table 2. Although Chicago received over one-third of the relocatees, the percentage of those remaining there was much lower than for those remaining in the California cities and other cities.

TABLE 2

NUMBER OF ROSEBUD PEOPLE RELOCATED, AND NUMBER AND PERCENT REMAINING IN RELOCATION AREA, FISCAL YEARS 1952-59

RELOCATION AREA	NUMBER RELOCATED	RELOCATEES REMAINING	
		Number	Percent
California cities	276	144	55.2
Chicago	270	74	27.4
Other cities	207	98	47.3
Total	753	316	42.0 (Av.)

Most of those who returned to the reservation did so in less than one year. There is considerable speculation about whether a downturn in business activity forces people to return to the reservation. Our best reading of the situation is that recessions and urban conditions keep people from moving to the city because city relocation officers relay information back to the reservation. Thus subsidized movement to the cities is influenced by a set of new circumstances over which the reservation Indian has no control and for which he is usually in a disadvantaged position because of his lack of skills.

Of the 222 units relocated during fiscal years 1952–59, 149 were breadwinners with dependents and 72 were single; the 149 breadwinners were responsible for a total of 680 persons leaving the reservation. Of the 149 family units, 79 units, or 53 percent, remained in the city by the end of fiscal year 1959. Of the 73 single units, 34, or 26 percent, remained. The relationship between family size and units remaining in the city is shown in Table 3. No sharp conclusions can be drawn from the figures except to note the similar rate of return for the single relocatees, the family with no children, and the family with one child.

TABLE 3

NUMBER OF ROSEBUD UNITS RELOCATED BY FAMILY SIZE AND PERCENTAGE REMAINING IN THE RELOCATION CITY, FISCAL YEARS 1952–59

Family Size	Number Relocated	Percent Remaining in City
1	73	46.0
2	24	41.7
3	27	44.4
4	30	36.7
5	29	31.0
6	12	33.3
7	17	58.8
8 and over	11	18.2

Age selectivity of migrants is shown in Table 4. The age group under thirty has the highest percentage of those who remain in the city. Those over forty-five years of age appear most disadvantaged in making the urban adjustment. Table 5 reveals a positive correlation between educational status and remaining in the city.

A total of 129 breadwinners who relocated were veterans—127 males and 2 females. Veteran status was unknown for 12 males. Armed service experience did not affect the breadwinner's adjustment to relocation: 51.9 percent of the veterans and 53.1 percent of the nonveterans

TABLE 4

AGE DISTRIBUTION OF ROSEBUD UNITS THAT RELOCATED AND NUMBER AND PERCENT
REMAINING IN THE CITY AS OF JUNE 30, 1959

AGE GROUP	NUMBER RELOCATED	REMAINING IN CITY	
		Number	Percent
15–19	8	4	50.0
20–24	61	33	54.1
25–29	52	30	57.7
30–34	43	21	48.8
35–39	27	13	48.1
40–44	15	7	46.7
45 and over	16	5	31.3
Total	222	113	50.9 (Av.)

remained. Rosebud data refute the clichés that all the veterans have been drained off the reservation by relocation and that veterans adjust easily to the city.

Although sketchy, information on jobs the relocatees obtained in the city indicated that 61.2 percent of the unit heads with skilled or semi-skilled jobs remained in the city, while only 46.7 percent of those who worked on unskilled jobs did so.

Since the economic position of the full-blood Indian is especially weak on the reservation, let us look at the relationship of degree of blood and off-reservation movement. If out-migration were a random process in which the degree of Indian blood did not influence the decision, it could be assumed that close to 50 percent of the relocatees would be full-bloods, for one out of every two adults over twenty-five on the reservation is a full-blood. Table 6 shows that only 30 percent of all family heads who left the reservation over the years 1952–59 were full-

TABLE 5

EDUCATIONAL ATTAINMENTS OF RELOCATED ROSEBUD UNITS AND NUMBER AND PERCENT
THAT REMAINED IN THE CITY AS OF JUNE 30, 1959

EDUCATIONAL ATTAINMENT	UNITS		
	Number Relocated	Remained in City	
		Number	*Percent*
Less than 9th grade	89	38	42.7
9th–11th grade	77	42	54.5
12th grade and over	56	33	58.9
Total	222	113	50.9 (Av.)

TABLE 6

DEGREE OF INDIAN BLOOD OF ROSEBUD UNITS THAT RELOCATED AND NUMBER AND PERCENT THAT REMAINED IN THE CITY AS OF JUNE 30, 1959

DEGREE OF INDIAN BLOOD	UNITS		
	Number Relocated	Remained in City	
		Number	*Percent*
¼	43	27	62.8
½	57	37	64.9
¾	54	29	53.7
Full	68	20	29.4
Total	222	113	50.9 (Av.)

bloods. In addition, the table provides evidence that full-bloods find city adjustment more difficult, for only 29.4 percent of the full-blood family heads have remained in the city, compared with 62.8 percent of Indians with one-quarter degree of Indian blood. Every married full-blood breadwinner who left between 1952 and 1955 came back to the reservation.

We arrive at the conclusion that the economic problems of the full-bloods will have to be solved mainly "in place," or on the reservation. As has been found in many migration studies, much of the hardship of adjusting to a new situation, particularly in urban areas, falls upon wives and mothers. This is a major factor leading to reservation return.

Adult Vocational Training Service

The second program administered under the Relocation Branch of the BIA is the Adult Vocational Training Service (AVTS), which was authorized under Public Law 959, enacted August 3, 1956. The purpose of the service is to help adult Indians from eighteen to thirty-five years old to obtain permanent employment by subsidizing their tuition, transportation, and living expenses while they attend full-time instructional vocational training. The amount of school training provided Indians depends on the nature of the course. There are 343 approved occupational courses involving 131 different vocational schools. Typical courses are automobile body repair, baking, barbering, bookkeeping, stenography, and welding. Courses range from six to twenty-four months in duration. The maximum grant period is twenty-four months. The grant is a cash sum of money advanced to an individual or married family head on the basis of the number of dependents. A single person received an average of $120 per month; married persons receive additional money per dependent. Transportation costs to the training centers, room and board, tuition, and related costs are generally provided each student.

The first Rosebud Sioux left the reservation under the AVTS program in February, 1958. Many of the twenty units (forty-six persons total) attended school in Chicago and California during 1958. Even though all expenses were paid, eleven of the twenty family heads returned to the reservation during 1958. Nine of the eleven returnees had not completed their required training. However, it appears that the vocational training attempt offers more economic security to Indians for a longer period of time in the city than does Bureau relocation, and will enable them to move from the traditional unskilled to the semiskilled job market. The tribal council and the Rosebud people have endorsed this program. Its most apparent drawbacks are that its upper age limit of thirty-five is too low, and that the applicant must live on trust land.

The AVTS reflects a return to the policy of the pre-1934 period, which trained high school students for off-reservation employment. During the IRA period and for sometime thereafter the emphasis was on training the youth for on-reservation livelihoods. Thus, the group of adults, ages eighteen to thirty-five, who were trained in BIA high schools in the 1940s to "love the land and cattle," were then subsidized by the Bureau to attend vocational training courses and prepare themselves for lives off the reserve.

CONCLUSIONS

In historical review we saw that after the reservation relief programs were halted in December, 1941, Rosebud people found employment opportunities in small prairie towns such as Sioux City and Rapid City. The beginning of the war enabled Indians to make a fairly satisfactory move even though they usually left the reservation for economic reasons and returned because of problems of social adjustment. After the war, many of these same Indians moved into seasonal work. Indeed, by the time of the 1956 BIA survey, most Rosebud people were seasonal workers. This may be contrasted to the fact that most Rosebud people were on government relief work in 1940. Seasonal work is far from satisfactory: although it provides employment, it adds new social problems as children are taken out of school and families follow nomadic lives. Moreover, the prospects for seasonal work are declining as machines replace Indian labor.

What of permanent employment opportunities? With fewer and larger ranches, and in the absence of any appreciable change in government employment, the permanent employment opportunities declined. We find the same rate of permanent unemployment at the end of the period as at the start: about one-third of the fully employable labor force.

Although the Bureau, in its efforts to combat unemployment and underemployment, has fostered new industry and subsidized out-migration, the results are disappointing. New industry has not been forthcoming and subsidized out-migration has been far less successful at Rosebud and other Plains reservations than previous reports had indicated. Nevertheless, the important factor which emerges is that relocation has had a selective effect according to the degree of Indian blood—or, what is roughly the same, the degree of acculturation of the relocatees. The relocation process is highly selective according to age and degree of Indian blood and, to a lesser extent, to the educational status of the individual. Full-bloods have been extremely unsuccessful; mixed-bloods have been moderately successful. This suggests that the full-blood Sioux's economic problems will have to be solved *on* the reservation while relocation should be expanded to offer more services to the younger mixed-bloods. Another important consideration in out-migration is that movement from an overpopulated agricultural area (even when the movement is subsidized) is highly sensitive to changes in the business cycle. At best, subsidized labor transfer facilitates movement from reservation to city during periods of high national employment. But the major determinant of a successful move and of a high out-migration rate is the job opportunities provided by an expanding national economy.

Despite a decade of experimentation and introduction of four new services—relocation, industrial development, adult vocational training, and job placement service—substantial imperfections persisted in the functioning of the reservation labor market in 1959.

REFERENCES

EICHER, CARL K. 1960. Constraints on economic progress on the Rosebud Sioux Indian Reservation. Ph.D. dissertation, Harvard University.

EWERS, JOHN C. 1938. *Teton Dakota: Ethnology and history.* Rev. ed. U.S. Department of the Interior, National Park Service.

HAGAN, EVERETT, AND SCHAW, LOUIS C. 1960. The Sioux on the reservation. Mimeo. Massachusetts Institute of Technology Center for International Studies.

HEADY, EARL. 1957. Adaptation of extension education and auxiliary aids to the basic economic problem of agriculture. *Journal of Farm Economics* 39:112–27.

HOWARD, JAMES H. 1966. The Dakota or Sioux Indians. Part III: The Teton or Western Dakota. University of South Dakota *Museum News* 27, nos. 9–10.

MEKEEL, H. SCUDDER. 1943. A short history of the Teton-Dakota. *North Dakota Historical Quarterly* 10:137–205.

MERIAM, LEWIS, et al. 1928. *The problem of Indian administration.* Baltimore: Johns Hopkins Press.

Nineteenth Annual Report of the Board of Indian Commissioners. 1887. Washington, D.C.: G.P.O.

PENNSONEAU, CLYDE W. 1957. Existing status of the Bureau's Agricultural Extension Service activities. Paper read at Bureau of Indian Affairs Conference, February 11–15, 1957. Mimeo. Washington, D.C.: BIA.

REIFEL, BENJAMIN. 1952. Relocation on the Fort Berthold Indian Reservation. D.P.A. dissertation, Harvard University.

Report of the Agricultural and Conservation Committee, South Dakota Legislative Research Council. 1958. Pierre, S. Dak.

SCHULTZ, THEODORE. 1956. Agriculture and the application of knowledge. Battle Creek, Mich.: W. K. Kellogg Foundation.

South Dakota Farm Placement Service. 1958. *Annual farm labor report.* Aberdeen, S. Dak.: Employment Security Department of South Dakota.

U.S. CONGRESS. 1957. Senate Subcommittee of the Committee on Banking and Currency *Hearings on bills to assist areas to develop and maintain stable and diversified economies,* May 14, 1957. Washington, D.C.: G.P.O.

U.S. Department of the Interior, Bureau of Indian Affairs, Rosebud Agency. 1952. Withdrawal programming report. September 15, 1952.

U.S. Department of the Interior, Bureau of Indian Affairs, Fort Berthold Agency. 1959. Progress Report, July 1, 1952–January 1, 1959.

USEEM, JOHN, MACGREGOR, GORDON, AND USEEM, RUTH HILL. 1943. Wartime employment and cultural adjustment of the Rosebud Sioux. *Applied Anthropology* 2: 1–9.

USEEM, RUTH HILL. 1947. The aftermath of defeat: A study of acculturation among the Rosebud Sioux of South Dakota. Ph.D. dissertation, University of Wisconsin.

Dakota Diet: Traditional and Contemporary

Ethel Nurge

INTRODUCTION

HUNGER AND NUTRITION have lately come to be newsworthy, following several reports that there are untold millions in the United States who are either hungry or malnourished. This paper is about one such group —the Dakota, or Sioux, Indians. The first part is about the Sioux in general and is derived from historical sources; here the specific tribe or band can only occasionally be identified; the second part is about the Sioux on Rosebud Reservation and is based on field work I did among them. Guidelines to the organization of the paper have been the food quest, food processing, and food consumption. These three processes are considered first for the early nomadic days and for the first years on the reservation. Thus, "Part One—Traditional" contains material both on the free-roaming life and on some of the initial experiences on the reservation. "Part Two—Contemporary" contains material on studies from later reservation days (Crow Creek in the 1920s, Pine Ridge in the 1930s, and Sisseton in the 1950s) and also, of course, my observations on Rosebud in 1962.

PART ONE—TRADITIONAL

Food Quest

The Sioux in the days of the flowering of Dakota culture were primarily a hunting people; throughout the year they sought the herds: buffalo, mainly, but also other ruminants. From the earth they took many items: roots, tubers, and fruit; and, all things considered, they had a rather wide range of foods to choose from, although they did not always have sufficient food. Food intake was expanded by the bounty of one season and limited by the scarcity of another, and this applies to game as well as to the fruits of the earth. More about this later. Earlier in their history, while the Sioux still lived in the east in the Woodland area and before they were so heavily dependent on buffalo, they collected wild rice and raised a little corn (Meyer 1967, p. 22) and beans (Jenks 1900, p. 1087). But first, the hunt.

Hunting, Fishing, Gathering, and Collecting. Throughout the Plains area large game formed the bulk of the diet of the nomads for whom Lowie describes four techniques of hunting: stalking on foot, disguised in an animal skin; winter hunting with snowshoes during which the hunters tracked the animals and killed them when they became embedded in deep snow; and, of greater importance than these two, the collective hunt of two types—the surround and impounding. In the surround, which became increasingly popular when the horse became common among the Plains Indians, game was driven over a cliff and encircled by fire. To impound, a corral was constructed with an opening approached between two converging lines. On foot and on horseback the hunters herded the game in. Some hunts included a combination of impounding and driving down a cliff (Lowie 1954, pp. 13 f.). The extent to which Dakota Indians used any of these techniques is problematic, but it is a fairly safe assumption that they used all of them. Denig (1961, p. 18) stated that the Brule Sioux were the only band to kill antelope by driving them over a cliff, but other writers show that other tribes followed the same practice. Of all the hunts, the buffalo hunt, carried out with discipline and caution, was the most important; it was invested with preliminary ceremony by men who solicited the deities for success.

Other animals hunted by the Sioux were "elk, black and white tail deer, big horn, antelope, wolves of several kinds, red and grey foxes, a few beaver and otter, grizzly bear, badger, skunk, porcupine,

hare, rabbit, muskrat, and a few panthers in the mountainous parts"
(Denig 1961, p. 13).

It was not only the adult males who hunted. Boys about the camps
killed birds, rabbits, and other small game (Dodge 1959, p. 278).[1]
One account lists rabbits, squirrels, and grouse as the most common
items and includes a surprising variety of birds, including a wood-
pecker and baby cranes (Eastman 1914, pp. 48–57).[2]

The portion of the diet which was the spoils of the hunt differed
not only by seasons but also changed in the course of each tribe's
history. When they hunted on foot and with aboriginal weapons,
the kill was less than when they acquired the horse, which opened a
new ecological niche. The horse greatly extended the hunting area
and made it possible to carry much more weight than formerly, when
the only transport animal was the dog, domesticated early in pre-
historic times as a pack and draft animal. Readers interested in the
introduction of the horse should see Haines (1938) and Roe (1955).

The portion of the diet which was the spoils of the hunt also depended on hunting practice. Conservation practices of sparing the
females either when they were with calf (mid-April until late June)
or at any other time did not exist; when game was found, a lavish
use rather than a conserving ethic prevailed:

> The Indians often, for the mere sport, make an onslaught, killing great
> numbers . . . and having a plentiful feast of "Ta-Tonka," as they call the
> buffalo meat. They use no economy in food. It is always a feast or a famine;
> and they seem equally able to gorge or fast. Each man selects the part of the
> animal he has killed that best suits his own taste, and leaves the rest to decay
> or be eaten by wolves, thus wasting their own game, and often suffering
> privation in consequence. [Kelly 1872, p. 76][3]

Others, however, have argued that the Indian was not so wasteful
(Roe 1951).

[1] Dodge's book, first published in 1877, was about the previous three decades. I
suspect Dodge exaggerated to create a dramatic effect.

[2] Eastman, an Eastern Sioux who had a B.A. and an M.D. degree, writes a highly
credible and satisfyingly detailed account, although he does tailor his writing to white
prejudices. Thus, he writes sentimentally of the sacrifice of a dog to the Great Spirit,
but in his story, the dog is not eaten. Without prior or additional knowledge, the
reader would not know that eating the animal was an integral part of the ceremony.

[3] Mrs. Kelly's account is written in a romantic, florid style, but her statements can
be taken with a good deal of confidence. She was captured by the Sioux west of Fort
Laramie in 1864. She learned the language during her captivity and much of what

Buffalo meat was the preferred food, of course, and it is interesting that hunting tribes often express preference for the flesh of big game and more often have to live on gathered and collected foods, which are their reliable staple (Kaberry 1939). When the Sioux were successful in their hunt, no part of the buffalo was without use—for food primarily, of course, but also for shelter and clothing. Indeed, an ingenious use of the by-products of the kill enriched Sioux life.

> Every part of this animal is eaten by the Indians except the horns, hoofs, and hair. . . . The skin is used to make their lodges and clothes, the sinews for bow strings, the horns to contain their powder and the bones wrought into dressing tools, or pounded up and grease extracted. When the hair becomes seasonable, from the beginning of October to the first of March, the skins are dressed with the hair on, and either worn by themselves or exchanged with the traders for various necessaries. [Denig 1961, pp. 13 f.]

From another account, we learn that flesh of the animal was eaten when newly slaughtered, was dried for winter use, and in its dry state could be pounded and mixed with other foods. The hide was used for tipis, bedding, lariats, containers, boats, garments, leggings, and foot-wear. From the skeleton, the Indian made shovels (of the scapula), grooved adzes, scrapers, flint-chippers, spoons, needles, and awls; the skull was used in ceremonies and the hoof points for rattles. The horns were used as ornaments, drinking vessels, and club heads. The sinews furnished thread, bow strings, and rope. There was, in addition, fuel from buffalo chips; the bladder became a storage container; and the hair was used for stuffing (Moorehead 1914, p. 307). And, finally, fat: fat was eaten and might also be dropped on the fire to give temporarily increased illumination (Parkman 1910, p. 167).

Several writers have noted that hunting or gathering peoples may live primarily on one staple at a time (Herskovits 1950, p. 248; Denig

---

she reports has been borne out by later investigators. Accounts by females from the nineteenth century are rare and are especially helpful in the search for data on food since, then as now, one of the primary functions of women was the preparation of food. Consequently, they noticed and paid attention to detail.

Roe takes issue with Kelly and other writers who state that the Plains Indians were wasteful and improvident in their use of the buffalo. According to him, the part the Indian played in the extermination of the herds was minor, even though the introduction of rifles and plentiful ammunition increased the numbers of buffalo the Indians could kill. Roe feels that it was the popular demand by the whites for buffalo hides which led to the efficient and speedy killing of thousands of buffalo and the resultant near extinction of the species (Roe 1951, p. 451).

1961, p. 12). What foods, other than game, were important to the Sioux? Fish were never a staple in Plains Indians' diet, but some tribes fished when meat was scarce. There is no evidence that the Western Dakota fished, although "the Eastern Dakota . . . consumed quantities of turtle and fish, but did not like to have them for their fare to the exclusion of meat. They hooked, speared, and shot fish with arrows" (Lowie 1954, p. 17).

Earlier in their history the bands who had inhabited the area which is now Minnesota gathered wild rice in the autumn (most plentiful in August, September, and October). Women collected rice from canoes pushed through the water where the grain stood thick; with a stick they bent the stalks over the edge of the canoe and gently struck the heads (Winchell 1911, p. 496). It is desirable but difficult to find statements about what proportion of the diet rice was. We do know that it was used less west of the Mississippi (Jenks 1900, p. 1045) and that fall hunts began soon after rice harvest. If the hunting was good, it was possible to save a greater proportion of the rice for the rest of the year. On the other hand, in times of scarcity of game, the people might live wholly on the wild rice while the supply lasted. Also, as with people everywhere, we may expect that some individuals were more provident than others; some disposed of much of the cured grain for trinkets and ornaments. We are fortunate in that we have one estimate of wild rice users:

> Considering all the data presented, it is probable that the estimate of 2,000 wild rice producing Dakota Indians is too conservative for the earlier part of the nineteenth century; and it is believed that between 5,000 and 7,000 Dakota Indians used wild rice at the time the Ojibwa were nominally in control of the territory east of the Mississippi. None of the Dakota Indians on reservations have access to wild rice at the present time. [Jenks 1900, p. 1047]

Another evidence of the widespread provenience of rice is etymological. Winchell (1911, p. 495) contends that:

> The prevalence of lakes and streams named *Rice Lake* and *Rice Creek* indicates the wide distribution of wild rice (*Zizania aquatica L.*) in Minnesota. . . . Among the Dakota, two of the "moons" of the year took their names from the rice harvest, one (August) signifying the *moon of the ripe rice*, and the other (September) the *moon of gathering the rice*. One of the Sioux villages "of the east," named by Le Sueur in 1700 was *Psinoumaniton*, village of wild rice gatherers, and one "of the west" was *Psinchaton*, village of red wild rice,

while still another "of the west" was *Psinoutanhinton*, the great wild-rice village.[4]

Etymology also yields evidence of the eastern origin of the Dakotas in the fact that the Dakota name for wild rice was transferred to a prairie turnip (*Psoralea esculenta*) which may have had a comparable importance in their diet once they moved out of wild-rice territory (Gilmore 1911–12, p. 56). The Dakotas called the tuberous plant *teep se nah*, and Denig (1961, p. 11) thought it a considerable item in their bill of fare, though mainly in times of scarcity. Besides being known as the prairie turnip, it had a common name of *tipsin* and was called by the French *pomme blanche*. Eaten raw or boiled, or dried for winter use, it was also sometimes pulverized into flour. The turnip ranked as a prize subsidiary food; large quantities were dug in early summer (June and July), peeled, braided into strands, and dried for winter use (Lowie 1954, pp. 18 f.). Another less common method of preparation was to split the roots and dry them. Difficult to dig, the prairie turnip grows in unyielding prairie soil; the enlarged root is several inches below the surface. Tipsin was so plentiful and collected in such quantities that it was traded; it was traded so commonly that an equivalent had been arrived at for shelled corn: one *hunansadu* of shelled corn was valued at four strings of tipsin roots or one *hunansadu* of split roots of tipsin. Also, one *hunansadu* of corn was worth one good buffalo robe or two packs of dried meat; and, finally, one meat pack was two cubits in length, one cubit wide, and one cubit thick (Gilmore 1911–12, pp. 92 f.). Other roots on which the Sioux were often heavily dependent were *Psincha* and *Psinchincha*, two bulbous esculent tubers, which grew in lake bottoms and which were dug by both men and women, but more frequently the latter (Winchell 1911, p. 496). *Mdo*, which resembled the sweet potato, is a leguminous land plant, scarce and difficult to find. The root was called *pomme de prairie* by the traders (Winchell 1911, p. 496). In the beginning of the summer the Indians ate a turniplike vegetable, *Arisema triphyllum*, which had an acrid juice.

Lastly, there were fruits. West of the Minnesota area the buffalo berry grew in greater abundance than any of the other berries. Utilized fresh in season and dried during the winter months (Winchell 1911, p. 496), it also served as ceremonial paraphernalia in girls' puberty rites (Gilmore 1911–12, p. 106). Plums and chokecherries occurred in abundance, but Juneberries and wild strawberries were rare (Gilmore

[4] Winchell based his report on the study of collections made by J. V. Brower and on field surveys and notes of A. J. Hill and T. H. Lewis.

1911–12, p. 84; Denig 1961, p. 12); whortleberries, raspberries, service-
berries and elderberries were found; *grain de beouf*, a small, red, acid-
tasting berry occasionally substituted for cherries in pemmican (Denig
1961, pp. 11 f.). When fruit was available and plentiful, vast quantities
were eaten.

A practice sounding like an adventure from a child's story of little
people is the collection from the nests of field mice of *omane'cha*, or wild
peas or beans. Young and tender mushrooms were also collected
(Gilmore 1911–12, p. 62).

Food Processing

Preservation, Preparation, Storage, Meat Packing, and Cooking. Before a
society has any preservation and storage of food, two prior conditions
must be met: there must be a surplus, and the society must have
developed techniques of preserving, such as drying, smoking, salting,
or freezing, and of storage, such as in bins, caches, granaries, or cold
storage. This also implies the development and use of containers such as
trays, baskets, and boxes. The Sioux had wooden troughs, blankets,
mats, bags of skin or woven bark, and baskets. In general, it is agricultural and sedentary peoples who have the surpluses and the developed techniques for preservation and storage, but collecting people
may also have this advantage.

Not all products can be stored, and among those that can the "shelf
life" varies greatly, according to both the innate properties of the
product and the method of preparation before storage. Wild rice must
be cured and dried; two techniques are described. "The Dakota
Indians of Titoha village, about 50 leagues west of St. Anthony Falls,
Minnesota, early in the eighteenth century, sun-cured their rice"
[Jenks 1900, p. 1064]. A later method was to build a scaffold from
twenty to fifty feet long, eight feet wide and four feet high, cover it with
reeds and grass, and spread the rice grains on it. A slow fire burning for
about thirty-six hours slightly parched the hull (Jenks 1900, p. 1065).

Once rice is dried, it is thrashed. Early in the eighteenth century the
Dakotas trod out their grain in a wooden trough (Jenks 1900, p. 1069).
Holes were dug in the ground and lined with skins and slabs of wood.
The moccasin-clad laborer treading upon the grain sometimes used a
wooden stake to steady himself; sticks also were used like flails and
churn-dashers (Jenks 1900, p. 1070). Men did the thrashing but
women did the gathering and winnowing with the help of the wind or
winnowing baskets. We have no information on the shelf life of rice,

stored, dried and hulled, in caches (Winchell 1911, p. 496); but Jenks (1900, p. 1070) writing of the Titoha band of Dakotas in the early eighteenth century, described their practice thus:

> [They] carry away as much of it as they think they need and store the rest in the ground. They also put some to rot in the water, and when they return in the spring they find it delicious, although it has the worst kind of odor.

The preparation of meat for storage is more difficult than that of grain. After the buffalo was killed, the man's work was done, the woman's begun. Animals spoiled very quickly if not eviscerated, and some hunters tried to regulate the kill according to the woman power available to prepare meat and hides. Sometimes after a big kill, this meant working all night (Dodge 1959, p. 253). The women worked long and hard to skin and cut up the dead animal as quickly as possible. Allowed to dry unstretched, the skin could never be straightened again. Some accounts from observers:

> The meat, cut as closely as possible from the bones, is tied up in the skin, and packed to camp on ponies. The entrails, emptied of their contents, form the principle food of all during the hunt, not only being the most delicious morsel, but not requiring a waste of time in cooking. [Dodge 1959, p. 254]

We get greater detail from Kelly:

> The squaws accompany the men when they go to hunt buffalo, and as fast as the animals are killed, they strip off their hides, and then cut off the meat in strips about three feet long, three to four inches wide, and two inches thick; and such is their skill that the bones will be left intact and as free from meat as though they had been boiled. The meat is then taken to camp and hung up to dry. It is most filthy, being covered with grass and the excrement of the buffalo. [Kelly 1872, p. 178]

Another account either reflects less attention to detail or describes another technique for jerking meat:

> The process of jerking consists in cutting the meat into long strips as thin as possible to cut raw meat. These are then hung upon poles to dry, and when dry are exceedingly brittle, breaking readily into chips. In the process of drying, and before the meat becomes too hard, it is lapped over into flat packages or bricks, which in turn are so arranged as to form a large flat package, which is finally wrapped up in the raw hide or skin. [O'Reilly 1889, p. 32]

Meat was also preserved by being cut into thin sheets which were dried in the sun (Parkman 1910, p. 164).

The buffalo filled his skin after death as well as before. The hide, cut to the required length, stretched, and allowed to dry, became as hard as iron and maintained whatever shape it was dried in. Dodge (1959, p. 254) writes:

> As soon as these parfleches or trunks are ready for use, . . . thoroughly dry meat is pounded to powder between two stones. About two inches . . . is placed in the bottom of a parfleche, and melted tallow is poured over it. Then another layer of meat is served in the same way, and so until the trunk is full. It is kept hot until the whole mass is thoroughly saturated. When cold, the parfleches are closed and tightly tied up. The contents, so prepared, will keep in good condition for several years.[5]

It is an economical process; nothing is lost. The flesh of the older animals becomes as soft as the flesh of the younger animals, but, Dodge (1959, p. 255), continued:

> All meat is so utterly spoiled by the process that there is no longer room for comparatives, good or bad. This [parfleche] is the true Indian bread, and is used as bread when they have fresh meat. Boiled, it makes a soup not very palatable but nutritious. So long as the Indian has this dried meat he is entirely independent of all other food.

Too little is known of the types of cooking containers the Dakota Indians had in early times, but some extrapolation of the specific techniques used in cooking is possible. Certainly they did not bake or oven roast, and broiling without a container was known but not common. Probably they did not fry food, although such a procedure is common today. It is also highly probable they boiled food before they had the white man's cauldrons; other Plains tribes had stone boiling, a technique wherein a hide was hung over four low posts, filled with water and food, and heated by stones, not fuel. The stones were heated in a separate fire, dropped into the hide container, and periodically removed and reheated. Slowly but surely boiling was accomplished.

Rice cooking presented special problems: Jenks tells how wild rice was washed three or four times before cooking (sometimes a small quantity of soda was added in the post-Columbian era) and different kinds of rice had several preparations. Green wild rice was adequately cooked by pouring boiling water over it. Parched wild rice was boiled for about half an hour, while fire-cured or black wild rice required

---

[5] The trunk-shaped parfleche was an aberrant development among the Santees, Iowas, Poncas, and Otos. By far the more common form was a flattish container shaped like a square envelope or an oblong-shaped object with the two ends folded in the middle (Lowie 1954, pp. 64 f.).

nearly an hour. The amount of water used was doubled for preparation as a gruel (Jenks 1900, p. 1086). Rice was used to thicken soup and to make a type of stew; sometimes dog meat was added to the latter (Jenks 1900, p. 1084). At other times rice was mixed with blueberries to prepare a delicious soupy dish. Another dish featured wild rice, corn, and fish boiled together; this was called *tassimanonny*. Rice was sometimes pounded to meal and boiled in water to which grease was added. Either boiled or roasted grain was eaten plain. Sun-dried whortleberries were added as a seasoning (Jenks 1900, p. 1085). In addition, rice was used as a cereal much as corn is used to boil and make hominy today; it was also parched and eaten. Rice was used to make a pudding; boiled and mixed with maple sugar, it was considered delicious. On the whole it may be said that the Indians prepared rice in any fashion and with any type of meat so long as it was palatable (Jenks 1900, p. 1084).

When boys killed birds, rabbits, and other small game they prepared and ate the food themselves; but sometimes a mother preempted a kill, which she prepared simply by raking a hole in hot coals and ashes and thrusting the bird or animal in. After thirty minutes or less, it was pulled out, beaten a few times against the earth to remove the ashes, the feathers or skin pulled off, and the prey eaten, entrails and all. Dodge (1959, p. 178) attests to the juiciness of game so prepared.

Both men and women cooked, but the circumstances of their cooking and their techniques differed: in camp, women preferred boiling meat to any other technique of preparation and did all the cooking; men, on the hunt, prepared meat by broiling on coals or on a stick over the fire (Dodge 1959, pp. 271 f.). In the days and nights of the chase, certain delicacies were enjoyed by the hunters—"marrow guts," "hump ribs," and "marrow bones" (Dodge 1959, p. 273). What these were exactly is not always clear, but the first was intestines, either eaten raw or wrapped around a stick, sprinkled with salt, and held in a bright blaze until the fat streamed down (Dodge 1959, p. 273). Broad slabs of ribs from which the meat had been rather closely cut were roasted before a fire of hot coals, turned, basted, and roasted some more. Large bones of the hind legs (femur, tibia, and fibula?) were thrown upon glowing coals or pushed under hot embers. In addition to the meat clinging to the bones, the marrow was eaten with enjoyment (Dodge 1959, pp. 273 f.).

For either men or women, there was no point in the cooking procedure at which a meat was considered "done." Rather, hunger or other considerations seemed to dictate when the pot should be removed and the contents eaten. All crowded around and helped themselves with knives, fingers, a stick, or a wooden ladle (Dodge 1959, p. 272). No judgment was passed on the rawness or overcooking of the meat; the primary consideration was the quantity and quality.

We have so far considered meat and rice preparation. What of other foods? Ripe corn was prepared by pounding to a meal, by hulling with lye from ashes to make hominy, and by parching (Gilmore 1911–12, pp. 67 f.). Wild artichokes, called *panghai*, grew on marshy river banks and were eaten raw, roasted, or boiled, but were not dried or preserved. Wild peas, boiled "with fat meat, [made] good soup, and [were] perhaps the most palatable vegetable" (Denig 1961, p. 11).

Red plums, called *cauntah* by the Sioux, were best when eaten ripe but were also dried and, at some later time, boiled and eaten (Denig 1961, p. 11). Chokecherries, which were plentiful, were dried and used in soup and also as one of the components of pemmican. Rosebuds were once plentiful and were eaten raw and boiled. A favorite dish was blood boiled with brains, rosebuds, and scrapings of rawhide stewed until it became the consistency of warm glue (Denig 1961, pp. 12 f.).

Other delicacies are described by Denig (1961, p. 12):

Pounded cherries boiled with meat and sugar and grease added is considered a dainty and eaten with great relish. The prairie turnip, sliced, dried, and boiled with the dried paunch of the buffalo, or the peas extracted from the mice's nests cooked with dried beaver tails or a good fat dog is also much admired and considered fit for soldiers, chiefs and distinguished visitors.

The fungus *Polyporaceae* was boiled when young and tender (Gilmore 1911–12, p. 62). Hazelnuts were either eaten raw with honey or used to thicken soup (Gilmore 1911–12, p. 74). Several tubers, one known as the Indian potato, were eaten either cooked or uncooked (Gilmore 1911–12, p. 94), and were prepared either by boiling or roasting. A berry called *tim' poo tah* by the Sioux was used in the preparation of pemmican; so was chokecherry, called *cham pah'*. The latter berry was

pounded with the seeds, and cooked in various ways, occasionally made into soup, but more often mixed with dried buffalo meat bruised and marrow grease added. This is what is known among the voyagers as pemican [*sic*]. It is convenient to carry, nutritious and rather more desirable than most of their dishes. [Denig 1961, p. 12]

Water was the main beverage of the Indians, mostly unadulterated, but they also did some steeping. Wild mint was prized for its medicinal values and also as a tea of pleasing aromatic flavor (Gilmore 1911–12, p. 113). Among the Oglalas the leaves of the purple prairie clover were also used to make tea (Gilmore 1911–12, p. 94). Elderberry blossoms were also utilized to make a very pleasant nonalcoholic beverage (Gilmore 1911–12, p. 115).

Those who early collected information on Indian diet did not, unfortunately, collect recipes. If they had, we might have had more information on flavorers: sweeteners, condiments, and seasonings. Maple and the box elder were a source of sugar. Gilmore (1911–12, p. 101) writes that in September, 1916, he "found a grove of trees [box elder] on the Standing Rock Reservation in North Dakota, of which every tree of any considerable size showed scars of tapping which had been done the previous spring in sugar making." Jenks also said maple syrup was drawn (1900, p. 1047). Winchell (1911, p. 497) provides information on species and provenience:

> Maple sugar was made from the sap of the sugar maple, *Acer saccharinum*, and of the box elder, *Negundo aceroides*. These trees were common throughout the wooded portion of the state, and the latter also is common along nearly all the streams in the prairie portion.

Wild mint was used as a flavoring in cooking meat and was placed between the layers in packing dry meat (Gilmore 1911–12, pp. 112 f.). The contents of an animal's gallbladder might be used as a condiment:

> The liver of a very fat buffalo or elk will not unfrequently become granulated and broken up by overheating in a long chase. This, with the contents of the gallbladder sprinkled over it, is one of the most delicious of all morsels that can titillate an Indian palate. [Dodge 1959, pp. 276 f.]

Wild onion was either eaten raw and fresh as relish or used as a flavoring for meat and soup. Gilmore also reports it fried (1911–12, p. 71). Lamb's-quarter, while young and tender, was cooked as pottage (Gilmore 1911–12, p. 78), while the tuber yellow lotus was peeled, cut up and used as spice for meat or hominy (Gilmore 1911–12, p. 79). Dodge said that all the Indians he had ever known used salt and there is considerable evidence from other sources that this was true. Quantities of black and red pepper were consumed; the old men liked black pepper in tea or coffee, claiming it invigorated them (Dodge 1959, p. 276). Hackberry and its seeds ground fine provided flavor for meat; the Dakota Indians called this spice *yamnumnugapi*, and they called black pepper *yamnumnugapi washichu*, or white man's *yamnumnugapi* (Gilmore 1911–12, p. 76).

Food Consumption

Gratification and Control of Hunger. Many psychological factors enter into gratification and control of hunger: people may have an adequate (or surplus) supply of some item of food and still feel hungry, or they may be trained to a sufficiency or excess of food. The Sioux were trained both to scarcity and to engorgement, as Eastman's account (1914, pp. 16 f.) shows:

> I once passed through one of these hard springs when we had nothing to eat for several days. I well remember the six small birds which constituted breakfast for six families one morning: and then we had no dinner or supper to follow! . . . I had only a small wing of a small bird for my share! Soon after this, we came into a region where buffaloes were plenty, and hunger and scarcity were forgotten.

Training in stoicism, for its own sake, may be an ideal. Eastman (1914, pp. 38 f.) writes: "I was not allowed to have beef soup or any warm drink. The soup was for the old men. General rules for the young were never to take their food very hot, nor to drink much water." The fortitude of the Sioux in the face of privations of food and water is documented. On a march of several days during which they were without water most of the time, the Indians carried little sticks in their mouths; they chewed these to stimulate the flow of saliva and thus lessen thirst (Kelly 1872, p. 69).

The opposite also obtains. They drank copiously, greedily, if water was available before they began such a march. And as to food intake, Dodge (1959, p. 274) reported that they had a tremendous appetite, and were not ashamed of gorging; especially on ceremonial occasions, it was not uncommon for an Indian to eat from ten to twenty pounds of meat in one night without indigestion or any other observable ill effect (Dodge 1959, p. 281).

Scarcity or superabundance with but little regulatory control by man leads to inability to schedule food intake. Times and the circumstances of eating are important to Westerners, but Parkman, noting that the Indian did not schedule meals and that one hour of the day served as well as any other, gave a feast to his Indian friends at eleven in the morning (1910, p. 169). Hans (1907, pp. 100 f.) corroborates the absence of patterned daily scheduling: "There are no regular hours for meals. A kettle of meat is put on the fire, and when cooked it is taken off and set on the ground." However, while it was true that the rhythm was different from that of the Western observers, there was nonetheless a general pattern:

> The Indians . . . followed the "No Breakfast Plan" even when food was plenty. When travelling they would start without eating and stop at noon for a rest and informal lunch. If in the camp the men would get up early and leave at once for the hunt or chase without the formality of breakfast. The principal meal was in the evening after the hunters returned with their game. The women would go out, get their share of the meat, which was equitably divided. Then while they prepared it the men rested and smoked. [Barton 1919, pp. 85 f.][6]

So it was not exactly impulse eating, but meals were tied more or less to the camp and the women. Being the individualists that the Sioux were, and are, the men got up of a morning and went out breakfastless. They might carry light storage foods for a noonday meal, but their principal intake was in the evening and in the village. Such a pattern of eating seems to be a common practice among hunting peoples and one which has great tenacity. Strict meal scheduling as is common in Western society fits best into a highly industrialized, mechanized society where food supply is controlled and regular.

We have said the Sioux were trained to scarcity or engorgement. It follows that there were scarcity, or famine, foods, as they are sometimes called, that is, items of diet which are not generally preferred but which are eaten when nothing else is available. It may even be that some items are neither defined, nor used, as food except under unusual circumstances. The Dakotas ate acorns and the vine of the bittersweet, but only in times of extremity. Several travelers in the northern region of Minnesota mentioned the use of tripe-de-roche as food, again only when nothing more desirable was available (Winchell 1911, p. 496). Another item eaten in hard times was the stems of prickly pears. The fruit, not the stems, was regularly eaten when found (either raw once the spines were removed or dried and stewed), but in times of famine the spines were removed from the stems, which were then roasted (Gilmore 1911–12, p. 104).

What feasts did they have and what feast foods? The Dakota Indians are mentioned in an article about the function of feasting as a

---

[6] J. P. Williamson, whose life story Barton tells, grew up among the Sioux. He was a boy of five among the Minnesota Sioux in 1840. In 1860 he joined the Redwood or Lower Agency of the Santees, or Mdewakantonwans, as a missionary.

part of ceremonies designed to cement ties: the Chippewas adopted rites, including singing, dancing, the lavish giving away of goods, and feasting, from the Hurons; the Dakotas were sometimes important participants. One writer notes that the Feast of the Dead was the last of a series of ceremonies held in 1660 by the Dakota and the Saulteur (Hickerson 1960). A Canadian Indian agent, who had worked for Hudson Bay Company, mentioned what are essentially first fruit ceremonies:

> The first corn or wild rice of the season, the first duck or goose killed when they appear in the spring, are all reserved for the feast, at which those Indians only who are entitled to wear the badge of having slain an enemy, are invited. [Cited by Jenks 1900, p. 1091]

Similar ceremonies were common among the Ojibwas in the same area. Another writer records that two Dakota Indian ceremonial features were weeping upon entering the lodge and feeding the guest three ladlesful of food. The food, in this instance, was rice (Jenks 1900, p. 1085). In the ceremony of adoption, participants smoked a pipe and ate rice presented on birch bark plates (Jenks 1900, p. 1085). Speaking of a white dog feast, Parkman tells how two kettles of soup slung on a pole were carried to the center of the lodge and ladled (the ladles made of the horn of a Rocky Mountain sheep) into the wooden bowls which the Indians had brought with them. Later they had bread in the same bowls, and still later, tea, amply sweetened, but spoiled for Parkman's taste by the addition of soot "to make it look strong" (1910, p. 169).

I want to deal in this section with a number of diverse matters: dog sacrifice and the dog as food, entomophagy, cannibalism, narcotics and stimulants, and the nutritive content of the pre-Columbian diet, not only in reference to the exotics just listed, but *in toto*. A number of authors have written of the extent to which the dog was used as food. This is usually understood to be the domesticated dog, but Belden (1870, p. 162) says that the prairie dog was hunted and eaten also. As a companion to the Sioux, Belden ate dog meat frequently; he became fond of it and considered keeping a supply of dogs in order to have meat in all seasons, but he gave up the idea because he "wished to remain respectable in [his] own eyes, and retain some resemblance of civilization" (Belden 1870, p. 165). He wrote that "each Indian family keeps from six to sixteen dogs" (Belden 1870, p. 162). The appearance of Indian dog meat is reported to be very fine, resembling the flesh of a calf or antelope, and not black or coarse. Belden (1870,

p. 164) mentions a dog meat stew prepared with corn and wild arti-chokes which he found palatable. For a few trinkets Parkman acquired a white dog once when he wanted to give a feast to a Sioux band. A preference for a white dog rather than a colored animal is congruent with the reverential awe in which the white buffalo was held. Park-man's men killed the dog, singed it on a fire, chopped it up, and threw it in two kettles to boil (Parkman 1910, p. 168).

Catlin, one of our more romantic and colorful sources, opines that dog meat was inferior to buffalo meat or venison, although the Indian ate it even when he was well supplied with fresh and dried buffalo meat (1947, p. 231).

> The dog-feast is given, I believe, by all tribes in North America; and by them all, I think, this faithful animal, as well as the horse, is sacrificed in several different ways, to appease offended Spirits or Deities, whom it is considered necessary that they should conciliate in this way; and when done, is invariably done by giving the best in the herd or the kennel. [Catlin 1947, p. 231]

In a society which includes domesticated animals in its cultural inventory, a wide variety of attitudes toward the beasts may be found. They may be treated with indifference, brutality, or affection. If the domesticated animal occurs in any numbers, some of their number may be (temporarily or for some time) treated as pets. The Sioux were fond of their animals and this very fondness was part of the sacrifice when slaughter was ceremonial:

> The dog, amongst all Indian tribes, is more esteemed and more valued than amongst any part of the civilized world; the Indian who has more time to devote to his company, and whose untutored mind more nearly assimilates to that of his faithful servant, keeps him closer company, and draws him nearer to his heart; they hunt together, and are equal sharers in the chase—their bed is one; and on the rocks, and on their coats of arms they carve his image as the symbol of fidelity. [Catlin 1947, p. 230]

Since no one else has ever reported that the dog was a symbol of fidelity to the Sioux and the notion that they have a coat of arms is definitely erroneous, Catlin is both displaying the ethnocentrism of his day and romanticizing. Kelly (1872, pp. 90 f., 110) verifies the affection and esteem in which dogs were held and writes that the best of "the kennel" was chosen for sacrifices, but she also notes that dogs, horses, and cattle which died of natural or unknown causes were eaten. When a man was adopted into a Sioux tribe, a feast of buffalo tongues and roast dog was given him as well as horses, saddle, bow and arrows, a quiver, and other gifts (O'Reilly 1889, p. 31). Dodge noted that the dog was eaten as food during the 1870s when starvation among Plains Indians was common, and also that the dog might be prepared in a sacred ceremony. An extension of the liking of dog to the liking of wolf—"When very fat, wolf is considered nearly, if not quite, as good as dog" (Dodge 1959, p. 277)—is surprising in that this is the single statement to that effect.

An item of diet not palatable to contemporary Americans but important in the diet of some peoples is insects. A scholarly work on this subject contains no evidence that the Teton Dakotas were insect eaters; in fact, the only Plains tribe mentioned are the Cheyennes, of whom it was said that they ate vermin picked from each other (Bodenheimer 1951, p. 288). However, there is direct evidence of entomophagy among the Dakota Indians in an account by Kelly, who reports that one very hot day in an Indian village, a storm of locusts came.

> To catch them, large holes are dug in the ground, which are heated by fires. Into these apertures the insects are then driven, and, the fires having been removed, the heated earth baked them.
>
> They are considered good food and were greedily devoured by the famishing Sioux. Although the grasshoppers only remained two days, and went as suddenly as they had come, the Indians seemed refreshed. [Kelly 1872, pp. 123 f.]

Another item of diet which it is difficult to consider objectively is a fellow human:

> Cannibalism as a rite and also to allay hunger . . . is an obscure subject, which has not . . . been very deeply investigated. . . . The act must have required tremendous courage. . . . Among the Missouri River Indians, cannibalism was "almost unknown," save from hunger: "Ioway and Sioux" instances [are] known. . . . It had been known among the Bloods, but apparently from hunger alone. [Roe 1951, p. 890]

Roe associates cannibalism with ritualism and sacrifice and makes a connection between cannibalism and the torture of prisoners. He referred to a report submitted in 1840 by a Dr. Gregg who said that cannibalism among the Plains Indians was rare, and had been abandoned by the prairie tribes at the time of his writing (Roe 1951, p. 890). And then there is the other side of the coin: being eaten. Jenks, citing a document from 1840, tells that the Ojibwas sometimes cooked the flesh of their enemy, the Sioux, with rice (Jenks 1900, p. 1084).

Food, whether it be a member of our species, a more distantly related animal, or the grain of the plain, is not all that pleases the palate. There are also narcotics and stimulants. The Sioux smoked. According to a distribution map prepared by Wissler, the Sioux had various tobacco usages; pipe smoking was the most common (Wissler 1950, p. 26). Murray (1962, pp. 1–44) has given us a detailed and focused study of pipe smoking and tobacco use; he indicates an early and widespread usage throughout the Northern Plains.

The use of peyote apparently came in the late nineteenth century to the Sioux; in the twentieth century the Dakotas were diffusing the drug (both eaten as a button and drunk in a broth) and other features of peyote cult to the northern Utes (Aberle and Stewart 1957, p. 108).

What of the nutritive value of the exotic items of diet we have been considering as well as the more prosaic foods which formed the bulk of intake among the Indians we are describing? While direct evidence is impossible to secure, it seems highly probable that the Sioux have suffered periodically from inadequate and unbalanced diets for a very long time. On the other hand, their stature in general and the vigor of some individuals in particular attest to adequate nutrition at least some of the time. The whole subject of the nutritive value of pre-Columbian diets is one which has not been systematically investigated and which is fraught with difficulties, perhaps of sufficient magnitude to make such investigation unfruitful. There are, however, some things that can be said. The amount and the variety of items are important considerations when making judgments about the adequacy of diet, and we have already seen that the diet was much wider in range than formerly thought. Wide range is basic to nutrition. What we cannot with any confidence speak about is the amount of food, of either a wide or a restricted range, which the Indians had. Another indicator of the adequacy of a given diet is the nutritional value of selected items. Here, too, our knowledge and information are less than we wish they were. However, it can be said that "wild rice is the most nutritive single food which the Indians of North America consumed" (Jenks 1900, p. 1083), more nutritious than other foods which wild-rice-producing Indians had access to (maize, berries, and meat). Very rich in carbohydrates and crude protein or the albuminoids, wild rice is also more nutritious than any of our common cereals such as oats, barley, wheat, rye, and domesticated rice (Jenks 1900, pp. 1080 f.).

The Indian diet of this grain, combined with maple sugar and with bison, deer and other meats, was probably richer than that of the average American family today. Of course, this diet lasted a limited part of the year only. [Jenks 1900, p. 1081]

If the diet was periodically both rich and sufficient, at other times it was neither. We have seen how the Sioux were trained to stoicism and restraint and how their ability to fast and to endure privation impressed several authors. Roe describes Indians as "champion fasters of the human race" (1951, p. 659). Perhaps this characteristic of their diet, centuries old, is sometimes lost sight of in the furor of modern clamor for "change." Nutritional imbalance in long-range diet, inadequacy of food supply, and sheer absence of food are an ancient characteristic of the Sioux: a characteristic which must be fought and changed in today's diet.

Myths and the Indian Diet

The preliterate peoples of the world have a wealth of oral literature, some of which lingers on as part of their cultural heritage long after they have adopted writing and other modern media of expression. It is not surprising that many myths contain items about origins, about the respect and deference due certain supernaturals, and about the qualities of plants and animals that were eaten (or avoided although edible). The Dakotas had their share of origin myths. While still in Minnesota, and part of a Woodland culture complex, they had stories about the origin of maize, wild rice, tobacco, and the bow and arrow (Winchell 1911, p. 508). Another kind of origin myth, about the beginning of knowledge, tells how a woman collecting tipsin roots was resting under a cedar tree and was given the knowledge of how to make baskets, and—what's more and what's better—baskets that walked alongside the gatherer and did not have to be carried. This endearing quality was lost when a later food collector, a greedy and inconsiderate woman, found a "winter storehouse of the bean mouse people," and took all their food without replacing any:

So she filled her basket with the wild ground beans, which are so delicious when cooked with bits of meat. She cared not that it had cost the bean mouse people many weary hours of hard work to dig these beans and bring them together in this place, nor did she care that without them the bean mouse people, their old people and their little ones, all would be left destitute of food and must perish from famine. [Gilmore 1929, pp. 65 f.]

Some tribes believed the herds emerged each spring from the earth (Roe 1951, p. 643). This was not a belief confined to the Dakotas. Many Plains Indians, perhaps all, believed that the buffalo originated in a country underground where they lived in countless numbers. "Every spring the surplus swarmed, like bees from a hive, out of great cave-like openings" (Dodge 1959, p. 286). According to Gilmore, each species of plant and animal life had for the Dakotas its own particular song which was its soul:

> The earth was poetically and mystically regarded as Mother of all living things, all plants, animals, and human beings. The sky likewise was re- garded as Father, and the Cardinal Points as the Paths of approach of the Powers which are all about us in this world. [Gilmore 1911–12, p. 81. See also pp. 85 f.]

In such an orientation man is of nature, not superordinate to it, nor him to it; all the good things of nature are his friends and kindred. All the qualities of nature are qualities that might be his. It is in this context that we can understand why the Indian would not eat turkey unless on the verge of starvation. "He believed it would make him cowardly, and [make him] run from his enemies, as the turkey runs from his pursuers" (Dodge 1959, p. 278).

On the Reservation

Sometimes the layman thinks that on a certain date the reservation system was created and the Indians moved from their free life to settlement and enduring frustrations. Historians and anthropologists know better, and any of numerous excellent accounts can show what a long-drawn-out affair becoming reservation Indians was, and how the patterns of free movement over the land lingered on after the change until, even in the 1960s, some Indians are nomadic in the sense that they prefer roving among rodeos, powwows, and give-aways, rather than staying at home tending a garden and canning foods. One can sympathize with this point of view, which is also part of the appeal of the writings of Jack Kerouac and the charm of the life of international flower children. What happened to the Sioux subsistence pattern in the transition from free-roaming days to the reservation? What of the items and behavior of the food quest, food preparation, and food con- sumption in such a basic change of a way of life?

Diet changed, of course, and the ways of seeking food and preparing food; but these modifications, like the rest of the changes the Indians underwent, were slow and incomplete. Perhaps daily life was most like the old life when the Indians were still almost wholly supported by rations and a good part of that ration was beef. At least this was the beginning of the change, and there are illuminating examples of the conservatism of old practices: for instance, as they became a reservation people, techniques used to hunt buffalo were inappropriately transferred to the slaughter of cattle. In the early days, under the ration system, beef came onto the reservation on the hoof. Several writers have given accounts (Pancoast 1883; Holley 1892; Hyde 1956). The following is from Pancoast (1883, pp. 22 f.):

> At Rosebud about once a week the trader issues to the Indians their supply of beef. These animals are not butchered in the usual way, but hundreds of them are driven out of the corral on the hills, where the Indians await them and shoot them down. The day after my arrival happened to be "issue day," as they call it. About ten o'clock the Indians began to assemble on their ponies, armed with pistols and short rifles, and very soon the hills were bright with gay groups of horsemen. Suddenly there is a scattering among the riders, and over the sharp edge of the hill, plunging down the slope in a wild, irregular gallop, come the cattle, fierce Texas steers with huge horns. With remarkable precision each Indian selects his victim and separates it from the throng. The scene that follows is a quick succession of beautiful, shifting pictures. The huge maddened, clumsy brutes racing aimlessly over the steep slopes, lashing their tails and tossing their heads, foiled at every point by their nimble adversaries, who wheel about them glorious flashes of color. There is a stirring abandon and daring in the way the men dash up and down the tumble of hills. Every few minutes comes a puff of smoke and the sharp crack of a rifle, then you wait and watch. Some heavy beast thunders on, staggers, stumbles, and his great bulk tumbles in a convulsive heap. After it is over come the squaws, like the stragglers on the field after a battle, knock those that are yet alive on the head with a tomahawk, and cut up the slain for their expectant families.

The irregularity of food intake which has been described already, continued on the reservation. Upon receiving rations the reservation Indians would hurriedly consume the food that was allotted for a week or ten days, share widely with the extended family, and then go hungry until the following ration day arrived (Hyde 1956, pp. 178 f.). Another cultural pattern carried over from nomadic days was in food preparation. The beef rations were dried and stored as had been the buffalo meat (Dodge 1959, p. 255). Another carry-over was food gathering and collecting; as to fruit, for many decades the Indians continued to prefer the wild species to the dried fruit introduced by traders (Denig 1961, p. 12).

In the third quarter of the nineteenth century when many Indians were being settled on reservations, the concept of culture was not popularly known, nor was the tenacity of cultural patterns well understood, not even by the anthropologists who befriended the Indians and certainly not by many other friends of the Indians. In a mood of optimism and, in many cases, a spirit of genuine benevolence, efforts were made to "civilize and Christianize the Indians." There were few, if any, who understood that a unilateral attempt at far-reaching culture change was doomed to failure and—what is worse—took a heavy human toll. Although there are instances when substantially different societies modify their culture to approximate that of the technologically more advanced culture, the number of societies who cannot make this change outnumber those who do. Plains Indians, as indeed most American Indians, were among those who clung tenaciously to the old way of life. Not understanding the nature and function of that tenacity, the people who had responsibility for the Indians tried to "civilize" them by substituting agriculture or stock herding for the old hunting and gathering way of life.

Before we consider either the introduction of agricultural or stock-herding programs, we need to note that when the Sioux were in Minnesota they were sporadic agriculturalists. Agriculture was an ancient subsistence base for many aborigines of America before the white man came, and the variety of crops grown was not inconsiderable. Europeans first got corn, potatoes, and tobacco from American Indians (jokesters say of the last, "They knew what they were doing!"). Many of the great pre-Columbian American civilizations were possible and developed only because of a firm agricultural base, and often the basic crop was corn. Although, thanks to the labor of archaeologists, we know that corn was widely grown, it is not so well known that it was grown as far north as the Dakotas (and indeed recent archaeological work in Canada shows that it was raised in southern Ontario). Before contact times, maize had reached the limits of its possible migration in almost all directions, limited in its spread only by peculiarities of soil and climate. At the northern and southern boundaries of the area, and at high altitudes, the growing season was also a limiting factor. The prairies and the plains did not produce maize, primarily for two reasons: buffalo herds were dense and made agriculture both difficult and unnecessary, and any part of the prairie which had the proper soil and climatic conditions for maize growth had a ground cover of sod-forming grasses and other tough-rooted perennial plants. In fact, the plains were not cultivable by man until the introduction of the iron plow, and indeed, some areas were not put to agriculture until little more than a century ago, with the coming of the steel-moldboard plow drawn by horses or oxen (Weatherwax 1954, p. 53).

One interesting exception . . . was in the northern part of the Great Plains. When the French explorers first visited the territory now included in the Dakotas, they found the northern limit of corn cultivation at the Knife River villages of the Hidatsa Indians in western North Dakota, at latitude north, 47°30'. [Weatherwax 1954, p. 51][7]

The use of maize by the Dakota Indians in prereservation days appears to have been sporadic and of minor importance. From tribes which made a greater use of it we know that all general types (dent corn, flint corn, flour corn, sweet corn, and pop corn) were extant. Purity was maintained from generation to generation by selecting typical ears for seed and by planting varieties at some distance from each other (Gilmore 1911–12, pp. 67 f.). While crop production figures are so rare as to be almost nonexistent, Lowie (1954, p. 19) points out:

> Probably the Eastern Dakota were the least productive of the farming groups; except near Lake Traverse (between Minnesota and South Dakota) most of their villagers planted so little corn that . . . "they probably did not raise enough annually . . . to feed the whole population more than a week or two." . . . in 1878, a good year, the Santee are credited with having raised 25 5/7 bushels per acre, and in a fair season the villagers of the Upper Missouri produced 20 bushels.

If the Sioux in their Woodland stage were indifferent agriculturalists, they still had developed a liking for corn, and there are ways to obtain a product besides raising it. The village tribes (Mandans, Hidatsas, and Arikaras) are agriculturalists today and have been for a long time; there is a good probability that the Dakota hunters traded with them for corn. Matthews speaks of the nomadic tribes who came in to trade with the Hidatsas at harvest time. A truce would prevail from the time they came within sight of the village until they had again disappeared (Matthews 1877, p. 27).

By custom and preference, then, the Sioux economy was based on hunting and gathering, and every indication is that they would have liked to keep it that way on the reservation. But as their territory diminished and the game disappeared, the hunting life became increasingly more difficult and less productive, and the Bureau of Indian Affairs made numerous valiant attempts to initiate an agricultural program. With no foreknowledge of how difficult and lengthy a task this was to be and how limited the degree of success possible, planners and administrators assumed their task with vigor and optimism. Given

[7] Weatherwax writes of the American agricultural scene as it was in the sixteenth century—what the early Spanish explorers saw or might have seen.

this belief in the possibility—nay, the inevitability—of change, and given the imperatives of bureaucratic existence, each year the resident Indian agent wrote sanguine reports of the progress of the agricultural programs. The mood of the time, the unrealistically optimistic point of view, is well expressed by V. T. McGillycuddy, of the Pine Ridge Agency, South Dakota, who, as early as 1884, said:

> The Indians' attempt at farming has succeeded better the past year than ever before, there having been double the acreage under cultivation, and the return in produce of all kinds has been such as to encourage the hope that in the future, under more systematic and enlarged efforts, this may prove a valuable and bountiful agricultural region, and the Sioux in farming and stock-raising attain a successful result in his efforts at self-support. [Commissioner of Indian Affairs 1884, p. 38]

Similarly hopeful reports were submitted by the agents of the Sioux located at the Cheyenne River, Rosebud, Standing Rock, and Sisseton agencies. As late as 1912 the report submitted by the Commissioner of Indian Affairs indicated the continuing efforts to move the Sioux and other tribes to a substantially changed subsistence base (Commissioner of Indian Affairs 1912, p. 7) under programs undertaken at tremendous cost and with very little success. Optimism, good faith, sustained and/or changing programs are not enough. The agricultural programs introduced to change the Dakota way of life failed for many reasons, cultural persistence being only one. Drought, fire, insects, and other hazards of farming conspired against any Sioux who could be persuaded to try farming.

Stock raising fared a little better. Caring for cattle was more in consonance with the old hunting way of life and there were a few satisfying similarities, although they were outweighed of course by the dissimilarities. Slowly some Indians drifted into the business of cattle growing and selling. However, pastoral activities were, at best, intermittent and practiced only by an unestimated portion of the Sioux. Those who found cattle raising satisfactory and advantageous faced the competition of the whites who well before World War I began running their herds (unofficially) on reservation lands (Meyer 1967, p. 196). Toward the end of World War I the selling of beef became so profitable that white ranchers became emboldened. By means never clearly explained, the government rules which were meant to protect Indian lands were set aside; grazing permits were given to non-Indians; and the Sioux lived gloriously but briefly on rents, the while he lost his herds (Hyde 1956, pp. xl f.).

The years on the reservation, then, were very difficult ones for many reasons. Accommodations and adaptations had to be made daily. In diet this was as true as with any other facet of culture. In the beginning meat constituted a larger proportion of the rations that the Indians got than later was the case. Indeed, the Sioux had a meat diet for most of their history; even after they were on the reservation and after the disappearance of the buffalo some had built up fairly large cattle herds, but most were dependent on rations. After 1916 beef was no longer included in rations, and this was the first time the Sioux had a lengthy experience living without meat.

Feeding refugees or displaced or relocated persons is a difficult task. Barton tells of 3,000 Sioux virtually held prisoners at Crow Creek in 1863 and 1864 before the government was able to give them adequate care. The Civil War worsened the situation.

> The Indians were told to come in the morning when the whistle blew, bringing their pails, and they received a ladleful for each member of the family. . . . [The soup] was strongly flavoured with green cottonwood and was very thin and unpalatable, but it was their food for the day and all that they had. [Barton 1919, p. 79]

As refugees, displaced persons, and then reservation dwellers, the Indians experienced a change in diet which was a long, slow process with clearly observable deteriorative effects. Cleanliness in the Protestant ethic sense was not part of Indian precontact culture, but what had been previously a kind of untidiness degenerated into squalor under reservation conditions. In large measure, choice was gone. Writing of the hardships of the late 1870s, Dodge says (1959, pp. 278 f.):

> The Indian who only ten years ago contented himself with nothing but the very choicest portions of animal food, now pinched by hunger, eats any and everything. Dogs, wolves, reptiles, half-decomposed horseflesh, even carrion birds, all go to appease the gnawings of his famished stomach.

Indeed, after 1870, starving Indians could be found all over Indian country, scavenging slop barrels and dump piles, eating dead horses, begging the raw blood and offal from butcher shops, and stripping the small patches of corn, vegetables, pumpkins, and melons they cultivated before they were mature (Dodge 1959, p. 281).

Their gardens did not provide enough food and the agricultural programs were not successful enough to bring them into the money economy. So began the long period when a substantial portion of their diet was government-provided rations.

The main articles on the list of free rations were low-grade beef, low grade salt or pickled pork, and a very low-grade flour, specially milled as Indian flour and of a quality that no white family would use. The cheapest grade of green coffee beans were added and rough brown sugar. [Hyde 1956, p. 178]

Boiling remained the cooking technique preferred for food preparation:

Everything went into the huge tin kettle that was always simmering: meat and any vegetables that could be obtained. The Sioux preferred shelled corn, as they could boil the corn with their meat or make it into hominy. A great deal of the flour ration was wasted; the rest was made into tough pan bread, baked in a skillet. [Hyde 1956, p. 178]

There is more data on the rations diet later, but here is one more view, this time from the early 1900s.

In 1908, Alex Hrdlicka, a pioneer physical anthropologist, investigated health conditions of five selected tribes for the Indian Office and the Smithsonian Institution. Of the Oglala Sioux at Pine Ridge, he noted that they ate much meat; especially beef:

They cook this fresh, or cut it into strips and dry it on cords stretched outside their dwellings. Other common articles of diet are badly made wheat bread and large quantities of coffee. When they have money they purchase crackers and canned foods. They eat very irregularly, both as to time and quantity. During feasts and when visitors are present, they not infrequently use the same wooden spoon or other utensil, one after another, and eat from the same dish, the bones and other remnants being freely strewn over the floor. [Moorehead 1914, pp. 270 f.]

From a consideration of unsanitary and unhealthy conditions, we move now to a concept of sickness and therapy in the old culture, more specifically, to the use of plants as medicine.

The Use of Plants as Medicine

This section is a description of the use of plants as medicine among the Dakotas. No systematic search of the literature was made for this information, as originally it was not part of the research planned. However, the inclusion of this subject is justified because it is of such intrinsic interest and because, to the degree that plants or other substances are taken internally in therapy, the investigation of such practices is part of the investigation of dietary intake. The data in this section are almost all from a single source (which will be cited by page number only), but that source is an excellent one: "Uses of Plants by the Indians of the Missouri River Region," a work which includes a glossary of the scientific names of plants, the common English name, and, when available, the Dakota, Omaha, Winnebago, and Pawnee names (Gilmore 1911–12, pp. 139–52). In the material that follows, the common English name is most frequently used.

A prairie mushroom, commonly called the puffball, was used as a styptic and for application to the umbilicus of the newborn (p. 62). Fruit and leaves of the cedar tree were boiled together to make a potion which was drunk as a remedy for coughs. Twigs from the same tree were burned and the smoke inhaled with the patient's head enveloped in a blanket for a head cold (p. 63). In 1849–50, the Oglalas, faced with a new disease, Asiatic cholera, treated it with various cedar-leaf decoctions, which they drank and also bathed with (p. 64).

Down from the common cattail had many uses which cotton has in our society: as a dressing for burns and scalds, as an application to infants to prevent chafing, and as a soft bed on which to lay the newborn (pp. 64 f.). Sweet grass was burned in many ceremonies to induce the presence of benevolent supernaturals; sage was burned to exorcise evil powers and malevolent supernaturals (p. 66). Sweet flag (*Acorus calamus L.*) was widely esteemed for its medicinal uses. It was taken as a carminative; a decoction of it was drunk for fever; the rootstock was chewed for toothache and as a cough remedy; and it was inhaled in a smoke treatment in the manner already described. According to Gilmore, mystic powers were ascribed to this plant (pp. 69 f.). The plant *Lilium Umbellatum pursh*, chewed or pulverized and applied as an antidote for the bite of a small poisonous brown spider, was reported to give rapid relief from inflammation and swelling (p. 71). Soapweed was used as soap, especially for washing the hair.

Any species of oak might be used for "bowel trouble." The bark of the root was scraped and boiled and the potion, when drunk, was purported to be especially effective with children (p. 75). The fresh inner bark of the slippery elm or red elm was boiled and the potion drunk as a laxative (p. 76). The *Humulus americanus nutt*, or hops, had several medicinal uses: a part of the root which had extended three or four feet into the ground was chewed and applied to wounds either alone or in combination with other medicines, and the fruit was steeped to make a drink to alleviate fevers and intestinal pains (p. 77). Another plant which was boiled and the potion drunk to allay fever was wild four-o'clock. Mixed with the roots of another plant, it was boiled to make a vermifuge to be drunk four consecutive evenings before retiring. Wild four-o'clock roots were boiled with those of another plant to make a remedy for swelling of arms and legs; the concoction was rubbed in a downward motion on the swollen part. After delivery the mother drank the preparation to reduce abdominal swelling (p. 78). Sprouts or young growths or the wild plum tree were used by the Teton Dakotas in a prayer offering for the benefit of the sick. The sprout, used as a wand, may have been painted; and the offering proper was fastened near the top of the wand. Any material acceptable to the supernatural spirits, such as tobacco, was used. Sometimes an altar was prepared and the wand set upright on it (p. 87).

The Dakotas, Omahas, Poncas, Winnebagos, and Otos used the bark of the root of the Kentucky coffee tree in an enema solution for constipation; also, the bark, pulverized and mixed with water. If, on being put into the water, the powdered bark settled quickly to the bottom, it was interpreted as a bad omen for the patient; if the powder, on touching the water, began to circle to the right and gradually mixed in, it was taken as a favorable prognostication (pp. 89 f.). The Indians had syringes in pre-Columbian times. An animal bladder served as the bulb and a hollow cylindrical bone formed the tube, the two attached by sinew wrapping.

For toothache the Teton Dakotas chewed the root of wild licorice and held it in the mouth. The leaves were steeped and then applied to the ears for earache. In addition, the roots yielded a potion which was given to children for fever. Lastly, a poultice was made for the sore backs of horses by chewing the leaves (p. 92). The roots of *Psoralea tunuiflora* were mixed with those from two other plants, boiled, and given in a potion to patients with consumption (p. 93). *Parosela aurea*, called a "bitter medicine," was used as a decoction for colic and dysentery (p. 94).

The dried root of the purple mallow was pulverized and fired, and the smoke was inhaled for a head cold. A potion was made from un-fired powder to bathe aching parts of the body. A potion made from the boiled root was drunk for internal pains (p. 103). A plant with the common name of red false mallow has a mucilaginous property. The members of a Dakota curing society called the *heyoka* chewed this plant to a paste and then rubbed it over their hands and arms. It gave them a temporary immunity to scalding water and enabled them to fish pieces of food out of boiling kettles without burning themselves. Also the plant was chewed to a salvelike consistency and applied to inflamed sores and wounds, on which it had a cooling and healing effect (p. 103). Another plant with a mucilaginous property, the prickly pear, was used on wounds; the stems were peeled and bound on the wounds as a dressing (p. 104). The stems of the *Nuttallia nuda* were stripped of their leaves, pounded to extract the gummy yellow juice, boiled, strained, and applied externally for fever (p. 103).

The gentian was called "yellow medicine" by the Dakotas because of the color of its roots. A decoction made from the root was taken as a tonic, and it was also used in combination with other ingredients as a medicine (p. 109). It seems that the Dakotas almost always boiled their medicine. Wild verbena was boiled to make a drink taken as a palliative for a stomach ache. The same plant was used by the Omahas, who merely steeped it to make a decoction (p. 111). For abdominal pains the flowers and leaves of horsemint were boiled together (p. 111).

Another cold remedy was an infusion of the leaves of the rough pennyroyal. This was also used as a special item in the diet of the ill (special dietary items for the ill are, unfortunately, rarely mentioned). Rough pennyroyal was used as a tonic appetizer and to add flavor to the food (p. 112). Wild mint, steeped in water and with sugar added, was drunk as a carmative and also merely because it was pleasant (p. 112). Weak or inflamed eyes were treated with a potion made from steeping the leaves of the wolfberry (p. 116).

Gourds or various squashes were, and still are, important in ceremonials. Pumpkins, gourds, melons, and squash (*Cucurbitaceae*) will now be considered. The wild gourd, *Pepo foetidissima*, was held in high esteem as a medicine by many tribes. It grows only in the drier parts of the Great Plains, was regarded with reverence and awe, and required careful, circumspect handling because of its mystic properties. In fact, it was considered dangerous to dig it up or handle it without knowledge and ritual. Offerings of tobacco were given to the spirit of the plant, prayer accompanied the act, and great care was exercised not to wound the root in removing it from the earth. The root was likened to the human body; for an ailment in a certain section of the body, a portion of the root in a similar section was used: "For headache or other trouble in the head some of the top of the root was used; for abdominal trouble a bit of the middle of the root; and so on" (pp. 116 f.).

Boiled sunflower heads were used by the Teton Dakotas for pulmonary disorders (p. 130). The comb plant was used as an antidote for snake bite and other venomous bites and stings and poisonous conditions, and as a smoke treatment for headache among humans and distemper in horses. It had further uses: a piece was kept on a painful tooth until there was relief; it was applied to enlarged glands as in mumps. It was also reported that "jugglers [*sic*]" bathed their hands and arms in it so they might grasp pieces of meat from boiling kettles without suffering pain. Finally, burns were bathed in juice from it to alleviate the pain, and the plant was employed in the steam bath to make the heat more endurable (p. 131).

Grindellia squarrosa, or sticky head, was prepared as a fluid and given to children for colic (p. 133). The little wild sage is known in the Dakota language as "woman's medicine" and was used in bathing and also taken internally for menstrual irregularities (p. 134). Wild sage, viewed as having special cleansing powers for both sexes, was used for ordinary bathing as well as if a person had broken some taboo or unwittingly touched some sacred object. Believed effective against malevolent powers, it was often used at ceremonies to drive away evil powers. Sometimes a decoction of wild sage was prepared for stomach trouble (p. 135).

Weatherwax (1954, pp. 114 f.) contends that corn silk was used as a cure for some types of dysentery in some areas and also as a medicine in the case of urogenital disorders, while the corncob when burned was used as a remedy for empyema.

PART TWO—CONTEMPORARY

Recent Studies

Section One is drawn from early accounts of the Sioux and deals primarily with life before they were put on reservations. Section Two is concerned with more recent reports, and particularly with reservation life. In addition, I present material from my field work.

In the early 1920s when the Crow Creek Reservation was studied by Jesse Anderson Stene (1927), it was popularly believed that the American Indian was the vanishing American, a race whose numbers had been so decimated by warfare, disease, and reservation life that the aborigines, the Sioux among them, literally would soon cease to be. Stene began her research with these assumptions: that (1) the change from an active outdoor life to one of restricted physical exertion was only part of the reason for decreasing population; and (2) a more probable cause for population decline, and one which had not been adequately explored, was nutritional factors.

In evaluating the study, it is relevant to know that the author's family lived near the reservation and that she had excellent rapport with government officials, storekeepers, and schoolteachers, whom she interviewed. She also constructed and administered a questionnaire to Indian families on the reservation and verified and supplemented family information by searching government records.

Of a population of 900 Indians, the survey covered 67 families (323 individuals, or about one-third of the Indian population of the reservation). One-third of the families studied were on welfare. As part of welfare care, rations were issued once a month to each person as follows: beef, twenty-five to forty pounds; salt pork, issued in lieu of beef twice a year, ten pounds; flour or hardtack (alternated), fifteen pounds; sugar, two and one-half pounds; coffee, two and one-half pounds; rice or beans (alternated), two and one-half pounds; baking powder, one-fourth pound; and laundry soap, one pound (p. 27). The kind and quantities of food issued in rations through the years of reservation status have been a contributing factor to the food preferences and habits of the Sioux today.

While water is not directly an item of diet, its use in food preparation and the maintenance of standards of cleanliness, and the relation of both of these factors to health, is of interest. Forty-nine families obtained their water from the Missouri River. The water was very muddy and appeared dirty; however, repeated analysis failed to show the presence of pathogens. Of the remaining families, eleven obtained water from wells, five from a creek, and two from springs. Methods of water storage were unsanitary.

Food preparation was a simple affair, particularly in the summertime. To cook, the Crow Creek Sioux dug a hole in the ground, banked it with stones, and placed a grate over it. Her kitchen cutlery, a single butcher knife, was strapped to her waist and she used a stick for stirring. Each member of the family had a tin cup for soup or coffee. Mrs. Stene tells us that it seemed to be a rule that many Indian families never removed a coffee pot or a pot of soup from the stove: the vessel stayed there, a permanent, blackened fixture. There was little scheduling of meals and little budgeting of resources, a condition already noted as derivative from the hunting life of precontact days. If food was plentiful, people ate to repletion; more often, unfortunately, food was scarce, and then the Indians went hungry or subsisted on black coffee and bread or hardtack. More than half the families had no regular hours for meals and over 60 percent ate between meals. About two-thirds of the families never ate at tables, while almost 20 percent of the remaining ones did so only occasionally. Much bread was used, but fruits, vegetables, eggs, and butter were used very little. Meat, much desired, was not often obtained in amounts large enough to satisfy the Indians.

The use of specific items of diet may now be considered. Oatmeal was the favorite cereal; fifty families ate it. The rest of the families (seventeen) were without any kind of cereal most of the time. Among the fifty families who used oatmeal, there were some who occasionally purchased corn flakes. Cereals, served with sugar and milk if the family had fresh milk, otherwise black coffee with canned milk in it, was eaten by all members of the family, even the youngest (pp. 46 f.).

Bread was an important item in the diet, and sixty-six families made their own; of this number, twenty also bought bread. All of the bread, whether made at home or purchased, was from white flour issued by the government; the Indians either did not know of the less highly refined flours or had not cultivated a liking for them. It is not clear whether the Indians had any kind of an oven. Twenty-seven families made grease bread, which is bread or biscuit dough fried in deep fat. In the majority of such families light bread and biscuits were also made; these lessen fat intake. Biscuits made of flour, salt, baking powder, grease or lard, and water were a favorite with many, and for one-fourth of the families it was the only breadstuff used. Measurements were crude and exact proportions never obtained, but through experience they knew approximately how much of each material to use. Some families received cornmeal in rations, and a few reported making corn bread once in a while (pp. 48 f.).

Very few families had a vegetable garden, despite the fact that the government issued seed. Sometimes a small patch of corn or a few potato plants, not necessarily tended, were found. Those who planted gardens put in navy beans, corn, squash, and potatoes. Local storekeepers did not keep fresh vegetables on hand because they found no sale for them among the Indians: one-third of the families used no vegetables at all and seven families had potatoes and navy beans as their only vegetable. The remaining thirty-six families (little more than half of the example) used vegetables other than potatoes and beans; but twenty-five of these families did not have more than two vegetables, leaving only about one out of six families with any variety among vegetables.

Of canned vegetables which the traders were able to sell, tomatoes were the most popular, with peas second. People had an idea that canned food was poisonous and caused stomach trouble. This may have had a basis in fact, since bulged cans or otherwise defective and inferior grades of goods were sometimes sold to Indians. Vegetables were used for the most part in soup. Squash and corn were generally dried, either by placing in the sun or hanging above the stove. Some Indians reported that formerly they had gone to the hills and dug wild turnips (p. 51).

As with vegetables, fruits formed a very small part of the average Sioux Indian diet. Eleven families used no fruit at all. One old lady, asked if she ate fruit, replied that she was not a baby any longer. Twenty families ate only dried fruit such as raisins, peaches, prunes, and wild chokecherries which they had picked and dried. Over half of the families reported having both fresh and dried fruit, but only in small amounts. Those who did use some fresh fruit stated that they bought about twenty-five cents worth of oranges or bananas once or twice a month. Grapes, chokecherries, and plums grew wild in this section of the country, and a few of the younger women used them to make jelly or canned them for sauce. The older women dried fruit and later cooked it in a large amount of water sweetened with sugar, with flour added for thickening. Called gravy, this was considered delicious served on bread.

Candy and sweets are always a favorite. The children especially spent a good deal of the little money they had on cookies, crackerjacks, and candy. The storekeepers said that because they had so little to eat, they obtained quick energy and a temporary feeling of fullness from these items. Among the older Indians a few found the sweet tastes foreign and did not consider them delicious. The age at which children were considered old enough to begin eating candy was about one year (pp. 52 f.).

According to Stene, coffee drinking was very well established in the year she was doing her research. Of the sixty-seven families none served coffee less than twice a day, while some reported that they drank it all day long. Two-thirds of the children under seven also drank coffee and those over seven drank coffee as regularly and as freely as adults. In a few cases, mothers reported giving coffee occasionally to babies who were only four or five months old. Other hot drinks, originating in precontact times, were peppermint tea and a tea made from cherry tree bark, both steeped in hot water and considered medicine (pp. 54 f.).

Since in native Sioux diet dairy products played no part, what use was made of butter, milk, and eggs at the time that Stene did her research? Although each family might have raised chickens with little trouble, only twenty-one families did so; most did not want to take care of young chicks or feed hens, and were apt to kill fowl rather than plan for eggs in a time of scarcity. Although her survey was made in the late summer when eggs are generally plentiful, only one family had eggs to sell. She thought it highly probable that many families had no eggs whatsoever in the winter. Of the forty-six families who did not raise chickens, eighteen, or more than one-fourth of the total number, had no eggs, while the other twenty-eight bought them in small quantities. Among those who bought eggs the use was not heavy— about one-half dozen to two dozen a month in their cooking was common. None were eaten as eggs. On the other hand, families who raised chickens used eggs both for cooking and eating as well as in baking.

The average Indian family used much less butter than the average American family; many did not like it, but more could not afford it. Fifty families used less than one-third of a pound of butter a week per person. Some families (in one case a family of seven) used as little as a pound a month; twelve families made no use of butter whatsoever. In spite of the fact that most of the Indians lived on farms, only one family (with a considerable infusion of white blood and diffusion of white culture) made their own butter.

Butter aside, the Sioux made generous use of other fats, especially lard. Nine families used over a pound of lard per week per person; of these nine, one reported using over two pounds a week for each member of the family (pp. 55 f.). Conversely, nine families, among the poorest on the reservation, used only grease fried out of the meat which was issued to them. The Indians made no cookies or other kinds of pastries, so fats were used entirely for making grease bread or frying other foods.

The government had gone to great expense and trouble to promote the production and use of milk, and yet home production was less common than that of meat or eggs. Twenty years prior to Stene's appearance on the reservation, a thousand purebred cattle had been distributed; they had disappeared. Only five families of the sixty-seven studied took milk from their own cows, and four of them had milk only about three or four months of the year. About a third of the families used no milk at all, about a third used canned milk, and about the same number used fresh milk. Some separated milk was obtained from white neighbors. In Stene's estimation a conservative statement about milk use would have been that less than half the families had milk, either fresh or canned, more than half the time (p. 66).

Milk was not used in cooking; it was principally for drinking or for use in coffee. Children drank very little milk. Fifty-six children, considerably over half, did not drink milk at all. The rest drank small quantities at intermittent times. Furthermore, Stene doubted that the fresh milk used came from tuberculin-tested cattle (p. 67).

In the later days of their recorded history, when they were in the Dakotas, the Sioux subsisted primarily on a meat diet. Therefore it is interesting to note how they used meat in Stene's time. Poverty restricted them to much less than they would have preferred. Meat, said her informants, is "healthy for Indians." When they were first put on the reservation and the government began issuing rations, beef (they did not like mutton) was the main item. In view of these two factors—their primarily meat diet in prereservation days and the continuity of that diet in the days of rations—it is not at all surprising that meat has a psychological as well as a nutritional meaning to the Sioux. They feel hungry if they do not eat it (p. 59).

Thirty-six heads of the sixty-seven families were reported as farmers, but of those only six reported that they slaughtered. Of the families who did not kill their own meat, thirty-seven (a little over half) bought their meat, while the remaining twenty-four families received meat rations from the government.

Some indication of the quantities of meat which were eaten would be valuable. Stene interviewed older persons on the reservation whose memory of the Indians of the 1860s was that they had had great quantities of meat. The same old-timers felt that they should have meat at least twice a day and that in the ideal situation it would be on the fire all day long. Stene had difficulty in getting accurate estimates of consumption for particular units. Although the government issued set amounts to certain families, the families themselves did not consume them. The day for the reception of rations was also visiting day. Families not on the ration rolls would visit those who were, and often the visit lasted until the friend's or relative's meat was gone. Stene found that the number of families who used either large or small quantities of meat was greater than the number who used an average amount. No family used between three and four pounds a week per person, but the number of families who used five and a half pounds of meat increases significantly from a middle point. All who used less than three pounds per person per week were in actual poverty, and the amount used was dependent on the cash they were able to raise. On the other hand, those whose financial condition made it possible for them to eat or kill all the meat they wanted consumed more than four pounds per week per person.

The finding seems to be that the desire for meat was great, but the amount actually consumed depended on economic circumstances (pp. 60 f.). Another factor about the cycle of consumption that she and other investigators have noticed is that large amounts were eaten for a short period and then there were long periods in which the Indians went without any meat until the next ration or cash distribution day. Finally, how meaningful any of these figures may be in the light of the ethic of sharing is problematic. Stene suggests that there is quite a bit of equalizing of the amounts because of the visiting and hospitality.

Meat preparation is of interest. All of the older families and many of the younger ones dried the meat before using it. In the winter they hung it above the stove and in the summer it was put out in the sun. They did not have a particular place to hang it, but it was kept out of reach of the dogs. Stene saw it hanging on barbed wire fences, wagon boxes, and other "no more desirable" places (pp. 63 f.). Decay, maggots, and flies attacked the drying flesh. After drying, the meat was prepared several ways, the favorite of which was to cook it in a large amount of water. Another way was to pound or pulverize the meat and add fat or bone marrow and chokecherries. Known as *wasna*, this delicacy was served on special occasions or formed into little balls, dried, and stored away.

Stene's account of five hours of observation at a slaughter house is eloquent:

> Five hours of observation at the slaughter house on issue day gives one a little insight into several phases of the Indian's life. If the men are along, they usually are on the inside of the slaughter house watching the animals killed and cut up. The women form in groups on the outside waiting for their turn to get their meat. When a name is called, the woman enters the slaughter house and comes out dragging a huge piece of meat over the board planks on which the animal walked only an hour previous perhaps. Another woman often comes to her rescue and helps her lift it into the wagon. Some of the women have old blankets, not at all clean looking, to wrap around the meat. The women take turns at getting the paunch (cow's stomach), which they say makes the very best soup; and unborn calves are considered especially desirable. When the Indians leave the slaughter house, the horns and the hoofs are all that remain—everything else is taken for food. On cool

autumn days a fire is built nearby and after pressing the fecal material out with the fingers, the intestine is wrapped on a stick, cooked over a fire for a short time, and then eaten with much relish. This is a rare treat but seldom obtained. [Pp. 64 f.]

Nowadays most Indians are ashamed of their tribe's custom of eating dog; in Stene's day young dog was still eaten by quite a few. To prepare it, they skinned the animal, cooked it in soda water for a short time, then threw the water off, put fresh water on, and cooked it again. Again drained and cooked a third time, the meat was considered good to eat and made into a soup (p. 65).

Stene had searched the literature before her field studies; and one tentative conclusion she came to was that in precontact times the Indian's winter diet of meat provided an unbalanced diet which may have been a causative or contributing factor to the sometimes reddened or sore eyes they had in the wintertime, for it seems that some were partially blinded seasonally. These eye conditions passed away in the summertime when the Indians added some fruit and vegetables to their diet. Another conclusion of Stene's was this: because there is a diversity of opinion among writers in regard to the food eaten by Plains Indians, the generalizations found in the literature must be used with some caution. This diversity of opinion is due partly to the fact that the writers studied different tribes of Indians and at different seasons of the year. Finally,

for the tribes who ate much meat, and all parts of the animal—including all the internal organs, bone marrow and gristle—and had a liberal supply of wild turnips, whole corn and wild berries, it is fairly safe to say that the members were getting an adequate diet, at least in the summer. But if the Indians did not dry an ample supply of vegetables and fruits for winter use, their diets would be lacking in some of the necessary constituents. On the other hand there were tribes of Indians who had less food than this and it is certain that for these tribes the diet was inadequate, ... [Pp. 18 f.]

Another relevant study is based on information collected by questionnaire in 1955 in the Sisseton Reservation area. With a sample of 160 households out of the 350 (plus) found in the area, 1,100 people, or nearly 50 percent of the Indian residents, were included (McPartland 1955). The study, made to determine some of the factors necessary to understand the socio-economic standing of the Sisseton-Wahpeton Sioux, included food as one of the subjects investigated. Respondents were asked about their food intake in the twenty-four hours previous to the administration of the interview; this was *not* a standardized twenty-four-hour recall survey. In addition a few questions on expenditures for food and on noncommercial food resources were asked.

McPartland attempted to make an estimate of nutritional adequacy in terms of dollars spent. Assuming that ten dollars per month per person is a practical minimum for an adequate diet, he found nearly one-third of the families in the survey were living below that minimum; in fact, only one-tenth of the families in the survey spent that much for food.

He essayed some statements on the crude nutrient content of the diet. Forty-three families (27 percent) had had no common protein food in the twenty-four hours before the interview. The remaining 73 percent reported some meat or similar food as part of at least one meal. All families reported a high proportion of carbohydrate intake. Three-quarters of the households reported that they derived some part of their food from noncommercial sources such as gardens, gathering wild food, hunting, and fishing. Although it is impossible to tell from the report, it seems improbable that questions were asked about in-between-meal snacking, and indeed, it is unlikely that the informants had the three scheduled meals which McPartland presumed. It also appears likely that no attempt was made to assess the size of portions of food or to check the reliability of the statements made.

Less than 15 percent of Indian households (24 families) had running water in their homes. Of the remaining 136 households, 48 had wells and this water was reasonably certain to be pure, but more than half of the families in the survey (88 households) had neither running water nor wells. These families depended upon natural sources such as springs, streams, and lakes or had water hauled in from some distance, all sources which are inconvenient, limit water use, and are sometimes impure. The water supply of 85 percent of the households in the Indian community was below the minimum national standards.

In another study, one of acculturation among the Rosebud Sioux, Useem (1947) related the degree of blood (full, three-quarters, one-half, one-fourth, less than one-fourth) to various beliefs or behaviors. Of four thousand males and females fifteen years of age or older on the reservation, six hundred were included in the sample. Useem found that the crude death rate of the South Dakota Sioux Indians was twice that of the South Dakota whites. Tuberculosis was the largest single contributor to mortality; in the four-year period 1938–1941 inclusive, tuberculosis accounted for 28.6 percent of all deaths, or 33.7 percent of deaths for persons over the age of one year. Useem asked, "Is the high tubercular rate based on an inherent weakness of the Indians as a race, to meagre diet, ignorance, or inadequate care of the afflicted?" (p. 64). She decided that contributing factors were: (1) inadequate treatment and isolation facilities; (2) the recency of the establishment of the Department of Health (1924) and lack of sufficient staff to educate the population; (3) inadequate diet; (4) the low level of living (homes were small and did not permit isolation); and (5) the fact that the tubercular person was not considered a less desirable mate because of illness; furthermore, among married couples there was no voluntary limitation of the number of offspring.

Food habits learned from the whites had brought certain nutritional imbalances. In precontact days the Sioux had some habits which were nutritionally sound but which aroused the disgust of the whites and which were discontinued through ignorance on the part of the whites. For example, the Indians used to eat the internal organs of animals. This aroused the horror of the white schoolteachers, who shamed them for it. As the knowledge about nutrients advanced in white society, it came to be understood how valuable these parts were. An attempt to teach the Indians to eat again the organs which they once had, met with little success (pp. 75–77).

Useem gives a table of rations for a thirty-day period as they were issued on Rosebud Reservation during 1933–39 (p. 77). They are shown in Table I.

In regard to the items listed, Useem adds that the flour was white and not whole grain, that the rice was polished (thus lacking two sources of the vitamin B complex), and that there were no vegetables. The hope was that the Indians would raise fresh vegetables in their garden plots, but vegetables did not rank high as a food preference and the majority did not thus supplement their diet.

It is often noted that food habits are among the habits more difficult to change, but the Sioux have had to eat white man's food by necessity and now many of them have come to prefer it. However, a considerable number still like to eat distinctive Indian dishes. Useem asked:

1) Should Indian food preparation be kept?
2) Did you learn how to cook Indian way from your parent?
3) Did you teach your children how to cook the Indian way?

For all degrees of blood more than half of each group answer affirmatively to question 1. For the other two questions, the percentages fell off, but a greater proportion had learned to cook the Indian way from their parents than were then teaching their own children this skill (p. 175).

TABLE 1

RATIONS FOR A THIRTY-DAY PERIOD ON THE ROSEBUD RESERVATION, 1933–39

ITEMS	ADULT	CHILD OVER 12	CHILD UNDER 12
Cereals and legumes			
White wheat flour	24 pounds	12 pounds	12 pounds
Oatmeal	2 pounds	4 pounds	4 pounds
Polished rice	2 pounds	———	———
Dried beans	2 pounds	2 pounds	———
Soybeans	1 pound	1 pound	1 pound
Meat			
Brisket or jowl bacon	4 pounds	2 pounds	2 pounds
Fruit			
Dried prunes	5 pounds	5 pounds	———
Tomatoes	5 no. 2½ cans	3 no. 2½ cans	3 no. 2½ cans
Milk			
Dried whole milk	2 pounds	4 pounds	4 pounds
Sugar			
Cane sugar	3 pounds	2 pounds	2 pounds
Cane sorghum	1 quart	1 quart	1 quart
Coffee	1 pound	———	———
Yeast form	1 package	———	———
Salt	1 pound	———	———

Useem gave as examples of Indian food *wasna*, *tanigha*, dog, and buffalo. Her data indicated very little preference for Indian foods alone; rather, there was a steady increase toward the use of white food alone. It appears that the desire to keep Indian patterns was more symbolic than functional as the degree of Indian blood decreased. That is, individuals paid lip service to the value of the old patterns while increasingly practicing the new.

In an unpublished report, Cardwell (n.d.) has a wealth of data on the Oglala Sioux. Among other things, he notes that it is the children of post-weaning but preschool age who suffer most from malnutrition. He attributes this to the fact that nursing infants draw what nutrition they need from their mothers and that babies are regularly fed supplements of soup and gruel. School-age children usually receive free lunches or snacks which, while not robust meals, are nutritionally balanced. Cardwell also notes that the Sioux have definite likes about milk: the canned variety is most often bought because of its convenience when refrigeration is lacking; the taste is not disliked, but fresh milk is also enjoyed; the taste of powdered milk is not liked (p. 41).

Finally, attention must be drawn to dietary studies undertaken by nutritionists and home economists. Their data are more specialized and may be examined by beginning with a report on the nutritional status of adolescent Indian girls in boarding schools in the Dakotas (Talcott 1960). The interested reader is referred particularly to chapter two of the Talcott work for a recent review of the literature. The reports of the nutritionists amply document dietary deficiencies. In fact, Bosley (1959, p. 905) says of reservations in general that people can be found on them who are almost untouched by present-day concepts of nutrition.

Rosebud, 1962

In the summer of 1962 I took up residence on the Rosebud Reservation for six weeks. I lived in the boarding school and took my meals at first in town and later with the boarding school personnel. My techniques in data gathering were observation and formal and informal interviewing; no questionnaires were used; no sample was purposively drawn.

The Rosebud Reservation in 1962 spanned four counties (Mellette, Todd, Tripp, and Gregory) and included twenty-five communities in the sense that they were recognizable entities. Only twenty-two of these were political entities in that they had a spokesman to represent them. They are: Corn Creek, Black Pipe, Parmelee, He Dog, Upper Cut Meat, Soldier Creek, Timber Reserve, Grass Mountain, Rosebud, Spring Creek, Two Strike, Swift Bear, Horse Creek, Ring Thunder, Bad Nation, Butte Creek, Antelope Creek, St. Francis, Okreek, Ideal, Bull Creek, and Ponca. The three without representation are Hidden Timber, Little Crow, and Keyapaha.

Food Quest

Annual Cycle. The Sioux today are no longer a hunting and gathering people. The estimate of one official is that 80 percent of the Rosebud Sioux receive government surplus commodities. In addition to this, purchases are made at a modern, air-conditioned supermarket at Rosebud, the agency town, and in supermarkets in Winner and elsewhere. A lesser range of food supplies may also be purchased at a number of small stores on the reservation. A few people hunt and trap a little, and a few practice limited agriculture and maintain small gardens.

The annual cycle today, then, bears little relation to the old one. No longer attuned to the migration of the buffalo herds and the ripening of fruits and tubers, the cycle today is geared to the dates of distribution of commodities and to the receipt of cash from programs of government welfare. These include old-age assistance, Aid to Dependent Children, aid to the blind, unemployment insurance, and grants from the Indian Bureau to welfare. To a considerably lesser degree, the annual cycle is modified by opportunities for employment, or individual exploitation of the resources of field and stream.

Distribution of Surplus Commodities. Under section 32 of the Agricultural Adjustment Act, an agency known as the Agricultural Marketing Service makes payments to commercial exporters and others to encourage export of surplus commodities. Funds obtained from customs receipts are used in the distribution of surplus commodities to school lunch programs, institutions, and welfare agencies which include American Indians in their programs (U.S. General Services Administration 1964, p. 275). The Agricultural Marketing Service is one of a series of social experiments brought about by an agricultural surplus.

In theory, a surplus of agricultural and dairy products can be prevented by production control; or the surplus may be destroyed or diverted from the normal channels of trade. However, both production control and destruction have been unpopular courses with the American public, and farmers and nonfarmers alike prefer the use of surplus products for such constructive purposes as feeding the hungry at home and abroad (Waugh 1962, p. 15).

The diversion of surplus commodities to needy families and to institutions provided a major outlet before World War II. During World War II, and for fifteen years thereafter, the amount of commodities distributed was greatly reduced. In the late 1950s the twin factors of additional farm surpluses and increasing unemployment led to renewed consideration of distribution as a solution. In 1961 direct distribution of food to needy families was increased and pilot programs involving the use of food stamps were begun (Waugh 1962, p. 30). In 1953 the distribution program was reaching 100,000 persons in family units. In 1959, the United States Department of Agriculture distributed 707 million pounds of surplus food. In 1960 a typical monthly donation for a family of four persons was (Waugh 1962, p. 38):

Commodity	Pounds	Retail Value
Wheat flour	10	$1.12
Corn meal	10	1.31

Rice	$2\frac{1}{2}$	.47
Dried milk	$4\frac{1}{2}$	1.35
Lard	3	.56
Beans	4	.66
Dried eggs	$3\frac{1}{4}$	4.55
Total	$37\frac{1}{4}$	$10.02

Distribution to institutions increased steadily, reaching 1.3 million persons in 1953 and 1.5 million in 1960.

In considering who is to receive surplus commodities, standards of need are determined by local welfare officials. Each state determines at what income level applicants are eligible for aid; in so doing, previously determined levels for families already on public assistance are used in defining the needy to whom commodities may be issued.

The federal government makes available to the states these commodities accumulated in its long-range price-support operations: wheat, corn, rice, dry milk, cheese, and butter. The government also makes available, intermittently and when they are in short-term surplus, fruits, vegetables, and livestock products. Recently a limited number of products have been added with the special intent of improving the nutritional content, variety, and attractiveness of the donation program; these include some vegetable fats and oils, peanut butter, and canned meat (Paarlberg 1963, pp. 2–15).

This is the program in general. What can be added specifically for the Rosebud Reservation for 1962? As stated previously, 80 percent of the on-reservation Indians receive commodities. What proportion of the total diet commodities are, is problematic. A more detailed study of the problem would move in from the societal perspective and focus on households or families, and should include estimates and figures of cash spent on food as well as of groceries bought on credit. Also, some household budgets with estimates of the amount of welfare money received, how the budgets vary with the seasons of the year, and what proportion is used for food would be helpful. Estimates of the amount of food obtained through poaching, in ceremonies, and from other tangential and infrequent resources might also be made.

Actually, of course, Indians have been receiving rations since the first treaties were signed with them, but the present-day distribution of surplus commodities has more in common with the governmental practices of feeding the poor in the 1930s than it does with the governmental practice of feeding the Sioux in the 1880s. Certain changes have come about. The Sioux have entered the world of paperwork, and must act as individuals, or at least as families, in a bureaucracy. In the old days, the leaders parleyed with the whites and only the leaders made their marks on the treaties. Today each family must operate for itself in the food quest. A family desiring help fills out a form which gives the names of the applicant and his spouse and the number and ages of children who eat at home (this last because some of the children are fed at boarding school and some have some meals at day schools during the school year). An economic classification, a statement on the condition of need, the applicant's signature and that of a councilman who vouches for his need complete the document.

According to a memorandum from the director of the school lunch program, 903,786 pounds of food worth $187,880.24 wholesale was shipped to the Rosebud Agency in the fiscal year 1962. What this means to a family may be seen from the following list of commodity and portion distribution per person per month.

Commodity	Portion Distributed per Person per Month
Print butter	1 pound
Lard	1 pound
Packaged dry milk	1 pound
Dried eggs	1 pound
Pea beans	2 pounds
Rice	$\frac{1}{2}$ pound
Cornmeal	1 pound
All-purpose flour	5 pounds
Rolled oats	1 pound
Rolled wheat	1 pound
Pork and gravy	5 pounds (canned)
Chopped meat	$30\frac{1}{2}$ ounces (canned)
Processed cheese	$1\frac{1}{4}$ pounds
Peanut butter	$\frac{1}{2}$ pound

What proportion of the total diet these commodities represent depends on what other resources the family has. The director of the program at Rosebud thought of the recipients as two kinds: the "average working family," that is one which has a regularly salaried member, and those who were day workers with much unemployment. The day worker might make ("as high as," said the informant) six dollars a day but work only three days a week. To such families the commodities would be the mainstay and staple of their diet, and for such workers the volume of food is sufficient but nutritionally unbalanced. An average working family of six members might make fifty to sixty dollars a week but would have to pay rent and other expenses, including the cost of other food, out of this. Other families might have small cash welfare income, all of which was spent for food.

Attitudes toward, and uses of, commodities differ, of course. One man who is a conservative practitioner of the old ways cooperates sufficiently so that he is pointed out as a prototype of the old-time Indian. He still wears his hair long and is the only man on the reservation to do so. He fasts and takes peyote and has had visions; furthermore, he is training a three-year-old boy in dance and mythology. With the aid of a stick and the sand, he told a story:

> A man was giving food to a horse and a bear. He gave the bear hay and the horse meat. Pretty foolish, huh ? We eat those rations [surplus commodities] and we follow the directions but it doesn't make any difference. We get sick from it. And the meat in stores. It stays in a refrigerator for two weeks. That's stale. Indians like fresh meat. We should have fresh beef.

Food Distribution other than Commodities. At a dance at Okreek the family of one of the more politically prominent Indians prepared food for all participants and watchers. The food was cooked in the family home and brought to the dance grounds in a station wagon. Men carried in heavy cooking kettles which contained stew, and women brought tins of cake. There were cartons of bread and rolls and containers of coffee. Over the public address system, the college-educated son of the family invited the people to eat. The guests brought their own dishes, generally a soup plate and a cup and perhaps a plastic bag for the bread. Guests formed a double line and were quickly and unostentatiously served. In about forty minutes, the inhabitants of fifteen tents plus a few non-camping visitors had been served. In addition to the food being given away, there were two concessions for the sale of soft drinks; children were the main customers.

The Jesuits of St. Francis School at Mission distributed food on the celebration of the first mass of a new priest. They gave away one hundred pounds of buffalo meat, potatoes, and cabbage. These were boiled together by the recipients, who also received coffee, sugar, bread, rice, and raisins.

The exchange of food at organized ceremonial is an old Plains Indian pattern. How much of it still exists on the Rosebud Reservation is problematic. Agency officials say it is decreasing and that when such a give-away occurs, it is mainly to give public notice of a death. One was also held to celebrate a youth's graduation from college.

Hunting and Trapping. The amount of hunting and trapping that is done is negligible. It would be difficult to get accurate counts both of the amount of various kinds of game taken and the nutritional value of the parts consumed. I do not have such data. What I do have data on, and what is interesting, is the Indian and white attitude toward the game resources on the reservation.

The tribal council sets the policies for hunting and trapping. The hunting regulations, including licensing and the establishment of the season, are patterned after those of the state of South Dakota. A general state hunting license cost sixty cents (1962) and is all that is needed for hunting on deeded land. For hunting game animals on tribal land, a tribal hunting license is needed. (A stamp is an additional requirement for duck hunting.) A small-game license cost two dollars; one for large game was five dollars. According to tribal council law, everyone is expected to buy a license; this is the theory. However, in practice it can be seen that the whites and the government-employed Indians are expected to, and do, buy the licenses and the reservation Indians ("back-area Indians," said the informant) are not expected to, and do not. This double set of expectancies and behaviors is in part rationalization and in part sensible in the circumstances. It is attested by Indians and whites alike that the "back-area Indians" who do take game do not do so deliberately and with forethought. Neither for food nor for sport do they seek game in the ordinary sense of hunting. A white man says: "They carry a gun in their car and if a deer crosses their path, they will shoot it, but they don't get out and walk the canyons." The fact that this is not hunting, in the sense that the white man understands it, puts a different perspective on the shooting for the Indian. "If some poor Indian out there is starving and he shoots a deer, nobody is going to arrest him because he has no license. If he needs meat for subsistence, we are not going to take him to court or anything," says an Indian.

This dual view of the same phenomenon is illustrative both of factors of the food quest and of the perspective of various categories of people on the reservation. For present purposes, we may think of these categories as the whites and government-employed Indians, and the rural Indians. An Indian speaks, "You know, it used to be that if white men wanted to come in here and hunt, we couldn't stop them. They used to come in from Winner in an airplane. And one guy would be spotting the deer and signaling to a car on the ground. Then they'd chase them up a ravine and slaughter them." A white man says, "I hunt a lot and I rarely see them [Indians] out hunting. Hunting can be a lot of work and they actually don't get out and do it."

With our dual perspective, let us see how an Indian and a white informant perceive what proportion of the diet may be large or small game. The Indian:

> Overall, fishing and hunting would not figure much in the average family diet. It depends on the area. For Indians that live out along the river, the deer would begin to figure. They would kill a deer every now and then when the opportunity presents itself. I suppose they get their share, or more than their share, you might say. Small game is insignificant. I don't believe they go out much and do any hunting. Just what they happen to come upon. They aren't like whites who come in with dogs and high-powered equipment.

In contrast to this, a white man speaks: "There are a few rural families we notice have deer all year round, because of all the salt they buy. They'll go to town and buy twenty-five pounds of salt and we'll say, 'Was it a doe or a buck?'" The white man also made the point that the licensed hunters give away a portion of their kill so that some of what they take goes to a "common pot." One informant (white) said that the more efficient and affluent hunters have a round of families to whom they bring food. The Indian emphasizes the exploitation of the game resources by the white man; the white man emphasizes that hunting is a sport and that he contributes most of his kill to the needy.

All the killing of game, whether it be large or small, sport or opportunistic slaying for meat, is done with guns. According to the estimate of one white man, probably every rural family has a gun. Twenty-two rifles and shotguns are popular. No use of traps or snares was reported.

Fishing. The regulations for fishing are also set by the tribal council. Fishing is permitted year round, but appears not to be a factor in the Indian diet. As in prereservation days, the Indians do not care for fish. All of the lakes and two of the streams on the reservation are stocked.

Trout is most common, although trout will not spawn in some of the waterways because they are too shallow; a few streams are stocked with bass and bluegills. Most, if not all, of the fishing is done by the whites˙ and a few of the government-employed Indians, who are also the men who buy fishing lures. A fishing license costs two dollars.

Collecting. Collecting was presumed to be of secondary importance in the aboriginal diet and it is of considerably less importance as a food source today. There still is some collecting of turnips, and a portion of these are consumed by the collectors, but some are also sold to the more prosperous Indians. Chokecherries, buffalo berries, wild grapes, and plums are collected, but not in any quantity. They are shaken from the branches on to a canvas below. In the recent era before automobiles, a family might take a wagon out to a distant spot, stay overnight, and return the next day with fruit which could then be canned and made into jellies or sauces. One very poor family ate rosebuds.

On Ghost Hawk Road from thickets thick with plums almost ripe, the writer and friends picked and ate fruit which tasted much like domesticated plums except for the smaller proportion of fruit to pit. Wild grapes were also plentiful but not yet ripe in August, 1962.

Agriculture

There is no formal agriculture in the sense of the raising of extensive crops either for personal use or for cash. According to an unpublished report by the Rosebud Agency of the Bureau of Indian Affairs, in 1959, 10.2 percent of the total allotted land on the reservation was under cultivation, mostly by non-Indians. Most of this land was in the eastern part of the reservation and was in fodder (hay or alfalfa). There was some small grain grown. The typical pattern was to raise cash crops rather than on-site feed. I saw one site that was contour farmed and one haying party. Men and women of one extended family came to work on a large field and were fed a cold lunch by a matron of the family resident near the land.

If there is no formal agriculture, there is a fair amount of gardening, although it is probably limited to the more acculturated families and the more industrious and energetic women. One woman, about seventy, spoke of a prize garden she had had. In a maximally productive year she had grown three hundred pounds of navy beans and sold one-third of them. I saw one garden which had been jointly planted and was cooperatively tended by two families of government employees; there was corn, squash, pumpkins, green beans, and tomatoes. One woman spoke of a garden she used to have; she had sent corn and tomatoes to a mission school.

Food Processing

Preservation and Storage. The greatest portion of the preserved and stored food that the Sioux eat today is that which comes from the surplus commodity program; none of these are fresh or unprocessed foods. What the Sioux purchase also includes a good portion of preserved and stored foods, of course. In purchased foods, the techniques of preservation include freezing, cold storage, chilling, canning, bottling, smoking, pickling, and drying. Neither to receive stores nor to buy groceries do the Indians need to know or practice the processes of preservation.

Some preservation is still practiced by individuals and families, however. In 1961 a stock truck was wrecked near White River; the cattle were injured and had to be killed. Before they were shot the Indians had gathered to collect the windfall; drying meet could be seen all up and down the valley. Meat which has to be purchased is still dried by the old techniques, but not very often. A family may prepare some for a festive or ceremonial occasion, but two factors are responsible for the trend toward the disappearance of the practice of outdoor meat drying. First, it is not practical for small cuts of meat; one needs at least a five-pound roast. To some Indians the cost of such a cut looks like an investment would look to whites. Second, the knowledge of sanitation and the role of flies in carrying disease has been disseminated through the schools and other agencies. Even those who discount the notion that flies transmit disease are aware of the censure of those who accept the theory.

Another occasional windfall is the sale of elk by the National Park Service when they cull the herds. The Rosebud Sioux sometimes have a chance to purchase very cheaply, rough-dressed game (guts removed but feet, head, and hide on) from Yellowstone and Custer State Park.

Home drying of foods is an ancient art, and modern Indian housewives still dry fruit. Plastic cloths and containers are used, and chokecherries are ground in a meat grinder, although at least one mortar is still in use. But the essential process of drying fruit and preparing them later by adding moisture remains the same. Plums are also dried; both chokecherries and plums may also be canned. Buffalo berries are especially liked among the more acculturated Indians and/or, according to individual preferences, the fruit may be pitted; it is also made into jellies. Prairie turnips are still prepared in braided strings; they may be dried indoors or out.

Most of the homes outside of the agency town do not have refrigeration. Perishable foods like fresh milk may be bought in town but are consumed on the spot. Lack of refrigeration is probably not felt as a problem. The commodities do not need refrigeration, nor do canned foods, and short-term storage was never important in the old Sioux food pattern.

Food Preparation. The most common cooking techniques today are boiling and frying, although there is also some baking. Modern cooking techniques and paraphernalia have all but supplanted the old. The girls are taught how to can, and the more provident and acculturated families can a variety of foods. For some, the lack of jars, rings, vinegar, sugar, or other ingredients makes canning impossible.

Among the commodity foods, oats and wheat are made into gruels; rice is prepared in soup or as a pudding; pea beans appear in soup or baked. With rice and beans, the question of firewood becomes important. Beef boils quickly and does not need much fuel to sustain it at a boil, but rice and beans require long, slow cooking and not all families have enough firewood for this. Flour is used primarily for fried and baked bread but also thickens soups. Dried eggs, used in baking, are liable to quick spoilage and if not thoroughly cooked may cause illness. Not every recipient likes cornmeal: when it is used, it is made into bread or muffins; some mix it with flour for bread. Peanut butter is primarily a spread for bread and crackers, despite attempts on the part of home economists to diversify the uses of this nutritious item. Butter is a spread and a cooking and baking ingredient. Lard is used only for baking and frying. The meats, pork and gravy and chopped meat, may be eaten cold out of the can, baked, or fried.

Among purchased foods, kidneys are fried, put in stew, and occasionally eaten raw. Pork chops are fried. Bacon is used in boiled dishes but is not fried. Dry salt bacon is boiled with beans, potatoes, and in soups. Fat stewing hens are boiled. Despite the former beliefs about turkey, they are now sometimes roasted on holidays, usually by families who get together at one house.

A highly nutritious food is *toniga*, or soup made from tripe. Although a small amount of tripe is prepared for sale in American markets, in general it is not liked and may not even be considered food. When cattle are butchered by local white butchers, they consider the tripe offal and throw it away. On the contrary, many Sioux are fond of it. It requires a lot of water for cleaning and then is prepared in a green soup.

Food Consumption

When considering purchased foods, it should be noted that for families who have sufficient income, and especially those who live in Rosebud, the agency town, the diet is not different from that of an average middle-class white family. However, for the rural Indian and those with lesser income there are substantial differences. Much, but not all, of the following information was given me by the owner of the Rosebud supermarket and his wife, Mr. and Mrs. Terrance V. Paulhamus. In fresh meat, beef is the most frequently sold item, and boiling beef is more popular than other types. When possible, it is bought every day and is a staple of the diet. Lean beef is preferred, but tenderness is not a quality sought in the meat. Mostly the plates are sold, but the front quarter is also cut up for boiling beef. Good roasts and steaks are bought by those who can afford them. Occasionally a poorer family will buy a roast for drying in the old Indian way. Kidneys are much in demand and liver is the second biggest item in terms of volume of sale, but brains, hearts, and tongues also sell well; tongues are not as well liked as the other organs. Only beef liver is bought. The Sioux do not like pork in general and pork liver in particular. In an average week (summer, 1962) seventy-five to one hundred pounds of kidneys were bought and forty to fifty pounds of beef liver. Kidney fat is bought. Suet and bones are given away and are so well liked that there is a waiting list. Veal is not stocked; it has not sold. Lamb and mutton are equally disliked. During the depression years when lambs were slaughtered in the Southwest, some were shipped to the Dakotas, who would not eat it; they fed it to their dogs.

Among the canned meats a fair amount of South American corned beef in the twelve-ounce cans is bought, as are other canned meats. Vienna sausages are well liked and the cheaper sardines and salmon. Some cold cuts (luncheon meats) are bought and consumed in town as snacks.

Among the starch staples, red potatoes are a favorite; sweet potatoes are not liked. Since rice has been given away among the commodity foods, it has reentered the Sioux diet and they now buy it. They also buy macaroni and cook it with the commodity cheese, sometimes adding tomatoes. Every grocery order includes bread, rolls, and buns; especially liked are sweet rolls. Among the home-baked breads are big rolls and fried bread. Saltines, soda crackers, and another cracker rather like hardtack are appreciated for their storageability.

As a general rule the Rosebud Sioux do not buy many fresh vegetables outside of potatoes, although they do use a lot of onions. They like corn, and put cabbage in soup. They also like big hubbard squash, but they raise them more often than they buy them. As to canned vegetables, corn is the most frequently used, tomatoes second, and string beans third.

Fresh fruits are bought by only those who can afford them, and this is not many people. Apples and oranges are most frequently bought; some bananas are purchased, and, in season, peaches, grapes, and plums. Citrus fruits are craved. Once in a while school children buy lemons and suck them. One bought a teacher a lemon as a gift. The morning after drinking, some men ate oranges and cookies. Sugar-deficient diets and an abnormal need for sugar may be related to alcoholism. The consumption of dried fruits used to be greater, but dried fruits have become relatively high priced. The Sioux today eat a small amount of prunes, raisins, and dried apples. Among canned fruits, peaches are most popular, and then various kinds of berries. Blackberries may be eaten when someone has diarrhea. Anomolously, while the full-bloods like apples, they do not like applesauce.

The cereals eaten are primarily the commodity foods, rolled oats and wheat. Some cold, dry cereals are bought, and they are eaten with canned milk.

A decade or two ago, the Plains Indians refused dairy products, but today only a few of the old-timers do so. The boarding schools have played a part in changing food tastes, and so too have the various governmental agencies concerned with nutrition. Today dried, canned, and fresh milk are consumed, and commodity cheese is baked with macaroni. They are not favorite foods, however. Hardly any dry milk is purchased and only a bit of cheese. Neither oleomargarine nor butter is much purchased. Ice cream and popsicles are well liked, but usually they are bought and consumed only in town. Many eggs are bought, but I do not know if they are much used by the poorer families.

Far too many sweets are consumed: soda pop, cookies, and candies. A nursing child was observed drinking pop from a bottle with a nipple on it. The children are much indulged and sometimes they are bribed or paid for running errands, so that they receive or buy many sweets. Snack foods like potato chips and popcorn are also disproportionately eaten.

As to condiments, an average amount of salt and mustard are used, ketchup is heavily used, and very hot peppers are much appreciated.

Among the changes wrought by medical personnel and nutritionists is the introduction of canned baby foods and milk formulas. When a new doctor arrives on the reservation and prescribes a new formula, the old favorite remains on the grocer's shelf and the new one is much in demand. Special baby foods are purchased only when income is adequate, of course.

Diet

We have noted that the food cycle on the familial level is geared to the distribution of commodities and the receipt of welfare checks. On the individual level and among children, there are also changes when school begins in the fall. It is especially instructive to watch the beginners. For the first six weeks they generally eat only what they ate at home. All too often this means no green vegetables, and some of them, oddly enough, do not like meat. Several observers have reported that the children come to school with a long-term hunger, and in the beginning and in the midst of plenty, they tend to overeat. At the onset of the fall term it takes four to six weeks to fill them up. By Christmas time their cheeks fill out, their eyes brighten, and the first urgency is past. At the same time, they gradually come to accept, with more or less enthusiasm, the foods that are new to them. They learn not only to eat new foods but also something about their preparation and serving. In the bright, clean kitchen of the Rosebud boarding school I observed these preparations: steak had been fried and was basted and put into a large oven to keep warm until serving. Potatoes were boiling in institutional-size kettles. Canned corn, cottage cheese with pineapple chunks, and jello with whipped cream were prepared to complete the menu. Five girls, ages thirteen to fifteen, were mashing the potatoes with an oversize spoon-ladle. Next they whipped two quarts of cream. They set the bread on trays, from which it was served with gloved hands. Boys set the tables, putting on two quarts of milk to a table seating six. All helpers were aproned and wore something on their heads, and all knew their tasks well and bent to them with good will. The children were orderly but spirited and ate with gusto. Meat, vegetables, and dessert were served one portion to a child, but seconds of bread and potatoes were allowed. Meat had to be cut up for the little ones; and the children of all ages helped in the chore of food distribution; they stood in line, carried trays to the serving line and later to the dishwashing area, and poured their own milk. In a smaller day school at Spring Creek the children were equally well fed and also were introduced into the posture, manner, and behavior appropriate to a well-stocked table.

Meals are rarely scheduled in the homes. The pot is on the stove and unless a visitor is being fed, eating is casual and unplanned. Cardwell (n.d., p. 40) reports that although some Indians have three meals a day, most families have two, a morning and an evening meal. However, a hungry person may eat anytime during the day whenever food is available.

A priest of the Mission school points out that children in the summertime get up about nine or ten o'clock, do not eat much, play hither and yon, and probably eat one good meal a day, although they drink quantities of soft drinks and eat too many potato chips, cookies, and candies. Come the fall, they begin their nine months in school where federal requirements for school lunches are met, and this daily meal does much to restore the ravages of the summer's diet.

The Relevance of Modern Diet in the Total Picture of Sioux Today

One of the reservation dentists observed that malnutrition is reflected in the four-year-olds in the development of their secondary teeth in the incidence of hyperplasia, or undeveloped enamel; more rare is hypoplasia. The incidence of caries is highest in the premolars. Nutritional levels are not the only reason for the general poor condition of the teeth, of course. Also contributive are the large amounts of sweets that are eaten; the disinclination, or the inability, to make use of the government services for tooth care and repair; and, in some instances, too little time between the births of siblings, in which case the mother does not have sufficient time to rebuild her calcium supply.

A priest also commented on the children's bad teeth, poor eyesight, stunted growth, and susceptibility to respiratory disease like tuberculosis. When they enter school in the fall, many have iron deficiencies.

One important consideration is that in the old diet, organ meats were well liked, and today they still are. They are, however, difficult to obtain, and most Sioux lack storage facilities. Organ meats are low-prestige items among the whites and the Indians know it. In addition, the Indians like to eat them raw and know that the whites disdain such a habit. If something could be done to make these cheap and nutritious foods more common in the Sioux diet, that would be an improvement. Similarly, if the entrails which are discarded by whites at slaughter time could be made available to the Indians, possibly at convenient pick-up spots (and ideally near a source of water under good pressure for cleaning), this, too, would add a valuable and a valued food to the diet.

Finally, to put all of this into perspective, we will look at some health statistics as they are cited by Talcott (1960), taken from 1957 reports of the United States Department of Health, Education and Welfare. Considering the United States Indians as a group, the degree of Indian mortality in relation to that of all races varies at different ages. During the ages one to four years, Indian mortality is five times higher than for all races. Among adults twenty-five to thirty-four years of age the mortality rate is three times as high. The Indian life expectancy in 1950 was at the level of that of the white population in 1930. High Indian infant mortality accounts to a considerable degree for this discrepancy. The major causes of death among the Indian groups are influenza, pneumonia, tuberculosis, and certain diseases of early infancy; these caused one-fourth of the Indian deaths in the 1951–53 period, whereas they caused only one-tenth of the deaths for all races in 1952. Maternal mortality rates for Indian women are higher than for the rest of the population. During the 1949–53 period, 23 Indian women per 10,000 live births died, while only 7.5 from the rest of the general population died for the same number of live births (Talcott 1960, pp. 40–41). Nutrition, then, cannot be treated as a separate topic in the overall health picture, but has been so considered because it has been my interest. Any programs to alleviate the malnutrition and hunger suffered by American Indians must take into account a total picture of the social factors involved.

REFERENCES

ABERLE, DAVID A., AND STEWART, OMER C. 1957. Navaho and Ute Peyotism, *University of Colorado Studies, Series in Anthropology*, No. 6.

BARTON, W. W. 1919. *J. P. Williamson: A brother to the Sioux*. New York: Fleming H. Revell Co.

BELDEN, G. P. 1870. *Belden, the white chief; or, Twelve years among the wild Indians of the plains*. Cincinnati: C. F. Vent.

BODENHEIMER, F. S. 1951. *Insects as human food: A chapter of the ecology of man.* The Hague: Dr. W. Junk, Pub.

BOSLEY, BERTLYN. 1959. Nutrition in the Indian health program. *Journal of the American Dietetic Association* 35, no. 9: 905–9.

CARDWELL, WARREN. N.d. *An introduction to the modern Oglala Sioux.* Department of Health, Education, and Welfare, Public Health Service, Division of Indian Health. Mimeo. Aberdeen, S. Dak.

CATLIN, G. 1947. *Letters and notes on the manners, customs and condition of the North American Indians.* London: Tilt and Bogue.

Commissioner of Indian Affairs. 1883. *Annual report to the Secretary of the Interior, 1883.* Washington, D.C.: G.P.O.

———. 1884. *Annual report to the Secretary of the Interior, 1884.* Washington, D.C.: G.P.O.

———. 1912. *Report to the Secretary of the Interior, 1912.* Washington, D.C.: G.P.O.

DENIG, E. T. 1961. *Five Indian tribes of the Upper Missouri: Sioux; Arickaras; Assiniboines; Crees; Crows.* Norman: University of Oklahoma Press.

DODGE, R. I. 1959. *Thirty-three years among our wild Indians.* New York: Archer House, Inc.

EASTMAN, CHARLES A. 1914. *Indian child life.* Boston: Little, Brown & Co.

GILMORE, M. R. 1911–12. Uses of plants by the Indians of the Missouri River region. In *Annual report of the United States Bureau of Ethnology,* vol. 33. Washington, D.C.: G.P.O.

———. 1929. *Prairie smoke.* New York: Columbia University Press.

HAINES, FRANCIS. 1938. The northward spread of horses among the plains Indians. *American Anthropologist* 40: 429–37.

HERSKOVITS, M. J. 1950. *Man and his works.* New York: Alfred A. Knopf.

HICKERSON, H. 1960. The feast of the dead among the seventeenth century Algonkians of the upper Great Lakes. *American Anthropologist* 62: 81–107.

HOLLEY, F. 1892. *Once their home; or, Our legacy from the Dahkotahs.* Chicago: Donohu and Henneberry.

HYDE, G. E. 1956. *A Sioux chronicle.* Norman: University of Oklahoma Press.

JENKS, A. E. 1900. The wild rice gatherers of the upper lakes. In *Nineteenth Annual Report of the Bureau of American Ethnology, 1897–98,* pt. 2. Washington, D.C.: G.P.O.

KABERRY, PHYLLIS M. 1939. *Aboriginal woman: Sacred and profane.* London: Geo. Routledge & Sons.

KELLY, FANNY. 1872. *Narrative of my captivity among the Sioux Indians.* Hartford, Conn.: Mutual Publishing Co.

LOWIE, ROBERT H. 1954. *Indians of the plains.* New York: McGraw-Hill.

MACGREGOR, GORDON, WITH HASSRICK, ROYAL, AND HENRY, WILLIAM E. 1946. *Warriors without weapons.* Chicago: University of Chicago Press.

McPARTLAND, THOMAS S. 1955. *A preliminary socio-economic study of the Sisseton-Wahpeton Sioux.* Institute of Indian Affairs, Vermillion, S. Dak., December 1955.

MATTHEWS, W. 1877. *Ethnography and philology of the Hidatsa Indians.* U.S. Geological and Geographical Survey Misc. Publications no 7. Washington, D.C.: G.P.O.

MEYER, ROY W. 1967. *History of the Santee Sioux*. Lincoln: University of Nebraska Press.

MOOREHEAD, W. K. 1914. *The American Indian in the United States, 1850–1914*. Andover, Mass.: Andover Press.

MURRAY, ROBERT A. 1962. A brief survey of the pipes and smoking customs of the Indians of the Northern Plains. *Minnesota Archaeologist* 24: 1–44.

O'REILLY, HARRINGTON. 1889. *Fifty years on the trail*. London: Chatto and Windus.

PAARLBERG, DON. 1963. *Subsidized food consumption*. American Enterprise Institute for Public Policy Research, Washington, D.C.

PANCOAST, HENRY SPACKMAN. 1883. *Impressions of the Sioux tribes in 1882 with some first principles in the Indian question*. Philadelphia: Franklin Printing House.

PARKMAN, FRANCIS. 1910. *The Oregon Trail*. New York: A. L. Burt Co.

ROE, F. G. 1951. *The North American buffalo: A critical study of the species in its wild state*. Toronto: University of Toronto Press.

———. 1955. *The Indian and the horse*. Norman: University of Oklahoma Press.

STENE, JESSIE ANDERSON. 1927. Diets, methods of living, and physical condition of the Sioux Indians of the Crow Creek Reservation. Master's thesis, University of Chicago.

TALCOTT, MARGARET I. 1960. Study of dietaries and nutritional status of adolescent Indian girls in boarding schools of the Dakotas. Master's thesis, South Dakota State College.

USEEM, RUTH HILL. 1947. The aftermath of defeat: A study of acculturation among the Rosebud Sioux of South Dakota. Ph.D. dissertation, University of Wisconsin.

WAUGH, FREDERICK. 1962. *Managing farm surpluses: A statement by NPA Agriculture Committee and a report*. Planning Pamphlet no. 117. Washington, D.C.

WEATHERWAX, P. 1954. *Indian corn in old America*. New York: Macmillan Co.

WINCHELL, N. H. 1911. *The aborigines of Minnesota*. St. Paul: Minnesota Historical Society.

WISSLER, CLARK. 1950. *The American Indian: An introduction to the anthropology of the New World*. New York: Peter Smith.

Changing Society: The Teton Dakotas

Gordon Macgregor

MANY ANTHROPOLOGICAL STUDIES have been made of the culture change of the Teton Dakotas in their historical contact with American society, but none have made full analysis of a Teton Dakota tribe and the Indian agency as two separate entities or social systems in interaction.

The federal relationship with the Teton Dakota tribes has been so focused historically upon the transformation and destruction of Indian culture that students of the impact have been more concerned with the nature and extent of the cultural loss and resultant social and psychological maladjustment of individuals than with the process of Indian groups becoming restructured communities. Although the Teton Dakotas on reservations are even now far from attaining economic self-sufficiency, social order, and local autonomy, they are becoming more self-directed and communities are becoming more active. Leadership by younger, better-educated men and constructive association with government agencies other than the agencies of the Bureau of Indian Affairs, with private industry, and with private social groups are occurring. The greatest significance of these new relationships lies in the opportunity for the Indians to avoid the historic pattern of the strict paternalism of the Bureau of Indian Affairs and to promote democracy among their own people.

A Theoretical Framework for Analysis

In retrospect, one can now see that the Teton Dakota tribe has passed through four periods since 1800, characterized by (1) independent and great cultural growth; (2) defeat and confinement on reservations, reinforcing deep enmity toward the white man; (3) accommodation to reservation life with extensive adoption of the white man's material culture; and finally, (4) acceptance and the beginning of integration into American society. Rejection, dependency, apathy, and profound personal disorganization mark the latter periods of this cycle.

To understand and analyze the process of these changes, a conceptual framework permitting the ordering of events and facts is needed. The framework used in this paper is adopted from *Culture and Community*. In it a tribe or community is perceived as a social system (Arensberg and Kimball 1965, pp. 267–71). As a social system the community is made up of a series of interdependent sub-systems, that is, groups of people organized to meet the needs of their members or those of the community. A system is "composed of individuals united by ordered relations, existing in time and space, each individual responding in a customary manner toward others in the system (or outsiders or events which impinge on the system). The nature of the interaction (ordered relations and customs) being an expression of the values affected by the situation or event which stimulated the response" (Arensberg and Kimball 1965, p. 270).

Each sub-system possesses three components. The first is a structure of interaction or patterned set of relationships in which the members relate more intensively or more frequently in pursuing the group's primary interests than in their interaction with individuals of other groups. Second, a system is characterized by a set of customs or approved patterns of behavior for individuals dealing with each other according to his status and role and membership in the social system. Third, a system possesses a set of values which dictate individual behavior and group activities, and these in turn reinforce and express the values. The system as a whole shares values which give meaning and direction to life for the entire population.

The reservation is comprised of two systems, the Indian community and the government agency, each having its own structure and sub-systems. The government agency functions to meet the needs of the Indian population and to carry out the broad policy objective of the federal government, which is the assimilation of the Indians into American society and culture. This policy, whether it be characterized as civilizing, assimilating, or encouraging participation, has sought and continues to bring about social change of a very drastic order. The nature and impact of this change becomes clearer if we examine the systems and social processes of the two communities (the government and the Indians) in interaction. (It is appreciated that a third community, that of local whites surrounding the reservation and sharing reservation lands has also been highly influential in social and cultural change among Indian tribes. It is the more extensive and concerned interaction of social systems of this community and the local state government, with the addition of federal agencies serving both white and Indian populations, that is now affecting the course of assimilation and participation of Indian groups in America. Some effect of the new groups is discussed at the end of this paper.) The Indian population and the federal government each form a community composed of closely integrated groups with common as well as particular customs and sets of values. How social change has been stimulated, received, or rejected over a period of time is essential knowledge for analysis and for conducting future constructive relationships. The overall processes of the changes that have occurred and are occurring and the major and unanticipated and often disastrous results are the focus of our interest.

The concept of a community as a system of interdependent subsystems provides us with a tool for understanding the change that has occurred among many reservation populations, change which ultimately affects the individual, altering his social and economic roles and his relation to others. To help those serving Indians to understand and to bring some guidance to the individual in a changing society, let us look at those systems in which the individual participates. Let us analyze how the individual is directly affected and how his dependency upon and interrelationships with other systems modify his behavior. It is necessary to determine where points of stress occur within, and between, systems and how tension and strain undermine the balance and customary functioning of the community of sub-systems.

Where change has been imposed to bring about cultural assimilation, it is to be expected that this experience will have caused deep individual suffering and will have been disastrous to the original social organization. Where cultural institutions are suppressed and become functionless, the individual may find little purpose in carrying on the customs and relationships, now disparaged by outsiders, or in expressing values that no longer give meaning to his life. For the Teton Dakotas the loss of the buffalo herds that ended group hunting activities and the prohibition of military exploits ended those activities through which the men had realized one of the primary cultural goals—personal prestige and honor—and left them angry and without avenues for achievement (Macgregor 1946, p. 121). The substitution of an agricultural economy brought an occupation that proud warriors looked upon as women's work, since the gathering of wild plants and fruits was traditionally part of a woman's duties. Agriculture on a family-homestead basis lessened dependence on the extended family, which had been functional in a nomadic hunting economy, a life of military exploits, and cooperative and protective relationships.

The first experience in directed culture change, introducing a sedentary life of farming, was an intolerable break with the old culture. Changes in techniques and individual land ownership have since deteriorated rather than developed. Since the Indians were not allowed participation in making adaptations to meet basic and perceived needs, they manipulated the resources and practices offered them in an attempt to follow traditional ways and to maintain their primary social systems. The defeat and confinement in the first years of reservation existence and the later realization of the meaning of their loss resulted in increased feelings of hostility and anger and increased striving to maintain Indian identification. The emptiness of reservation life with its poverty and dependence has brought accumulated bitterness and strong opposition to programs for change and to the proponents of such programs. Those who would help the Tetons identify with a better life were looked upon as the enemy and the source of their dilemma.

Periods of American and Indian Interaction

The effects of interaction between local agencies of the Bureau of Indian Affairs with tribes of the Teton Dakotas, if represented on a progress chart for 1800 to 1967, would at first show a rapid upswing, reflecting the enrichment and development of Plains culture, and then a long descent toward cultural and social disorganization. From about 1950, a slight upturn would depict a positive effort on the part of the Sioux leaders to bring about greater cooperation with many outside agencies, which has led to some reduction of poverty and dependency.

Autonomy, 1800–76

The first influence of the white man's civilization upon the Teton Dakotas was metal trade goods and then, somewhat later, firearms. The horse and the gun enabled the Indians to move farther onto the High Plains and to hunt with greater efficiency. In the nineteenth century, with an abundant food supply and armed to meet other competitive tribes, the Teton Dakotas entered a period of great cultural development and extended their hunting territories.

The acquisition of the gun and the horse also brought the Teton Dakotas great wealth in herds of horses captured from other tribes and increased through breeding, and from stores of food and buffalo skins. This wealth, however, was unequally accumulated and distributed. The number of horses owned enhanced the prestige of individuals and was a primary value of the Teton Dakota culture. Desire for higher and higher status led to an increase in traditional personal rivalries and group violence, a not uncommon characteristic of aboriginal Sioux behavior. The fighting and occasional murders that marked the affluent period were held in sufficient check, however, to maintain the group cooperative patterns in hunting and welfare.

After 1850, the herds of buffalo began to decrease under a wasteful slaughter by the Indians as well as the white hunters. The impact of the white man was intensified by the growing number of settlers and the U.S. Army to protect them, the railroad work gangs, and the emigrants moving westward. Treaties permitting the building of forts and east-west roads followed, and it appeared that Indians and settlers were at peace. But pressure from whites upon Indian lands and occasional killings on both sides provoked greater hostility among the Indians. War was no longer conducted to achieve traditional values of bravery and honor, but to kill and drive the invaders from the Indian country.

This era of conflict and autonomy culminated in the battle of the Little Big Horn in 1876, in which General Custer and all his forces were annihilated. The confederated Indian tribes immediately withdrew from the scene to go on the hunt instead of consolidating their victory. Some bands drifted to the reservations for food. In 1877 the hostile bands of these tribes were either defeated or else fled north into Canada to escape punishment. By 1880, the last great herds of buffalo had disappeared from the Plains, and with them the only resources that would make it possible for the Plains Indians to maintain a semblance of independence. Starvation more than military defeat drove them to settle on the reservation. The days of an integrated and stable way of life were terminated.

Although the days of great material wealth had led to internal tribal conflict, the later threat to survival by the white man had had an opposite effect. When tribes allied to drive off a common enemy, their characteristic aggressiveness was directed outward. Visitors during the war period frequently noted harmony within the Indian camps. Violence returned with a deepening in-group tension and discord as a result of confinement on the reservation and disagreement among leaders as to ways of coping with the federal government. The internal sanctions for social control collapsed and the aggression to which the Sioux were conditioned in early training turned against themselves (Goldfrank 1943, pp. 67–83).

Confinement, 1877–99

In the first years on the reservations, the Teton Dakotas were under military control and treated virtually as prisoners of war. The civilian government which later attempted to train them as farmers was looked upon with disdain. Those who were to try farming soon learned, as did many homesteaders, that cultivation of the land under conditions of limited and unpredictable rainfall would not provide an income or subsistence. It was easier and more reliable to depend on rations. In the Pine Ridge Reservation the tribal camp, filled with idle and unhappy men, was so fraught with quarreling that the government broke up the tribal circle and scattered the band groups to settle separately on the reservation.

The chief event marking this period was the Sioux attempt to regain their independence, restore the buffalo, and drive out the white man. This took form in the Ghost Dance, a cult in which dancing led to trancelike states in which many fell to the ground in complete exhaustion. Thus were the supernaturals invoked on behalf of the tribe.

The final event occurred when a band of Sioux traveling to Standing Rock Reservation was intercepted by a troop of cavalry, who attempted to disarm them. A shot was fired and the soldiers poured down from the hillsides on Wounded Knee Creek to massacre the Indian men, women, and children. The Ghost Dance as a spiritual means of defeating the white man was suddenly ended; the spirit of the Sioux was broken.

Accommodation, 1900–1928

Although Congress in 1887 enacted a law to allot reservation lands in small acreages to individual Indians, this pattern of creating homesteads was not carried out in Pine Ridge and other western Sioux Reservations until the turn of the century. In manipulation of the government program, many Indians exchanged their allotments so that their lands might adjoin those of their extended family, thereby maintaining the residence pattern of native bands in a consolidated community. Maintaining the fundamental group based on kinship ties was deemed more valuable than the land or farming opportunities. Thus the native band, or *tiospaye*, of Sioux social organization was perpetuated as the first reservation community.

The fact that local Indian agencies did not recognize traditionally functional groups as potential units through which economic change could be achieved and leadership and cooperative efforts fostered handicapped many succeeding economic and administrative programs. What did happen was that agents or superintendents sought to destroy the power of the chiefs and to concentrate authority in their own hands. By so doing, government efforts were focused upon individuals and families, thus adding to the dissension and rivalries accompanying confinement on the reservations.

Education was the second major effort to bring about the adaptation of the Sioux to the white man's life. Schools had been promised as one of the benefits to be received for the relinquishment of lands. To go to school, older children were taken away from their families and communities and sent to distant localities. The curriculum of the twentieth century stressed vocational training for Indians in order to help them to become laborers and household domestics. Employment with white families during the summers gave them experience in American life but also avoided a return to the influence of Indian custom. The conflict engendered with earlier, native child training was entirely unappreciated by teachers and administrators. In addition, the expectation that the young men and women graduates would enter off-reservation employment was rarely realized.

Customary patterns of child training continued among the full-blood families and led to the culturally prescribed personality necessary to conform with and to carry on the hunting-fighting way of life. An anachronistic child-training system unsuited to the new reality has been carried on (Erikson 1950, p. 138). Children arrived at adolescence equipped with the tools of the three R's and some ability in the English language but with no strong incentive to choose the white man's life. The deeper and less conscious drives stemming from early childhood experience and associations with some measure of affection and security in the home led the older child to return to his family instead of seeking new paths. Correlatively, the atmosphere of hostility and hate constantly exhibited by Indian adults almost always meant that the early generations of reservation-born children consciously or unconsciously resisted assimilation and remained with their own people in an increasingly empty life on the reservation.

In this environment the basic personality of the Teton Dakota has become almost schizophrenic. Individuals were torn between desires to gain status and role outside the reservation and to enjoy warm, stable, and positive social interrelations by remaining at home. Through failure to realize either goal, many of the younger generation slipped into a life of apathetic resignation and passivity that had as its only and questionable satisfaction the defeat of the efforts of the white men to effect cultural changes. For reservation populations as a whole, the result has been to come close to social and psychological destruction.

The Period of Acceptance and Potential Integration, 1929–65

In 1928 the Brookings Institution of Washington carried out a survey of the conditions of the American Indians for the Secretary of the Interior and made several recommendations for changes. Poverty, bad housing, and the discouragement of Indian peoples were underscored as the result of indifferent and biased administrators. The survey led to a change in policy and a more humanitarian approach to Indian affairs.

The impact of this critical report culminated in the passage of the Indian Reorganization Act of 1934, which provided the right for Indian tribes to approve constitutions, elect councils, and appoint business committees. The law also authorized funds for loans to finance agricultural and business enterprises, and to provide loans for higher education. It is possible now to see that the restoration of confidence among Indian leaders and their willingness to be spokesmen of tribal interests was one of the most significant effects of this law. There is now greater expression by Indians of their own needs and wishes and also greater cooperation with federal, state, and private agencies concerned with improving aspects of Indian life and health.

The redirection of Indian Service policy also diminished concern with assimilation and brought a respect for the meaning and values of Indian cultures. It was at this time that professional anthropologists were appointed to full-time positions as advisors in the central office of the Bureau. A new atmosphere of permissiveness and empathy (often mistaken by outsiders as an attempt to preserve or restore former

cultures) pervaded the administration. Nonetheless, it was clearly foreseen by Commissioners of Indian Affairs of the time that normal or
enforced processes of acculturation with the larger society would
inevitably continue.

In 1934 a Human and Economic Dependency staff was appointed,
with the cooperation of the then newly formed Soil Conservation
Service of the Department of Agriculture, in order to determine the
condition and quality of Indian range and farm lands and Indian
forests, and to plan for their restoration, proper utilization and management, either by Indian owners or by outside enterprises. Anthropologists, economists, and demographers assessed the related Indian
practices, attitudes, and reasons for nonuse of natural resources as data
for planning economic programs and increasing Indian employment.
This activity occurred during the depression and drought of the 1930s,
when the erosion of the Great Plains was a chief concern of the nation.
The Sioux, like the white man, was deprived of his primary natural
resource. Indians saw that their achievements in learning to raise
cattle and farming were of little practical value. Many interpreted the
disaster caused by climatic changes as another manifestation of the
lack of wisdom and integrity of the white man.

In the latter part of the 1930s, the Civilian Conservation Corps was
established. One of the aims of this program was to provide jobs to the
nation's unemployed youth. On Indian reservations the program had
one distinction: unemployed married men were allowed to live at home
and go out to the forest or the range conservation project, or to vocational training school. Many young and middle-aged Indian males had
regular work and wages for the first time in their lives. The CCC
program brought relative affluence and a new status to husbands and
fathers in the eyes of their families. Among the Teton Dakotas the
program brought a change in attitudes and experience: employment
for wages on the reservation and residence among their own people
was a new way of life and one that has become the occupational ideal
of Indians.

World War II gave to the Teton Dakotas two new experiences. Young
men and women went off to war, many to see foreign countries, and
all to live in and observe the world outside the reservation. Older men
and women went off in greater numbers to work in the potato and beet
fields, in the construction of military installations, and in industries in
urban centers. These experiences led many Sioux to feel competent in
coping with the outside world. But for many others, especially those in

migrant labor work, the experience was that of prejudice, indifference, and the low esteem with which Indian, Mexican, and Negro labor is generally regarded. For these Indians the reservation remained the preferred place of residence (Useem, Macgregor, and Useem 1943, pp. 1–9).

At the end of the war, most of the Sioux in the armed forces came home. Activities in which Indians had been working in off-reservation employment closed. On the reservations the Indian agencies undertook two economic programs to give employment to resident and returning Indians. The first, in part inspired by a return of a favorable climate to the plains, was a program of loans of money and cattle on a basis of repayment in kind. This was done in the hope of reestablishing families on the land. The second program was the recruitment of men and women for training in vocational schools in the urban centers, and for employment in industries in the cities. Indians proved competent employees, but at first an unexpected number returned to the reservations. They were unprepared for, and unwilling to accept, the social isolation of the city, and there was prejudice toward and from their neighbors in the lower-class, low-rent areas where they lived. The problem of isolation and the preference for social relationships with other Indians is now being met in urban centers by clubs and social gatherings which symbolize Indian cultural loyalties and identification. Of all the tribes in the city the Sioux appear to be among the most unstable and the most frequently migratory between the city and the reservation. The chief cause for this appears to be their poor psychological adjustment.

In the 1950s a new policy, supported by both Congress and a new administration of the Indian Service, was adopted to resolve the Indian problems. A program of progressive termination of the services of the Indian Bureau and disposition of the reservations by incorporating them as counties or by placing them under private management was proposed. The increasing cost of Indian administration and the continuing poverty, illiteracy, low educational achievement, poor health status, and many other causes were advanced as reasons. Tribal members with a small fraction of Indian blood and living off the reservation brought pressure to have tribal resources liquidated and individual shares distributed in cash. The pressures for termination and liquidation were, in one sense, expressions of a general desire to promote rapid assimilation and thus eliminate a problem that had been troubling the American conscience for a century. The effect upon the

Teton Dakotas on reservations was that of arousing great anxiety and doubts concerning the word or intentions of the white man. They became demoralized by the fear of abandonment to an unfriendly and unprotecting world (Hagen 1962, p. 487).

The pressure to resolve the Indian problem this way, although it would almost force Indians into becoming undifferentiated members of American society, is still strong. However, many inside and outside the federal government are clearly aware that such a movement would leave the uneducated and unskilled Indians at the bottom of society and with less opportunity than at present to improve their condition and to escape from a state of dependency.

The Department of Interior modified this policy with the announcement that no move would be made without the advice and consent of the Indians. The present administration has extended the policy and seeks the full participation and leadership of the Indians in planning and carrying out procedures for achieving higher educational and economic status and a greatly improved level of living on the reservations. This new relationship, begun in 1962, has restored much of the faith of Indians in the intent of the Bureau of Indian Affairs and its agencies.

A strong effort is now being made to attract and establish industries on Indian reservations. The Sioux reservations have already received several. Employment and a steady wage have led to family stability and improved the economic status of Sioux men. This and the program for off-reservation employment, while far from resolving the unemployment problem or overcoming the unemployability of many able-bodied adults, has at least started a trend that is raising the unbelievably low average family income of Sioux families. One unanticipated result of the establishment of industrial plants on the reservation has been the return home of many off-reservation, employed Sioux. The desirability of working and living in their own communities has attracted from three to four thousand Sioux back to Pine Ridge in the last few years.

Several federal agencies with programs organized for the assistance of the poverty-stricken throughout the United States are now assisting Indians in cooperation with the Bureau of Indian Affairs. The Federal Housing Administration appointed housing authorities to build and administer low-rent Indian homes, welfare housing, and community halls. The responsibility for independent direction of a program has led to an awareness that Indians can manage and participate with outside agencies and without the paternalistic supervision of the agency. Similarly a program of home and business loans to Indian farmers by the Farm Administration of the Department of Agriculture has taught Indians that they can obtain government aid by independent action of their own.

From the beginning the Office of Economic Opportunity has dealt directly with Indian groups to bring its training, work, and educational programs onto reservations. Indians have taken the leadership in requesting projects to relieve the poverty of reservation families. Indian women in the Headstart Program are teaching Indian children both new habits and a knowledge of English. This early preparation for school and for life in American society, if guided by persons understanding the psychological needs of Sioux youngsters in their early years, will have a positive effect on personality as well as on social adjustment. It is important not to let these programs become meaningless work. (Sioux teenagers were recently observed policing tribal and agency grounds.) The result of "make-work" can only be negative and another deterrent to a needed sense of purpose in what is now the most psychologically maladjusted age group.

The leaders of the tribal councilmen show a clear and assured ability to manage their own business affairs. With support from federal and state agencies and in control of their tribal funds, they are (1) putting into effect plans drawn up by the Indian Bureau years ago for the consolidation of land holdings for cattle ranges, (2) loaning funds for family enterprises and for college education, and (3) negotiating with private businesses and state agencies for industrial and social programs.

In spite of the apathy and despondence that still pervades the more culturally unchanged Indian segment of the reservation populations, a motivation to accept and benefit from the economy and way of life of the dominant society is gradually developing. In view of the impatience of some members of Congress and some assimilated Indians who seek the conversion of rights to tribal properties to cash payments, time is the most critical factor in achieving better adaptation.

SUMMARY

The long-term effects of the relationship of the dominant society administered at the reservation level by the agency staff needs now to be evaluated in greater detail. The efforts to bring about change has reached all segments of the traditional culture and affected the social

character. Pressures for assimilation weakened the native social
institutions and produced psychological disequilibrium of varying
intensity in each individual.

The first traumatic experience was the loss of the game resources and
the territory on which the Sioux hunting culture had been built. The
second came about inadvertently through the allotment of lands to
individuals. Pressed to start a family farm or herd cattle, the nuclear
family became more important than previously, and at the same time
the traditional bonds and functions of the extended family were undermined. Although the satisfactions of personal relationships, the mutual
obligations, and the security found in the extended family have been
perpetuated to some degree, they become decreasingly significant in a
society of small farmers and wage workers. With the ending of war, the
military societies of men and the ceremonies honoring feats of valor have
disappeared. The suppression of native religious ceremonies and growing realization on the part of the Dakotas that the supernatural power
has given them no support or release add to their desolation. Old
values can no longer be expressed in daily life and have no place in
reservation existence.

Loss of traditional leadership, subordination to officials assuming
complete authority, and a dependence on the government for life itself
have undermined the motivation needed to introduce innovative adaptations. Indian leaders who complain of government treatment have
been ignored or opposed. Furthermore, the new leadership must now
compete with the long held attitude that those who cooperate with the
government betray the tribe.

Few substitute social institutions have been formed or accepted.
Except for wage work the economic opportunities have been rejected.
All who visit the reservations today and see the Teton Dakotas in their
poverty and ill health and with their broken families decry the maladjustment.

Most Bureau officials still see the solution to this problem as improvement in education, vocational training, more jobs, and better
housing. These are undoubtedly necessities, but they have been offered
to previous generations without marked success. They have not offset
the increasing deterioration of reservation societies and the personal
maladjustment of individuals. The underlying causes of this patho-
logical condition have not been sought out, and the contributions of
extensive social science research explaining the social behavior of the
Sioux has not been heeded.

The basic cause of the problem of the contemporary Sioux appears to be the early training and social experience of the child. Another cause is the historical unwillingness of the federal government to relinquish full authority and responsibility to tribes, despite the fact that increasingly the people themselves and their leaders demonstrate their capacity for managing their own affairs. In the history of the reservation experience the Teton Dakotas have moved from the position of a feared enemy to that of a group held in low regard. The loss of respect from outside and from within one's own society has had a crippling effect. The low status and resultant feeling of inferiority have caused anxiety and led the Indian to identify with his former culture, his only source of pride and sense of equality.

Although lessened in its intensity, the persistence of the federal government to press the Teton Dakotas to adopt the model of the white man continues to antagonize and create anxiety. The constant pressure deepens and promotes personal maladjustment and social disequilibrium.

In spite of the despondent and belligerent view which the majority of Teton Dakotas maintain toward the white man's world, there are some individuals emerging among the middle-aged and younger adults who are seeking to assist their people in realistic ways and who are planning their economic, social, and education development. They see the poverty, illness, and despair, but they are unaware of the psychological forces and the areas of conflict between two cultures that underlie these conditions. The safety sought in passive action and the restraint placed on rage and their own actions as a means of revenge are not perceived. Certainly the crippling acquisition of unambiguous and unconscious tendencies in infancy and childhood, as Hagen (1962) describes it, which contributes to failure of adjustments to reality, has not been discussed or understood by Indians or their mentors. An understanding would be of great benefit to young leaders who may have learned the principles of modern psychology in their education.

New leaders, however, are making significant contributions to the reservation scene. They are models of action and a purposeful life to the younger Indians. They are also giving confidence and hope to others who desire to improve their lot but who see no way out of their complex predicament. Indian leaders are beginning to fulfill the promise of the better life that is constantly sought but rarely realized through government programs. The new leadership is beginning to overcome the suspicions among the rank and file of reservation populations as they demonstrate in successful tribal cattle operations, in new industries, and in decisive and active councils some fulfillment of their people's basic needs. However, agents of the federal government relinquish their authority slowly and do not change the binding laws and regulations in a way which would support further development of Indian leadership and local autonomy.

Motivation leading to innovation by young leaders is fundamental to any great social change in the Teton Dakota communities. In spite of all that has been said of the retreatism and hostility of contemporary generations, the desire among all Sioux to escape their poverty and unhappiness and the equally strong desire that their children shall be prepared for a better life are fundamental supports for change. The speed with which and extent to which great change can take place depends on the wisdom and understanding of officials in dealing with the deep psychological handicaps and the social factors which are the sources of negative adaptations. Willingness to transmit greater responsibility to those who are proving their commitment to and ability for social change is also mandatory. In the last analysis, the paternalistic relationship between the dominant and subordinate systems must be reoriented to one providing greater equality and enlightened guidance to people advancing through self-motivation and their own effort.

REFERENCES

ARENSBERG, CONRAD, AND KIMBALL, SOLON. 1965. *Culture and the community.* New York: Harcourt, Brace and World, Inc.

ERIKSON, E. 1950. *Childhood and society.* New York: Norton.

GOLDFRANK, ESTHER S. 1943. Historic change and social character: A study of the Teton Dakota. *American Anthropologist* 45: 67–83.

HAGEN, EVERETT E. 1962. *On the theory of social change.* Chap. 19, A case in point: The Sioux on the reservation. Homewood, Ill.: Dorsey Press.

MACGREGOR, GORDON, WITH HASSRICK, ROYAL, AND HENRY, WILLIAM E. 1946. *Warriors without weapons.* Chicago: University of Chicago Press.

USEEM, JOHN, MACGREGOR, GORDON, AND USEEM, RUTH HILL. 1943. Wartime employment and cultural adjustment of the Rosebud Sioux. *Applied Anthropology* 2: 1–9.

Cultural Change and Continuity in the Lower Brule Community

Ernest L. Schusky

INTRODUCTION

LOWER BRULE is one of the smallest Dakota reservations in size and population.[1] It lies in central South Dakota on the west bank of the Missouri River. Families were once scattered over the reservation, occupying their allotted lands, but they gradually moved into the town of Lower Brule, site of the former agency. The old agency town is located on bottom land. The nucleus of the site is a square surrounded by former agency buildings. Except for one or two houses maintained by the Bureau employees, the other houses are dilapidated. Indians occupy them more or less as squatters.

The agency center is described in such vivid terms by older men that one feels a "Golden Age" must have existed when the superintendent resided on the reservation with a staff of whites who taught school, instructed men in blacksmithing and farming, and carried on the routine tasks of administration. With the transfer of agency headquarters to Pierre, Bureau representatives at Lower Brule were reduced to three teachers and a policeman. Only their houses have been maintained to conform to middle-class standards.

[1] The author is indebted to the Institute for Indian Studies, University of South Dakota, Vermillion, South Dakota, for funds to make this study. Field work was conducted from March to September, 1958, with periodic visits in 1959, 1960, and 1967.

107

Two rows of clapboard houses line a street north of the square. They were built in the 1930s as part of an economic development scheme which would convert the Brule to truck farming and canning. Traces of irrigation ditches remain, but the Brules never showed an interest in farming. The cannery stands as a tribal recreation and meeting hall. Most of the houses belong to the tribe, and there are constant squabbles over who has rights to a building. Expensive central heating units have been replaced with oil space heaters; a number of houses have burned. Other houses, scattered to the west and south of the agency square on the remaining bottom land, are less desirable. Completing the town are the Catholic and Episcopal churches and the combination store and post office. The priests for the churches are white and a white couple manage the store.

Altogether about one hundred families or four hundred people live on the reservation. Close to eighty of the families are in the town of Lower Brule. For the purposes of this report the community of Lower Brule consists of the Indian families living in the town of Lower Brule plus some of the families elsewhere on the reservation. Excluded are the seven whites residing in the town and a few families who can claim Indian descent, who belong to the tribe, but who live as whites and have little intercourse with Lower Brule.

Lower Brule is most useful for analysis because the reservation can be seen as a community; the outside social systems which interpenetrate the reservation penetrate the community as a whole. In contrast, only some communities of the Pine Ridge and Rosebud reservations are in contact with nonlocalized social systems. The qualities used here to define Lower Brule as a community are distinctiveness, smallness, and homogeneity. A common language, Teton Dakota, distinguishes Lower Brule from whites; in addition, the Lower Brules believe there are a few differences in dialect which distinguish them from Teton speakers at Pine Ridge or Rosebud. Also, the community is marked by a distinct social structure. Social relations within the community differ sharply from those in the white community. Furthermore, the people of Lower Brule have distinct kinds of relationships with people in social systems at the state and national levels. Most important, however, is the group consciousness of the Lower Brule people. Although legal and territorial definitions of "Lower Brule" confuse the outsider, the Indians know and readily agree upon who is a "real" Indian member of the community. The agreement and knowledge are possible because of the small size of the community. The one hundred families are all intimately acquainted; moreover, long intramarriage has related them in a complex network. The Lower Brules frequently express this relationship with the saying "We are all relatives here." The homogeneity of the community depends in large part upon these feelings of kinship. A few Indian ranchers have adopted white values on such a scale that they differ sharply from conservative Indians. However, this change and their income differences do not contribute significantly to heterogeneity. In dress, housing, and general style of living the ranchers do not stand out from the most traditional members of the community. Certainly in contrast to the small white community, with its immediately apparent social-class differentiation, the Lower Brule community exhibits a major degree of homogeneity.

CHANGE AND CONTINUITY IN THE COMMUNITY

One initially suspects that the smallness of Lower Brule would make it susceptible to assimilation and that long contact with whites and increasing accessibility to the white world would add to the susceptibility. A review of culture change theory in regard to Indians is in order. An early conviction that Indians were a "vanishing race" biased culture change theory and influenced data collection. A later antithesis may have emphasized too strongly the persistence of Indian culture traits. In the late nineteenth century assimilation of the Indian was assumed to be inevitable, and Congress sought all means to expedite this highly valued end. While legislators were confident of the course Indian communities would follow, anthropologists made few explicit statements. In fact, anthropologists at the turn of the century agreed with the legislators at least implicitly. Students were urged to collect ethnographic data rapidly lest the tribes soon vanish. Indeed, the Indian population had declined radically and some tribes had become extinct. Moreover, a number of the structural features of Indian tribes were being lost, and a host of white social systems were beginning to penetrate the reservation. In about 1930 anthropologists began to show a serious interest in assimilation and acculturation as processes of culture change. *Acculturation in Seven American Indian Tribes*, edited by Ralph Linton (1940), for the most part emphasizes changes in the direction of the larger society and gives the impression that the tribes would be absorbed in a few generations. In evaluating the seven studies, editor Linton concurred (1940, p. 462).

The Social Science Research Council Summer Session on Acculturation (1954) suggested that change generally may be a much longer process than formerly assumed, but nonetheless held on to the dictum of inevitable assimilation. Minorities which persist within a large society are referred to as cases of "arrested fusion," "incomplete assimilation," or "the failure of two cultures in contact to lose their autonomy." A stronger statement of the persistence of culture was issued from a conference of anthropologists on the American Indian. Provinse and others (1954, p. 388) concluded:

> Most Indian groups of the United States, after more than one hundred years of Euro-American contact and in spite of strong external pressures, both direct and fortuitous, have not yet become assimilated in the sense of a loss of community identity.... The urge to retain tribal identity is strong and operates powerfully.... Group feeling and group integrity among the American Indians are as likely to gain strength in the decades ahead as they are to lose it.
>
> ... The Conference agreed that despite external pressures, and internal change, most of the present, identifiable Indian groups ... will continue indefinitely as distinct social units, preserving their basic values, personality, and Indian way of life, while making continual adjustments, often superficial in nature, to the economic and political demands of the larger society.

A few years later other anthropologists were expressing a belief in the persistence of Indian culture in stronger terms. In the *Annals* on the American Indian, Evon Vogt (1957, p. 137) said: "It has become apparent to the social scientists studying the American Indian that the Indian population of the United States is markedly increasing and that the rate of basic acculturation to white American ways of life is incredibly slower than our earlier assumptions led us to believe." Another anthropologist, examining the rate of change, concluded: "Indian groups residing on reservations (homelands) will continue indefinitely as distinct social units" (Dozier, Simpson, and Yinger 1957, p. 165). Although some aboriginal traits have persisted surprisingly long, the striking aspect about Indian communities is their continuity as a distinct unit. This distinctiveness results not only from persistence but also from change; that is, culture change has occurred in great degree but has not necessarily been in the direction of the larger society. Indeed, some of the dominant social systems imposed on Indian communities largely for the purpose of fostering assimilation have led instead to the creation of unique cultural forms. These adaptations are illustrated by examination of similarities and differences between Lower Brule and the larger society.

CULTURAL SIMILARITIES

One sees readily why Lower Brule Indians might be thought on a path of assimilation, because they are like whites in many ways. Furthermore, the similarities in material culture, technology, and economic life are easily observable and striking. Lower Brule operates on a cash and credit basis; most men perform some farm work during the year; a few are full-time ranchers; and some hold permanent government jobs with the Bureau or tribal council. There is little reliance on hunting or gathering, except for one or two families who sometimes subsist for short periods on fish, pheasant, and berries; and men or their families may leave the reservation for a temporary job outside the community. Again the pattern is similar to that of neighboring towns.

The formal education of children is also like that of whites. Children attend the first seven grades at a Bureau-operated day school within the community. Although there are only three teachers for the school, their qualifications, the student-teacher ratio, and physical facilities are as good as or better than those for rural white children. The teachers make a few adaptations to their Indian pupils, but in general the curriculum, books, and activities are comparable to those of neighboring schools.

The formal governing body of Lower Brule is the tribal council. The council is an elected, representative body operating under a constitution and bylaws. In form and procedure it acts much like a city council in a white town. Most of its time is spent in approval of small expenditures for the community, discussion of community problems, or conferences with Bureau officials. A major task of the council is to vote for or against purchase of land which Indians or whites within the reservation wish to sell. Large expenditures of tribal money are involved; not all land offered for sale can be purchased. It appears that the decisions of the tribal council are quite important, but there is reason to review the decision-making power of the council later.

The churches at Lower Brule resemble the political body; only overtly are they much like white churches. Catholic and Episcopal missionaries have long been active among the Dakotas, and the community is nominally one hundred percent Christian. Services and ritual are those of the dominant society, although the Dakota language is used occasionally in the services and frequently in hymns. Ordained white priests serve the churches, and, as on the national scene, they take an increasing interest in social problems once outside the scope of churches.

CULTURAL DIFFERENCES

As noted above, most material culture of Lower Brule is white; however, symbols of "Indianness" are seen. Dresses, particularly of older women, are longer; men frequently wear a silk scarf around the neck. Distinctive "Indian" foods are occasionally prepared. Although the ingredients of fry bread all derive from the larger society, it is regarded as distinctly Indian. Much the same could be said of Indian homes. Even though they may be frame and the interiors furnished with sofas, tables, and chairs, there are subtle Indian symbols which distinguish the home as "Indian."

In economic life, the give-away persists as a form of exchange; the flavor of the give-away is also reflected in church-sponsored events such as basket socials. However, the major difference in the economy of Lower Brule is its source of income. The Lower Brules depend in great part upon welfare payments. Aid to the aged, aid to dependent children, and general relief provided by the Bureau are major sources of income for the community. Government surplus foods, or commodities, are a vital supplement to the subsistence of most families. This pattern, of course, is true for most reservations which have little or no resource base.

In formal education, differences from the larger society are even more apparent. Only the classroom shows many resemblances to the familiar white pattern. The teachers do not participate in any other community activities, nor are they under the usual informal pressures found in the small white community. Most apparent is the lack of parental knowledge about and interest in activities or the content of the program. Although parents take great pride in the education of their children and make sacrifices to keep their children in school, they have little understanding of what is involved in the process. Most parents have attended school in their youth, but they realize that their experience was quite different. Rigid discipline, emphasis on learning English, and technical training are no longer the basis of education. The absence of parental participation is understandable enough when one recognizes that no community control of the schools is possible. The Waxes (1964) and others, describe in detail the lack of community power in Rosebud, which is similar to Lower Brule.

The Lower Brule political system is influenced by the tribe's relation with the federal government. The tribal council is the only political body and, as noted above, appears to have the power to make important decisions on land purchases. However, the Bureau of Indian Affairs has developed a land consolidation scheme for the Lower Brules under which tracts within consolidated areas can be bought. The Bureau must approve the council's decision for such a purchase. If the council should attempt to acquire other tracts, it is doubtful that the Bureau would approve. In short, what seems to be an important responsibility of the council is actually a routine matter. The Bureau, by its master plan, has already determined which tracts of land can or cannot be purchased. The council holds little real power, and thus in its functioning it cannot be compared to the governing bodies of white communities. The lack of self-government is notable on all reservations, and it is a problem that a number of anthropologists examine in detail in other parts of this volume. It suffices here to note that the lack of political power makes Lower Brule quite different from other American communities.

The Catholic and Episcopal churches at Lower Brule are missions. The priests, as missionaries, are obligated economically to mission boards rather than their congregations. As a result, many parallels between religious and political organization can be drawn (Schusky 1963). In brief, the Lower Brules lack power in their church organization just as in their political system. As a result, they show similar attitudes of apathy, if not antipathy, and hostile dependence.

Christian dogma and belief are accepted in large part, but much of the former religion persists. Those Indians who are most like whites believe in the effectiveness of shamans in a past generation. They tell of miraculous Yuwipi cures, discoveries, and predictions. They rationalize that many past practices are Christianlike and imply that the old religion was inspired by the Christian God; for example, a crosstie on the sun-dance pole makes it a cross. Indians least like whites still hold firm beliefs in Yuwipi powers, and shamans from other reservations have been invited to Lower Brule to solve crimes, cure illnesses, and hold meetings simply for the general welfare. One man who sponsored some of these meetings is thought to be fasting and seeking visions in order to find supernatural power; he is also one of the most active members of the Episcopal church and well versed in Christianity. On occasion he conducts services when the priest and lay minister are both absent. His sincerity in Christianity cannot be doubted. The point illustrated is that two religious beliefs—Indian and white—do *not* exist. Christianity forms the core of Lower Brule religious organization; aboriginal practices and beliefs are grafted to this core in various ways for different individuals. Thus, the community is basically Christian. Missionaries spend their time in social service, not proselytizing; and other whites recognize the community as Christian. However, the Indian elements are so integral, although covert, that religious life is distinct from that of the larger society. The distinctiveness stems not only from the existence of different beliefs, but also from the fact that external social systems, represented by the missionaries, govern most policy in the churches.

Probably the most overt difference between Indians and whites is to be seen in kinship. With a cash economy, the establishment of permanent houses, and intermarriage with whites, the nuclear family became the basic unit. The use of English kinship terms further emphasizes the importance of this group. However, as the old Dakota system broke down, a generalized obligation to kin developed, and recognition of relatives was greatly extended. In fact, when Dakota terms were reported by many informants, they extended terms for father and mother to all uncles and aunts. That is, the aboriginal bifurcate merging terminology was changed to generational terminology. Old terms for cross-uncle and cross-aunt are being applied to anyone "who feels like a close relative to you." The terms are also used when one is making a request of another. However, to the outside observer, unfamiliar with the Dakota language, Lower Brule kinship appears much like that of whites. The household units, composed largely of nuclear families, further contribute to the superficial and misleading similarity.

Processes in Change and Continuity

Customarily one speaks of the changes described above as a result of two cultures in contact. Actually, of course, it is people who are in contact—Lower Brule Indians and whites—not cultures. Moreover, the individuals are in social systems which significantly structure the kind of interaction occurring. The whites who live in Lower Brule and have daily contact with Indians are in social systems which invest them with authority. Indeed, from the beginning, most whites in long contact with Lower Brule have held statuses which restricted interaction between the two peoples. This situation accounts in large part for the continuation of a distinct Indian culture.

Obviously, the interaction of white social systems with Indian ones brought much culture change. The material culture became almost solely that of the white world. Hunting and gathering techniques were virtually lost; a cash economy with wage labor and ranching became the basis of subsistence. A formal education system has been transplanted from the dominant social system with little modification. The Lower Brule governmental body resembles a white model and follows the Western procedures of elected representatives. In operation the tribal council organizes committees, makes motions, resolves actions, and follows Robert's Rules of Parliamentary Procedure about as closely as most small-town political bodies. Nominally, all of the Lower Brules are Christian, and the Catholic and Episcopal churches are an integral part of religious life. Even in family life many changes occurred which made these Indians much like whites.

Yet there are many differences between Lower Brule and neighboring white communities. One readily observes personality differences between Indians and whites, even in small children. On first acquaintance the young seem excessively quiet. Although this shyness lessens with greater familiarity, children are quite reserved before adults, waiting to be "spoken to before speaking." Whites frequently comment on the good behavior of Indian children in this aspect. On the other hand they note that Indian parents spoil their children and whites anticipate spoiled behavior. Indian children are overindulged in terms of the larger culture. Lee (1959), however, shows how Dakotas inculcate responsibility in the child almost from birth through ways which whites interpret as spoiling. Lee and others (Erikson, 1939; Macgregor, 1946) have so well outlined the patterns of Dakota enculturation that further exploration here is unnecessary. It is important, however, to realize that a personality is being developed in the young which keeps the next generation distinct from whites. Furthermore, one must understand that this personality is not simply the aboriginal one. The process of enculturation results in individuals who can accommodate to the white world but still remain distinct within it. The formal education system is vital in this process, but parents make many important accommodations in the informal educative process. The term biculturation has been suggested as descriptive of what occurs (Polgar 1960, p. 233). He notes that "neither the conception of the adjustment to the dominant culture as a mask or veneer nor the marginal man theory has been found to fit the Mesquakie situation." Instead, a process of biculturation, or enculturation into two cultures, develops personalities that fit a situation of stabilized pluralism. Certainly a particular enculturation is basic in the processes which serve in the continuity of a distinct culture for Lower Brule.

Another difference between Lower Brule and white communities is the degree of isolation. Physically the community is more removed from highways and other towns than most South Dakota settlements. A snowstorm or heavy rainfall easily cuts off the Lower Brules. Most of the mass media fail to reach the community, although radios are becoming more common and a few television sets have appeared. However, the major separation is social isolation. First, few whites live in Lower Brule; of greater importance is that all of those whites—the trader, priests, and school teachers—are in positions of authority. The trader, operating largely on credit, is somewhat feared by his debtors. The teachers not only are Bureau representatives, and therefore suspect, but also voluntarily isolate themselves. They look to nearby Chamberlain for their entertainment and their friends. The authority of the priests may not have had to interfere with close contacts, but the Catholic priest spends most of his time at an orphanage off the reservation; the Episcopal priest labored conscientiously to attain a warm personal relationship with Indians, but he stayed only a year and had the added disadvantage of being considered too young for the job. Much of what happened in the community was hidden from him for fear he would condemn a practice as pagan or immoral. Thus, the Indians, potentially friendly, outgoing, and able to interact intimately with strangers, are prohibited any extensive contacts. The local whites are in social systems which have built-in barriers to intimate interaction. The statuses of whites in Lower Brule prevent their active participation in Indian social systems.

Another factor which makes Lower Brule different from non-Indian communities is the relationship between the reservation and the federal and state governments. This relationship results in a general lack of interest in many institutions of considerable importance to other Americans. Rarely are Lower Brule interested in or enthusiastic about even those matters which the tribal council has the authority to determine. The people are prevented from participating in activities which influence such community institutions as health, education, law and order, and welfare. A variety of formal organizations influence these institutions. The U.S. Public Health Service provides medical care and advises and aids in health measures such as providing pure water. The state government is becoming more involved with education and law enforcement; it is responsible for much of the welfare program. The social systems of these organizations are composed of highly diversified personnel with much variety in their experience, values, and philosophies. Yet the reaction of the Lower Brules to all of them is much the same. In all cases Indians find themselves in a state of dependency and subject to rules and regulations of the dominant social system, over which they have no control; their reaction is withdrawal and lack of interest. This apathy on the part of the people makes the community distinct, and the control of the community imposed by outside social systems differentiates Indian communities from all other American ones.

Migration is another important process which accounts for the continuity of a distinct Lower Brule community. The individual Indians most likely to introduce important aspects of white culture are those who leave the community. Therefore, the influence of acculturated Indians is slight. Those who migrate short distances and return to visit frequently meet with much resistance because of differing interests in the tribal estate. The effect of migration in culture change has been noted by other anthropologists. Evon Vogt (1957, p. 138) terms it a "drifting out" mechanism and says: "In some cases, this rate of migration has been great enough to involve almost all of the Indian population; but in many cases, it has had the effect of 'draining off' the most acculturated segment of the population each generation and of leaving a conservative reservoir of more traditional culture carriers intact to carry on their Indian way of life."

Discrimination is another process which maintains the distinctiveness of Lower Brule. Many persons generally have assumed that Indians would be assimilated because discrimination against Indians is minor, especially as compared with that against Negroes. But the emphasis given to the attitudes of the majority often masks the importance of the attitudes and values of the minority itself. Unlike the immigrant groups which sociologists usually study, American Indians made no explicit choice to assimilate by movement to this country. This factor alone makes them a case quite different from European immigrants. Groups like the Lower Brules have lived in the same locale for a hundred years or more. A history of their community has developed which serves to tie people to their home. Some of this history now appears as rationalization, and there is much selective "forgetting" so that the past serves as a source of pride for community members. Such a value acts as a positive force for maintenance of the community, in addition to the negative values of surrounding whites. The interplay of these two factors is found on many reservations besides Lower Brule, of course. It is vividly described by Lisa Peattie (1950, p. 14).

It is a source of pride for the Fox that they have a separate cultural tradition; they are a People. Yet the younger generation of Mesquakie are acutely aware that they live in a world which is run by whites, where the whites have power and they do not. In such a world, the superiority of Fox culture comes strongly into question. In technology, there can be no doubt, and here the Mesquakie have made the obvious choice.

Yet the Mesquakie are, willy-nilly, part of one society; even if they could escape it, escape is difficult. Here is where they feel that they are accepted as belonging. Even those who are most interested in "getting on" in the eyes of whites tend to feel strongly their identification with the community and wish to see it perpetuated.

It is necessary to detail the nature of this feeling of "getting on" in order to understand the behavior of some Lower Brule mixed-bloods. A number of these individuals are well educated and accept many white values and attitudes. However, they remain at Lower Brule not only because of economic opportunities in ranching but also because only in this community do they have a chance to lead and to acquire prestige. Among whites, these persons would not have similar opportunities.

The relationship, then, between whites and Indians is one which accounts for the preservation of Lower Brule as a community. Obstacles are placed in the path of full acculturation, and "an ultimate ceiling is still firmly clamped down by our persisting Anglo-American 'racial' attitudes" (Vogt 1957, p. 145). In reacting to this discrimination, the Lower Brules assert a pride in their traditions and history and identify themselves with other Indians. This reaction makes the community distinct from neighboring white towns.

Finally, the social structure of Lower Brule is highly important in the continuity of a distinct culture. Anthropologists have long recognized the importance of structure in the rate of change, but explicit statements about the part it plays are limited. The Social Science Research Council on Acculturation (1954, p. 976) notes that some societies have special types of "boundary-maintaining mechanisms"; and "flexible and rigid" structures have been compared on a theoretical level. In somewhat more detail Wolf (1955, p. 456) describes the resistance to change of peasant corporate communities in Latin America. He says that "persistence of 'Indian' culture content seems to have depended primarily on maintenance of [a corporate] structure. Where the structure collapsed, traditional cultural forms quickly gave way to new alternatives of outside derivation."

Factions, basic in Lower Brule structure, have been reported as the significant structural feature for many North American tribes. However, critical analysis of factionalism has been minor. Macgregor (1946) emphasized that among the Pine Ridge Sioux the differences are sociological rather than biological, but his analysis of dissension between the two groups is limited. He mentions that the division results from a difference in attitudes toward the administrative policy of the Indian Reorganization Act. Implicit in his work is the belief that other differences are highly important, however, for he says (1946, p. 25): "The division of outlook within the tribe has brought an increasing amount of conflict of one group against the other. It appears in every new issue the Sioux face and tends to retard their economic and social development."

At Lower Brule the division between mixed-blood and full-blood goes beyond political differences. Although mixed-bloods are more likely to discuss political plans for the future while full-bloods stress settlement of old treaties and wrongs committed by the federal government, the major issues involve other differences which can best be understood through a description of the two groups and an analysis of what determines group membership.

Everyone in the community is either a full-blood or a mixed-blood. A person claims descent solely from other Indians, or from one or more white ancestors. The former are regarded as full-bloods, the latter as mixed-bloods. Each group has derogatory terms for the other. The part-whites, or mixed-bloods, speak of the "backward full-bloods." They maintain that the full-bloods have kept the Indian, meaning themselves, from progress. On occasion the term "conservative" is applied to the full-blood to connote the resistance to progress. The full-bloods make derogatory reference to the mixed-blood in the use of such terms as "half-breed," "breed," or, in Lakota, *washica chinks* (white man's son). The full-bloods often propose "kicking the breeds off the reservation" as a solution to the "Indian problem." The use of epithets is only one means of maintaining the solidarity of each group. The solidarity and interaction between the factions is analyzed further elsewhere (Schusky 1960, pp. 60–77).

It is sufficient here to note that the structure allows continuity of distinct culture content. It is not a rigid system nor a corporate one. Although the tribe is incorporated, it acts this way only insofar as tribal council business is involved. The structure which has developed is the result of culture contact, but it has reached a point of accommodation which makes change in the direction of assimilation unlikely.

A basic part of this structure, and one which functions to keep Lower Brule distinct, is factional alignment. The mixed-blood faction is composed of individuals who have accepted some of white culture, but who when they attempt to bring innovations into the community are resisted by the full-bloods, who have not made similar changes. A balance of power between the factions maintains the status quo. If the factions were highly disruptive so that affairs led to an impasse or a breakdown of the social structure, acculturation might proceed rapidly, but a mutual dependence of the factions upon each other has developed. The full-bloods believe they must depend upon the mixed-bloods to interpret white culture and that the mixed-bloods serve as a buffer against the larger society. In turn, the mixed-bloods feel that many of the privileges which accrue to Indians are a result of the full-blood population. This relationship demands that some forms of interaction be worked out between the two groups, and in this situation the process of cooperation plays as important a role as the process of conflict, inherent in factionalism. The factions do cooperate sufficiently so that the community can determine ends and decide means to reach them. The process is one which not only allows Lower Brule to be a community but also makes Lower Brule distinct from non-Indian communities.

SUMMARY

A complex of mechanisms perpetuate a distinct community life for the Dakotas. An internal social system, the family, remains responsible for primary enculturation, and means have been found to prepare children for life in two worlds. In addition, Lower Brule's physical and social isolation and its governmental relations operate to foster continued distinctiveness. Migration and the adoption of white technology have not led to assimilation of the community, but rather they have aided the Lower Brules to maintain a separate social identity. Finally, past processes of culture change have helped to build a social structure which gives the Lower Brules a consciousness of kind and an organization adapted to a distinct style of life.

The maintenance of a separate identity and community does not imply a persistence of culture or the retention of aboriginal patterns. Culture changes at Lower Brule have been extensive and rapid as a result of contact with the dominant, white social systems, and it seems probable that further change will continue in the future. It does not seem probable, however, that the direction of the changes will lead to the absorption of the people at Lower Brule as a homogeneous part of the larger white society. The interaction between white and Indian social systems has brought about a distinct community, capable of change, but adapted to the continuity of a culture different from the surrounding world.

ADDENDUM, 1969

The field work that is the basis for these observations was conducted between March and September, 1958. Additional contact was maintained until the fall of 1960 while the author was at South Dakota State College. In 1960 construction of the Big Bend Dam was begun; its backwaters covered the town of Lower Brule described above. Since then, most of the Lower Brules have moved into a model town built as a replacement. The new site was carefully planned; its paved streets, new houses and apartments, modern civic buildings, and latest conveniences could serve as a model for town planning in the West.

However, a similar statement could have been made for the original town of Lower Brule when it was built in 1895. Soon after the opening of western South Dakota to homesteading, Lower Brule became one of the most attractive towns west of the Missouri River, but the development did little to change Dakota culture. The Lower Brules continued living much as they had before, changing slowly into the way of life described above. The most recent physical move may not produce much more change than the first one, but it is still too soon to determine how much change has occurred. In addition to modern physical facilities, a small electronics plant was built at the new town. Regular wage labor has significantly increased, and a new contact with whites has been established. A few Indians from other reservations, connected with the plant, are also now settled among the Lower Brules. Finally, the compensation for flooded lands made a large amount of cash capital available; in 1960 the Lower Brules had hoped to expand ranching operations with these funds.

Unfortunately, no intensive observation of these events has yet been made. On the basis of brief visits, the author has not noted any radical changes among the Lower Brules, nor does he see any significant changes in the processes described above that serve to keep the Lower

Brules a distinct community. Although increased employment, Office of Economic Opportunity work, and Headstart programs have doubtless changed the Lower Brule economy, other changes are not readily apparent.

REFERENCES

DOZIER, EDWARD, SIMPSON, GEORGE, AND YINGER, MILTON. 1957. The integration of Americans of Indian descent. *Annals of the American Academy of Political and Social Science* 311: 158–65.

ERIKSON, ERIK. 1939. Observations on Sioux education. *Journal of Psychology* 7: 101–56.

LEE, DOROTHY. 1959. Responsibility among the Dakota. In *Freedom and Culture*. New York: Prentice-Hall, Inc.

LINTON, RALPH, ED. 1940. *Acculturation in seven American Indian tribes*. New York: Appleton-Century Co.

MACGREGOR, GORDON, WITH HASSRICK, ROYAL, AND HENRY, WILLIAM E. 1946. *Warriors without weapons*. Chicago: University of Chicago Press.

PEATTIE, LISA. 1950. Being a Mesquakie Indian. Mimeo. Department of Anthropology, University of Chicago.

POLGAR, STEVEN. 1960. Biculturation of Mesquakie teenage boys. *American Anthropologist* 62: 217–35.

PROVINSE, JOHN, et al. 1954. The American Indian in transition. *American Anthropologist* 56: 388–94.

SCHUSKY, ERNEST. 1960. The Lower Brule Sioux. Ph.D. dissertation, University of Chicago.

———. 1963. Mission and government policy in Dakota Indian communities. *Practical Anthropology* 10: 109–14.

Social Science Research Council. 1954. Acculturation: An exploratory formulation. *American Anthropologist* 56: 973–1002.

VOGT, EVON. 1957. The acculturation of the American Indian. *Annals of the American Academy of Political and Social Science* 311: 137–46.

WAX, MURRAY, AND WAX, ROSALIE. 1964. Formal education in an American Indian community. Supplement to *Social Problems*.

WOLF, ERIC. 1955. Types of Latin American peasantry: A preliminary discussion. *American Anthropologist* 57: 452–71.

Representative Government:
Application to the Sioux

William O. Farber

CONTEMPORARY SIOUX tribal governments are good examples of the intermixture of inherited, imitated, and imposed organizational arrangements that have much in common with local government in the underdeveloped nations of the world and as such can be subjected to analysis as units of political and social modernization. This survey of Sioux tribal election machinery concentrates on the election process and its relation to democratic principles. Democratic principles, presumed to undergird American government, have long been scrutinized by political scientists, and basic theories have frequently been challenged. In a pragmatic sense, however, certain rather well settled rules have been observed as essential, and it is these rules that we have for the most part tried to communicate to the world.

Indians generally have been compelled to adopt traditional Anglo-American concepts even though representative institutions may not meet their needs or work satisfactorily. This has led to undue concern with how to compel adoption and adaptation and too little concern with natively based and accepted traditional practices. David Apter (1965, p. 3) correctly notes: "The preoccupation of political studies with the strengthening of democratic practices has obscured the need for an examination of the role of pre-democratic forms of government which, as a result, has received little attention."

In this study I shall attempt (1) to suggest the hereditary obstacles to acceptance of democratic principles as conceived by Anglo-American society and (2) to outline in some detail the problems Sioux tribal governments have encountered as they have attempted to adopt "democratic principles." Indian tribal governments have undoubtedly made remarkable progress since 1934 when the Indian Reorganization Act became effective, if such standards as stability, respect, and accomplishment are considered; nevertheless, a number of unresolved problems remain. What I attempt here is to delineate Indian and Anglo-American concepts of government and to survey the election machinery as the heart of the democratic process. The question arises of how in practice a synthesis of the concepts has been achieved and what problems remain.

ESSENTIAL DEMOCRATIC CONCEPTS

Our first task is, then, to consider briefly the essential characteristics of democratic government as conceived, accepted, and practiced by the dominant society. The need for qualification and accommodation becomes immediately apparent. Democratic government is based on the philosophy of majority rule. Theoretically, what 51 percent of the electorate desires ought to be the policy pursued. However, there are these questions: In determining the 51 percent do we count all members of the body politic, including children? If we exclude children on the grounds that they cannot participate in civic matters intelligently, then might we not also exclude senile persons and the mentally defective? What are the proper standards for the exclusion of unfit voters? Even in the case of the educated, how can participation be intelligent if propaganda, emotion, or terror have dictated the decisions? Should there be limits to majority rule? Should a minority be suppressed and silenced if the majority wishes it?

Democracy involves more than the above, and the following are advanced as minimum essentials:

1) The majority, considering all people as equals, must have the right, directly or through its representatives, to determine the basic policies of government.
2) The majority, directly or through its representatives, selects the personnel which runs the government.
3) Voters must have access to information so that the previous two functions can be performed intelligently and fairly.

4) The minority has both rights and obligations. These include freedom of speech, press, petition, and assembly, and the obligation to cooperate with the majority.

Democracy is thus rooted in the belief that all men are created equal, and the dictum "one man, one vote" is the cornerstone of democracy in action. Citizens are the best judges of what needs to be done and how government is working. They determine whether personnel and policies should be maintained or changed.

Unfortunately, in any large jurisdiction the voters cannot meet together at any one time and place to make laws. Such a meeting, an example of "direct" or "pure" democracy, existed formerly in the Greek city-states, Swiss cantons, town meetings in the United States, and sometimes in Indian tribal governments with few members. For the most part, however, law must be enacted by representatives chosen by the voters. We commonly call our republican form of government a representative democracy. About the only examples of direct democracy remaining in populous jurisdictions are the initiative, referendum, and recall, which will be discussed later in this study.

INDIAN GOVERNMENTAL CONCEPTS

A review of accounts of Indian tribal government prior to extensive contact with Americans indicates that these governments lacked many of the power characteristics of modern government. The significant political group was the band or *tiyošpaye*; the latter term means loosely "they live together." Stephen Feraca (1966, p. 2) has written: "Each of the *tiyošpaye* was headed by one or more chiefs. The 'tribal' council of that day apparently met rarely, only during time of crisis, and consisted of a number of band chiefs and leading men. There is no evidence that all of the bands which regarded themselves as Oglalas were represented at any councils held prior to the establishment of Pine Ridge Agency in 1878." The band itself thus was the political unit of importance, and the band chiefs and councils were the significant political systems. Apparently the chiefs were not elected by the councils but rather were self-made. The idea of election was forced on the Indian by American ideas of representation for treaty-making purposes. Pre-reservation politics included factionalism, violence, and political assassination (Feraca 1966, pp. 3–4; Howard 1966, pp. 3–4).

Sioux government was an extremely loose confederacy with almost unlimited home rule. Indians were not acquainted with a strong government physically removed from the band itself, and they were probably not conscious of being part of any area in a territorial sense which was controlled by a power other than the band. The Sioux nation rarely if ever met in its venerable assembly called the Seven Council Fires, and the annual sun dances of lesser groups resulted in few decisions. Indeed, "in practice, each division within the Sioux Nation was an autonomous system capable of functioning independently of the tribe" (Hassrick 1964, pp. 6–8, 26–28).

Two elements thus missing from Indian experience were (1) an overhead centralizing government and (2) a continuous, defined delegation of authority to a legislative (that is, council) representative. To this list may be added a third, the reaching of consensus by voting. From what accounts are available, it appears the Indians were accustomed to debate at great length until an agreement was reached. If this did not occur, dissidents might depart. The concept of deciding issues relatively quickly by a majority vote with peaceful acquiescence by the minority apparently was not a part of Sioux culture.

VOTING: CONSTITUTIONAL AND LEGAL CONSIDERATIONS

In the light of this background of Sioux Indian government and democratic concepts, what has been the experience of Sioux tribal governments in the most formal aspect of the democratic process, namely voting? In the summer of 1964 a survey was made of tribal practice in South Dakota, and the situation as it existed at that time is reported in the material presented here.

First of all, it must be noted that in determining the right of an Indian to participate in a democratic process by voting care must be taken to distinguish the jurisdiction (or level of government) which is involved. Thus an Indian on a South Dakota tribal reservation may vote for (1) federal officers: presidential electors, senators, representatives; (2) state officers: governor, lieutenant governor, secretary of state, state auditor, state treasurer, commissioner of schools and public lands, attorney general, superintendent of public instruction, public utilities commissioners, judges of the supreme and circuit courts, and state senators and state representatives; (3) county commissioners, clerk of courts, sheriff, county auditor, register of deeds, treasurer, states attorney, and county superintendent of schools; and (4) tribal officers as determined by (a) congressional acts and (b) tribal constitutions. In addition, a voter may participate in determining policy directly through the initiative and referendum on the state level and in tribal government insofar as authorized by the tribal constitution.

Because those may vote in national elections who may vote for the most numerous branch of the state legislature, state government has substantial powers to determine a wide variety of matters such as voting age, residence requirements, voting district, absentee voting, and the like. These requirements vary from state to state. In South Dakota, for example, a voter must be a citizen, twenty-one years of age, and must have resided in the state one year, the county ninety days, and the election precinct thirty days. These are the requirements for voting for federal as well as state and county officials.

Tribal governments have the power to determine who may vote in tribal elections, subject to the important restriction that if an election is held under the authority of a congressional act, there may be special requirements in connection with the conduct of the election. Section 16 of the Indian Reorganization Act of 1934 states:

> Any Indian tribe, or tribes, residing on the same reservation, shall have the right to organize for its common welfare, and may adopt an appropriate constitution and bylaws, which shall become effective when ratified by a majority vote of the adult members of the tribe, or of the adult Indians residing on such reservation, as the case may be, at a special election authorized and called by the Secretary of the Interior under such rules and regulations as he may prescribe. Such constitution and bylaws, when ratified as aforesaid and approved by the Secretary of the Interior shall be revocable by an election open to the same voters and conducted in the same manner as herein above provided. Amendments to the constitution and bylaws may be ratified and approved by the Secretary in the same manner as the original constitution and bylaws.

Thus, the Secretary of the Interior has special rights with respect to the holding of elections involving tribal constitutions and bylaws. In addition, there may be other elections where the Secretary has specified authority to prescribe regulations relative to the conduct of such election; voting on a charter of incorporation is an example of this. All elections held subject to the authority of the Secretary of the Interior are called secretarial elections.

In accordance with the Indian Reorganization Act, special rules governing elections involving the constitution and bylaws have been promulgated as federal regulations. These regulations are detailed and involve not only such matters as the minimum number necessary in voting if changes are to be made, but the time when elections will be held and what shall be done in cases of election disputes. Absentee voting is also regulated (Federal Register 1963, 6545–47; 29 F.R. 14359, 1964). Unless congressional acts specify otherwise, all remaining elections, including the selection of tribal officers, are held under the authority of the Indian tribal governments as set forth in the individual tribal constitution.

TRIBAL ELECTION PROBLEMS

The Voter and Voter Qualifications

Tribal governments do not escape the problem of who is entitled to vote either in the selection of tribal officers or in referendums. A survey of voting qualifications among the South Dakota Sioux tribes reveals three common classes of voting qualifications: membership, age, and residence. Each constitution defines membership. The following provisions of the Lower Brule Sioux tribe are typical:

Article II—Membership

SECTION 1. The membership of the Lower Brule Sioux Tribe shall consist as follows

(a) All persons of Indian blood whose names appear on the official census roll of the Tribe as of April 1, 1935, and, after the effective date of this amended constitution, only such other persons who are of Lower Brule Sioux Indian blood and whose names appear on the official census roll of September 2, 1958;

(b) All children born to any member of the Lower Brule Sioux Tribe who is a resident of the reservation at the time of the birth of said children but children born to any member after the effective date of this amended constitution and possessing at least one-fourth degree Lower Brule Indian blood shall be members regardless of the residence of their parents at the time of their birth.

SECTION 2. The Tribal Council shall have the power to promulgate ordinances, subject to review by the Secretary of the Interior, covering future membership and the adoption of new members provided only that no person may be adopted who is not a resident of the reservation.

The dates used for the original rolls differ, but in general the form of definition is the same, with the tribal council authorized to provide for additions.

The second general voting requirement is age. On all the reservations the minimum age is twenty-one, except for Crow Creek, where the age requirement is eighteen.

The final requirement is residence. At present the Cheyenne River Sioux and Pine Ridge require one year, whereas the other tribes have shorter time periods, or merely require residence at the time of voting. Lower Brule has a one-year residence requirement in voting for district councilmen; in all other cases the membership may vote on any questions regardless of residence. Cheyenne River has the added requirement of thirty days' residence in the election district in voting for council members.

It should be noted that Indian tribal constitutions do not contain restrictions on voting by occupants of state mental institutions, those with criminal records, illiterates, or those failing to pay taxes. The Standing Rock election code does have in it the interesting stipulation that "anyone under the influence of liquor shall not be eligible to vote."

Four principal problems face Indian tribal government with respect to voting qualifications. First, are the requirements as previously outlined satisfactory? No serious complaint has been raised with respect to them; nowhere do they appear to be a cause of nonvoting. The determination of membership is usually regarded as more important for possible economic rather than political rights, and definition is more apt to be considered from this point of view. The two might be separated, as indeed they are in state and tribal election voting.

The second and third voting problems faced by Indian tribal governments are more serious and are related: Should nonresidents be permitted to vote, and if so, under what circumstances? Should absentee voting be authorized, and if so, with what safeguards? The nonresident and absentee voting potential is substantial. John Artichoker (1956, p. 22) observed that in 1950 the estimated number of Sioux Indians on tribal rolls was 33,399, while the reservation census totaled 23,334. Thus, a third of the total tribal strength resided off the reservation. Should nonresidents be permitted to vote? We may distinguish two types of nonresidents: those who have permanently moved from the reservation but who maintain a residence in name only for voting and other purposes, and those who have moved away, usually recently, only temporarily, and who plan to return to the reservation. Many nonresidents are primarily interested in receiving benefits which may be available to tribal members, such as special educational grants, loans, or rehabilitation rights. Noteworthy is the recognition in the Sisseton constitution of a category of nonresidents who have never been residents of the reservation.

Related to the problem of nonresident voting is that of absentee voting. For the most part absentee voting is permitted, although the Standing Rock election code states specifically, "No absentee ballots will be accepted." On the other hand, the remaining tribal governments authorize or use absentee voting, although Pine Ridge does not permit it for primary elections. While some constitutions and election codes do not specifically provide for absentee voting, apparently, as in the case of Crow Creek, such ballots are counted. Lower Brule provided: "Qualified voters who are in the military service, penal institutions or college . . . shall be mailed absentee ballots of the appropriate resident district" (Election Rules and Regulations as Amended 1963).

A final problem is that of registration. Non-Indian communities have much more difficulty in this regard because no formal and complete membership lists are maintained as in the case of Indian tribal governments. Tribal government membership lists are maintained by the central office so that district lists can be readily checked. (The minutes of the tribal election committee, Fort Yates, North Dakota, August 23, 1963, contain the information that an enrolled Cheyenne had voted in the Bullhead District even though her name was not on the membership lists. Since no one knew the candidate for whom she had voted, it was decided to take one vote from each of the five candidates running for office!)

Bases of Representation: Reapportionment

The voters customarily have the opportunity to choose one or more tribal council members, and in some cases one or more executive officers. On the larger reservations, voters may also vote for district tribal officers and council members. In practice the number of tribal positions to be filled by popular voting is fortunately limited.

In South Dakota, tribal council members are selected by one of three methods: (1) at large, (2) by districts electing equal numbers of council members, and (3) by districts of unequal population electing varying numbers of council members.

The at-large method is found on the Yankton reservation, where all members are elected on this basis, and the Sisseton-Wahpeton reservation, where five of the twelve council members (the officers) are elected at large. Since the Yanktons meet as a tribe, and the Sisseton-Wahpetons use is restricted, the at-large system is of little consequence. If it were used more extensively, a problem would arise relative to the communication of ideas back to the individual communities which might not be represented.

The most common basis of representation is by districts electing equal numbers of representatives. On the Crow Creek and Standing Rock reservations, each district elects two representatives for two-year overlapping terms, while the Cheyenne River Sioux elect one representative from each district for four-year terms which overlap. Each of the seven Sisseton-Wahpeton districts elects a representative for a two-year term, not overlapping. The Lower Brule Sioux vary the representation of districts from one to three, the Oglalas from one to four, and the Rosebuds from one to two, all with two-year nonoverlapping terms. The Rosebud formula is that apportionment shall be "in the proportion of one representative for each two hundred fifty (250) members or a remainder of more than one hundred twenty-five (125), provided that each recognized community shall be entitled to at least one representative." The Oglalas use a similar system, except that the proportion is one for each 300 members, with an added representative if there is a remainder of 150 or more.

All of the tribal governments accept the principle that councils should be apportioned according to population. On every reservation, with the possible exception of Rosebud, a need for reapportionment exists if this principle is to be followed. Population shifts have occurred on the reservations as elsewhere so that the problem of securing reapportionment is a real one.

In the case of Indian tribal government three unusual factors influence the reapportionment problem. In the first place, the districts are established in some instances by the constitution itself, so that a constitutional amendment may be required to make a change. Some tribal officers are reluctant to recommend changing the constitution, since they feel this would add another unsettling factor to an already unstable situation. A second factor is related to the problem of communication. Some small communities are quite isolated, and strong feeling has been expressed that a reapportionment would destroy a needed link between tribal officers and these people. It has been argued that it would be preferable to enlarge the size of the council rather than deprive those communities of representatives. On the other hand, there was a feeling that the Oglala council was already too large for the effective conduct of business. (See page 132 for Council Composition data.)

Finally, there is the basic question of the extent to which voting districts should conform to *tiyošpaye*. On this point political scientists and anthropologists may well part company. The political scientists, contemplating future population shifts and realizing the legal necessity for serving the numerical equality of election districts, observe that no

TRIBAL COUNCILS

	No. of Dists.	No. Council Members	Term	Overlap
Cheyenne River	13	15	4	yes
Crow Creek	3	6	2	yes
Lower Brule	5	7	2	no
Oglala	11	32	2	no
Rosebud	21	21	2	no
Sisseton-Wahpeton	7	12	2	no
		(5 at large)		
Standing Rock	7	14	2	yes
Yankton	at large	9	2	no

amount of boundary juggling can make districts coterminous with *tiyošpaye*. The anthropologists, with equal cogency, appreciate that those outside the dominant *tiyošpaye* have no representation and are in effect disenfranchised in local elections. Only a change in political and cultural orientation can ameliorate this situation.

It can be anticipated that the obstacles to reapportionment will be overcome as the voter acquires a better understanding of the nature of constitutions and as communication improves with the spread of education. At the same time, a will to reapportion must be created in the council itself. As with most legislative bodies, this has not been easy to attain.

The other elected officers are in the executive branch. Two methods of selecting such officers exists, election by tribal councils and election by the voters on an at-large basis. The Rosebud, Crow Creek, and Lower Brule Sioux use the former method, the remainder the latter method. The advantage of council selection is that it would initially ensure that the officers have council support, which would tend to ensure effective cooperation. On the other hand, this system means that tribal chairmen may become excessively dependent upon the council. A chairman elected by the people, especially by a rather large margin, has an independent source of support. For the most part, recent theory and practice have favored increasing executive power relative to the legislative branch to provide for a more effective approach to modern problems.

Election Procedure and Machinery

The problems connected with the actual holding of an election cover a wide range, from the timing of elections to election machinery, from methods of nomination to restrictions on campaigning, from ballot forms to counting procedure. The problems encountered often seem trivial in themselves, but the outcome of elections may depend on how they are met, and improper procedure can be the cause of deep-seated conflict. Most tribal governments have found it expedient to establish special election boards or committees to supervise and conduct elections. A wide variation exists in the composition of such agencies.

The basic problem confronting those seeking the best election administration for Indian tribal government lies in the close political tie of the machinery to the tribal council. Election machinery should be nonpartisan, but this is difficult to attain when no nonpolitical institutions exist. The settlement of disputes by the council is not satisfactory, but since tribal courts are not independent, review by the courts, available in non-Indian jurisdictions, is not a satisfactory remedy and no tribal constitution provides for it. A more plausible alternative is appeal to the Bureau of Indian Affairs, but the reluctance of the Bureau to intervene in internal problems seems a bar to this type of review, though it has much to commend it. Only requests for this procedure by the Indian tribal governments themselves would make this step possible.

Nominations, Majorities, Pluralities, and Tie Votes

How do tribal governments provide for the nomination of candidates to tribal office? The simplest method is that found on the Crow Creek and Sisseton-Wahpeton reservations, where mere announcement of candidacy filed with the Secretary of the Tribal Council at a stated time prior to the election is sufficient. Lower Brule requires a petition signed by five members. On the Rosebud Reservation, 20 percent of the legal voters of the district must sign a petition if one is not nominated at a community meeting.

The other tribal governments have found it desirable to use either primary elections or runoff elections as means of ensuring that in the final election attention will be concentrated on two opposing candidates for each office. This has proved necessary since the number of candidates is often high, and to permit an election to go to the contestant with the highest number of votes might mean that he represented only a small proportion of the voters.

The problem of nomination procedure is thus connected with the problem of majority versus plurality elections. A plurality election is one in which the candidate with the most votes wins. The confusion

that often exists in Indian tribal government over the meaning of
majority and plurality is illustrated in the following contradictory
section of the Rosebud election ordinance:

> PLURALITY VOTES: Candidates receiving a majority of votes of those
> voting at a meeting of the Tribal Council shall be declared elected. It is
> defined to mean the candidates for the office of President, Vice-President,
> Secretary, Treasurer of the Rosebud Sioux Tribal Council. [Election
> Ordinances]

Some Indian tribal governments hold primary elections. Primaries
are used by the Cheyenne River Sioux, Oglala, and Standing Rock
tribes. While there is no provision for primaries or runoffs, the problem
of the tie vote is greater because of the scattering of votes. One way that
the number of candidates could be cut down is by requiring a larger
number of names on nominating petitions. It has already been pointed
out that the required number where primaries and runoffs are not used
is very small. Standing Rock and the Cheyenne River Sioux require
only ten names, and the Oglalas, with the highest requirement, sets the
minimum for council members at thirty and for tribal president at
three hundred.

With this sort of election procedure, the problem of tie votes is
certain to be significant. Rosebud, Cheyenne River, Pine Ridge, and
Sisseton make no provision for tie votes. The Lower Brule Sioux settle
tie votes by runoff procedure. Crow Creek provides: "In case of a tie
vote the winner shall be decided in the presence of the Tribal Council
by drawing a name from the hat. Drawing to be made by Chairman of
the Council" (Election Rules and Procedures 1964). In 1964 resort had
to be made to this procedure, causing considerable discontent. In 1964,
in a Pine Ridge election, despite the use of a primary, two candidates
for the Pass Creek District received the same number of votes. The
election report notes: "The tie between the two candidates from the
Pass Creek District will be determined by the Tribal Council" (Official
Reports General Election 1964, p. 1). In the case of tie votes in the
primary, the election ordinance provides that all three candidates will
have their names presented in the general election, and this had to be
done with respect to the office of tribal president in 1964, resulting in
the election of a candidate with less than a majority of the votes cast.

Election ordinances cannot anticipate all problems, but this survey
has presented sufficient evidence to show that the ordinances themselves
are needed, and they should provide definite and specific answers to

questions relating to majority and plurality elections, as well as to tie voting.

Election Protests

Indian elections are no different from elections elsewhere. Disappointed candidates frequently seek to change the result by contesting the legality of the election. Tribal elections have usually been protested on one or more of the following grounds, challenging (1) the accuracy of the count, (2) the qualifications of a candidate, (3) the qualifications of voters, or (4) the legality of the ballot or the election itself.

Tribal governments usually provide that the tribal council shall be the sole judge of the qualifications of its members, as is the case with most legislative bodies. At the same time, tribal constitutions and election ordinances may provide that decisions on elections made by election boards shall be final and not subject to further review. These apparently contradictory provisions appear to be resolved by regarding the tribal councils as, under any circumstances, appeal bodies. This applies to tribal officers as well as tribal council members.

A survey of tribal constitutions and election ordinances reveals considerable variation in protest procedure. No tribal government provides for appeal to any official of the Bureau of Indian Affairs or to any court. Despite this, defeated candidates have not hesitated to consult with superintendents or to send letters to area offices or to the Bureau of Indian Affairs in Washington. Since the Bureau works with and through tribal governments, and with monetary allotments involved, obviously there may be a need for a determination of what is the lawful government. This is a problem of supplanting the entire government, and it has not been done in South Dakota in recent years.

For the most part, while in theory the Bureau of Indian Affairs remains as a sort of court of last resort, in practice it prefers that tribal governments settle all election disputes and determine for themselves who their officers shall be. Thus, while the Bureau takes no direct action, it remains a potential check, and without question exerts great influence in the direction of keeping tribal elections honest and fair.

POPULAR GOVERNMENT: INITIATIVE, REFERENDUM, AND RECALL

Three devices have been developed whereby the voters can participate directly in the governmental process: the initiative, the referendum, and recall. The first two have a unique aspect in South Dakota, since South Dakota was the first state in the United States to authorize their use, in 1898.

All three of these devices of popular control are found in some of the tribal governments. The initiative used by Sioux Indian tribal governments is unusual in that the power to initiate an ordinance directly is not provided. Rather, in every case the constitution provides that the initiative can be used to demand a vote on any proposed ordinance. Presumably this means proposed to and in the tribal council. Since it should not be difficult to get an ordinance introduced in the council, this does not serve as a very important limitation. The Pine Ridge phraseology is typical:

> Upon a petition by at least one-third ($\frac{1}{3}$) of the eligible voters of the Oglala Sioux Tribe, or upon the request of a majority of the members of the tribal council, any enacted or proposed ordinance or resolution of the council shall be submitted to popular referendum, and the vote of a majority of the qualified voters voting in such referendum shall be conclusive and binding on the tribal council. [Constitution and By-Laws of the Oglala Sioux Tribe 1936]

The language employed in the Crow Creek and Lower Brule constitutions is similar except that the number of required signers is 50 percent. The Cheyenne River Sioux require three hundred names; Sisseton calls for 10 percent. It should be noted that the same requirements apply to enacted as well as proposed ordinances. Rosebud and Standing Rock do not provide for either the initiative or the referendum.

An unusual feature of the referendum as found in these constitutions is the absence of a time limitation within which petitions must be filed after the passage of an ordinance. Ordinarily, as the referendum operates in state and municipal government, petitions must be filed prior to the effective date of the statute or ordinance. For municipal government this is usually less than thirty days, in state government somewhat longer.

Tribal governments might well consider the desirability of limiting the time within which referral petitions might be filed. To permit referral petitions at any time increases instability in government and promotes uncertainty in policy.

All the constitutions require the referral of proposed constitutional amendments to the voters for approval or rejection. Twenty percent of the qualified voters can initiate a constitutional amendment on Standing Rock, two hundred voters on the Cheyenne River Reservation, and 10 percent for the Sisseton. Lower Brule, Rosebud, and

Crow Creek retain control of proposing amendments in the tribal council.

Recall procedure is provided in three constitutions: Cheyenne River, Pine Ridge, and Sisseton. The Cheyenne River provision is as follows:

> Every person elected to a tribal office by the Sioux Indians of the Cheyenne River Indian Reservation is subject to recall from such office upon petition of 40% of the electors of the reservation, or the district or voting precinct, qualified to vote for such office, but no recall election shall be held without the approval of the council. [Constitution and By-Laws of the Cheyenne River Sioux Tribe 1935]

The 40 percent requirement is unusually high for the operation of the recall, and the limitation that recall action must have tribal council approval is a rather substantial one.

The Sisseton-Wahpeton provision is as follows:

> Each district, by petition signed by twenty (20) per cent of the eligible voters of the district, may request the recall of their District Councilmen by the Tribal Council for improper conduct. The recall of members of the Executive Committee for improper conduct shall be by petition signed by twenty (20) per cent of the eligible voters of the whole reservation. [Revised Constitution and By-Laws of the Sisseton-Wahpeton Sioux Tribe 1959]

While the Pine Ridge constitution refers to "recall," a careful reading of the pertinent section reveals that this term is in reality a misnomer, and what is meant is impeachment. The section is as follows:

> Any officer of the council or any councilman shall be subject to recall from office under due process of law for cause. Any complaint against any officer or any councilman must be in writing and sworn to by the complainant. No person is to be impeached except by a two-thirds ($\frac{2}{3}$) vote of the council after the accused has had due notice of the charges against him and an opportunity to be heard in his own defense. [Constitution and By-Laws of the Oglala Sioux Tribe 1936]

An evaluation of direct popular participation by the use of the initiative, referendum, and recall is difficult. On all reservations where these devices have been authorized they were reported as little used. This is not strange in the light of the large number of signatures usually required to initiate the procedure. Moreover, the use of a required percentage of the eligible voters is itself questionable, since the number of eligible voters at any given time is uncertain.

It is also to be noted that while the council may be required to submit matters on petition to a popular referendum, no time is given when the elections must be held. The initiative and the referendum, to work satisfactorily, should result in elections held within time limits specifically determined by the constitutions or bylaws. Otherwise they too easily become dead letters, with their effectiveness dependent upon the caprice of tribal councils, the very branch of government they are designed to check.

In most non-Indian jurisdictions, the significance of these devices lies not so much in the number of times they are employed, but in the extent to which they keep officers responsible to the public. The initiative, referendum, and recall constitute continuous checks that make officials aware of their duties and obligations. The great need is probably educational; that is, the public needs to be aware of these means of popular control so that governmental officials will be more mindful of their potential checking effect.

SUMMARY

The characteristics of Indian tribal government election machinery and administration can be traced in part to the original constitutional provisions and election ordinances. Sometimes provisions are vague and important points not covered; but equally important, they are not workable because they have not been related to the Indian cultural background and reservation experiences. What clearly needs to be done is to reexamine each aspect of the election process with a view to determining what should be required and how it should be required. This second process involves determining whether the subject matter is properly to be incorporated in the constitution or in an ordinance.

How important are election problems in Indian tribal government? If the number of elections protested has any significance, then the evidence seems clear: election problems are frequent, serious, and need attention. On almost every reservation election contests have occurred during the past five years. A root difficulty in the administration of elections lies in the concentration of power in tribal councils. Indian tribal government knows no separation of powers; there is no independent judiciary. Furthermore, in most cases election disputes will involve membership in tribal councils, and these are the very bodies which settle such disputes.

Elections are important, not only because democratic government could not exist without them, but because they bring citizens into contact with their government. If procedures are faulty, lack of confidence in government will result. Fortunately, voting on the reservations is on the increase. This is true of both tribal elections and state and national elections. As the Indian becomes more and more a part of the American political system, he will become aware of the mechanics of democracy, the principles under which it operates, and the difficulties inherent in the translation of public opinion into law; but unless improvements are effected, many Indians will continue to find attempts to participate in the democratic process a frustrating and unrewarding experience.

REFERENCES

APTER, DAVID. 1965. *The politics of modernization.* Chicago: University of Chicago Press.

ARTICHOKER, JOHN. 1956. *Indians of South Dakota.* South Dakota Department of Public Instruction bulletin no. 67A.

Constitution and by-laws of the Cheyenne River Sioux tribe. 1935.

Constitution and by-laws of the Lower Brule Sioux tribe. 1935.

Constitution and by-laws of the Oglala Sioux tribe. 1936.

Election ordinances. N.d. Rosebud Sioux tribe.

Election rules and procedures. 1964. Crow Creek Sioux tribe.

Election rules and regulations as amended. 1963. Lower Brule Sioux tribe.

FERACA, STEPHEN E. 1966. The political status of the early bands and modern communities of the Oglala Dakota. University of South Dakota *Museum News* 27: 1–26.

HASSRICK, ROYAL B. 1964. *The Sioux.* Norman: University of Oklahoma Press.

HOWARD, JAMES H. 1966. The Dakota or Sioux Indians. Part III: The Teton or Western Dakota. University of South Dakota *Museum News* 27, nos. 9–10: 1–9.

Revised constitution and by-laws of the Sisseton-Wahpeton Sioux tribe. 1959.

Political and Religious Systems in Dakota Culture

Ernest L. Schusky

THE POLICY, PRACTICES, and personnel of the Bureau of Indian Affairs and the various mission churches on Dakota reservations vary considerably. Federal officials and missionaries often clashed openly in former times; today their relations range from cooperation to mild respect mingled with open criticism of each other. Certainly the social systems represented by the missionaries and the Bureau representatives differ considerably as to their goals and definitions of what is "best for Indians." Yet, the effects of both the dominant political and religious systems on the Dakotas have been remarkably similar, and the Dakota reaction to both is much the same. A comparison of the operations of these two systems reveals a covert similarity in exercise and effects of authority despite the many overt statements of differences between the organizations.

Catholic, Congregational, Episcopal, and Presbyterian missionaries have proselytized among the Dakotas for more than a hundred years. Today the Indians are almost all Christians, but mission work continues. Mission boards no longer are interested in proselytizing, but rather provide certain services that Indians cannot provide for themselves. Churches on Indian reservations remain, for the most part, mission churches because local congregations cannot support them. Salaries of missionaries, maintenance of the churches, and other programs are financed largely by national organizations. The mission boards are aware of their new role, but have failed to understand the consequences that follow from their position of economic control.

This control makes the relationship between the missions and the Indians much like the relation between the Indians and the federal government. An underlying assumption of all federal policy has been that special relationships between Indian communities and Washington would eventually be terminated. Under one administration, plans called for Indian communities to be economically independent and self-governing; other administrations have sought for assimilation of Indians both on and off reservations. Whatever the outcome, Bureau of Indian Affairs officials foresaw ending the relationship of dependency in which Indians find themselves. Likewise, most mission policy is in anticipation of a time when Indian churches no longer need to depend on outside support. The personnel of both social systems, churches and government, generally fail to understand the effect of the present period of dependency and how this dependency negates many of the efforts toward independence.

The nature and consequences of these dominant systems are best understood in the government's relationship with the Indians. This relationship is detailed at length in this volume for several reservations, and social scientists have devoted much work to its analysis throughout the country. A critical factor in the federal government's involvement is the trust status of most Indian property. Because of this status, the Bureau must act much as an executor responsible for property inherited by a minor. The Secretary of the Interior supervises or approves the use of trust property and is responsible for the expenditure of income derived from it.

Furthermore, because this property is tax exempt, the federal government provides services assumed elsewhere by the state or county. The BIA, for instance, has taken responsibility for education and law enforcement, while the U.S. Public Health Service manages hospitals and other health services on reservations. Although many Indians are employed in the agencies, authority in these social systems remains outside Dakota communities. And as long as the Indian Bureau or PHS remains responsible for their activities, it is difficult to see how they can transfer their authority to a local social system such as a tribal council. The short phrase "subject to the approval of the Secretary of the Interior" appears innocuous in tribal constitutions, but its insertion is enough to protect the government in its role of executor. It is also enough to make true self-government and independence impossible.

The structure of the relationship between the Bureau of Indian Affairs and Indian tribes is likely to continue because of implicit values in the dominant society about economic independence. Dakota reservations lack a natural-resource base and trained manpower, and show little potential for economic development. Even for a minimum of services, such as education, an outside social system must provide financial assistance. Under present legislation, the responsibility, and therefore authority, for this assistance is vested in the Bureau of Indian Affairs or other government organizations. It is conceivable that the financial aid could be divorced from the authority, but many Anglo-Americans appear reluctant to entrust Indians with monetary responsibility. Implicit in their view is an argument that anyone who is not financially independent is irresponsible. The historical circumstances which led to Dakota poverty are neglected. It, of course, does not follow that Indians are necessarily irresponsible simply because they are poor. Yet they are denied self-government because of the trust status of property, and the trust status is maintained largely because of their poverty.

Although the Christian denominations do not have a relationship with Indian communities that is highly structured by legislation, their position is strikingly similar to that of the Bureau of Indian Affairs. The denominations which have a policy of centering power in local congregations or regional organizations are also faced with the dilemma of providing money without retaining control over its expenditure. In no case on Dakota reservations were mission boards able to separate financing from authority. Thus, they are in much the same role as the BIA, and a number of Indian informants pointed up similarities between national missions and the federal government.

Furthermore, behavior and attitudes toward national mission boards correspond with those toward the Bureau. A national office is conceived of as a far-off and somewhat hostile force, even though individuals personally known in the organization are generally liked and respected. Individuals within the BIA are regarded in the same way. Also, a national board serves as a scapegoat for many local matters over which it has little control, just as the Bureau is often blamed for events of which it has no knowledge. Plans or even suggestions coming from either of these distant offices are regarded with suspicion, apathy, or outright hostility, simply because they are associated with an outside social system in which Indians lack any significant voice.

The relationship between the dominant social system and indigenous communities frequently leads to misunderstandings and distrust. A specific case illustrates the point. In the summer of 1961 the Presbyterian National Board of Missions planned to combine the all-white Black Hills Presbytery with the all-Indian Dakota Presbytery. Personnel of the National Board spoke of the plan as "merger," but it was clear that integration movements in the South had sparked this attempt at Indian-white integration. The Indians, however, reacted to the merger as a move that was being forced upon them; therefore, they resented and resisted the plan. The resistance was a kind which the Dakotas have worked out over the years to block innovations offered by the Bureau of Indian Affairs. Little overt opposition appeared; instead, spokesmen requested a postponement in order to discuss plans further. Opposition was expressed primarily by refraining from doing anything. In their silence, the Dakotas were again expressing the belief, "Here is one more white man's plan forced upon us about which we can do nothing." Actually, the Indians were doing something. They acted in ways which completely blocked the proposed innovation and defeated it through gossip, apathy, and ridicule. However, they failed to recognize even this limited extent of their potential control within the dominant social system. Resentment and suspicion of the Board of Missions did not diminish after merger plans were withdrawn.

The relation between the political or religious social systems and the Indian communities also highly structures the status of the contact agents in the formal organizations. The federal government gives special encouragement to Indians to enter the Bureau of Indian Affairs. Many of the civil servants within the Bureau are Indian, and a few Indians have become reservation superintendents. For a while the area director of the Dakotas was an Indian. Likewise, the denominations have offered special inducements to Indians to become missionaries. Most of the Presbyterian and Congregational ministers are Indian, and the Catholics and Episcopalians have trained a number of Indian priests. However, Indians do not appear to be any more effective than whites in their roles as either missionaries or civil servants. The Indians' command of the Dakota language is a definite advantage, but whites can generally manipulate better the dominant social system for Indian ends. In short, the social significance of race is minor for the contact and change agent.

Far more significant is the structuring of the status which derives from the nature of the dominant social systems. In the case of the religious systems, the presence of a missionary, either Indian or white, identifies a church as a mission and means outside financial assistance and control. This support leads to a particular relationship between minister and congregation on the one hand and ministers and board of missions on the other. The process of explaining merger plans in the Dakota Presbytery, for example, illustrates the dilemma faced by contact and change agents within dominant social systems. Local congregations were almost unanimous in opposing the merger. The ministers felt they should represent and respect this view. Yet, as missionaries, they also had strong loyalties to the National Board of Missions and felt bound to introduce national plans. The missionaries were truly "men in the middle" who were being criticized by church members for simply trying to please the mission board while mission board officials questioned their failure to achieve a merger.

Although some of the misunderstandings in this case could have been resolved by better communication, the present system contains an inherent paradox. A missionary owes some loyalty to his employer. When he differs with a particular policy of the National Board, he must feel some guilt, even though he is supporting his congregation's and his personal viewpoint.

Government agents at the local level occupy a comparable position. Several anthropological surveys have described how schoolteachers are divided in their loyalties between the Bureau system and the community they are supposed to serve. However, participation in the Bureau social system demands a very high degree of conformance to it; missionaries cannot create almost totally isolated social lives for themselves on reservations as do Bureau personnel. Employees at Pine Ridge and other large reservations have created for themselves a community within a community. The social systems described above have been, in the opinion of some, the creations of the dominant society, but they have been modified in many ways through experience with Indians and by the Indians themselves. The loci of power and final authority are clearly within the dominant society, although personnel within the political and religious systems are frequently Indian at the local level. When an occasional Indian rises in the hierarchy, he is obviously one who is committed to the values of the dominant system and oriented toward it, not the Indian community. There are, however, indigenous religious and political systems. The formal organizations which represent these systems have their origins in, and have been created in part by, the dominant systems, and the form they take is similar to that of comparable white organizations. Yet the function and meaning of these groups are distinctly Indian. It is possible that the present groups may be more an outgrowth of aboriginal associations than usually suspected, but few data are available. The nature of the aboriginal associations was formerly thought to be understood, but now is being questioned. Still less is known about the transition, if indeed it was a transition, to modern forms.

The present associations within the political and religious systems are the tribal councils or business committees and various church groups. The church groups follow fairly rigid age and sex lines and function as social as well as service associations. It is the church associations which are most reminiscent of aboriginal forms such as the warrior societies.

The Brotherhood of Christian Unity, for instance, is an Episcopalian men's association that grew from an all-denomination grouping. Younger men may join, but active participation is confined to males of about thirty-five to fifty years of age. The group is responsible for minor and regular routine duties around the church; in this function the group is relatively unimportant. On occasion, however, the men may assume major responsibility for a task, and their activity becomes of much importance to them and other Indians. For example, in the summer of 1958 the Episcopal Convocation was scheduled to meet at Lower Brule. Delegates from all the Episcopal mission churches of South Dakota met for three days; attendance was well over a thousand. The Lower Brule congregation of fifty to sixty families assumed full responsibility for the meeting. Planning and fund raising started the first of the year; they raised over a thousand dollars. Women's groups arranged special sales; the BCU made collections; and even youth groups participated. In the late spring the BCU painted the church and parish house, constructed a large shade for outdoor meetings, cleared a campground and prepared sanitary facilities, arranged for a pure water supply (Lower Brule residents take their water from the Missouri River but realize that it makes Indians sick who are unaccustomed to it), brought electricity to the outside site, and persuaded the Bureau to make road repairs. During the meeting the Lower Brules provided three meals a day for those in attendance, policed the camp-grounds at night, arranged recreation for teenagers, and managed all the many details arising from such an occasion. Responsibility and work were delegated to various associations, although in such subtle fashion it was difficult for an outside observer to note details of the delegation. Moreover, the division of labor was not strict; men helped the women even in such traditionally female occupations as cooking, for instance. But with termination of the convocation, the associations quickly lost their importance.

Tribal councils operate in a similar fashion. Although councils often include a few elderly men and occasionally a woman, membership is confined largely to the thirty-five- to fifty-year-old men. In this respect they probably resemble the informal political bodies of aboriginal times. Today, however, the organizations lack power to make any major decisions; they serve largely in an advisory role to the Bureau. Originally the Indian Reorganization Act meant these groups to be the organ of self-government. The reasons for failure to achieve self-government through the IRA have been detailed many times elsewhere; the present function of the councils is well described by Robert Thomas in Schusky (1965). He shows how councils are circumvented in decision-making and how Indians are fully aware of the ineffectiveness of their indigenous government. Basehart and Sasaki (1964) provide a comparable case from the southwest. Yet, at least the councils provide a minimum of political expression and an opportunity for learning some political behavior for modern conditions. Indeed, it is surprising how much pressure Indians can bring upon the Bureau, given the present structured relationship. This pressure must be attributed largely to well-skilled individuals who have learned much about political maneuvering as members of the tribal councils.

Another example from Lower Brule illustrates this point. In 1954 much reservation bottomland had been flooded by the Fort Randall Dam. In 1958 the council was in the process of negotiating a settlement. The flooded land was evaluated at about a million dollars; the Lower Brules had formulated a plan to make the reservation self-sustaining. The plan required an approximate two-million-dollar investment. The second million would have covered any claims against the government from past treaty injustices (no such claims had been entered in court, but some were feasible), or Congress could recognize the extra money as an outright grant. At that time the federal government was following a policy of termination; that is, it wanted to end special relationships between tribes and the government. Almost all tribes had expressed strong opposition to the policy; the Lower Brule request for termination must have had much appeal to the congressmen who favored the policy. Certainly it was a most opportune time to ask for an extra million. Lower Brule politicians were well aware of their political advantage and exploited it fully. Bureau officials likewise were aware of Lower Brule's position and had had a major voice in construction of the plan, but since the council was supposed to be the spokesman for the community, its testimony before Congress carried much weight. Unfortunately, the outcome of this maneuvering cannot be known. Before a settlement was reached, construction of another dam began. Attention became focused on settlement of direct damages for it. Moreover, Congress rejected the termination policy in 1960, and Lower Brule lost its advantage in requesting an end to special services. Still, it is obvious that some Lower Brules have become adept politicians. Although they are strictly limited in what they can do, they have learned to maneuver fully within the limits.

Clearly the relationship between the dominant and the indigenous social systems prevents the Dakotas from determining all of their goals or the means to the goals. The situation has often been described as paternalism or colonialism. The Bureau of Indian Affairs is generally made the scapegoat for allowing such a development; Indian Commissioners, in particular, are a frequent target of criticism. Little cognizance is taken of their problems. Extensive hearings on Indian rights by the Senate Judiciary Committee has finally extended certain civil rights to Indians but not self-government (Schusky 1969).

A comparison of religious and political systems illustrates that it is the structure of the relationship between dominant systems and Dakota communities that limits Indian action or the development of effective indigenous systems. Personalities within the systems vary in their dedication or concern, but individuals are of little consequence. When final authority and responsibility are vested in the dominant systems, such as the BIA, PHS, and mission boards, then the community or indigenous organizations, such as tribal councils, can do relatively little. Indeed, it is surprising that the Dakotas have learned as much as they have since they have been denied statuses with meaningful power or duties.

REFERENCES

BASEHART, HARRY, AND SASAKI, TOM. 1964. Changing Political Organization in the Jicarilla Apache Reservation Community. *Human Organization* 24: 283–89.

SCHUSKY, ERNEST. 1965. *The right to be Indian.* Vermillion, S. Dak.: Institute of Indian Studies.

———. 1969. American Indians and the 1968 Civil Rights Act. *America Indigena* 29: 369–76.

The Dakotas in Saskatchewan

Alice B. Kehoe

APPROXIMATELY SIX HUNDRED and fifty registered Dakotas live in the Canadian province of Saskatchewan. They constitute less than 3 percent of the total number of Indians registered in the province and occupy only four tiny reserves. Through five generations, however, they have maintained their tribal identity. Now the swelling tide of pan-Indianism is lapping at the bulwarks of Dakota nationalism. Some Saskatchewan Dakotas are tentatively probing the numerically dominant Crees' invitation to unite against the enveloping Euro-Canadian society. A new period in the Dakotas' adjustment to Canada seems to be emerging.

The theoretical importance of the Canadian Dakotas is potentially great, for they constitute a comparative group for testing hypotheses derived from studies of the Dakotas on United States reservations. To date, little advantage has been taken by anthropologists of this ready-made control. This paper suggests and delineates some of the insights that could be gained from directed field studies.

The Minnesota Uprising of 1862 initiated the influx of Dakota settlers into Canada. Fearing reprisal, Dakotas involved in the Uprising fled into southern Manitoba. More refugees trickled in as other conflicts between Dakotas and Americans threatened trouble for the Indians. The most famous, and largest, group of Dakota refugees was Sitting Bull's band, seeking safety in southwestern Saskatchewan after their victory in the Battle of the Little Big Horn in 1876.

Several factors made Canada a desirable haven for the Dakotas. The most obvious advantage was that the United States Army could not pursue the Indians across the forty-ninth parallel. The North-West Mounted Police, the select and well-disciplined force guarding Canada's western territories, were believed by the Indians to be just and understanding. They were sought out as protectors by the border tribes, their jurisdiction becoming a sanctuary for Indians who felt persecuted by American authorities. Indian confidence in the good faith of the North-West Mounted Police was demonstrated when the Police succeeded in persuading Sitting Bull and his followers to return to the United States.

During the period when the Dakotas were moving into Saskatchewan, their safety was linked to the lack of white settlers in western Canada. Not until 1896 did a demand for land become apparent in what were to become the prairie provinces (Card 1960, p. 8). Farming had been conducted only around the few missions and in the scattered settlements of the Metis (Indian half-bloods, principally French-speaking Catholics). Anglo-Canadians filtering into the western territories perceived the Metis to be their chief competitors for land. The Metis, who formed an organized opposition to Anglo-Canadian sovereignty in the two Riel rebellions (1869 and 1885), served as a buffer between the white homesteaders and the Indians. The slow expansion of Canadian agriculturists and the delaying actions of the Metis, politically more sophisticated than their Indian cousins, permitted the western Canadian Indians to retain their freedom longer than the American tribes.

A favorable human climate in the Canadian territories was underlain by an ecology very similar to that of the Dakotas' homeland in Minnesota and North Dakota. Following the climatic belts, which extend northwest onto the Canadian prairies, the Dakotas moving into southern Manitoba and Saskatchewan remained in the type of environment they were skilled in exploiting. Only the Teton Dakotas, adapted to the semiarid plains, were less at home, for their type of land occurs only in southwestern Saskatchewan and in Blackfoot-dominated Alberta. These differences in geographical conditions may have contributed to the Tetons' eventual willingness to return south, in contrast to the Eastern bands' tenacity in remaining in Canada.

Although the Canadian government was reluctant to force the Dakotas to recross the border, and indeed would have been unable to do so without a large expenditure of money and military manpower, it was unwilling to legitimatize their residence in Canada by registering them and granting them reserves. Living as squatters, the Dakotas petitioned the Canadian government to allot them land for farming and homes. As the buffalo began to disappear, and the flow of white settlers to increase, the Dakotas' pleading became more urgent. Their requests were seconded by recommendations from both North-West Mounted Police officers and from civilians, favorably impressed by the Dakotas' diligence and good order.

The government in time acceded to the Dakotas' desires and eventually granted them these reserves: in Manitoba, Birdtail, Oak Lake, Oak River, and Long Plain; in Saskatchewan, Standing Buffalo, Moose Woods, Sioux Wahpaton (generally known as Round Plains), and Wood Mountain.[1] Of the Saskatchewan reserves, Standing Buffalo is the largest, and is located in the grassy Qu'Appelle River valley entrenched in the prairie wheatlands. Moose Woods lies on bush-covered sand dunes near the South Saskatchewan River, south of Saskatoon. Round Plains is on the edge of the transitional coniferous forest near the forks of the Saskatchewan River. Tiny Wood Mountain is on the border of the semiarid plains of southwest Saskatchewan. All except Wood Mountain were predominantly, though by no means wholly, composed of Eastern Dakotas. Standing Buffalo and Moose Woods, also known as White Cap, preserve the names of the leaders of the settling bands.

Until 1869 the area in which the Dakota reserves lie had been Rupert's Land, protected fur domain of the Hudson's Bay Company. Because the company had discouraged European settlement in its territories, the Indians retained possession of their hunting grounds until the establishment of Canadian sovereignty. Even then the territory was considered so remote from the seat of government in Ottawa that the Metis challenged Canada's right to incorporate Manitoba into the Confederation, but the surveying and administration of the West proceeded. In the 1870s a series of treaties were concluded with the tribes occupying the newly acquired lands. Treaty No. 1, dated August 3, 1871, effected the transfer of much of southern Manitoba to the Crown.

---

[1] Population of Saskatchewan Dakota reserves, as of December 31, 1963 (Indian Affairs Branch report):

Standing Buffalo	396
Moose Woods (White Cap)	121
Sioux Wahpaton (Round Plains)	81
Wood Mountain	50
Total	648

The Qu'Appelle Treaty, No. 4, September 15, 1874, brought southern Saskatchewan under Crown control, and No. 6, August, 1876, added central Saskatchewan. The Dakotas did not take part in the treaty-making, since they were not indigenous to Canada.

The treaty dates reflect the lag in Canadian westward expansion as compared to that of the United States. The Canadian Indians were negotiating their first treaties at the time that United States tribes were fighting last-ditch battles to regain the autonomy they had lost. The Canadian tribes were culturally within the fur trade period until the 1880s, nearly a generation longer than the American.

The Dakotas had come from a frontier where they had become acquainted with segments of Euro-American society, and their sophistication impressed the Canadian authorities. Methodist missionaries visiting White Cap's band at Moose Woods in May, 1889, spoke of "the industrious habits of these red men, and the fact that they had built sixteen log houses, and were anxious to have a school, and assist in the building of it" (Black 1913, p. 750). If the Canadian government had hoped that the Dakotas would lead the indigenous, less acculturated tribes into assimilation with Euro-Canadian society, however, they were disappointed. Once domiciled among the Crees, Saulteaux, and Assiniboins of Canada, the Dakotas tended to conform to the general culture of the Indians around them, rather than move closer toward European norms.

In Voget's (1951, p. 221) terms, the Dakotas were in a "native-modified" phase of acculturation when they came to Canada. They remained in this phase as the indigenous Indians entered it more fully and consolidated their new cultures. There was little real pressure on the Dakotas to develop the traits that would place them in the "American-modified" phase. The minimum of agriculture and schooling and nominal Christianity that permitted a living congruent with aboriginal standards seemed to be all that the Dakotas in Canada really wanted.

The Canadian government's handling of Indian affairs was, in general, based upon the treaty agreements. Each family of five persons was given one square mile of land incorporated in its band's reserve. The men were instructed in agriculture and provided with necessary tools and the stock and seed required to begin farming. Treaty Indians retained the right to hunt and fish on Crown lands. Children were to receive a standard Canadian education. Annual payments of twenty-five dollars per chief, fifteen dollars per band councilor, and five dollars per individual registered Indian were promised in perpetuity. The Saskatchewan Dakotas were eligible for all these benefits except the annuities, which were considered to be compensation for surrendered lands.

At the beginning of the reserve period, many Indians sincerely attempted to become farmers. They cooperated with the instructors the government placed on the reserves, and they worked long and hard in their fields, but drought, hail, grasshoppers, and frosts attacked the crops and discouraged the novice farmers. Not unreasonably, the Indians frequently interpreted their crop failures as signs that the Great Spirit did not favor Indian agriculturists. Even modern civil law regards natural disasters as "acts of God."

When farming failed, the Indians had no alternative but to beg the government for rations. The buffalo herds had been the staple of prairie life, but they had disappeared. Deer and antelope had always been too sparse to support the comparatively dense populations relying upon the buffalo. There are few fish in the shallow prairie waters, and wildfowl are only intermittently abundant. The hungry Indians slaughtered their breeding cattle, and when these were gone, were forced to depend upon relief rations.

The government had not foreseen the extinction of the buffalo herds. Beset by the manifold problems of a new nation, it nevertheless did its best to relieve the distress of its wards. In spite of the difficulties of transporting food immense distances, often in oxcarts, quantities of beef, flour, and bacon were distributed to the Indians. These rations staved off serious hunger, but they formed a depressing diet for people accustomed to fresh buffalo meat. Worse, the diet was nutritionally inadequate, and caused a degree of malnutrition that predisposed the population to illness.

Not only the diet but many other features of reserve life must have been depressing to the Indians relinquishing their nomadic freedom. Discouraged from farming, finding very little to hunt, unable to obtain jobs in a territory of self-sufficient pioneer homesteads, the Indian man had too little to do. The government had banned all native dances on the grounds that they were pagan, wasted time and supplies, and were likely to stir up rebellion. (The Cree chiefs Poundmaker and Big Bear were alleged to have planned their part in the 1885 Riel Rebellion during a thirsting dance held jointly by their bands.) Most native rituals did continue sub rosa, but could not be held often or with large gatherings. Life seemed empty. As Wissler (1916, p. 869) observed at the time, "Many young men were so overwhelmed by the vacuity of the new life that they . . . [threw] their lives away."

On the Canadian prairies, as elsewhere, the Indians developed a "reservation culture" that differed in important respects from their aboriginal cultures, yet was, and is, remarkably different from the Euro-Canadian cultures around them. White homesteaders staked out the prairies from about 1896 until after World War I; towns and a few small cities were established; the prairie grasslands became the breadbasket for millions of people, but only the Metis (who had no treaties) were forced to adjust to the incursion of western society. The Indians were encapsulated in their reserves. They kept their traditional understanding of the nature of man and the universe, their recognition of Power (*wakan*) and respect for nature. The band system, built upon the dual principles of kinship ties and personal leadership, endured. Reserve life consisted of intermittent hunting and fishing, occasional wood- and hay-cutting, and odd jobs and chores. The Indians danced for recreation and in the rituals that still seemed relevant. Fortified by government paternalism, each little reserve became a microsystem.

The physical welfare of the Indians became the concern of the Indian Affairs Branch of the federal government. All registered Indians were, and are, entitled to complete free medical care, given by Indian Health Service doctors, nurses, dentists, and public health nurses, or by provincial personnel paid a fee by the Indian Health Service. In Saskatchewan, the Indian Health Service has one public health nurse for every one thousand Indians, five times the province's ratio. The Service also conducts an intensive campaign for the diagnosis and care of tuberculosis and a program promoting maternal and child health through education and sanitation; tuberculosis and infant gastrointestinal disorders are the only two categories of disease of which there is a higher incidence among Indians than among whites in Saskatchewan. Children with handicaps are aided at the Moose Jaw Training Institute and at provincial physical rehabilitation centers. Mental disorders are treated at Indian Health Service expense in the province's two hospitals for the care of the mentally ill. No special provisions are made for the treatment of Indians, other than the presence of interpreters for those who do not speak English. The comparatively low degree of acculturation on many Saskatchewan reserves suggests that the incidence and nature of Indian mental illnesses would differ somewhat from those of whites, but this has not been investigated.

Canadian Indians have not yet fully attained citizenship status. The right to vote came to them in 1961. Before that year, only those Indians could vote who had been war veterans or who had legally relinquished their status and rights as Indians. Indians could not buy liquor until 1956. (In 1965 bands still had the option to forbid liquor to be taken onto their reserves. Many reserves, including Standing Buffalo, are legally dry today.) An Indian agent can withhold money due an Indian and use it to pay the Indian's debts, regardless of his wishes. To achieve full autonomy, a Canadian Indian must renounce his inherited privileges, including his membership in his band and usufruct rights on his reserve.

Indians who retain their wardship status are being led toward greater autonomy, however, under recent government policies. Many of the internal affairs of the reserves (judgment of minor law infractions, disbursement of band monies) are now conducted by the elected councilors and chief of the band. The government builds small frame houses for Indian families on the reserves, may share the cost of building reserve roads, and has instituted community development projects. These latter, designed to enlist the participation of reserve residents in the economic improvement of their home, are expected to promote native leadership and a constructively aggressive outlook on the part of the younger Indians.

The Canadian government has from the first considered the education of Indian children one of its major tasks. The principle of this education has been to provide the Indian with a Euro-Canadian background. Since Christian missionary organizations had personnel and methods already adapted for this end, the government entrusted Indian education to those organizations. The Indian Affairs Branch regulations stipulate that each reserve shall be provided with trained teachers belonging to the church to which the majority of the band members belong. In practice, this means that the mission first on a reserve has the exclusive privilege of establishing the schools. Truly nonsectarian schools apparently cannot exist on Indian reserves: one illuminating case from the Battleford (Saskatchewan) district concerned a pagan Saulteaux band that, despite objections, was assigned a missionary for a teacher. As a concession to the band's religious beliefs, the teacher was ordered to refrain from evangelizing during school hours.

The policies of the Protestant missions regarding Indian education have been clearly stated.[2] Native beliefs and attitudes were to be eradicated and the children molded according to a British Protestant image, resembling the popular concept of the peasant—sturdy, hard-working, sternly moral, and content with the restricted world of farm and village. Canadians perceived the Indians to possess some of the characteristics of peasant societies: small, homogeneous, kin-based groups, living close to the land, the Canadian Indian bands reminded the British of European rural folk. Obviously, some essential characteristics of the peasant were lacking in the Indians: devotion to agriculture and commitment to hard physical labor, frugality, and Christianity. These deficiencies would have to be met by education. It was assumed that carefully developed school programs could correct the restlessness of the nomads' children and teach them to live happily and usefully in their native hamlets. This ideal may have harbored a less noble hope that the isolation of village life would minimize the contacts between the two races, promoting peaceful coexistence.

The first schools set up after the reserves were established were usually day schools, but the difficulty of forcing the scattered children to attend regularly persuaded the churches to favor residential schools. From 1892 to 1957, the government paid per capita grants for the maintenance and instruction of Indian children. Since 1957, the government has been taking a greater role in the operation of the schools, and day schools have come into favor again.

Canadian Indian schools have endeavored to develop programs that were believed to be especially well adapted to conditions of Indian life. Their philosophy has been that "the curriculum for Indian schools should be planned to prepare Indian youth for complete living in their future environment, that is to say, for the development of self-supporting community life on their Indian reserve" (Westcott 1943, pp. 283–84). The usual elementary subjects were taught, and, particularly in the 1930s, much emphasis was placed on the acquisition of manual skills as well. Boys were instructed in agriculture, carpentry, printing, blacksmithing, and shoemaking. Girls learned household skills,

[2] "The paramount aim of the missions, as might be expected from those who are themselves disciples of the Lord Christ, and keenly desire to bring all mankind into subjection to Him, is to impart unto all the Indians in Canada the truths of the Christian religion. . . . the ruling of our Lord that men should 'render to Caesar the things that are Caesar's' . . . places inescapably on these missions the obligation of fitting the Indians to conform to that ruling. . . . the Indian is to be qualified as a Christian citizen" (Westgate 1943, pp. 118–19).

including cooking, the making and care of clothing, and dairy work.

The secretary of the Church of England's Indian and Eskimo Residential School Commission painted an appealing picture:

> Not only do the residential schools develop both the bodies and minds of the children, but they help to remove the baneful influence of segregation, to elevate the standards of health and hygiene, and by daily contact with virtuous and educated men and women they gradually train these children to evaluate their own position as units in the great and complex world around them. [Westgate 1943, p. 120]

The Indians tell another story, one of strict discipline. Authoritarianism separated the white personnel from the Indian children, and absolute conformity to the rules was demanded. The schools intended to cut the children off from their ancestral cultures and to impress upon them the superiority of Euro-Canadian culture and its bearers. Their denigration of the children's parental cultures and the coercive measures used to ensure obedience to the teachers' plans contrasted unfavorably with the tolerance, affection, and respect the children found on their reserves. Thus, the schools often succeeded only in alienating the Indian children from the Euro-Canadian culture urged upon them. The Indians were not attracted to the role of peasants.

The Dakotas in Saskatchewan were no more willing to accept peasants' roles than were the indigenous tribes, but they were still beset by insecurity as immigrants. They realized that a demonstration of familiarity with English and with Euro-Canadian society pleased the government authorities and other whites with whom they came in contact. A knowledge of English and ease among Euro-Canadians also helped the Dakotas travel to other Canadian and to the northern United States reservations, with which they maintained social ties. Perhaps for these reasons, the general level of education is higher on Standing Buffalo than on most other Saskatchewan reserves. Most of the older adults have completed the fourth or fifth grade, and the younger generation the seventh or eighth, a level not far below that common for the province as a whole. One Standing Buffalo resident remarked that when he attended the school in the Qu'Appelle valley at Lebret, some thirty years ago, the Dakotas seemed to outnumber the children from other tribes, although their reserve was smaller. Nevertheless, Standing Buffalo has few high school graduates. Its young people are content to join the four-fifths of Saskatchewan teen-agers who do not complete high school.

In 1948, the government initiated a move toward integration of Indian children into the public day schools near their reserves. In 1957, further revisions of policy permitted the formation of school committees drawn from band members, in order to give Indian parents some voice in the operation of the reserve day schools. The new policies in Indian education reflect the current belief that Indians should be encouraged to become assimilated into Euro-Canadian society, instead of remaining a caste outside. The success of the revisions depends upon whether the local agents, both Indian agents and school authorities, agree with the government's new goal for its wards. Its success may also be affected by the Indian parents' unwillingness to foster assimilation. There is general agreement that preventing the internalization of patterns of segregation through integration of the immature will break down the caste barriers, but there are many of both races who do not accept the desirability of such a breakdown.

One Saskatchewan Indian agency, the File Hills-Qu'Appelle Agency overseeing Standing Buffalo and Wood Mountain reserves, among others, took the lead in actively promoting the integration of reserve children into the provincial school system. A precedent was set when the government contributed one-fifth of the cost of a new combined elementary and high school opened in the town of Balcarres, Saskatchewan, in 1964 to serve both Balcarres district white children and nearby Indian reserve students. There were reported to be nineteen other integrated schools in Saskatchewan at the beginning of 1964. At Standing Buffalo reserve that year, approximately fourteen children attended day school in the town of Lipton.

Indian parents decide whether their children are to attend integrated schools, if available. Several factors influence the parents' choice. Two paramount considerations are the parents' attitude toward assimilation and their concern over the child's adjustment to the alien school. The fear that children will be unhappy in the strange environment induces many parents to keep their youngsters in the familiarity of the reserve. Ahab Spence, a Saskatchewan Cree who has become an archdeacon of the Anglican Church and principal of the Indian Residential School at Sioux Lookout, Ontario,

> recalled his own sense of having been transplanted into a different world altogether. Always there is [a] completely strange environment, often a new language. . . . The greatest hindrance to integration, the archdeacon felt, was the deep-seated fear of the painfully shy Indian of making a mistake and thus exposing himself to ridicule. Often ridicule comes simply because

he is Indian and therefore "different." He carries a different food in his
lunch pail if he is lucky enough to have a pail, or he has to wear clothing
that is different. Nothing hampers a child more effectively than such fear.
. . . Equally upsetting is the effect of integration upon the parents of a child
attending a "mixed" school. Many habits must be changed. Better clothing
and white man's food must be supplied. The ancient diet of bannock and
lard has had to give way to bread and cake and apples and oranges. Space
and light for study must be provided in the one-room shack which over-
flows with grandparents and cousins and nieces and nephews. Chores must
take second place to homework. . . . With the closing of reserve schools the
parents lose touch with an invaluable—and sometimes their only—link with
the outside world, a personal contact with their children's teacher. [Report of
speech by the Ven. Spence to the Punnichy, Saskatchewan, (a heavily Indian
district), Home and School Association, *Regina Leader-Post*, January 19, 1963]

As their hesitation over accepting integrated schools indicates, many
Indians do not understand the currently fashionable Canadian concept
of ethnic pluralism as a national characteristic. The Indians assume
they still face the cruelly simple choice they were given as schoolchildren: Indians *or* white. Few realize they can maintain a selected
portion of their tradition, that which is compatible with Euro-Canadian
culture, as an ethnic group within Canadian society. They fear that if
their children are sent out of the protected reserve, they will disappear
under the overwhelming pressure to repudiate Indian ways. Therefore,
they oppose integrated education.

Reservation culture has developed in southern Saskatchewan into
a stable form of society. A core of aboriginal Indian values is carried by
groups bound to the sharply circumscribed worlds of their bands'
reserves. Neighboring towns may be visited, but the reserve residents'
principal contacts with the outside society are through their Indian
agencies. The reserves have become rural ghettos. Having elected to be
segregated with the indigenous tribes, the Dakotas in Saskatchewan
have come to share in this centripetal culture.

If population size were as stable as the reservation culture, the
Indian societies might continue to live as they have for the past several
generations. The Indian birth rate, however, is high (5 percent), and the
pressure of overpopulation is now felt on most reserves. Living standards,
already low, are being pushed even lower. The reserves cannot physically expand, and few have any resources that could raise the incomes
of the residents. The only solution to the problem of overpopulation
appears to be emigration. But even those who admit the problem—
and not all Indians do—usually do not wish to be the ones to leave.

Figures underline the extent of the problems facing Canadian Indians. According to the Indian-Eskimo Association of Canada, in the mid-1960s 75 percent of Indian families in Canada earned less than two thousand dollars annually, and 45 percent earn less than one thousand dollars annually. Each year 36 percent of the families require relief (ten times the national average), an expenditure now totaling nine million dollars. Unemployment is eight to ten times the national average. More than half the Indian families live in fewer than three rooms, and not one family in ten has indoor plumbing. Hospital care is given to twice the national average of persons, and mortality rates are three times the national average for adults and school-age children, twice that for teen-agers, and eight times the average for preschool children.

The gap between living conditions on the Indian reserves and those among the Euro-Canadians surrounding them has been widened since World War II, as a result of the changes marking the advent of an "affluent society" in the Canadian West. The postwar period has seen a shift from manual labor to mechanization on farms and in the construction industry, the two principal sources of temporary employment for Indian men. Coupled with the increase in the number of young Indian men, this mechanization has made it extremely difficult for the men to obtain jobs. Rural white youths are streaming into the urban centers because they can find no opportunities in the farm districts. Indian youths usually lack even the basic grade ten education demanded for semiskilled urban jobs. Before they can follow their white neighbors into the cities, the Indians must spend months in upgrading programs, recently instituted by Saskatchewan. The essentials of the curriculum through grade ten are taught to adults and older youths planning to continue vocational training. This need for preparation, in combination with the difficulties of adjusting to Euro-Canadian social norms and discrimination, discourages emigration from the reserves. Yet most Indians realize that the unskilled jobs they used to get no longer exist. Even their markets for cordwood and fresh fish, once a dependable though limited source of cash, have disappeared with the expansion of rural electrification, natural gas lines, and home freezers. Reserve conditions have worsened in direct proportion to the betterment of Euro-Canadian society.

Round Plains

A comparison of two Saskatchewan Dakota reserves, Round Plains and Standing Buffalo, will illustrate the reservation culture and point up some of the more pressing problems on these reserves today. These reserves, it should be remembered, are situated in a province that legally and culturally maintains the norms and values of the British working class, somewhat modified by American attitudes.

Round Plains, with a population of eighty-one, of which a dozen are Dakotas and the rest their Cree spouses and children, typifies the more conservative reserves of central Saskatchewan. It pictures conditions that were more general in the past. The region in which it is located was termed by Card (1960, p. 3) a "veritable moat of submarginal agricultural land which [in 1950] was still underdeveloped pioneer fringe." Prince Albert, the small city eight miles away, is called "the Gateway to the North," but it fronts on largely impenetrable bush inhabited by Indians who depend upon hunting, fishing, and trapping. Lumbering and mining are enterprises of limited potential, since Saskatchewan lacks valuable timber and high-grade ores, and the tourist industry has hardly been tapped.

Round Plains reserve is on the margin of the forest. Hunting, trapping, and fishing are too meager to support the population, and the Indians supplement these activities with day labor and by welfare. As Father André Renaud pointed out to the Ontario Conference of the Indian-Eskimo Association, November 22, 1964 (reported in Indian-Eskimo Association of Canada *Bulletin*), all these pursuits, including welfare, are forms of food gathering. They represent the continuation of the aboriginal way of life.

All the sources of subsistence available to the Round Plains people are in restricted supply. The jackpine forest that surrounds the reserve offers only a limited quantity of small game and berries, and there are no fishing lakes on the reserve. Welfare payments are kept to a bare minimum in order to encourage a search for employment. Round Plains residents will walk the eight miles to Prince Albert to look for jobs, but in the city they must compete with white and Metis laborers coming from all outlying districts. Their lack of fluency in English and a deserved reputation for unreliability (like so many Indians, the Round Plains people fail to comprehend the high value the Euro-Canadian places upon responsibility to a job) lead to a reluctance on the part of employers to hire Indians. As prostitutes, Indian girls find themselves in steady demand, but this trade cannot support them; unsophisticated girls from more isolated reserves sell their favors for a drink and a ride to town.

Indians who are willing to leave the reserve for a protracted period can find work in logging, commercial fishing, and bush work, particularly firefighting. This last occupation, a short-term group activity demanding bravery and endurance—rather like a Plains war party—appeals to the Indians. In the long run, however, none of these occupations are satisfactory, because all involve the sacrifice of the social pleasures and emotional rewards of the home community.

A few Round Plains residents have pursued an education with the hope of working at a skilled trade or clerical job. An education does not guarantee a job to an Indian, however, and those who do land one still face social discrimination. Girls especially are discouraged by their exclusion from the recreations of their co-workers, and are likely to accept in desperation the men who attempt to pick them up on the street. Thus even those Indians who qualify themselves for better jobs frequently return to their reserves, unemployed once more.

The leader of the Round Plains Dakotas exemplifies the difficulties encountered by the ambitious Indian. A full-blood Dakota, he is highly intelligent, meditative, and self-disciplined. He is comparatively well read, and speaks English with a sensitivity for nuances of meaning that makes him an ideal interpreter. He spent years working at the port of Churchill, Manitoba, and in other towns, but he has never been able to obtain more than an ordinary laborer's job. Consistently rebuffed by Euro-Canadians, he finally returned to Round Plains as to a sanctuary. White men who dare intrude onto his reserve find him openly hostile and profoundly distrustful. He has critically examined Euro-Canadian culture as he has met it, and he categorically rejects both its philosophy and its theology. Now he is consciously living a "native-modified" culture with his own people.

It is not quite sufficient to say that the discrimination he experienced induced this man to abandon his attempts at assimilation. Both Prince Albert and Churchill are still frontier towns, colonies composed of aggressive migrants come to wrest a living out of the virgin wilderness, and of marginal men who found little satisfaction in more stable communities. The nineteenth-century antithesis between the red son of the forest and the conquering white man still has some validity in these towns. To guard against the often alluring way of life presented by the indigenous people, the Euro-Canadians keep the boundaries of their colonies explicit and rigid. Discrimination is thus a mechanism to maintain an invading alien culture. The Round Plains man was repulsed not only by the overt discrimination, but also by the culture behind it. His own bias toward the values of his ancestors segregated him as much as did the color of his skin. Not rejection, but a decision to repudiate Euro-Canadian culture led him back to Round Plains.

The anomie of life on the margins of the frontier towns contrasts strongly with the microcosmic coherence of life within the reserve. The Round Plains Dakota community embodies a profound and meaningful integration of man and his world. It is a congregation, professing the Ghost Dance religion that was brought to them in the beginning of this century by Fred Robinson, an Assiniboin from Montana who married a Moose Woods woman. Robinson had been a disciple of Kicking Bear, the Assiniboin delegate to the meetings in which Jack Wilson (Wovoka) taught his revelations. The Ghost Dance that Robinson carried to Round Plains was devoid of the millenarian and militaristic tenets that precipitated the Wounded Knee Massacre. Instead, it stressed the necessity of leading a "clean, honest life," as they phrase it on Round Plains, which would be rewarded by reunion with deceased loved ones in an after life spent in a vast Dakota camp.

The Ghost Dance religion has a foundation derived from traditional Dakota beliefs: a mystical rapport with a universe pervaded by Power; deep respect for Power and its myriad manifestations; and a pharmacopoeia believed to be efficacious because prayers and offerings are made to the Power within the herbs. The interlocking traditional Dakota and Ghost Dance beliefs provide the Round Plains Dakotas with a complete philosophy congruent with their food-gathering way of life.

Whereas the Dakota culture successfully holds its members against the evangelizing of the distinctly alien Euro-Canadians, it cannot compete with the Cree culture carried by the majority of the southern Saskatchewan Indians. The Cree system of beliefs and practices is, like the Dakota, rooted in the aboriginal northern Plains tradition. It is coherent and vigorous. Its greatest strength lies in its adaptations to the stresses of Indian life in Saskatchewan today. Rituals not only emphasize the Cree identity of the communicants, in that respect paralleling the Ghost Dance rituals, but also serve a cathartic function, releasing the tensions besetting the Indians. A perceptive Cree shaman remarked of his religion, "It will never die. The Indians may go to the cities, but they still have their troubles." The Cree religion seems more viable than the Ghost Dance, because the latter is oriented to the past.

The small size of the Round Plains Dakota community (decimated by the 1918 influenza epidemic) and the kinship ties within it have forced it to be largely exogamous. Many Crees from the Prince Albert region have married into Round Plains. The children of the mixed unions tend to identify with the Cree culture that dominates the region.

They grow up speaking the Cree that is used in their homes, and turn to Cree rituals for religious expression and psychological help. The Ghost Dance religion has become "the Sioux religion" of the full-blood Dakotas. Only the latter attend the "prayer meetings" that constitute Ghost Dance worship on Round Plains today. Since the full-blood Dakotas are all middle-aged or elderly, the Ghost Dance religion seems destined to die out after this generation. An event that occurred in 1962 demonstrates the transition: A middle-aged half-Dakota, half-Cree Round Plains man dreamed that the Thunders ordered him to sponsor a sun dance for the health of his family. He fulfilled his vision by inviting leaders to conduct a Cree thirsting dance (the Cree version of the Plains sun dance). The Dakota Ghost Dancers watched the ceremony, but did not participate.

It appears that under the government pressure to acculturate to Euro-Canadian culture, the Round Plains Dakotas developed a solidarity with their fellow Indians, the Crees. Dakota and Cree are viewed as two variants of Indian culture, and little conflict is felt between them. The Round Plains Dakotas are being engulfed by the Crees; but looking upon the Crees as, literally, their brothers-in-law, the Dakotas do not seem very disturbed. Being Indian is more significant to them than being Dakota.

In this, as in more tangible aspects, the Round Plains Dakotas contrast with Standing Buffalo Reserve. Round Plains, hidden in its pine forest, looks like a page out of a turn-of-the-century ethnography. P. E. Goddard might have photographed its sturdy log cabins with the drying racks in front, festooned with meat; the weather-beaten buckboards around which dogs and ragged, sunburned children swarm; the women in long homemade dresses, shawls, and hair in two braids tied together at the ends. The scene seems generations removed from Standing Buffalo.

Standing Buffalo

The largest of the Saskatchewan Dakota reserves, Standing Buffalo, lies on the north bank of the Qu'Appelle valley, beside one of the string of Fishing Lakes that have been developed into provincial parks. A good gravel road links the community of government-built frame houses with the resort town of Fort Qu'Appelle in the valley, and with the rural village of Lipton on the wheatlands above. Euro-Canadian culture is literally spread out before the reserve in the vacationers' cottages fringing the lakes, and is reflected in the young matrons of

Standing Buffalo, encased in tight slacks and wearing fashionable hair styles.

In spite of its proximity to Euro-Canadian society, Standing Buffalo does retain a distinct air of Indianness. The geometric layout and landscaping that embody the European town ideal are absent from the reserve. The government-built houses had been placed in rows, but crisscross trails and haphazardly disposed outbuildings distract from the pattern. Instead of the aloofness that stems from the European concept of private property in land, Standing Buffalo exhibits communal behavior. Groups of women climb the hill with their water pails, groups of men stroll or chat here and there, more as in a band encampment with its flow of movement in and out of the tents than a town with each family closeted in its home.

With 416 persons, Standing Buffalo has a more formal social structure than does Round Plains. The latter has no official chief, but Standing Buffalo residents elect a chief and a band council. The man who was chief in 1964 claims that the band chief has become a public servant who with his council acts as the liaison between the agency and the band, transmitting the wishes of each to the other. The role of the modern chief is thus quite different from that of the traditional Dakota chief, who was a patriarchal figure. The traditional chief "was always preaching, advising. When the old people spoke, they expected everyone to say 'yes,'" explained Standing Buffalo's recent chief. Now, "everyone has his own opinions," he observed, and younger people do not hesitate to voice them in council meetings. Some band members still consider the chief a father, but most approve of the reduced authority of the modern elected chief. The government's former system of appointing chiefs for life is seen to have been an obstacle to progress, permitting elderly, ultraconservative men to decide matters for the entire community.

Standing Buffalo is divided into two groups, rather like moieties, the Up-the-hill and the Down-the-hill. Houses tend to cluster in two groups, roughly higher and lower on the terraced valley flank, but membership in the two groups is not strictly determined by geography. Membership is activated in elections and in social competitions, such as softball games. Until about 1960, the groups competed also during the Christmas season by riding in sleighs from house to house, singing powwow songs honoring the head of each house, and receiving in return a "lunch" from each. Men of the reserve are said to be usually loyal to one party in election after election, but the women's vote is considered to be influenced by the past performances and the campaign promises of the nominees for office. In the election concluded in February, 1965, out of 160 eligible voters, 72 voted for one party and 60 for the other, the remaining electors abstaining.

Interpersonal relationships in Standing Buffalo retain a family orientation, still couched in Dakota terminology. Cross-cousins are distinguished from parallel cousins, a man calling his brother's children ćiŋkśi (son) or ćuŋkśi (daughter), but his sister's children toŋśka (cross-nephew) or tuŋźaŋ (cross-niece). Marriage would not be sanctioned between parallel cousins, but would be between cross-cousins. In-law avoidance is still practiced, especially among the older people, and a relationship of respect is maintained between brothers and sisters. *Omawahetoŋ*, the relationship between the parents of a husband and the parents of his wife, is acknowledged, the four parents being united in a "oneness," as a Dakota on the reserve phrased it, a singleness of purpose.

Community dances used to be held in a reserve hall. Fewer are held now, and they are usually in the comparatively large home of one of the leading elders of the band. A schism between the generations is appearing in these dances, the older people preferring to perform the Indian social dances but the younger wishing to enjoy the twist and other popular Euro-Canadian dances. The schism disappears each summer when Standing Buffalo sponsors a powwow. The young people then dance the Indian dances and sing powwow songs in a Sioux language they hardly understand. Most of the Standing Buffalo residents participate in the powwow. It is less an intracommunity function than a device for joining the reserve to the network of intertribal visiting in the prairie provinces, North Dakota, and Montana. The "powwow circuit" permits friendships and the exchange of ideas among the northern Plains Indians, counteracting the centripetal tendencies of reservation culture. As more formal education gradually broadens the social universe of the Indians, the "powwow circuit" provides a satisfying in-group, larger than the reserve, yet still defiantly Indian—an alternative to assimilation. The young people who indulge in Euro-Canadian dances in the security of the reserve publicly reaffirm their Indian identity in the powwow.

Nearly all Standing Buffalo residents are nominally Roman Catholic, but only a small percentage believe exclusively in Catholicism. The Oblate Fathers (Oblates of Mary Immaculate, an order devoted to Indian mission work in Canada) established the first church and school on the reserve and have maintained the reserve school since. About twenty-five years ago, some residents wanted to build a nonsectarian school, but it was never accomplished. Recently a new threat to the Catholic monopoly has arisen as a result of several years of evangelical effort by a Protestant mission, the Full Gospel sect. About thirty Indians now form a Full Gospel congregation and have bought a building to use as a church. In early 1965 the band council faced a dilemma when the Full Gospel group asked for land on which to place their church. The council feared the Catholic authorities might refuse to bury Protestants in the church cemetery, the only one on the reserve, but did not want to allocate the band's meager acreage to a second cemetery. There were no other religious sects on Standing Buffalo in 1965. Bahai adherents have been active on neighboring reserves, but that religion has not come to the Dakotas. A few Standing Buffalo members have taken peyote at Montana meetings, but this rite has not attracted enough followers to form a church.

Dakota religious beliefs persist, though not too overtly. Probably most residents believe in *wakan*. Both shamans (*wapiye*, "fix-it man," as one resident translated the term) and herbalists (*wopiye yuha*, "possessor of a medicine bag") live on Standing Buffalo. The latter are often patronized, but the former now seldom employed. One resident felt that the relatively high fee expected by the *wapiye* discouraged patients, who would be inclined first to try the Indian Health Service hospital in Fort Qu'Appelle, where they would be treated without charge. While the Crees seem to dichotomize illness into diseases peculiar to Indians that can be treated only by shamans, and diseases common to all races that can be treated successfully by white doctors, the Dakotas seem to consider that only the extent of a doctor's power is the limitation on his ability to cure. Therefore, Euro-Canadian doctors can know much about curing, but faith healers, shamans, and herbalists may also be able to cure many diseases. The pragmatic, purse-conscious outlook of my informant is probably shared by many Standing Buffalo residents.

One *wopiye yuha* on Standing Buffalo has been performing some *wapiye* feats as well. This man, whose Saulteau wife is also a herbalist, is the son of a *wopiye yuha*. He had led a dissolute life, he says, until a beloved son died. Mourning for his boy in a lonely coulee, he saw a vision of Jesus and was instructed by that spirit to pray daily and promised the power to heal. The vision reformed his life. He abjured liquor and began to collect medicinal plants in the manner used by his father, praying to his guardian spirit (Jesus) to enhance the powers of his herbs. Now in his sixties, the man claims he has cured at least eleven persons through Jesus' aid, and has also been able to predict correctly the location of lost objects. He is paid for his efforts in cash, groceries, or both. This shaman calls himself a Christian, but will not join a church. He compares himself to the faith healer Oral Roberts, who, he notes, is part Indian. Because he follows the form of the Dakota rituals his pagan father used, because he bases his conviction of his power to cure and to divine upon a Dakota concept of *wakan* power, and because he considers participation in a sun dance a sacrifice that would enhance his power, this "faith healer" on Standing Buffalo seems to be a traditional-style Dakota shaman who has chosen Jesus as his spirit guardian. His choice of Jesus as a powerful *wakan* being reflects the present "American-modified" character of Standing Buffalo reserve.

In the economic sphere, Standing Buffalo is clearly reservation Indian. Before World War II, the residents obtained a little cash by selling wood and fish in neighboring towns and farms and by raising grain. Now only four families are supported by farming on the reserve. One of these men supplements his income by driving the school bus between the reserve and Lipton. As a fellow band member described these four farmers, "They're not putting any money away. They drive cars, but not good cars." The largest reserve farm has 237 acres of crop land, the next 200, the third 150, and the smallest 100 acres. The minimum acreage considered necessary for profitable grain farming in Saskatchewan today is 600 to 1,000 acres. None of the Standing Buffalo residents raise cattle. A few keep chickens for their own use. Fishing, trapping, and cutting wild hay have become negligible sources of income.

Although farming is not openly discouraged on the reserve, the mechanism by which the Indian farmer obtains capital restricts the initiation of new agricultural projects or the expansion of marginal enterprises. The Indian agency administers a revolving fund to lend Indians money for equipment, but insists that the borrowers put up one-third of the cost of equipment as a guarantee of good faith and ability. Few Indians are sufficiently prosperous to meet this requirement. The Indians realize that the small size of their reserves will not permit all residents to engage in farming. The lack of land and capital, present or potential, must aggravate the frustration and apathy of younger

Indians, yet more generous loan policies could only result in disastrous debts on the crowded reserves.

The Standing Buffalo band, like many others, receives most of its annual revenue from leasing land to white farmers. There is so little land available that only about three thousand dollars is obtained from this source. The money is used by the band council for projects benefiting the reserve as a whole, with a small sum allotted to help the reserve farmers. According to the chief in office in 1964, five hundred dollars was spent that year on wells, two hundred dollars for road graveling, three hundred dollars for snow plowing, six hundred dollars was given to the farmers (who used most of it for fuel), and the remainder went for similar needs.

Because Standing Buffalo is close to a rapidly expanding resort area, there is some outside employment available, especially in the summer. Three Standing Buffalo families work for most of the year on Euro-Canadian farms, but opportunities for this type of labor are few, since most Saskatchewan farms are family concerns relying on machinery for cultivation and harvest. The prewar demand for labor in planting, haying, and shocking grain has been severely attenuated, as has the use of manual labor in construction. Some compensation for this loss of income has occurred as the Fishing Lakes have attracted vacationers. Indians are used as handymen and gardeners, to bush and maintain the parks, and to work on the construction of summer cottages. Half a dozen find employment each summer at the tuberculosis sanatorium, Fort San, adjacent to the reserve. The Indians, however, are the last to be hired and the first fired on the seasonal projects.

Three Standing Buffalo women work all year as charwomen in Fort Qu'Appelle, cleaning stores on Monday, when retail businesses are closed, and homes the rest of the week. An additional six to twelve women find work cleaning summer cottages in season. The women, like the male laborers, receive the standard provincial wage for their type of work, but because the Indians seldom work long enough (or expect to work long enough) to qualify for unemployment benefits, they do not pay the unemployment compensation tax and lose this form of extra income.

For several years the Indian Affairs Branch has sponsored a program to bring Saskatchewan Indians to work in the sugar beet fields around Lethbridge, Alberta. The project is designed to wean the Indians from their reserves by accustoming them to seasonal work and to living under conditions conforming to the government's minimum standards of decency. One Standing Buffalo family was persuaded to go to Leth-bridge, but returned dissatisfied with their experience. They com-plained that they could work only in good weather, but were forced to pay board in the camp whether they worked or not, and therefore had been unable to save any money. This unfavorable report is said to have discouraged any other Standing Buffalo people from going to the beet fields. One resident added, "They are suspicious of anything the Indian Department offers—there must be something wrong with it."

Social welfare payments from the agency are the principal source of subsistence on Standing Buffalo. At one time the agency demanded proof of unavoidable hardship before it issued welfare relief. The now fashionable concern over the plight of Canadian Indians, which parallels the United States concern over its Negro minority, has modified the agency's policy, in the opinion of the former chief at Standing Buffalo. He believes that the agency now seeks to prevent hardship in order to avoid unfavorable publicity in the news media. Politicians have been using Indians' difficulties to attack opposing parties or to gain support for their own, and this also induces the agency to guard against actions that might raise allegations of neglect. The Indians on the reserve know this and use the threat of publicity as a weapon in demanding payments. If this weapon is ineffective, they then may beg for relief for their children.

An unhealthy proportion of the welfare payments are used to pur-chase liquor. The agency attempted to control this malpractice by issuing food vouchers instead of cash, but the Indians would sell the food, for half its value, and continue to buy liquor. The agency also tried to discourage drunkenness by requesting the Fort Qu'Appelle police to be strict with Indian offenders, but the Indians responded by going to Lipton to drink instead of to the agency town. As the former chief observed, "These people aren't dumb. They just spend money foolishly."

In a superficial analysis, drunkenness is the root of all evil on Standing Buffalo. Drunkenness causes quarrels, violence, and death from exposure in the winter. Drunkenness leads the young girls to sell themselves for a couple of dollars and a drink. Drunkenness leads to adultery and serious neglect of children, the latter becoming a major problem on the reserve.

Actually, drunkenness is only the immediate cause of the Indians' troubles. It may be suggested that one factor in the Indians' drinking is their identification of the reserve as the source of their security. The

Indian is first and foremost a member of his band. Only on his band's reserve is he fully accepted. Outside he encounters discrimination. The reserve is his world, but the reserve cannot support most of its population. If he wants to remain at home, to remain in his own world, the Indian must resign himself to accepting relief. Perceiving this, the Indians have no incentive to struggle to be self-supporting. They give themselves up to the pastimes of the idle poor, of which drinking is the effective way to dull the ache of boredom and futility.

The Indian is usually not an alcoholic in the clinical sense. Drinking is primarily a social activity on the reserve, as it was among Indians in the days before the treaties. Alcoholics Anonymous tends to become a cult movement among Indians, not a gathering of anonymous alcoholics (cf. Steinbring 1964, pp. 11–12). Though it has become a truism, it is worth repeating that drunkenness cannot be alleviated on the reserves unless the underlying socio-economic problems are ameliorated. Since most reserves offer little possibility of economic development, the most feasible course would seem to be training to assist the Indians to internalize their dependency in order to be able to work off the reserves. Integrated elementary education for reserve children may be able to effect this psychological change, teaching self-reliance and confidence in adjusting to alien patterns. Whether the limited exposure to Euro-Canadian personality norms in integrated schools will be sufficient to alter the deeply rooted Indian attitudes must still be demonstrated.

The problems enumerated above for Standing Buffalo reserve are shared by most other Saskatchewan reserves. A unique difficulty on Standing Buffalo is the apparent need to resist Cree domination. Round Plains Dakotas do not seem disturbed by Cree engulfment, perhaps because there are too few Dakotas to form a viable community, but Standing Buffalo residents are proudly Dakota and mean to remain so. Many of the present middle-aged Standing Buffalo men are married to Cree women, there apparently having been a low ratio of Dakota girls to men in that generation, but the children of these unions grew up speaking the lingua franca, English, and not Cree. In other instances in which Standing Buffalo people have seen a choice between Cree and an alternative, they again took the alternative: for example, the community chose to arrange annual powwows when interest in the sun dance declined, instead of joining in the thirsting dances on neighboring Cree reserves. One result of Standing Buffalo's opposition to the Crees is a lessened hostility to English. The Euro-

Canadians are not the only enemy, and perhaps not the most threatening. Young people on Standing Buffalo have been permitted to grow up speaking nothing but English, and their elders are now concerned that the Sioux language may die out.

Pan-Indianism is perceived by some Standing Buffalo leaders as an avenue to a broader Indian identification without risk of Cree dominance. At a meeting of the Federation of Saskatchewan Indians, a Standing Buffalo delegate protested the presentation of an address in Cree without translation. The acceptance of this objection by the other members of the meeting seems to have encouraged Standing Buffalo to participate more in Federation activities. In February, 1965, a young Standing Buffalo man was elected secretary of the Federation, the first Dakota to hold such an office. The same young man has been active in the National Indian Council of Canada. Pan-Indianism may thus counteract the younger Dakotas' tendency to accept Euro-Canadian cultural traits when they find traditional Dakota ways anachronistic.

Hopefully, pan-Indianism may also help reduce the Indians' dependence upon their reserves. Pan-Indianism fosters the image of the Indian as a member of an ethnic subgroup in North American society. When his world is no longer bounded by the confines of his tiny reserve, the Saskatchewan Dakota may be able to break the vicious cycle of futility and drunkenness. Camaraderie with Indians from other tribes living in the cities may give him the emotional support needed to pursue education, training, and a job off the reserve. Pan-Indianism can confuse tribal traditions, as when a Moose Woods family carves a totem pole for Saskatoon's Pion-Era fair (*Regina Leader-Post*, July 6, 1964), but it can also instill in the Indian a new confidence in his potentiality.

At the present writing, Standing Buffalo, like the smaller Saskatchewan Dakota reserves, is still very much an encapsulated society living a reservation culture. Although the Saskatchewan Dakota bands seem more closely knit than their much larger United States reservation groups, the people are as poor, frustrated, and basically insecure as their American cousins. A trend toward greater self-determination, both of bands and of individuals, has been rather belatedly felt in Canada. Popular outcry against Indian living conditions, the government's recently announced community development program, and pan-Indianism are all new influences on the Saskatchewan Dakotas. They promise radical improvement in the Indians' self-image and way of life. They will be effective, however, only if they relax the boundaries of the reserves and free the Indians from emotional bondage. This will not be easy, for while the Indians are beginning to understand which side their bread is buttered on, a century of withdrawal has palsied the hands reaching for the bread.

The history of the Dakotas in Saskatchewan has not been dissimilar from the development of the United States Dakotas, though the tempo has been slower. How many of these convergences are due to a common heritage, how many to international communication, and how many to ecological and political similarities in the two Anglo-American countries cannot be determined. Yet whatever the dynamics of Canadian Dakota history, these refugee bands should not be overlooked in any study of the Dakotas. Their communities preserve many of their ancestral traditions, and their present societies are examples of several varieties of Plains reservation culture.

REFERENCES

BLACK, NORMAN FERGUS. 1913. *History of Saskatchewan and the North West Territories*. Vol. 2. Regina: Saskatchewan Historical Co.
CARD, B. Y. 1960. *The Canadian prairie provinces from 1870 to 1950*. Toronto: J. M. Dent & Sons, Ltd.
Indian-Eskimo Association of Canada *Bulletin*. 1965. Vol. 6, no. 1.
Regina (Saskatchewan) *Leader-Post*. January 19, 1963.
———. July 6, 1964.
STEINBRING, J. 1964. Recent studies among the Northern Ojibwa. *Manitoba Archaeological Newsletter* 1, no. 4: 9–12.
VOGET, FRED. 1951. Acculturation at Caughnawaga: A note on the native-modified group. *American Anthropologist* 53: 220–31.
WESCOTT, A. E. 1943. Curricula for Indian schools. In *The North American Indian today*, ed. C. T. Loram and T. F. McIlwraith. Toronto: University of Toronto Press.
WESTGATE, T. B. R. 1943. The history, policy and problems of Protestant missions to the Indians in Canada. In *The North American Indian today*, ed. C. T. Loram and T. F. McIlwraith. Toronto: University of Toronto Press.
WISSLER, CLARK. 1916. General discussion of shamanistic and dancing societies. In *Anthropological papers*, vol. 11, part 12. New York: American Museum of Natural History.

Part II

Individuals in the Social System

The Lower-Class "Culture of Excitement" among the Contemporary Sioux[1]

Robert A. White, S.J.

SINCE THE MIDDLE of the nineteenth century the Sioux Indians have faced two major periods of social and cultural adjustment. From approximately 1865 to 1900 they experienced the painful transition of retreating to the reservations, giving up prestigious roles and the basic economy which had supported these roles, and learning a new life in the reservation situation. However, by 1900, in the isolation of their reservations, the Sioux had begun, quite remarkably, to reintegrate a "reservation culture" which was neither traditional Sioux nor

[1] The materials for this paper are based on research carried out on the Pine Ridge Reservation and in the Sioux Indian ethnic community in Rapid City, South Dakota, from 1957 to 1965. Besides a study of a selected community on the Pine Ridge Reservation in 1958, the research included interviews with 150 families in Rapid City in 1957 and 1958 and intensive case histories of up to twenty-five hours of recorded interviews with 20 selected Sioux families in Rapid City in 1962, 1963, and 1965. A general census of the Sioux ethnic community was made in 1963 and numerous smaller studies and surveys such as a survey of employers of Indians were carried out. Especially relevant for the present paper were life-history interviews with approximately 50 young Sioux boys and girls between the ages of thirteen and twenty-five and concentrated interviewing, participant observation, and observation through key informants among the Sioux lower-class subgroup in Rapid City. The research was supported initially under National Institute of Mental Health Grant MH 08227-01. Data analysis has been carried on under NIMH Grant MH 11353-01.

American, but largely the expression of traditional Sioux values in terms of American-derived institutions in the reservation situation. But the isolation of the reservations was not to be maintained, and from 1940 on, the Sioux began to have more direct contact with off-reservation American communities. As a result of these recent experiences the Sioux reservation culture has undergone a fairly radical transformation, and a new set of cultural orientations have come to be characteristic of the Sioux both on and off the reservations.

More precisely, a series of fairly distinct subcultures are emerging within the Sioux ethnic group. The acculturation process on the reservation has already produced a variety of cultural divisions among the Sioux. Now as they move off the reservation they find in the American communities horizontal, social-class divisions as well as vertical, religious and ethnic divisions which provide many different paths of assimilation into the American socio-cultural structure. Studies of the off-reservation adjustment of the Sioux indicate that they are taking on the cultural orientations of all levels of the American lower- and middle-class range (Hurt 1961–62, pp. 230–31; Kemnitzer, this volume). But those Sioux who come from a rural, traditional background on the reservation face great disadvantages in attempting to enter any but the lowest social-class levels off the reservation. Consequently, Sioux families of a rural, traditional orientation are tending to adopt American lower-class cultural norms. And since these more traditional families are in continual migration back and forth between the reservation and off-reservation communities, lower-class cultural norms play an increasingly important role in reservation life also. As the isolation of the reservation erodes, the unique reservation culture is giving way to a Sioux Indian version of the American lower-class culture.

The presence of the lower-class subculture in the Sioux ethnic group in Rapid City, South Dakota, was evident from my surveys in 1957. However, the process of how the lower-class culture developed among the Sioux began to be apparent only after detailed case histories of selected families had been made. By examining the remembered circumstances of the families on the reservation, their experiences in moving off the reservation, and the gradual acceptance of lower-class norms, it was possible to analyze the factors which influence the development of a lower-class subculture among the Sioux. In the present paper I will attempt to (1) trace the historical development of the lower-class culture among the Sioux, (2) analyze the factors which influence the development and persistence of this kind of subculture, and (3) describe the norms and central ethos of the lower-class subculture among the Sioux in Rapid City. In addition, I will attempt to elaborate further the theory of lower-class culture on the basis of the valuable insights offered by the case of the Sioux Indians.

Recent study of the way of life of low-income groups has elicited a variety of approaches to lower-class culture and has called into question the meaning of the term "lower-class culture" (Ferman, Korbluh, and Haber 1965).

Walter Miller (1958) has described lower-class culture as a series of six focal concerns: (1) trouble (law-abiding or -violating behavior), (2) toughness, (3) smartness (ability to outsmart, dupe, con), (4) excitement, (5) fate (trust in luck), and (6) autonomy (freedom from external constraint or superordinate authority). These focal concerns arise as a typical definition of a situation by members of the lower-class community. Miller prefers to use the term "focal concern" rather than "value" because the former denotes the quasi-quantitative amount of attention and importance of these activities in the lives of lower-class individuals. The concept of focal concern emphasizes that though a given attitude or activity (trouble, toughness, etc.) constantly engages the attention and emotions of individuals in the lower-class group, it may be given a positive or negative valence according to the circumstances. Value implies the notion of an official ideal, whereas the actual behavior may imply many different intracultural dimensions.

Miller has stressed that the specific concerns of the American lower class are by no means entirely absent from the American middle class, but that because of different ranking and weighting of concerns a quite different pattern of life emerges. The distinctiveness of lower-class culture does not imply, however, that its norms are simply the inverse of middle-class norms or that lower-class culture arises solely as a reaction to the middle-class norms. Lower-class culture has its own tradition centuries old and its own social integrity.

However, the point is also made that while the various social-class levels may have some distinctive value orientations there is a set of overarching American values which are common to all social classes. Hyman Rodman (1963, pp. 205–15) explains this apparent paradox by suggesting a "value stretch" across the lines of social class. Thus the lower class may have a commitment to the same general values as the middle class, but it is a much weaker commitment and frequently is adapted to the lower-class circumstances. In Rodman's view it is questionable whether lower-class groups have a cultural orientation entirely distinct from that of the middle class.

Oscar Lewis (1966, pp. 19–25) prefers to speak of the cultural traits of low-income groups as the culture of poverty. Lewis proposes that the culture of poverty develops in the context of a highly competitive cash economy with high rates of unemployment and underemployment along with low wages for unskilled labor; little organization and sense of social power on the part of the low-income group; a family system based on the nuclear progenitive family in a bilateral kinship system; and a dominant class that prizes thrift, the accumulation of wealth and property, upward mobility, and explains low economic status as the result of individual personal inadequacy and inferiority. The culture of poverty is viewed as both an adaptation to this situation and a reaction to the position of the poor as a marginal population in a class-stratified, highly individuated, capitalistic society.

Lewis sees four basic dimensions in the culture of poverty: (1) the disengagement and nonintegration of the poor with respect to the major institutions of the society; (2) the subcommunity which carries the central traits beyond the nuclear and extended family and hence powerless before its own collective problems; (3) a matrifocal family which offers little protection and security for the individual child; (4) in the individual an attitude of fatalism, helplessness, dependence, and inferiority.

The approach taken in the present paper owes much to Walter Miller and has many similarities to that of Oscar Lewis. We are assuming: (1) that a culture is a group-level phenomenon, not simply aggregative, and that a subcommunity, in so far as it forms a social system, will tend to have its particular subculture; (2) that the traits of the lower-class culture are not only areas of concern, but are normative for the individuals moving within the system and carry the sanctions of social control; (3) that a culture tends to be ordered in terms of central values and of derivative, supporting norms as the logic of the values works its way out in concrete situations. It is the basic methodological thesis of this paper that the lower-class groups define their situation in such a way that a powerful central ethos arises which gives meaning and structure to a whole series of normative traits and cultural institutions. Once the researcher has grasped what the central ethos is and how it has arisen, the lower-class way of life becomes understandable not just as a state of disorganization, but as a quite logical, positive reaction to a situation.

The lower-class culture as observed among the Sioux in Rapid City, South Dakota, has been termed the *culture of excitement* because the central ethos which gives meaning to the life of the members is the periodic experience of great emotional elation by getting involved in very exciting situations. The process by which the culture of excitement develops is quite complex. Certain Sioux families are predisposed to such an ethos by their reservation background. In part it is a reaction to the marginal position of Sioux urban immigrants in a competitive, progress-oriented society, and, in part, it is an ethos learned from other lower-class groups. But nearly all the norms of the Sioux lower-class culture are observed to be related in some way to a central ethos, these highly desired periodic bursts of excitement.

The Reservation Culture from 1900 to 1940

The kinds of adjustment that the Sioux are making in their direct contacts with American society are influenced to a great extent by the basic pattern of life and especially by the social structure that was established very early in the reservation period.

When the Sioux first came onto the reservations they gradually settled more or less in extended family groups along the creeks where water and firewood were available. In time there were located in each neighborhood a small rural school, a meeting house, a church, a government "boss farmer," and perhaps a small "trading post" store. In the years from approximately 1900 to 1940 these extended family neighborhoods tended to be maintained as relatively isolated, self-contained units (Macgregor 1946, pp. 35–40).

By 1910 a system of subsistence farming had developed, with small patches of corn, potatoes, a variety of vegetables, and perhaps some barnyard livestock being raised. On the (then) open ranges the "squaw men" and their mixed-blood descendants ran large commercial herds, and though few of the full-blood Sioux families operated commercial cattle enterprise, most had cattle in the herds which they slaughtered when they needed meat (Hulsizer 1940, p. 48). By 1912 most Sioux families were able to live well enough by subsistence farming and occasional wage work so that government rations were no longer really necessary.

Most Sioux families rarely traveled off the reservation and trips out of the neighborhood area were not frequent. For the more traditional

Sioux, life centered on a yearly round of extended family gatherings, native Sioux celebrations, and religious activities. The extended family met often for subsistence farming activities—rounding up cattle, slaughtering and drying meat, cutting firewood—and for ceremonial dances at the neighborhood meeting house. A series of reservation celebrations developed on the reservation—New Year's Eve, Washington's Birthday, Flag Day, Memorial Day, Fourth of July. Each was the occasion of colorful native Sioux dancing, ceremonial give-aways, oratory, and other festivities depending on the nature of the holiday (Mekeel 1936, pp. 11–13).

Religious activities were important in the rhythm of life, but a distinct "reservation Christianity" developed among the Sioux. The neighborhood gathered at the church each Sunday for a full day which included religious services, a common potluck dinner, a game of shinny in which all took part, from little children to grandmothers, and a simple supper before returning home. Christmas and other important religious holidays were celebrated in common at the neighborhood church. Each year large religious convocations were held by both Catholic and Episcopal churches with thousands of representatives from neighborhood churches on all Sioux reservations for a period of a week.

In this period all knew well the traditional kin relationships and the duties that went with them so that family life was relatively stable. The ties of extended family held the neighborhood together; excessive drinking and disorder were not serious problems (Mekeel 1932, p. 92). The wisdom of grandparents was listened to and life was guided by this wisdom. Social control was strong in the isolated neighborhoods.

It was during this period that the typical reservation social structure was forged. The socio-cultural groups that Voget described among the Crow Indians: native, native-modified, American-modified, and American-elite, were also observed among the Pine Ridge Sioux, with the addition of a distinct transition group between the native-modified and the American-modified (Voget 1952, pp. 88–93).[2]

The native-oriented group includes those elderly Sioux who grew up in the early years of the reservation when the old rhythm of life was still fairly integral. They listened to old men who had been warriors and hunters, and their imagination is still focused on that distant past.

[2] Vernon Malan, studying Sioux communities on the Pine Ridge Reservation in 1956 and 1957, characterized the types of Sioux acculturation as traditional, transitional, and transpositional. He describes the different types along lines similar to those used here. Cf. Malan (1958).

The native-modified, known on the reservation as the "full-bloods," were so socialized in terms of the fundamental Sioux values that their personality structure is thoroughly Sioux. But they have grown up within the institutions of the American-modeled school system, from league sports to school bands; they have been involved in the activities of the Christian churches; they have lived within the Bureau governmental structure; and they have had at least casual experience of wage earning within the American economic system. These Sioux learned subsistence farming, but never developed it into a farming enterprise; in fact, they had never really grasped the meaning of a money-market economy. Their life has centered around the activities of the extended family group, periodic celebrations, meetings, and interest in community and reservation politics. In spite of their poverty the reservation is their homeland where they can maintain their race and the traditions of the Sioux reservation culture.

The American-modified Sioux, by their relatively successful ranching and employment, have begun a commitment to the fundamental ethos of American culture, "getting ahead." On the reservation they are commonly called the "mixed-bloods." Though their basic orientation is American, not Sioux, they have participated in all the typical Sioux reservation institutions and are an integral part of the reservation social structure. The reservation is their homeland and they identify themselves as Sioux Indians, but they have a feeling of affinity for the larger white, American world outside the reservation.

Between the native-modified and the American-modified groups are those Sioux who are attempting to disengage themselves from the expectations of their native-modified friends and relatives and are attempting to adjust to the American socio-economic system with the underlying value commitments that this entails.

A final group is the American-elite, a group with relatively slight Indian ancestry who live on the reservation, but have practically no allegiance to the reservation as their homeland and move outside its social system.

The reservation cultural and social structure which developed after 1900 is still evident today, but the rhythm of life of the isolated extended family neighborhood—subsistence farming, church gatherings, and reservation celebrations—has changed so profoundly that one can say that it has almost disappeared. In the 1930s the rapid extension of government hospitals, consolidated schools, reservation maintenance facilities, and CCC programs developed the reservation towns, and the growing use of cars and summer migrant labor jobs began to take the Sioux off the reservations into nearby communities. Then during World War II the young men joined the armed forces en masse and the opening of defense installations in western Nebraska and South Dakota led to a veritable exodus from the reservations.

After the war many stayed in the off-reservation communities and those who returned to the reservations found it very difficult to adjust once more to the simple life of subsistence farming in the isolated neighborhoods after the fast, open life of the defense plant communities with relatively high wages. Gradually in the years following the war the young Sioux who felt that they could make a living off the reservation drifted back to the towns and cities where there were job opportunities—and a faster life.

Types of Adjustment in Rapid City, South Dakota

By 1955 approximately four thousand Sioux Indians had moved to Rapid City, where the expanding SAC defense installation and tourism provided many new jobs. As the number of Indian families increased, so did the consciousness of being a separate Indian ethnic group. The Sioux preferred to have their own churches; their centers for recreation, medical attention, and family services; their political action groups; and a number of their own clubs and organizations.

Though the Sioux form a distinct ethnic subcommunity in Rapid City, they come from a variety of socio-cultural orientations on the reservation, from native to American-elite, and they are entering the Rapid City community on many social-class levels. When the first surveys in this research were made in 1957, Sioux Indian families were living in nearly all parts of the city: in the squalid Indian "camps" which formed as rural, traditional Sioux pitched tents and threw up shacks near the lumber mills; in the older lower- and lower-middle-class sections of the city; and in the pleasant new subdivisions of middle-class homes.

A thorough acquaintance with the life of many Sioux families in Rapid City indicated a quite close association between the exterior style of life—the ecological area of the city, the kind of house, and the furnishings of the house—and the socio-cultural orientation of the families. On the basis of this association an eighteen-point scale was drawn up recording differences in socio-cultural adjustment between the Sioux families living in the camps and the Sioux families living in the better middle-class subdivisions. Guided by this scale as well as an analysis of friendship preferences and social participation, three general types of adjustment were observed among the Sioux in Rapid City: the *Camp, Transition*, and *Middle-Class* Indian.[3] The Transition families are those which are in the *process* of moving into the various levels of American society, and consequently there are at least two distinct types of Transition Sioux: those moving toward the working and middle class, and those moving toward the American lower class, or what some would call the lower-lower, "outcast" group (Warner, Meeker, and Eells 1949, pp. 15–17).

The style of life of the Camp Indian is little changed from that of the rural, native-oriented Sioux on the reservation. Many of these families tend to move back and forth between the reservation and Rapid City, and they retain a lively interest in tribal and reservation affairs. From the beginning the white homeowners not infrequently complained of the littered yards, packs of dogs, the invasion of relatives from the reservation, and other reservation folkways. The city reacted strongly to the "terrible squalor" of the Indian camps within the city limits and has been condemning the shacks and eliminating the camps within the city. Gradually the Camp Indian families have been forced outside the city limits to a special "Sioux Addition" where they can live as they wish close to extended family members or at least close to familiar friends from their own reservation—in peace.

The Middle-Class Indian families report a life history indicating that they were clearly within the American-modified group back on the reservation. Through their experience as employees of the Bureau of Indian Affairs or in a small commercial or ranching enterprise (or through such experience in their family of orientation), these Sioux have already come to accept and comprehend the meaning of the urban economic and social system. In Rapid City they remain within the Sioux ethnic community, but they are accommodating their American-modified orientation by building onto it the *symbols* of middle-class life. They are insisting on buying a new, modern home and are ambitious about their children's education. The women join clubs for

[3] In 1963 approximately one-third of the Sioux Indian families were in the Camp or Lower-Class Transition group, one-third in the Middle-Class Transition group, and one-third in the Middle-Class Indian group. This is based on a special census of the Sioux ethnic group.

In the following discussion the kinds of adjustment of the Sioux in Rapid City are presented as ideal types. Considerable quantitative data describing various dimensions of each socio-cultural type are being prepared for a much more detailed publication at a future date.

TABLE I

PROCESSES OF SOCIO-CULTURAL ADJUSTMENT OF THE SIOUX IN RAPID CITY

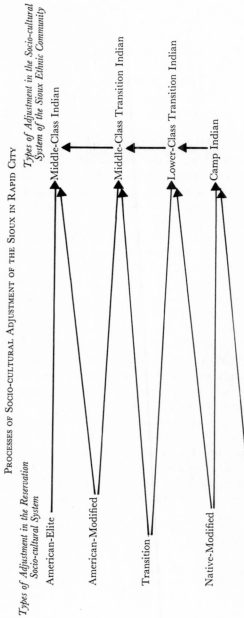

Types of Adjustment in the Reservation Socio-cultural System

American-Elite

American-Modified

Transition

Native-Modified

Native

Types of Adjustment in the Socio-cultural System of the Sioux Ethnic Community

Middle-Class Indian

Middle-Class Transition Indian

Lower-Class Transition Indian

Camp Indian

self-improvement; they become very conscious of tasteful home decoration and are anxious about careful housekeeping. The men, for their part, are proud of their skills, and though most are of the blue-collar group, it has become a definite status symbol to make a step ahead by opening their own small business.

Many of the Middle-Class Transition Indian families are young couples of an American-modified background just getting established in the city, but are successfully seeking the middle-class symbols. However, some of the families which could be considered Middle-Class Transition are those who tried to make the middle class, but have come from a native-modified or transition group on the reservation and have found that the mobilization of their lives so as to adjust from a rural, reservation background to American middle class is beyond them. They emphatically do not want to live in the camps, but must be content to accommodate themselves to the urban situation in a social and cultural position between Rapid City's lower and middle classes.

The Lower-Class Transition Sioux

We have already seen that when the culturally conservative, rural Sioux move off the reservation they find the adjustment to an urban socio-cultural system very difficult, and the tendency has been to live their life apart in the camps at the edge of the city. But even though they may live much of their life isolated from the mainstream of community life, they are one part of the urban social system and are being swept into the rhythm of that system. This is especially true of the younger generation of Camp Indians which is growing up in Rapid City and knows little of the life of the isolated reservation neighborhood.

Most of the Camp Indians lived the very simple life of the rural native-modified cultural group on the reservation with little formal education and little knowledge of the outside world, but this did not necessarily put them into a lower social class. The reservation was their homeland and either formally or informally they were the leaders there—indeed, more so than the more acculturated mixed-bloods in many instances. They carried themselves with pride as lords of the land.

However, when these Sioux move off the reservation and come into direct contact with the American competitive social-class system, they are immediately at a disadvantage. They are a racially and a culturally distinct group classified by whites as inferior. Theirs has been a totally different cultural tradition with a much stronger personal orientation, a culture attuned to harmony with nature rather than interpersonal competition in the domination of nature. The slow pace of a subsistence farming or occasional wage labor existence has not provided them with the driving aspirations of the rest of the community. They accept the simplest and worst housing of the city. By tradition their external manner is reserved, and quite frequently they speak a broken or less refined English. They dress rudely, are less demanding in their habits of cleanliness, and are not attuned to many middle-class niceties. In short, they continue their rural reservation life without really comprehending how much this puts them at a disadvantage. Most likely, most of them simply do not understand what the motivations and expectations of the dominant society are.

When these families come in contact with the competitive social-class system, they can only be perceived as and classed as "the failures." They feel hopelessly out of place within middle-class social circles. It is easiest to move among those groups where the middle-class social niceties and the appearance of being prosperous and respectful are not so important. They move in areas where other "failures" move, that is to say, on the lower-class levels. Thus, wherever the rural Sioux families come into direct contact with the American social-class system, they tend to move into the lower-class socio-cultural group. This is both a spontaneous reaction to their conditions of life and a learning process through communication with the lower-class milieu of the communities they enter.

The Lower-Class "Culture of Excitement"

What is lower-class culture as observed among the Sioux in Rapid City? If we look at the Camp and Lower-Class Transition Sioux in the context of the whole community, we see them as a people outside the mainstream of a competitive, progress-oriented society. These are people who have little or no sense of building the community around them. Nor are they conscious of achieving a personal career or family aspirations. Their life is mainly one of day-to-day survival. The odds against substantially improving their lot in life are so overwhelming that their aspirations are realistically very low or very weak. Their ethos has traditionally been present-oriented, and most do not feel the urge to "get ahead." They are not conscious of "losing their reputation" by living in a shack or meeting their friends in a cheap bar. The social controls of the larger community do not reach them. Most feel rejected by the dominant society and are suspicious of the official institutions of the community, politicians, welfare workers, police, etc. They create their own community with their own norms.

The life of these people is above all one of perpetual insecurity. One is never sure what calamity the morrow might bring, and without financial resources or prestige within the community to command respect and protection these Sioux are at the mercy of events. Life for these people cannot be an orderly series of little events leading to a more or less predetermined goal. It is a life of violent changes and violent emotional experiences. And in a life of constant violent emotional experience, no experience is felt unless it is strong. The subtle shades are not noticed, only the brightest contrasts. Gradually emotional reactions become strong in whatever direction they may be.

In this atmosphere of goalless, almost monotonous, day-to-day survival relieved only by explosive bursts of emotional excitement, the only experiences that have real meaning are the bursts of excitement. These periods of emotional elation may not be altogether pleasant since they involve physical violence, personal calamities, brushes with the police, etc., but they are something which distract from the sense of failure and provide something to talk about and perhaps much to laugh about. Gradually the high points of one's life are the bursts of excitement. A strong need for these emotional outbursts develops in the personality structure of individuals—perhaps as a discharge of tension built up by fear, monotony, and frustration. When a group of individuals tend to define these periodic experiences of excitement as the most significant and desirable aspects of their life (more or less unconsciously), the emotional elation accompanying this excitement becomes a central goal of life. In time the group develops a set of norms centered around this ethos of excitement (Miller 1958, p. 11).[4] From the beginning the rural, traditional Sioux immigrant was marginal to the mainstream of community life. But as these Sioux enter into the culture of excitement, they are alienated even further from the dominant

---

[4] Walter Miller has also pointed out that *excitement* is the concern around which most lower-class activities are centered. "Many of the most characteristic features of lower-class life are related to the search for excitement or 'thrill.' Involved here are the highly prevalent use of alcohol by both sexes and the widespread use of gambling of all kinds—playing the numbers, betting on horse races, dice, cards. The quest for excitement finds what is perhaps its most vivid expression in the highly patterned practice of the recurrent 'night on the town.' This practice, designated by various terms in different areas ('honky tonkin',' 'goin' out on the town,' 'bar hoppin''), involves a patterned set of activities in which alcohol, music, and sexual adventuring are major components" (Miller, 1958, p. 11).

society where norms are centered around an ethos of personal career and community progress.

The case histories of the Lower-Class Transition families reveals that a kind of culture of excitement was developing among the men on the reservation in the late 1930s, especially among the men working with the reservation CCC projects. These men worked in groups, usually away from their neighborhood and its social controls. They had a regular cash income, perhaps for the first time, and after working together all day they might decide to spend the evening in the little off-reservation towns. Though the sale of liquor to Indians was prohibited, bootleg was always available and heavy drinking almost always was a part of the evening (Hurt and Brown 1965, pp. 222–30).[5]

At the beginning of World War II many left their families on the reservation and went to work at off-reservation defense projects. These Sioux had more money in their pockets than ever before, but as described above they found it easiest to move in circles where a rough, fast life was the norm. Heavy drinking and carousing during after-work hours became the pattern of their life, and for the Indian man who had had little job experience before, saving money and job stability were less important.

In Rapid City the young Indian boys had already begun to move into a rough gang in the late thirties, and it soon became an all-Indian gang. When the big influx of families began during and especially after World War II the culture of excitement was already well established among many of the Camp Indians. When the bars were allowed to sell liquor to Indians in 1953, a line of cheap bars on Rapid City's Main Street became the center of the lower-class subgroup among the Sioux.

As in the case of any subculture, the culture of excitement varies in its emphasis. Many Camp families preserve some of the stability of the old reservation neighborhood, and although they like to visit the bars occasionally, they will not have much to do with those involved in the culture of excitement. Others may exhibit only certain characteristics of this culture. In Rapid City the norms of the culture of excitement are

[5] In a recent publication Wesley Hurt and Richard M. Brown show that contemporary Sioux drinking patterns have been in the process of formation since the Sioux first began to use alcohol in the tribal period. Excess drinking was not untypical of Sioux men from the beginning of the reservation period, and missionary conferences, for example, speak of it as a perennial problem. However, a reconstruction of patterns of life on the reservation from 1900 to the 1930s indicates that excessive drinking was not nearly so characteristic of the Sioux as has been true since the Sioux have had greater contact with off-reservation American communities. (Cf. Hurt and Brown 1965, pp. 222–30.)

exhibited most fully by the young men of a Camp Indian background between the ages of fourteen and thirty, and more and more by the young women of this age group.

The Sioux who move within this subgroup have a tight code of loyalty to each other. They have their own lingo, styles of dress, favorite hangouts, and set tastes in music, dancing, etc. These norms are strikingly like those of lower-class Negroes, Mexicans, and other lower-class groups in larger cities across the country. Denver has had a particularly strong influence on Rapid City. When someone returns to Main Street in Rapid City after several months in Denver, he brings all the latest news of what the guys really in the know are doing in Denver, and one can expect the new fads to sweep through the Main Street group. But more in particular, what are the folkways of the culture of excitement among the Sioux?

For the Sioux Indian one of the most important is chronic drinking to excess. This is the easiest way to quick elation and excitement, a way to relax and forget the fears and insecurities of one's life. It is also a means for the Sioux, who by tradition is dignified and reserved, to be loud, raucous, and cocky in his repartee. In his elation he forgets any sense of inferiority and gains a feeling of power and assurance—ready to accept any dare.

A second important norm is readiness for physical violence. Among men and women whose physical strength is their most important economic asset, prestige is measured by reputation of physical prowess. Differences of opinion, a personal slight—all are settled immediately and physically. Both men and women are equally ready to fight physically. And a good fight is, of course, a source of diversion and excitement in itself.

Violation of the law or vandalism is another source of excitement. Such incidents usually begin with drinking and a dare from companions, and are looked for out of a desire for excitement rather than any real economic need.

Constant travel, frequently to distant cities, is important, especially for young men past twenty. The ability to con some hapless cowboy or construction worker out of money for drinks in the bars is also a highly prized ability. The subgroup has its sexual code operative for both men and women; success in sexual exploits according to the group norms is not only a mark of prestige, but an important source of excitement.

The Sioux lower-class subgroup with its focal point on the line of bars on Rapid City's Main Street tends to be a world apart even from the rest of the Indian community. In the bars one can meet friends and

find out "what's going on around town." The group has a strong sense
of who belongs and who doesn't belong on Main Street and its own
informal prestige and leadership structure based mainly on "who can
take on just about anybody on Main Street."

The culture of excitement in Rapid City is shared by men and
women of all age groups, and the norms generated by the lower-class
situation—heavy drinking, physical violence, conflict with the law, etc.
—are accepted to some extent by all who move within the subgroup.
But the nuclei of the Main Street subculture and the basic carriers of
the values of the culture of excitement are the small, tightly knit group
of young men between the ages of seventeen and twenty-five. This peer
group plays a striking role in the life of the young Sioux men of the
lower-class group.

The young Sioux feels the need for "my gang of fellows" when he
reaches the age of thirteen or fourteen, and it is at this age that these
groups begin to exert a dominant social control in their lives. In the
majority of cases the boys come from family situations where the parents
are of rural, reservation background with relatively little compre-
hension of the urban situation or where the father or mother or both
have become involved in the culture of excitement and are neglecting
their roles as parents in the home. Especially typical of the latter is the
derelict or absent father and the mother working to support the family.
With this family background the boys tend at this age to find greater
security and ability to cope with the environment around them if the
focus of their life is in the strong loyalty of peer groups. In Rapid City
the Sioux boys tend to stick to their Indian friends, and generally the
groups are composed of brothers and/or cousins or at least boys with a
kin tie in some sense—their fathers came from the same reservation
neighborhood, their fathers or mothers were close friends, and so forth.

The peer group rises to meet the pervasive concern with physical
violence which is one of the fundamental presuppositions of the lower-
class environment. Whether going to school or just hanging around up
town it is best to go in groups or at least, it is important to know where
loyal friends can be found. Loyalty to one's friends becomes a central
consideration of the young Sioux and in a crisis one's time, money,
fearless defense or whatever is asked is at their disposal.

A second aspect of lower-class culture which reaches into their lives
is the harsh emotional tone, the boredom and frustration of their life
and the need for high-pitched, exciting diversionary experiences. When
the group meets for the evening, there is always an uneasy tension as

plans are laid—a silent challenge of each other to suggest the most daring and exciting plan. Usually this begins with drinking "to get in the mood." Then later on someone will challenge the group, "Let's go get so and so," or "Let's break the street lights in so and so's part of town," or "I bet you wouldn't break into so and so's fixit shop, get a bicycle tire, bring it out, show it to the group, and put it back again." So an evening of some drinking, possible vandalism, theft, and physical violence begins—"just for the excitement of it."

For most of the boys, especially when they reach sixteen or seventeen, the evening of excitement may include sex play. But the principal loyalties are to the group, and when the time comes that one is really serious about a girl a choice of loyalties is placed before the young man and there begins a period of conflict in his life.

When the young Sioux reach the age of eighteen or nineteen the group continues to be very important, but its activities gradually change. There is more heavy drinking, more fighting and physical violence, more possibility of serious crime, and much wider traveling. At a time when young men of a more middle-class background are thinking of a life career and marriage, the life of these young Sioux becomes an ever more violent series of bursts of excitement. Especially notable is the travel of this age group—to Denver, Los Angeles, Chicago, living with Indian friends or relatives, occasionally working to pick up extra cash, but eventually drifting back to Rapid City and the gang on Main Street.

Around the age of twenty-five or thirty the crisis of marriage and establishing a family along the lines of a middle-class model presents itself most forcefully (Miller 1958, p. 14).[6] The young man must decide to accept the husband-father role, which involves loyalties toward the

[6] The one-sex peer group as a basic social unit appears to be a general characteristic of lower-class social structure. Walter Miller observes the conflict between the one-sex peer group and the conjugal unit. "The nature of the social groupings in the lower-class community may be clarified if we make the assumption that it is the *one-sex peer unit* rather than the two-parent family unit which represents the most significant relational unit for both sexes in lower-class communities. Lower-class society may be pictured as comprising a set of age-graded one-sex groups which constitute the major psychic focus and reference group for those over twelve or thirteen. Men and women of mating age leave these groups periodically to form temporary marital alliances, but these lack stability, and after varying periods of 'trying out' the two-sex family arrangement, gravitate back to the more 'comfortable' one-sex grouping, whose members exert strong pressure on the individual *not* to disrupt the group by adopting a two-sex household pattern of life" (Miller 1958, p. 14).

nuclear family, or to continue with his principal loyalties to the peer group and the life of excitement. If a man's loyalties continue to be with the Main Street group, he frequently succumbs to chronic drinking or alcoholism, is in and out of jail, and holds a job only sporadically. He may continue to live with his wife and family—usually supported by the wife's work or by her family—or he may eventually cut all family ties and simply drift in the culture of excitement which exists in the other "Main Streets" of the towns in the off-reservation areas. These men are usually lone individuals who seem to have few social ties of any kind.

Also drawn into the group are wives of the men who move in the culture of excitement and are unable to assume the husband-father role in the family. With their marriage wrecked, they are frequently supported by the state welfare's Aid to Dependent Children and are not employed. The long struggle with a drunken husband and the marriage breakup has made it difficult for them to move as single women among the husbands and wives of more middle-class-oriented groups. An evening on Main Street with acquaintances, a few drinks, laughter, and music all help to ease the sorrow and break the monotony of their lives. Corresponding to the boys' peer groups are the groups of young Sioux girls looking for the boys and excitement on Main Street. The Main Street area is also a mecca for the young men stationed at the nearby air base, the cowboys in from the western South Dakota ranges, and traveling construction workers. Many young Sioux women find it very easy to pick up a "friend" who will support them as long as he is in the Rapid City area.

At the bottom of the group (in status as well as the meaning of life) are the women who have become prostitutes and the complete derelicts known on Main Street as the "winos."

The Lower-Class Matriarchal Family Structure

Even in the reservation society the family tended in many instances to be mother-centered because of the lack of a solid male economic role to define the husband-father role within the family (Macgregor 1946, p. 57). But as the Sioux men become involved in the culture of excitement, the conflict of the husband-father role with loyalties to the drinking groups brings about a definite Sioux matriarchal family type.

Most of the young men of the Lower-Class Indian group begin to marry in their early twenties, but these marriages are often quite unstable. Few of these men have any definite plans for establishing a family, much less a life career. They are still living in the rhythm of their friend groups, moving from one exciting evening or week end to the next. Their drinking and carousing carries over into the home, and the young wife may find herself cooking and caring for the gang while they sober up. They almost never hold steady, skilled jobs, preferring short-term work with little responsibility in order not to interfere with plans for a trip or drinking spree. The wife and children remain secondary to the peer group. Family income is unsteady and the young wife has to depend on relatives, claim ADC, or go to work.

In some cases the wife can bring pressure on the husband by the threat of leaving him. There may also be the pressures of in-laws, law officers, clergymen, school officials, welfare workers, and often his own "reformed" friends. Some of the young men who were the center of the Main Street group at the beginning of the study in 1957 had, through these various pressures, begun to reject their Main Street group and were accepting a middle-class ethos. They were typical young Middle-Class-Transiton Indian families.

In many cases, however, the marriage breaks up and the young mother seeks a more stable husband. In other cases the husband, in spite of his drinking bouts and brushes with the law, manages to support the family more or less. But unless a man can separate himself from the Main Street group, his drinking tends to grow heavier over the years and frequently develops into a problem of chronic drinking or alcoholism.

In the matriarchal family the instability of the family situation as well as the harsh emotional struggle with an unpredictable husband have made the home an unpleasant place. The children seek their emotional security in adolescent peer groups outside the home, and the cycle of loyalty to peer groups and involvement in the culture of excitement begins anew. Within the strictly matriarchal Sioux family the relationship of the mother to the boys is observed to be unusually salient, while in the boys there is frequently a dislike, even contempt, for the absent father or the present but worthless father.

The Culture of Excitement and the Problems of the Sioux Today

The value of describing the lower-class culture in terms of a central ethos, the culture of excitement, lies in its greater power in explaining the pattern of activities of certain lower-income groups. Indeed, because this approach ties together in such a meaningful way so many disparate

observations of lower-class behavior, it may well be a correct step
toward building a theory of lower-class culture.

As Oscar Lewis and others have pointed out, the cultural patterns of
certain low-income groups and ethnic or regional groups are not
simply a matter of deprivation or disorganization, but a design for
living adapted to their situation (Lewis 1966). Likewise, much of the
behavior of the Sioux today, which appears so contrary to establishing
a viable, self-maintaining community life, is not necessarily attributable
to a state of cultural normlessness or personality disorganization. It is
an attempt to build a meaningful ethos by subscribing to the norms
derived from the value of excitement. It is contended that not infrequently behavior which is attributed to the remnants of traditional
Sioux values or to the conflict of Sioux and modern American values is
better explained by the acceptance of lower-class American culture.
The economic instability of many young Sioux men is due not so much
to the internalization of traditional Sioux values regarding time, a
money-market economy, and personalism in social relations, but rather
is explained by adherence to the norms of lower-class peer groups
dominated by interest in periodic drinking bouts accompanied by
violence and violation of law, the readiness to travel, and the norm of
living by one's "wits" (conning people, theft, etc.) rather than by
steady labor.

The sudden collapse of achievement and aspirations when the young
Sioux reach adolescence is influenced by the chaotic conditions and
perpetual insecurity of the family in the culture of excitement and
especially by the opposition of the norms of the peer groups to the
middle-class-oriented achievement norms proposed in the schools. The
world around these young people is perceived as so hostile and unpredictable that they soon become convinced that they cannot achieve
success in it except by luck.

A number of Pentecostal movements have proved very attractive to
the Sioux in the lower-class group in recent years. Many of the most
fervent adherents of these movements have moved (or still are) in
Rapid City's Main Street group. For these Sioux the nativistically
oriented Pentecostalism with its highly emotional music and singing,
dramatic testimonies of conversion, healings, gifts of tongues, and other
expressive rituals is more attractive than the older, more emotionally
conservative churches. It may be interpreted as a religious form of the
culture of excitement.

The question remains, however, of policy choices in view of the
present situation of the Sioux. The policies which were valid before

1940 when the Sioux were indeed a poor people are no longer valid now when they are not only poor but characterized by a culture of poverty. In considering policy we must try to pinpoint the causes which bring about a lower-class culture.

Stated in its briefest form the fundamental etiology of the culture of excitement lies in the rejection of the Sioux by the dominant white community because they do not meet certain minimum standards in a highly competitive, upwardly mobile system. They play no meaningful role in maintaining or developing the larger community or any organization in the community off the reservation and only to a limited extent on the reservation. Consequently the goals of the community have little significance for them. Because of their poverty and marginal position, these individuals have little or no power in their social transactions with the larger white American community and have far less control over the events of their life. These events seem to succeed one another in chaotic and unpredictable fashion, and there appears to be no protection from the terrible emotional jars that are experienced from day to day. Most important, these emotional experiences are not subordinated to or integrated into a pattern of realistic life goals, and become, themselves, the significant events of life.

Many of those involved in the lower-class culture of excitement are no doubt the "failures" of our society, those who either have not the capacity or the inclination to enter the competitive race of upward mobility. However, the present study has shown that the lower-class culture of excitement developed among the Sioux as they came into more direct contact with the social-class structure of American communities. Having an identity as an Indian or being from a reservation is not in itself a key factor, because many reservation Sioux are making a successful transition to an American middle-class orientation. The Sioux who adopt lower-class norms are those who (1) maintain their rural simplicity in language, dress, manners, and lack of education; (2) have a present-oriented view of reality; (3) were accustomed to an economy of subsistence farming or dependence on government rations; (4) have a quite negative concept of themselves and their capabilities of success in American communities; (5) have little or no sense of directing their own social system because of government paternalism; (6) have a deep fear of and hostility toward white American society. Individuals from this kind of socio-cultural background will find themselves in a marginal and powerless position when they enter into the modern industrial social-class system with its orientations of competition and progress. I advance the proposition that in any situation where these conditions exist—immigration to cities from poverty-stricken areas, in the rapidly developing countries, in colonial societies or societies where backward minorities are being brought under an exploiting centralized government—the culture of excitement will develop.

Among the Sioux the culture of excitement is most accentuated in the off-reservation Indian subcommunities. But more and more many Sioux are traveling back and forth to Rapid City; Cheyenne, Wyoming; Scottsbluff, Nebraska; Denver; and other cities—and always moving on the lower-class level—so that the heavy drinking, violence, and other aspects of the culture of excitement are typical of the reservation as well. The Sioux are rapidly losing their distinct reservation culture and are becoming part of the American proletariat, the lower-lower category of the American social-class structure. Instead of being a culturally and socially distinct group with a simple rhythm of life, they are classed with the "failures" of American society.

The lower-class culture of excitement has grown out of the economic, social, and cultural deprivation of the Sioux reservations. If one approaches the problems of Sioux adjustment with the strategy of simply moving the Sioux off the reservation without attempting to change the reservation situation itself, then we will be training recruits for the off-reservation welfare rolls indefinitely. As I have noted above, the Sioux families who were able to have experience with employment and some of the cultural advantages that steady employment on the reservation brings have generally made a successful adjustment off the reservation. There is strong hope that with the current emphasis on the development of the reservation environment itself—employment opportunities, better housing, more imaginative recreational facilities, a new orientation in education, and especially the development of local leadership and local government so that the reservation communities need not be so dependent on the paternalistic care of the Bureau of Indian Affairs—a new generation of Sioux will come forth much more capable of successfully entering the American social-class system at a desirable level.

REFERENCES

FERMAN, LOUIS A., KORBLUH, JOYCE L., AND HABER, ALAN, EDS. 1965. *Poverty in America*. Ann Arbor: University of Michigan Press.

HULSIZER, ALLAN. 1940. Region and culture in the curriculum of the Navajo and the Dakota. Federalsburg, Md.: J. W. Stowell Co.

HURT, WESLEY R. 1961–62. The urbanization of the Yankton Indians. *Human Organization* 4, no. 4: 226–31.

HURT, WESLEY, AND BROWN, RICHARD M. 1965. Social drinking patterns of the Yankton Sioux. *Human Organization* 24, no. 3: 222–30.

LEWIS, OSCAR. 1966. The culture of poverty. *Scientific American* 215, no. 4: 19–25.

MACGREGOR, GORDON, WITH HASSRICK, ROYAL, AND HENRY, WILLIAM E. 1946. *Warriors without weapons.* Chicago: University of Chicago Press.

MALAN, VERNON D. 1958. *The Dakota Indian Family.* South Dakota Experiment Station bulletin no. 470. South Dakota State College, Brookings, S. Dak.

MEKEEL, H. SCUDDER. 1932. A modern American Indian community in the light of its past: A study of culture change. Ph.D. dissertation, Yale University.

———. 1936. *The economy of a modern Teton Dakota community.* Yale University Publication in Anthropology no. 6.

MILLER, WALTER. 1958. Lower class culture as a generating milieu of gang delinquency. *Journal of Social Issues* 14.

RODMAN, HYMAN. 1963. The lower-class value stretch. *Social Forces* 42, no. 2: 205–15.

VOGET, FRED. 1952. Crow sociocultural groups. In *Acculturation in the Americas: Proceedings and selected papers of the XXIX International Congress of Americanists,* ed. Sol Tax, pp. 88–93. Chicago: University of Chicago Press.

WARNER, W. LLOYD, MEEKER, MARCIA, AND EELLS, KENNETH, EDS. 1949. *Social class in America.* New Haven: Yale University Press.

Cultural Identities among the Oglala Sioux[1]

Robert E. Daniels

I. INTRODUCTION

The Reservation

PINE RIDGE RESERVATION in southwestern South Dakota is the home of the Oglala Sioux. The reservation is equal in area to approximately three rural counties.[2] The landscape is typical of the high plains:

[1] This paper is based, in part, upon observations made during a ten-week visit to Pine Ridge Reservation during the summer of 1961 and upon field work for a like period in 1963 made possible by a grant from the Department of Anthropology, University of Chicago. In addition to the members of this department, I am indebted to Drs. Murray Wax and Ernest Schusky, who corresponded with me prior to and during the field work; to Stephen Feraca, who shared both his intimate knowledge of the Sioux and his hospitality during my visit of 1961; and to Robert V. Dumont, Jr., for similar aid during the summer of 1963. An earlier version of this paper was submitted to the Department of Anthropology, University of Chicago, in partial fulfillment of the requirements for the degree of Master of Arts.

[2] The reservation is currently considered by the state to be two unorganized counties, Shannon and Washabaugh, although it was originally subdivided as three. An appreciable amount of land within these areas is now owned by non-Indians. A fourth county, Bennett, formerly a part of the reservation, was opened to homesteading and is now a typical wheat-growing area. Some land in Bennett County remains in Indian ownership and is under the jurisdiction of the tribal government and agency offices. The Bureau of Indian Affairs reported that Pine Ridge Agency had jurisdiction over 1,628,831 acres, or approximately 2,544 square miles in 1960 (Hagen and Schaw 1960, pp. 2–13 n).

rolling grassland marked by creeks lined with dense stands of deciduous trees and bushes, and by ridges with scattered pines. The northern section of the reservation consists of tableland and vast areas of erosion. Most of the land is suitable only for modest ranching, with farming generally difficult, if not impossible, especially in the areas of Indian ownership.

The majority of the Indian population lives scattered throughout the countryside. Most live in log houses or frame shacks. Some live in tents, a few in old car bodies. Few of the "country Indians" live in houses of substantial construction. The vast majority of the rural homes are some distance from paved roads and are without electricity or running water. Kerosene lamps supply light. Many homes use bottled gas stoves for cooking. Virtually all are heated by wood stoves. Most of the rural families haul water from pumps inspected by the Public Health Service, but many rely on creek water.

Pine Ridge town,[3] near the southwestern corner of the reservation, is the site of the vast agency complex of governmental offices, the federal boarding school and high school, and the Public Health Service hospital. The town is likewise the seat of the tribal council and the Shannon County public school system, and the center of much of the missionary activity on the reservation. The town is sharply divided into two sections. To the west of Highway 18 on tree-lined streets stand the government buildings, the schools, the hospital, and the government-built housing for federal employees. To the east stand the churches, cafes, stores, and filling stations. Beyond this "main street" are the makeshift homes of hundreds of "town Indians," and two suburban-style housing projects built between 1961 and 1963 by the tribal government in cooperation with the Federal Housing Authority. They are rented to members of the tribe, screened by the Housing Authority Committee. Approximately half of them were occupied in 1963. The pattern of Pine Ridge town is repeated, in microcosm, in the several small federal installations throughout the reservation.

The Problem

It is commonly agreed that the reservation is the home of "Indians." It is also widely agreed that the majority of the people on the reservation are "Indians." Everyone agrees that either (1) these people live

[3] Both the reservation and the main town, which is the site of the agency, are named Pine Ridge. To avoid confusion, the phrase "Pine Ridge town" is used here. Throughout this paper "*on* Pine Ridge" refers to the reservation and "*in* Pine Ridge" refers to the town.

differently from their non-Indian neighbors because they are Indians, or (2) these people are Indians because they live differently from their non-Indian neighbors. Even the casual visitor to the reservation soon finds that beyond such general statements there is a great diversity of opinions as to just who the Indians are, and why they are considered Indians:

> Today there are probably more people claiming Indian identity than ever before, and on Pine Ridge Reservation, such terms as *Indian, Whiteman, Mixedbloods*, or *Fullbloods* are heard on every hand. At the same time, the question of who is an Indian, or more precisely, who is what kind of an Indian becomes increasingly vague and elusive. . . . We would like to suggest that this seeming confusion and disagreement about definitions of identity is, in itself, an extremely significant datum. [Wax et al. 1964, p. 29]

The Focus

All studies of recent conditions on Sioux reservations have stressed the breakdown of native social groups[4]—the large amount of behavior which is in agreement with neither the traditional nor the introduced normative systems and the resulting uncertainty and instability of both social roles and individual personalities. Yet it is widely asserted that the Sioux have been able to maintain social groups that are somehow distinctly "Indian" and exhibit cultural and psychological patterns that are somehow distinctly "Indian."

Ideally this situation should be studied on two mutually interdependent levels. On the one hand, it is necessary to study patterns of social interaction among all the inhabitants of the reservation in order to determine the frequencies and types of interaction which reveal social boundaries. On the other hand, it is necessary to study the cultural patterns of the people, the sharing of normative patterns, the presumptions about the human condition these patterns make, the conceptualizations about social roles and social groups, etc. While the mutual adjustments of these two levels, and the discrepancies between them, are of interest in a "stable" society, they are crucial to an understanding of the modern Sioux, who have experienced major changes, often of a disorganizing nature, in both these aspects of life. A discussion, for example, of the "marginal man," who is to be found among

---

[4] A social group is here defined as a number of people who share certain norms of behavior (and agreements concerning the application of these norms, i.e., membership) and whose interactions with each other, guided by these norms, are distinguishable in quality from their interactions with nonmembers of the group.

all the *categories* of people on the reservation, would be incomplete if not based on both social patterns of interaction and cognitive patterns of identity. Further, it is argued that because so much of the behavior of the reservation's inhabitants is significant to them precisely because of its symbolic value in their cognitive systems, a discussion of cultural identities is necessary for an understanding of the events of reservation life.

Unfortunately, the vast amount of systematic data necessary for a thorough study of social interaction is lacking, and much of what is available is marred by the failure to separate these two approaches in discussing Sioux social groups and analyzing the behavior of their members. The social *categories* represented in the cognitive frameworks of the Sioux are too often taken to be identical with the social *groups* sharing norms of behavior.[5]

Therefore this paper will discuss the various typologies of identity employed on the reservation, their logic of classification, and the data

[5] A good example of the difficulties that can follow this method of analysis is "The Aftermath of Defeat" (Useem 1947), a study of "the relationship of degree of Indian blood to acculturation" (p. 8). Based on the premise that "the biological and physiological manifestations of man which have repercussions on the social organization have to be held constant in order to make valid sociological generalizations" (p. 49), this study stratified the reservation universe into five blood groupings: full-blood Indians, and those with three-quarters, one-half, one-quarter, and less than one-quarter Indian blood (rounding off fractions in eighths and sixteenths). Individuals were categorized according to the degree of Indian blood they *claimed* for themselves (p. 10). The author writes: "The importance of blood groups for social organization is the main theme of this thesis" (p. 54). Qualification of terms then follows (all italics added):

> Degree of Indian blood [as used here is] *a bio-social construct.* [p. 9]
> It is to be understood that when terms such as "Indian blood" or "white blood" are used, the author does not imply that the actual blood is any different. The terminology is a highly useful way of describing the *racial* types of a person's *progenitors.* [p. 9]
> Almost without exception, residents of Indian reservations know, *or think they know,* what degree of Indian blood they are. The main reason for this is in determining *legal* status. [p. 10]
> Indians are *legally* and not biologically a *race.* [p. 70]
> In addition to its bio-social basis and legal use, degree of Indian blood also has a *social* connotation. . . . Degree of Indian blood is a popular way of summing up the relative influence of Indian *culture* and white *culture.* Full blood and mixed blood and white are adjectives which indicate *ways of life.* They designate *roles* which members who are *deemed* to have certain biological inheritance are expected to play. [p. 12]

each considers significant in making classifications—the symbols which manifest these identities. It is thus a discussion of conceptual models which structure, and are themselves structured by, the behavior of the reservation's population. The data consist of those items of behavior and circumstance which are defined by the conceptual models as signaling membership in one or another of the typological categories. Following a discussion of the symbols of cultural identity, the analysis will be applied to a discussion of the behavioral complex here called "Sioux Nationalism."

II. OGLALAS IN THE WHITE WORLD

Isolation

As has been pointed out explicitly in one study (Wax et al. 1964) and implied in all other recent studies of Pine Ridge Reservation, the Oglalas live in considerable isolation from their non-Indian neighbors. Geographically the reservation is removed from the densely settled areas of South Dakota and Nebraska. Rapid City is approximately one hundred miles from the agency. Larger cities are hundreds of miles farther away. On the reservation, the vast majority of the population live "out in the communities." The agency town of Pine Ridge is in the southwest corner of the reservation, over one hundred miles from the most distant Indian communities. Moreover, although the rural Indian population is too dense to be supported by the economic resources of the land, it is definitely "thin and scattered" for the purposes of central administration. The current rural residence pattern poses severe problems for such basic governmental organizations as the police and the schools. In addition, it is often noted that the major differences in life style among the Indian population are between the "country Indians" and the "town Indians." It is usually added by white observers that the more rural a community of Indians is, the more traditional it is in its cultural patterns. As expressed by the Bureau employees, the rural Indians are somehow perversely "backward" about coming to the benefits of civilization, or are "deprived" of them because of the fact of their remoteness and could be "helped" more effectively if they were closer at hand. As explained by Wilcox (1942, p. 32) for Devils Lake

---

Residents, both Indian and white, use in conjunction with these physical traits [skin color, patterns of hair growth], *social traits* for the *identification* of persons— dress, manner of speech, body movements, and *attitudes*. [p. 13]

The present paper is an attempt to unsnarl these difficulties of analysis.

Reservation, North Dakota, this pattern reflects the fact that the rural population (as opposed to the majority of "town Indians") is living on land that they own and from which they receive lease payments. Hence they are less dependent upon employment for a cash income, and can live where there is less need to conform to the standards of the agency.[6] While it is true that most rural families need less cash than families living in Pine Ridge town (Wax et al. 1964, p. 20), the rural pattern is by no means homogeneous. At one community I visited, the people get almost all their food from the distribution of surplus commodities, from gardens and by gathering wild fruits, and from illegal deer hunting, while in other rural areas some households are deeply involved in a cash economy for such necessities. Because of the size of the reservation, most rural families can as easily shop in the surrounding white farm towns as at the stores around the agency (i.e., in Pine Ridge and White Clay, Nebraska). Wax suggests that many rural families prefer to shop in farm towns, even if farther away, in order to avoid the embarrassing contacts with the mixed-bloods and the "White people who look down on you" to be found at the agency (Wax et al. 1964, p. 35 n). Even if a rural family finds that it needs a greater cash income, the strict demands of living in the agency town can be avoided by seasonal agricultural work in South Dakota and Nebraska, or by sporadic work in an off-reservation town (Mekeel 1936).

A discussion of "remoteness" on the reservation is always a discussion of the distances between whites and Indians, as seen from the *white* point of view. While Pine Ridge is "off the beaten track" for a tourist driving to see the sun dance, it is centrally located for an Indian participant coming from another Plains reservation. While few Indians on the reservation live directly adjacent to paved roads, almost all of them can be reached by cars in all but the worst weather. Indians, with cars that are much less reliable than those of the Bureau, pay much *less* attention to the distances between communities. Similarly many of the "country roads" leading from the highways into "remote" Indian communities bear a surprisingly heavy traffic in Indian cars. The distances traveled on the reservation by Indians while visiting and attending summer dances demonstrate that the "lack of accessibility"

[6] This pattern, and the various attitudes associated with it, have probably been in existence since the first efforts of the last century to get the Sioux to "give up their wild ways and come in to the fort and settle down." Once on the reservation, those who rejected white cultural patterns were (and occasionally still are) said to have "returned to the blanket."

of a community is basically a matter of social contacts and personal
motivation and not transportation.[7] Indeed, it is often necessary to
know the names of Indian communities on other reservations in the
state and in adjoining states in order to follow a discussion of summer
travels. Social distance is maintained even when geographic distances
are small, whether in the town of Pine Ridge or in one of the agency
"outposts" out in the districts. During the summer of 1961 I spent
several weeks in the "town" of Allen. While I was living at the federal
day school, my social contacts were limited to the families of the school
principal (white), the school maintenance man (white), the storekeeper (white), and secondarily to the one teacher in residence (Negro),
the tribal policemen, the two bus drivers, and the school cook (all
"mixed-blood," i.e. marginal, Indians). This was considered to be the
whole town. Although I spent the days with children of the rural
Indian families, I never saw any of their parents around the federal
buildings, and met them, only nominally, when accompanying the
school personnel on bus routes. The situation was drastically altered as
soon as I traveled in the company of a local, non-school-affiliated
"full-blood." The situation is repeated in each of the other government
locations, although it may not strike the visitor as quickly in Pine
Ridge because of the size of the non-"full-blood" population there. In
Pine Ridge there are many Oglalas who will gladly engage in conversation on the street or in the stores, but most of these people are merely
acting out a superficial contact role which is lacking in the repertoire
of the average rural Indian. A few of these townspeople can be "white
men's Indians" with much relish and consummate skill.

The Basic Cognitive System of the Whites

The primary method of categorization exhibited by the white population of the reservation is based on the concept of blood descent. This
scheme of symbolizing behavioral reality has changed during the
reservation era less than the analogous Oglala conceptual schemes discussed below. One could speculate that American Indians, even in the
case of the Teton Sioux, have not provided a challenge great enough to
force a change of this concept, still evident in the thinking of the
majority of American society. Even among the personnel of the local
Bureau of Indian Affairs agency, for whom the Oglalas are ostensibly
the *raison d'être*, the whites are in a position of dominance which does
not demand a general readjustment of their concepts to those of their

[7] Visiting is, of course, restricted by the limits of social ties. The major mechanical
consideration for those having cars is the amount of gasoline available.

wards and customers. The contact situation has been defined for over a century as placing the burden of acculturation on the Sioux. If the whites on the reservation are to change their framework of blood descent, it will probably be in response to changes in American society generally, rather than in response to the conceptualizations of the Oglalas. The frequent usage made in the spoken English of the Oglalas of such terms as "white man," "full-blood," and "mixed-blood" reinforces the whites in the belief that they are describing Oglala social groups in a realistic manner. The isolation that exists between the white BIA employees and the Oglalas amounts to a situation in which the whole of the Oglala framework, and hence the basic differences between the two modes of conceptualization, are not apparent from the point of view of the whites. Because most members of the white enclave in Pine Ridge are both representatives of the greater American society (and the teachers of Oglala children) and the administrators of federal power, the disruptive influence of their concepts of group membership with respect to the social structure and personality structure of the other elements of the reservation population is disproportionately strong.

Blood descent is a rather straightforward concept which presumes physical ancestry to be the critical dimension of socio-cultural differences. Unlike much of American thinking on Negroes, which sees variations in the degree of Negro blood to be of secondary importance, the use of blood descent with respect to the Oglalas is primarily interested in the variations in degree of Indian blood. Being concerned not only with "race" but "degree of race," they consider the distinction between the categories of full-blood and mixed-blood to be crucial.

Intermarriage between Teton Sioux and whites (the "squaw men") was a historical fact long before the establishment of federally controlled reservations. Certainly some individuals of mixed ancestry had developed styles of life in the prereservation era which synthesized elements of the cultures of the Oglalas and of the frontier. The Sioux recognized the existence of such differences among individuals (see below, p. 221; for a discussion of the question of mixed-blood social groups, see p. 212). For the federal government, which defeated the Teton Sioux and placed them on reservations, social structure was not a concept, and the structure of Teton society was neither recognized nor acknowledged in the struggle to civilize and individualize the Indians. Naturally those individuals who had some familiarity with both cultures and (in many cases) a stake in both societies were of importance to the government. Out of this situation came the pattern of governing according to blood descent. Today the government keeps census records which try to record the degree of Indian blood (expressed in fractions) of each individual Oglala. Qualification for special legal status depends on a variety of definitions, most frequently on being "of one quarter or more Indian blood." To give an example of the financial advantages of being legally Indian, during the biannual bidding for the contracts to rent Indian-owned land (controlled by the agency), the bids of tribal members are increased (on paper) by an established percentage prior to being considered in competition with the bids of non-Indians. Tribal membership also means access to a whole series of federally operated services, from free education to free medical care. Moreover, for many it offers a potential share in the reactivated Oglala dream of the Black Hills claim against the federal government (Wax et al. 1964, p. 31). The settlement they are hoping for, equal to the value of the Black Hills in 1876 (including the value of all gold and minerals which have been mined there) is astronomical. Such are the real and imagined aspects of reservation life which hinge on the legal definition of one's degree of Indian blood.

Even if the correlation of one's biological and cultural heritage were one to one and immutable in one's lifetime (which it obviously is not), there are several factors of reservation life which would defeat the empirical utility of blood descent as a guide for dealing with the Oglalas on their terms. The relatively high incidence of paternity which is indeterminable (at least to the government census keepers) and the frequency of cases of people who have a series of mates, both with and without legal marriage (the latter known locally in English as "illiciting") obscure the recording of biological ancestry. Blood descent also fails to record differences in the genetic inheritance of full siblings. Several other factors, among them the practice of placing children in the care of people other than the parents and the pattern of adoptions among the Oglalas (which are seldom noted on legal documents) confuse attempts to judge an individual's cultural inheritance in terms of the identity of his parents. Nor does the system allow for the fact that full siblings are born into differing social positions, although in the history of some families these differences have included which language, Lakota or English, the child learns first, whether his childhood friends include non-Indians, and similar factors which affect the cultural identity and orientation of the adult.

For most whites in the area, the use of the terms of blood descent does not imply a purely racial explanation for the underlying behavioral differences. The general criteria used in applying the terms "white," "mixed-blood," and "full-blood" are based in part on an ethnocentric evaluation of the behavior of individuals. Before discussing this, however, it must be mentioned that there are some individuals in the surrounding farming communities and among the agency personnel (the few I met were all involved in maintenance of natural resources and agency property rather than in positions relating to Indians) who adhere to purely racial arguments to explain the—to them—strange and unpleasant behavior of the Sioux.

Stereotypes and Symbols of Identity

To the non-Indian personnel of the Pine Ridge agency, the social world of the reservation is explicable in terms of a series of stereotypes. Whites, quite obviously, are "whites," and no further definition is considered necessary, although in fact there are significant differences in the patterns of Bureau personnel, storekeepers, missionaries, and local ranchers and farmers. Socially, agency personnel have virtually no permanent contacts with those local whites who are not officially involved with Indians, and in most cases no contact with the missionaries. Nevertheless, all whites are spoken of as being uniformly industrious, clean, thrifty, sober, law-abiding, etc. Needless to say, it is often quite easy (even for the socially distant Indian) to observe deviations from these ideals. During the summer months the "work" of many of the school personnel could be characterized as marking time rather than as accomplishing something. It is also generally held by whites that the prohibition of alcohol on the reservation (a decision of the tribal council) does not really apply to non-Indians (because, unlike Indians, whites can "hold their liquor"). Alcoholic beverages can be found in the homes of many of the schoolteachers (where "real Indians" are almost never invited); the Pine Ridge town dump, serving federal personnel, contains an extraordinary number of beer cans (where anyone can observe them). Similarly, behavior differing from the other ideals are often notorious subjects of gossip.

Within the Bureau there are a few black employees, who are obviously "Negro": "Everyone knows what that means"; "Negroes are not whites, but they are just like them, at least the ones on the reservation."[8]

---

[8] The fact that such Negroes are a part of the white (Bureau) society of the reservation, since there are not enough of them to form or be considered as forming a distinct Negro social group and since any real or imagined behavioral differences are overshadowed by the white/Indian contrast, is probably a major attraction of their jobs.

Then there are the Indians. Even in the eyes of those employees who have been on several reservations, they are seen behaving as "Indians," not as "Sioux" or "Oglalas." As everyone on the reservation knows, there are two kinds of Indians: "full-bloods" and "mixed-bloods." The following two paragraphs are a composite of the *stereotypic views* held by many reservation whites (not opinions of the author):

> Full-bloods live in poverty because they don't care, are slow-witted, waste their money on alcohol and no-good relatives, and waste their time on dances and fooling around the countryside in cars they don't maintain. Full-bloods have no respect for personal property, either their own or other people's. Full-bloods are unreliable employees because they are always late (on "Indian time"), are lazy, and can only be given limited responsibilities. Full-bloods prefer to make a living, miserable as it is, by deception, by sexual immorality (through Aid to Dependent Children welfare checks), and by seeking federal and tribal handouts rather than holding down an honest job or putting their land to use. Full-bloods will say one thing but do another, or do nothing. Full-bloods spoil their children with candy and with toys that are soon broken and neglected, but they don't care enough to see that the children are properly fed or get a proper education. Full-blood children go undisciplined.
>
> Mixed-bloods, on the other hand, are better employees and often prove satisfactory as bus drivers and school cooks. Many mixed-bloods, at least, desire the bare necessities of electricity and plumbing, and are likely to have food in the house.[9] Mixed-blood children do better in school because their parents, in a limited way, want them to make something of themselves. Mixed-blood politicians are smart enough to fool the full-bloods into electing them, but are basically corrupt and have no understanding of the higher purposes of public office.

Such are the stereotypic perceptions heard daily on the reservation. They are not, of course, systematic. For example, if one wishes to complain about mixed-blood politicians one would comment that the full-bloods, especially the old men, are scrupulously honest (those of former generations being considered saintly for the purposes of such comparisons). Like all stereotypes, they are based on both ethnocentric observations of behavior and largely on false information. Thus, from

[9] One often hears that full-bloods never have food in the house from day to day. While it is true that many full-blood families do not keep large stores of food and many do face shortages of food, the statement is surprising, because most "traditional" Indians make a point of offering whatever food they have to everyone who pays them a *social* visit. The people who make such statements are never *guests* in such homes and, presumably, conclude that without refrigeration it is impossible to store food.

the point of view of the farmer who has "started from scratch" and endured the crises of South Dakota soil and weather, the Indian is a deplorable failure. As an example of the denigrating falsehoods one hears on the reservation, I was told that "full-blood women have no modesty. They'll take a bath in a tub outside the house right in front of everybody." From my observations, I would conclude that any sane[10] "full-blood" would be horrified at the thought of such behavior.

Beneath these stereotypes and the overt use of blood descent based on physical appearances, whites apply various behavioristic methods of categorization while expressing them in terms of "blood." Many aspects of life thus become symbolic of a person's "racial" identity. For the average white, a "white" home contains electricity and plumbing, a bedroom separate from the main family room, rugs and upholstered chairs, a garage, etc. Outside there is usually an attempt at a stand of shade trees and a lawn. For the school personnel of the day schools in the districts, the transplanted suburbia of a half-dozen mass-produced homes of aluminum siding, surrounded by lawns and omnipresent lawn sprinklers and sustained by their ribbons of asphalt and electrical wires, stand in stark contrast to the endless grasslands. Only in the relatively dense agency settlement of Pine Ridge town is it possible to find places where the plains do not strike the eye. The housing of the white agricultural families (who comprise most of the nongovernmental white population) is also marked by many of the same characteristics, expressed in a more rural style. A typical wheat farm may have a stand of one hundred hand-planted shade trees around the house and the complex of farm buildings. Conversely, according to my white informants, Indians are considered to live in shacks which lack characteristic white items. Indian homes are not perceived as being marked by any specific attributes except such negative things as old car bodies and other "junk" around the house (i.e., the absence of "order").[11]

10 If the various typologies presented in this paper are difficult to follow analytically, they are infinitely more difficult to live with. There are *many* people on the reservation whose psychological adjustments are unstable, and some who can only be described as violently disturbed. My informants claimed that the Public Health Service hospital offered no services for people with "illnesses of the mind," but that sometimes hopeless cases were taken "east river" (to eastern South Dakota) and "locked up in a crazy house." I observed no other evidence that the Public Health Service offered trained psychological counseling.

11 For an excellent discussion of this type of thinking among federal school personnel, see "The Vacuum Ideology" in Wax et al. (1964).

Family names are another indicator of cultural identity in the system used by the whites, since family names in white society are taken as prime indicators of ancestry. The people with the names of the first French "squaw men" are considered by whites to have "mixed-blood" names, for example, Janis, Pourier, Mousseau. People with these names number in the hundreds. Full-bloods are identifiable by "full-blood" names, for example, Standing Elk, Afraid of Bear, Imitates Dog, Pawnee Leggings.[12]

In the final analysis, economic status and economic behavior often override other indicators of "race" in the eyes of the whites. Those Indians who are economically self-sufficient by operating modest ranches are "not really Indians" despite any physical characteristics or family names. Thus, although the white concepts of race are a cultural fiction, and a fiction that is particularly unsuited to the reservation situation, they are not explicitly recognized as such by most whites. Rather, the negative data are discounted and the various categorizations are not interrelated in order to make the general scheme fit.

To some extent the recognition of economic behavior as crucial is (or more truly, *was*) an accurate assessment of the facts. The value system of the Oglalas, as developed during the period of the "horse culture," contrasts with the values of the BIA and the homesteaders, especially in the realm of economics. To the whites a nuclear family should be economically self-sufficient and should operate on a budget of cash provided by the labor of the "man of the family." Economic competition is considered natural. Hence Indians who attempt to preserve the patterns of economic cooperation among several households rather than use the money to increase the material assets of the nuclear family are "dragged down by their lazy relatives." To the Oglalas, who hold on to the traditional values of sharing, and who practice community generosity patterns and take part in give-away ceremonies, the whites appear stingy and disloyal even to their own relatives. Differences in economic behavior thus imply basic differences in family and community interaction, child-rearing patterns, and attitudes toward the use of material objects and the use of one's time.

One of the major tragedies of the present reservation situation is that such a distinction obscures the fact that the economic patterns of the

[12] Surnames which occur on Pine Ridge Reservation are used here only as examples of one type of cultural label. *No personal reference is intended* to anyone bearing any of the surnames mentioned.

rural Indians are as much a product of the cultural contact as a legacy of plains hunting life. Thus the definition of cultural identity by economic position becomes circular: poverty is a sign of "Indianness." The majority of the Oglalas who have remained on the reservation have chosen to remain in some cultural and social sense "Indian." Thus they are also subjected to the factors which account for poverty on the reservation (most especially the lack of a sound economic base for the concentrated population and the barriers to jobs around the reservation met by anyone classified as an Indian). To the whites, who are unaware of the real issue of cultural identity, the "choice" of poverty by the Indians only supports the conclusion that the Oglalas are inferior, and this inferiority is most often expressed in terms of the concept of race.

Variations in the Cognitive System of the Whites

While the above discussion of stereotypes and character judgments is, I believe, a true reflection of the thought patterns of the most powerful group on the reservation, the white federal employees, some qualifications are necessary. First, although these views appear basically hostile, there are many people who do not feel that they are condemning Indians per se. There is, as there has always been in Indian affairs, a difference between what is communicated cross-culturally and what one feels is being said and done "with one's heart in the right place." Second, there are also some federal employees who take a sincere unofficial interest in Indians, although it is usually of a very limited nature, for example, in the traditional religious ceremonials, and usually does not involve close personal contact with Indians. There are also some federal employees who have little interest in Indians and few strong opinions about them. And there are a few white employees who have formed personal friendships with Indians. The significant point is, however, that such rare individuals must deal not only with conflicting conceptual views and evaluations of the world, but also with a social system structured to prevent such contacts. Moreover, the Bureau employee finds such a position difficult because he is, by the fact of his employment, responsible to an organization which defines itself as being in the thankless and difficult position of determining what is best for Indians.

The members of the other major type of "civilizing" institution, the missionaries, also find themselves in such a position. There is a wide range of denominations and sects active on the reservation. It is possible on the same day to hear a sermon in which the native shamans are attacked, the concept of psychosomatic illness is introduced, and an explanation that ministers are the proper doctors of the soul and the Public Health Service the proper doctors of the body, or to hear a sermon in which the mystical elements of religion are stressed and the people are urged to stare at a Bible until the divine message comes to them (not unlike the vision quest). And within, at least, the larger churches (Catholic and Episcopal) there is a wide range of attitudes held by individual missionaries. There are, to be sure, some who carry a lot of culturally specific institutional baggage along with their theological teachings, but this does not mean that there are no missionaries who are culturally open-minded and able to relate closely with Indian individuals. Some missionaries have attempted the Lakota language, and a few have mastered it well and are deeply respected for so doing.

Those missionaries who live on the reservation and are actively involved with Indians appear to have a much better understanding of current Sioux social organization and community affairs than does the average Bureau employee. Most missionaries, however, use such terms as "white," "Indian," "full-blood," and "mixed-blood" in some variation of the standard white usage. The advent of Mormon missionaries in the early 1960s presents an interesting case of conceptual "dissonance" which is as yet unstudied.

The Position of Mixed-Bloods

Although all local conceptualizations of Pine Ridge society contrast mixed-bloods with whites and full-bloods, it must be emphasized that those people who are *generally* agreed to be mixed-bloods do not clearly form a distinct social group in the sense that there are distinct full-blood and white social groups. "Mixed-blood" is a term used to describe all those who are somehow standing between the two major cultural traditions, *or* social systems, represented on the reservation. While it has been mentioned that neither of these traditions is homogeneous or static, the possible range of syntheses (seen as being outside of both) is quite broad. As Useem (1947, p. 53) noted for the Rosebud Reservation, the term "mixed-blood" is applied equally to the child of a white and a mixed-blood or a white and a full-blood, or to a person of mixed-blood and mixed-blood or of full-blood and mixed-blood parentage. Thus, if the judgment is made in terms of the cultural identities *assigned* to the parents, the actual cultural environment of two "mixed-blood" children can vary greatly. A very sizable percentage of the reservation population has been legally defined as "mixed-blood" since the early days, and because of this a person may be, for example, officially of "one-half Indian blood" while having only "Indians" in the last three generations of his ancestry. Assuming no irregularities in paternity or socialization of children, a name of pre-reservation vintage such as Janis *may* indicate quite a different cultural background from that indicated by a name such as Smith. It is not surprising to find, therefore, different rural communities with differing conceptions of the term "full-blood," and to find that a community may be "full-blood" to those people living closer geographically and socially to the agency while being called "mixed-blood" by those more distant (Wax et al. 1964, p. 41).

It is also generally agreed that Indian federal employees are usually "mixed-blood." There are reasons for this actually being the case: "Here, of course, their legal identity as being an Indian brings them preferment in employment over Whites, while their superior 'know-how' and knowledge of English brings them preferment over Full-bloods" (Wax et al. 1964, p. 31). Yet "full-bloods" employed by the federal government may find themselves forced, by both their employers and their kinsmen, to sever ties with their home communities and thus become "mixed-bloods" by virtue of their employment.

The lack of one clear-cut mixed-blood group serving as intermediaries between the whites and the full-bloods, as is reported for Lower Brule Reservation (Schusky 1960), may be due to the relatively large size of the reservation, the relatively large number of jobs available with, *and outside*, the government, and to the lack of any permanent social control, on this level, in the prereservation social organization of the Oglalas (which might have effected the crystallization of two well-bounded social groups).

It is unwise to assume that all persons or groups with a "transitional" culture necessarily lack a systematized and distinct culture or social system. Yet it is true that many of the people who are recognized as mixed-bloods on Pine Ridge are in a marginal social position. As expressed by an observant rural "full-blood" (legally mixed-blood): "Those mixed-bloods are funny people. When they're with whites they call themselves Indians and when they're with Indians they call themselves Whites." In contrast to both the "whites" and the "full-bloods," the "mixed-bloods" on Pine Ridge (in either the narrowest or the broadest application of the term "mixed-blood") do not possess a distinct ceremonial life symbolizing a common cultural identity.[13]

III. The Cognitive Systems of the Oglala World

The Traditional Social Structure[14]

Confusion marks the usage of terms designating the political and cultural groupings of the Sioux, both in the historical and anthropological literature and in the speech of the reservation's inhabitants. The Sioux nation, or *Očeti-Šakowiŋ* ("the seven council fires"), separated in recent centuries into three divisions as follows:

Santee (or Eastern) Division
  1) *Mdewakaŋtoŋwaŋ*
  2) *Wahpekute*
  3) *Wahpetoŋwaŋ* (Wahpeton)
  4) *Sisitoŋwaŋ* (Sisseton)
Wičiyela (or Middle) Division
  5) *Ihaŋktoŋwaŋ* (Yankton)
  6) *Ihaŋktoŋwana* (Yanktonai)
Teton (or Western) Division
  7) *Titoŋwaŋ*

The members of each referred to their own division by the terms "Dakota," "Nakota," and "Lakota," respectively. This term, in its three dialectal variants, means, literally, "friends" or "allies." The three variants are also used to refer to the three dialects of "the Sioux language." Thus the Indians of Pine Ridge are "Lakota-speakers."

The Western Division, composed of the single *Titoŋwaŋ* tribe, appear in the literature as the Teton Dakotas, the Western Dakotas, the Teton Sioux, and the Western Sioux. The *Titoŋwaŋ*, with their superior numbers, their "high plains horse-culture" of the nineteenth century, and their dramatic military clashes with the United States Army, have stood in the minds of the American public as the archetype of all Sioux,

---

[13] For the best-rounded picture, this study should include a picture of white ceremonial life. It is hoped that some interested reader will undertake it.

[14] The two lists of tribes and sub-tribes which follow are adapted from Howard (1960) and Feraca and Howard (1963). In the lists I have included only those anglicized forms and French and English translations which are commonly found in the literature. The terms used in this paper for the various levels of organization differ somewhat from those in these sources.

indeed, for some, of all North American Indians. The *Titoŋwaŋ* were divided into seven groups as follows:

1) *Oglala*
2) *Sičaŋǧu* (in French, *Brulé*, Burnt Thighs)
3) *Itazipčo* (in French, *Sans Arcs*, No Bows)
4) *Sihasapa* (Black Foot)
5) *Minikoŋjou* (*Mnikondzu*, or *Hohwodzu*)
6) *Oohenoŋpa* (Two Kettles)
7) *Huŋkpapa*

The Oglalas were the largest among these sub-tribes.

The Term "Oglala"

"Oglala" means roughly "sprinkling (something) unto oneself or one's own." One man explained to me that when he poured sugar into his own coffee it was "oglala." Other explanations are that the term described the practice of putting ashes on a horse's saddle sores, or that it commemorates a quarrel between women in which they threw ashes (or sand) in each other's eyes. A mimeographed pamphlet put out by the Pine Ridge Agency offers the translations "scatter their own, or those who do not agree among themselves" ("Home of the Oglala Sioux" 1963, p. 4). None of the Indians I talked with gave this second meaning, nor does any other reference I have found. It is, however, easy to find many BIA employees who hold this view of the Oglalas, specifically in reference to tribal politics. The criticism is not unrealistic, although the factors contributing to the constant dissension evident on Pine Ridge as on several other reservations are related to the lack of communication and the lack of conceptual agreement on basic political matters between the Bureau and the Indians (Tax 1961).

The Term Sioux

"Sioux" is a French corruption of a Chippewa term meaning "snakes" or "enemies" (Riggs 1893, p. 176, *Nadouessioux;* Densmore 1918, p. 1, *Nadowe-is-iw-ŭg;* Howard 1960, p. 249 n, *Nátɔwèsiwɔk*). The original meaning was undoubtedly derogatory. Some Oglalas are aware of the derivation of the word. On one occasion I was strongly criticized by an old man for calling him a "snake." His information, most likely, was derived from whites, although I doubt if many of the whites on the reservation share his knowledge. It is, of course, the common term for English speakers to use both on the reservation and in the literature when talking about the descendents of the *Očeti-Šakowiŋ*. It is unfortunately used for several different levels of prereservation and reservation organization rather indiscriminately. The usage of the term "Sioux" by non-Indians on the reservation suggests little understanding of the complex historical divisions listed above.

"Sioux" is used in this paper to designate the Lakotas, Nakotas, and Dakotas collectively, rather than using "Dakota" to refer to *both* the three divisions taken together and the Dakota-proper, or Santees, as is done by Mekeel, Feraca and Howard, and numerous others.

Current Terminological Usage: Other Indians

The terms used by the Oglalas today to designate membership in Indian groups on various levels are different, and presumably more irregular, than the nineteenth-century terms listed above. This is due both to the introduction of English terminology, which is not in direct correspondence to the earlier native terminology, and which the Oglalas must use in their dealings with whites, and to the reorientation of Sioux political and social units caused by the creation of several reservations.

The Oglalas have no word which translates easily as "Indian." Oglalas refer to other groups among the Lakotas by their respective sub-tribal names, for example, *Sičaŋgu*,[15] *Hunkpapa*, etc. People in other divisions of the Sioux are referred to by either the division name, *Wičiyela*, Santee, or tribal names, for example, Wahpeton, Sisseton, Yankton, etc. Within the various Sioux groups, however, it is becoming common to identify people according to their home reservation, as is done by nearly all whites. Among the official names of the Teton reservation polities, the Oglala Sioux Tribe of Pine Ridge Reservation is the only one to preserve the original sub-tribal name. The Lower Brule Sioux Tribe of Lower Brule Reservation has adopted the common mixed English-French term, Lower Brule, analogous to the original name, *Kul Wičaša* (lowland people) of the *Sičaŋgu* (*Brulé*, Burnt Thighs). Pine Ridge Reservation and the much smaller Lower Brule Reservation are noteworthy because their inhabitants, in each case, are nearly all descendants of one prereservation social unit. Rosebud Reservation, east of Pine Ridge, has many individuals of Oglala ancestry and a few of mixed Lakota-Ponca ancestry. The official name of the reservation group is the Rosebud Sioux Tribe. Similarly, the populations of the two other United States reservations for Lakotas are

---

[15] The term most often found in the literature and in governmental papers, Brule, is not widely used by the Lakotas themselves (Feraca 1963, p. 1).

known officially as the Cheyenne River Sioux (*Minikoŋjou, Oohenoŋpa, Itazipčo*, and *Sihasapa* sub-tribes) and the Standing Rock Sioux Tribe (*Huŋkpapa* and *Sihasapa* sub-tribes and Yanktonai Dakotas).[16]

Informally the Oglalas often refer to people as Rosebud Sioux, Cheyenne River Sioux, or Standing Rock Sioux when speaking English. There is now, and evidently always has been (Mekeel 1943, p. 137), a fair amount of travel between groups. It is not unusual to meet a Lakota (in my experience usually a man) from another reservation who is living on his spouse's home reservation. In designating such a person by the reservation where he is legally an enrolled member, rather than by his original sub-tribe affiliation, the Oglalas indicate the currently important fact of where a person owns or may inherit land and thus the source of any checks for land lease he may receive. On the other hand (presumably in the absence of significant monetary income) a person may come to be recognized by the sub-tribal name of his reservation of residence rather than his reservation of descent. Thus some individuals who move onto Pine Ridge Reservation become "Oglala," and similarly for Rosebud Reservation become "Sičaŋǧu" (Useem 1947, p. 22), though their origins are never totally forgotten. Moreover, the traditional groupings are not fully understood by many Lakotas, particularly the younger people (Feraca and Howard 1963), and confusion results between such distinctions as Black Foot (*Sihasapa*) and the Blackfoot tribe of Montana, and between the Cheyenne River Sioux and the Cheyennes of Montana. Change is also shown by the fact that some people refer to themselves as "South Dakota Indians." The term "Siouxs" is frequently heard on the reservation, and despite the appearance of the word "Sioux" on virtually every official document, notice, sign, and poster, some Oglalas have difficulty with the unusual spelling.

In spoken Lakota, reference to non-Sioux Indians is also complex. If a person is known to come from a familiar neighboring tribe, the tribal name may be used in either the Lakota or English form, for example, *Šahiyela* or Cheyenne. For more distant tribes the Oglalas use the tribal names used by the BIA, for example, Navajo. Some Indians in distant areas are identified in conversation only by their location. If the tribe is not known, Lakota speakers may use a phrase that means roughly "he's from another tribe." Usually they will refer to a person as "Lakota" when it is obvious that he is not, thus rendering the

---

[16] All the information on reservations other than Pine Ridge is derived from Feraca and Howard (1963).

meaning "Indian" in a very general sense. When speaking English the
Lakotas of course use the word "Indian" widely, although they have
an understandably parochial interpretation of the word. The term
Očeti-Šakowiŋ is now used only rarely, usually with some confusion over
its meaning (Feraca, personal communication). In English "Sioux" is
used in this sense, although the referent is sometimes restricted to only
the Lakotas.

Current Terminological Usage: Non-Indians

The terms now used by the Oglalas to describe non-Indians, and the
way in which they are used, also reflect the introduction of one set of
categories on top of another during a period of rapid change. The term
now universally used for whites is *wašičuŋ*. The French explorer and
missionary Louis Hennepin recorded in his journal of his visits among
the Sioux in present Wisconsin in 1680 that the principal chief at the
time was called "Washechoonde" (Riggs 1893, p. 174). Riggs con-
cludes that "their name for Frenchmen was in use, among the Dakota,
before they had intercourse with them, and was probably a name
learned from some Indians farther east." It is generally agreed, however, that the term is native to the Sioux language.

Two translations of *wašičuŋ* have been suggested. One possible
meaning is "loudmouth" or "one who talks a great deal." This interpretation is perhaps supported by the term *iwašičuŋ*, meaning
"mouthy" (Feraca, personal communication). The other meaning
that has been suggested is "a person with (supernatural) power" or "a
worker of wonders." Evidence for this interpretation is presented by
J. R. Walker. He describes a "*sicun*" as "an immaterial God" which
can be "imparted to material things by a proper ceremony." The
sicun-object with its obligatory wrappings make a bundle called a
"*wasicun*"[17] (Walker 1917, p. 87). Sword, one of Walker's informants,
explains that a *sicun* is a type of spirit which guards its possessor against
evil spirits and gives him special strengths and abilities. Each individual
acquires a *sicun* at birth, but others could be obtained through visions
or ceremonies (Walker 1917, p. 158). This suggests that the term
wašičuŋ became associated with whites because their superior technology was interpreted by the Sioux as evidence of superior supernatural helpers. Relevant to this is Sword's explanation that he
converted from being a shaman, a medicine man, and a war leader to

[17] In the orthography used by Walker (1917, p. 55) *c* is equivalent to *ch* or *č*, and *s*
is equivalent to *sh* or *š*.

being a deacon in a mission church because he became convinced after fighting whites that their Great Spirit (*Wakan Tanka*) was "superior" (Walker 1917, p. 158).

Although I have no direct evidence to support this, I suspect that the two meanings of *wašičuŋ* might have been conceptually related in traditional Sioux thought. Practices such as recounting *coups* suggest that being an outspoken person and being a person recognized as possessing strong supernatural helpers were parts of the same behavioral patterns. For brevity, I will gloss *wašičuŋ* as "doers."

The term *wašičuŋ* was applied to the French quite early, and was extended to include other whites. Since the Sioux were not directly involved in the fur trade competition between the British and the French, but instead first met missionaries, explorers, and isolated traders, it is to be expected that differences of nationality among these early visitors would be of secondary importance. During the intensive contact of the nineteenth century, the whites were, of course, "Americans." Riggs, in his 1852 dictionary, defines *Wašičuŋ*, as "*Frenchmen, in particular; all white men, in general*" (p. 227). He also lists *Wašičunhiŋča* (literally, "very *wašičuŋ*") as "a Frenchman from France" and *Wašičuŋhokšidaŋ* as "*a French boy*, the common name for the Canadians in the Dakota country, *any one who labors*." As the contacts with whites changed, the term *wašičuŋ* shifted meanings. The name of one of the famous Oglala leaders of the early reservation era, *Wašičuŋ Tašuŋka*, is translated proudly as "American Horse." The general application of the term can still lead to occasional confusion; one man told me that his great-grandfather was "a Frenchman named Billy Thompson."

When the Oglalas first met Negroes they called them *wašičuŋ sapa*, black *wašičuŋ* (Riggs 1852, p. 313; Neihardt 1932, p. 104 [for the year 1876]). As the Sioux came into closer contact with the whites, and as *wašičuŋ* came to be generally translated as "white man," the phrase *wašičuŋ sapa* was abandoned. Williamson (1902, p. 113) gives two Dakota terms for Negro: *wašičuŋ sapa* and "*hasapa*." The second term, *ha sapa*, is the one used today on Pine Ridge. Literally, it would translate "black skins." While "black *wašičuŋ*" is more descriptive of the social and cultural patterns on the reservation (see above, footnote 8), the translation "black white man" is too awkward to be used in speaking English (i.e., with whites who think in terms of blood descent). Although the whites on the reservation never mention degrees of blood in connection with Negroes, the Oglalas attempt to apply blood descent in such cases. In 1961 I spoke to two Negroes employed as teachers in BIA schools. Both mentioned with embarrassed amusement that the Oglalas expressed great curiosity on this matter, asking each repeatedly when they first arrived if he was mixed-blood or full-blood. The Indians must have had difficulty searching for symbols and behavioral traits which would have been meaningful to their methods of categorization. Virtually all of the few Negroes on the reservation are federal employees following middle-class white patterns identical to those of the "superior" whites.[18] However, many Oglalas speak of Negroes as inferiors, thus gaining some status for themselves out of the racial categories and prejudices introduced by the whites. Black Elk reports that a Lakota mortally wounded in the Battle of the Little Big Horn was named "Black Wasichu" (Neihardt 1932, p. 130). It is very doubtful that any Oglala would today accept the name "Ha Sapa."

Similarly, many Oglalas have an image of Jews as greedy and deceitful, based on the status of Indians as compared to whites and derived from the opinions stated by local whites, rather than from any real observations of Jews. Even here the label is used to categorize behavior: several times I have heard Indians use the verb "to jew" someone. Just as the whites on the reservation use the mixed-blood/full-blood distinction, the Oglalas in their minority position have picked up the divisions in the larger society while showing very little understanding of the bases for such distinctions.

Although all the terms under discussion here, and below, reflect changes in reference due to the influences of the non-Indian conceptual scheme, the shift from *wašičuŋ sapa* to *ha sapa* is the only case of an earlier term being replaced by one which is a literal description of physical, and not behavioral, characteristics.[19]

Current Terminological Usage: Pine Ridge Indians

In discussing the categories of mixed blood and full blood the Lakota speaker uses terms which are not linguistically parallel to those in English, either in origin or in current referents (see Table 1). A speaker who considers himself full-blood might use the term "full-

[18] Many Oglalas are involved with the psychological problem of resisting feelings of inferiority to whites. Their current interpretation of Oglala-white history is another major refuge from such feelings.

[19] The phrase *wičaša ska* (literally, "white man") is occasionally used in conversation with naive whites as a red herring, "to count coup." My informants emphatically denied that the phrase is ever used in ordinary conversation to mean Caucasians. *Wašičuŋ* is the term used when speaking both politely and derisively of whites.

TABLE 1

Usage of Group Labels in English and Lakota

	Categories			
	White	*Mixed-blood*	*Full-blood*	*Negro*
English (white speaker)	white	Indian mixed-blood full-blood		Negro
Lakota (prereservation speaker)	*wašičuŋ* (doer)	*lakota* (?) *iyeska* (interpreter) *lakota* (ally)		*wašičuŋ sapa* (black doer)
Lakota (present speaker)	*wašičuŋ* (white man)	*iyeska* (mixed-blood)	*lakota* (full-blood)	*hasapa* (black skin)
English (Oglala full-blood speaker)	white man	mixed-blood, half-breed	Indian, Sioux, full-blood	Negro

blood" in English to make it clear to a white that he dissociates himself from "mixed-bloods." If he does not feel that he will be misunderstood, he will call himself an Indian, implying that mixed-bloods are something else. In speaking Lakota (which almost always means that he is not speaking to a white) he will use the term *Lakota*, "allies."

In speaking of mixed-bloods, full-bloods will use either the terms "mixed-blood" or "half-breed" (or simply "breed"). "Half-breed" is the more derisive phrase, although in some situations neither one could be considered polite. The choice between the two phrases is based on matters of attitude rather than on any desire to indicate differing degrees of "blood." In Lakota there are no aboriginal terms for fractions other than one-half (Riggs 1893, p. 165).

The Lakota term for "mixed-bloods" is *iyeska*. The original meaning of the word was "one who speaks well," i.e., "interpreter" (Riggs 1852, p. 82; Williamson 1902, p. 92) and indicates the position of the early mixed-bloods. Today the term is used to mean "interpreter," but its more common meaning is "mixed-blood." Because it is used primarily in Lakota, and Lakota is often used as a sign of being "full-blood," *iyeska* generally has a derogatory connotation. One woman commented to her husband about the hiring of young men for the lucrative job of fire fighting (in English in my presence): "Yesterday they took three busloads; six were Sioux Indians, the rest *iyeska*."

As mentioned above, mixed-bloods show great situational variation in their use of terms to identify themselves:

> Indians who are themselves Bureau Employees. . . rarely say "we Indians" before Indians, lest some aggressive Fullblood challenge them. They will use the expression before Whites only if forced to do so, as when, for example, they are obliged to represent "the Indian" at a conference. On the other hand, when such persons spoke to members of our study they always implicitly made clear that they considered themselves Indians while at the same time, they always differentiated themselves from "residual families," "backward folks," or, if no words came, by an inclination of the head toward the heart of the reservation and the word, "them." [Wax et al. 1964, p. 34 n]

Another Lakota term, *wašičuŋčiŋča*, "white man's child," was used earlier by the Indians to refer to "mixed-bloods." It is not in common use today on Pine Ridge, perhaps because most of the mixed-bloods today are, in fact, children of mixed-bloods.

Symbols of Identity

Many items in reservation life have become identified with either an "Indian" or a "white" style of life. The example of houses mentioned before indicates the introduction of non-Indian material objects into a definition of "Indianness." To an Oglala an "Indian house" means a log house, and a "white man's house" means a frame house, of varying degrees of structural strength, covered with boards, tarpaper, or a variety of other building materials. Thus what whites might call a shack (as opposed to a cabin) is considered to be characteristically "white" by the Oglalas, although the material goods in and around it reflect an Indian style of life in both their nature and arrangement. The log cabin is considered a trait of Indian culture. An Indian cook for a rural consolidated day school told me that she would much rather live in the log house she was in than in the principal's modern prefabricated house next door. Her log house was in fact a substantial frame house with electricity and plumbing, built by the federal government years ago. But the outside was finished with logs and that was the significant fact for her, even though the logs were dressed and stained and were caulked with painted stucco. The new houses for Oglalas built in Pine Ridge and two "rural towns" are decorated with "Indian" designs on the shutters, and thus despite all the aluminum siding, lawns, curbing, fire hydrants, etc., they are "Indian homes" to all but the most traditional. For some material items being introduced by the government it would seem that manipulation of the *labels* of cultural identity may have a significant effect on the reactions of the Oglalas. The situation is much more complex for those symbols of identity which have a firm historical basis in Sioux culture.

The symbolism today attached to names by the Oglalas is indicative of the adjustments they have made during the reservation experience. Those Indians having family names which are translations (with varying accuracy) of the names of Indian ancestors consider these their "white names." They are always said in English, even when the conversation is in Lakota. Some bilingual Oglalas are not able to translate their "white names" rapidly and accurately.

When the government started to keep population records of the early reservation groups, they felt that it was necessary to establish an American system of family names among the Indians. Thus the family names that have survived today were once the personal names of men who were judged to be the heads of households (e.g., Standing Soldier and his wife, White Star, would be listed as Joe and Mary Standing Soldier). Confusion was immediate in the new records: Standing Soldier's brothers might have been Thunder Bear, Brings Him Back, and Steals Horses by Night (each of whom, incidentally, would have been "father," *ate*, to Standing Soldier's children).

Kneale, recalling his experiences on Pine Ridge during the period 1899–1901 (as teacher of a one-room schoolhouse in the center of the reservation) describes the continuation of this pattern of naming:

> When a child was brought to school for the first time, the teacher made inquiry of the parent as to its name. The response, almost invariably was the same: "It has no name." Then ascertaining the name of the male parent the teacher used it for a surname, placing what is termed a Christian name before it, thus giving the child a name. [1950, p. 40]

Kneale refers to these as "school names" which were not used by "the Indians of the camp." The children, of course, had other names at home. Today these "school names" or "white names" are the names used constantly. I did meet one young boy whose "Christian name" was never mentioned in an Indian setting and was unknown to his Indian playmates, who called him by a Sioux nickname. His situation, however, was unusual; his father was a white rancher living off the reservation and the boy therefore did not attend the local school with his Indian relatives.

If one asks an Oglala for his "Indian name," the answer will almost always be *not* a translation back into Lakota of his "white name," but a personal name that has been given to him. Not all Oglalas have personal names; some people are a bit unfamiliar with their own and might need prompting to remember it. The pattern of naming is based on the aboriginal procedure, although individuals may often be named after ancestors who had more of a chance to win honors in warfare and hunting. These "Indian names" are thought of in the Lakota form, and when they are translated a short explanation is usually offered (by contrast, most people lack an understanding of the contextual meaning of their "white names"). I do not know the current use of personal names; I suspect it is extremely limited. It is interesting to note in this context that the "Christian names" given to Sioux children are chosen with much greater individuality than is the case among the American middle class. Although there are many names of the "Tom, Dick, and Harry" variety, the following examples are typical of hundreds more: for males, Ambrose, Cephus, Lymon, Narcell, Zachary; for females, Angelique, Cleon, Delilah, Rosetta, and Verine.

The family names are used, of course, to trace some kin relationships and to help classify Indians who are unknown to the person making the classification. There are also statements about "full-blood" and "mixed-blood" names, but again the usage is not the same as that of the whites. A name is not a determining factor in classifying cultural identity as much as it is a particular label for a family whose position is agreed upon by some group for some period of time. Thus I was sternly corrected by a "full-blood," to use his term, for confusing "Cortier" ("That's a full-blood name") and "Cottier" ("That's a mixed-blood name"). Both "full-blood" and "mixed-blood" names are subcategories of "white names" (see Table 2).

In addition, some of the existing family names were the personal names of Indian leaders in the final stages of the armed conflict, and

TABLE 2

THE IDENTIFICATION OF FAMILY NAMES

The "White" System	The "Full-blood" Oglala System	
	Indian names (personal): e.g., Carries Him in Front	
Indian or full-blood names: e.g., Standing Elk	Full-blood names: e.g., Standing Elk, Cortier	⎫
Mixed-blood names: e.g., Cortier, Cottier, Janis	Mixed-blood names: e.g., Cottier, Janis	⎬ White names
		⎭
White names: e.g., Smith, Wilson	(names of non-Indians)	

the names are proudly remembered as indicators of the leaders' deeds. The controversies which flare up over who are the real descendants of such leaders are complicated by the American system of assigning names.

Because of the significance that the whites attach to his "white name," one Indian may change his name from "Yellow Bird" to "Wilson," while another will refuse to let school officials change his grandson's name from "Charles Bad Face." Still a third individual may go by two names, being called "Don Blue Shirt" by the members of his community and "Don Small" by the people at the agency where he serves on committees. A very few Oglalas maintain that rarified form of a "white name" known as a "show name." These are used only professionally, for dancing appearances at Disneyland, roles in motion pictures, etc. Ironically, they are chosen to strike the white audience as sounding particularly "Indian."

Language, or, more precisely, the choice of languages, also takes on symbolic value in many situations. The linguistic differences, and the correlated conceptual differences, between the white and Indian worlds have taken on increased significance due to the basically hostile position of the Bureau toward the Lakota language. The matter of languages has become a major impasse within the BIA schools (Wax et al. 1964). To some extent Lakota is used to exclude mixed-bloods, including a few individuals on the tribal council. But it is my impression that most people who are called mixed-bloods are to some extent bilingual. I do not know if degrees of facility in spoken Lakota are used to determine or preserve social distinctions.

English, in some form, is understood by almost everyone on the reservation. For a great part of the rural population, however, it is not used in the home or taught to children before they enter school. For such people it remains a language to be used haltingly in specific limited situations dealing with whites, and these situations are generally embarrassing. Most of the rural people are able to carry on a conversation in English on certain topics, notable among them politics. But the white visitor soon realizes that he is not hearing his native language. It is "Pine Ridge English" (Wax et al. 1964, p. 17) and differs from standard English (whatever that is considered to be) in both the phonemic and nonphonemic qualities of pronunciation, in items of vocabulary, in the meanings assigned to common English words, and in sentence structure, etc. The Oglalas are aware that it is considered "broken English" and many avoid using it when possible. Some, however, refuse to speak English on certain occasions as a matter of pride. I have observed an Indian, noted for his loquacity with visiting whites, call over a friend to act as an "interpreter," pretending that he did not understand the English questions being put to him. As his masterful performance unfolded, he doubled the insult by letting it be known, through gesture, that he understood the questions perfectly before hearing them in Lakota.

It is possible that "town Indians" use a more fluent and more "proper" form of English to differentiate themselves from the rural folk. I have not, however, observed this. In fact, the most eloquent English used by the Oglalas is heard over the loud-speaker systems at ceremonial gatherings, which are, broadly speaking, "full-blood" activities. And as noted by Wax et al. (1964, p. 108), this English is not directed at whites or English-speaking mixed-bloods, but at the "traditional" visitors from non-Sioux tribes. These announcers are the same people who are noted for their facility in Lakota oratory. Determination of cultural identity according to language, as with nearly every other facet of reservation life, is not a simple thing.

Group Boundaries and Social Control

From the above discussion it is clear that one individual may classify himself or another as being one of a variety of types (cultural identities) since he has several possible methods of classification to choose among and several possible levels on which to apply his choice. Naturally, the determination of an individual's identity is fairly stable within certain limits. Some people are generally accepted as being full-blood and others as mixed-blood, and these general classifications reflect general differences in life styles. Within a community it is possible to get a high degree of consensus about the identity of an individual when talking on a rather general level. To some extent this consensus is also a function of the tendency among the Oglalas to give outsiders a simplified picture of the complexities involved. The more they accept a white, or the more they have to deal with a white in power, the more discerning they become in their use of the terminology in his presence. When one asks about specific events, or asks persons outside the immediate group of interacting households, the answer to a question of cultural identity may vary greatly.

The application of these terms is also a means of social control. If "educated" Indians are embarrassed by a country cousin who is too demonstrative in his "backwardness," that is, participation in ceremonials or insistence on living "Indian style," they may deride him as being a "Big Indian." They face, however, the retort of being "*Wašíčuŋ*." To someone who considers himself "an Indian" it can be a grave insult. A fair-skinned individual legally considered to be Indian may be grudgingly accepted as Indian by an old man from a remote district if his political views are of a certain nature (and politics is the topic of discussion). He may be branded as a white illegitimately taking advantage of his legal status as an Indian (a frequent charge when discussing land rights), or he may be considered a mixed-blood because he refuses to lend money to the "full-blood" making the judgment, or because he drinks too much, or in the wrong places, or at the wrong time, or with the wrong people. It is important to take into consideration the relationship between the speaker and the person spoken of in any matter of criticism or social control. This is especially true on the reservation because there are many subdivisions of the population, each trying to see itself as the top stratum. If a "mixed-blood" is challenged as "acting like a white man" by someone he considers a "dirty Indian" the effect is quite different from when it comes from his "mixed-blood" brother.[20] This type of social control is truly effective only when it questions a social bond or position of social parity which both parties would rather preserve. A milder form of social criticism, not directly involving labels of cultural identity, is to call someone "crazy." From its usage, I would judge the meaning of this word as "acting like an outsider," that is, not acting responsibly in terms of the group. To the extent that it does not label a person specifically as a member of another (inferior) group, it achieves the same purpose with less strain on a common relationship. In a very real sense, the application of any term of membership either challenges the individual or bolsters his identity in a challenging world.

IV. The Differing Views of Human Nature

A discussion of the symbols of cultural identity reveals not only the differing methods of categorization and evaluation of individuals according to such categories, but also basic differences in the concepts

[20] "Thus a young man of our acquaintance claimed Fullblood status despite the fact that his mother was genetically a Mixedblood. He consistently spoke ill of Mixedbloods, though his wife was genetically less than half Indian. His mother, who claimed and generally was given *de facto* Fullblood status was once, in our presence, insulted by some persons of unimpeachable Fullblood status. 'Those are *real* Fullbloods,' she told us caustically, 'They walk right over you.' Later, however, she tried to convince us that these persons had been rude to her because she was associating with 'hated White men,' namely us" (Wax et al. 1964, p. 31).

held by the whites and the Oglalas concerning the nature of man. As has been pointed out by numerous writers (e.g., Wax et al. 1964, p. 36), the Oglalas view change of an individual's basic character as being something beyond his control. Changes in a person's life situation or enduring difficulties are due to such ultimately uncontrollable forces as supernatural power, early life experiences, disease, perfidious behavior by the powerful whites, and sheer luck. Full-bloods speak of their neighbors suffering from "hard times," rather than being "poor." An individual arrested for intoxication may cite his "bad luck" that he encountered the police. A teen-age boy I met, who shuns sports, associates with girls, and speaks in a feminine manner (it would be difficult to say if his blue jeans and sweat shirt were a "masculine" or "feminine" style among his peers), is admired by middle-aged women for his skills in beadwork, not unlike the berdaches of former times. There was no indication that these women saw his behavior as something unnatural, shameful, or to be corrected.

It is difficult to judge the extent to which the Oglalas feel their lives directed by supernatural commands. Such directives, in traditional forms, are still important factors in the lives of many (Feraca 1963) and parallels must surely exist in the lives of many of the "practicing Christians." Several people told me, in guarded words, of supernatural events they had witnessed. One boy explained to me that his brother (currently in prison for auto theft) was compelled to steal because as a child he had stolen something trivial during his mother's wake. The explanation followed that anyone committing a transgression during the period between the death and the interment of a close relative would be destined to repeat the act uncontrollably for the rest of his life.

Although the traditional Oglalas may consider a person's basic nature as unchanging, this does not mean that individuals are not held responsible for their actions (as shown by the above discussion of social control). The individual is expected to express his character in a manner that is *socially* acceptable. The respected person is the one who acts generously not only with material possessions and food at ceremonial distributions but also with his time, his experience, and his associations. It is high praise to say of someone that "he gets along with everybody," "he talks to people," or "he helps them out because he's got a big heart."

However, such behavior is rarely possible toward everyone that one is likely to meet. While whites often criticize rural Oglalas for supporting relatives who never reciprocate (whites limit this to material possessions), it has been my experience that even the most generous persons are anything but naive about such situations. Rather, it is a matter of placing primary value on social contacts and social prestige. Some people, of course, lie outside the boundaries of such generosity. All whites are initially suspect and usually remain so. Similarly, rural Oglalas tend not to form contacts with the Oglala townspeople. Those individuals who continually refuse to adjust to the group's attitudes are excluded in order to preserve what harmony exists. Even in the case of their very close relatives, traditional Oglalas will regretfully "give up on them." There is no sense in being generous and sociable toward a person who does not share one's appreciation of such good deeds.

On the other hand, traditional people may meet "mixed-bloods" or non-Indians who are willing to act in a socially responsible manner. Even the most rural families, who shrink from sight when a stranger approaches their homes, become gracious hosts if the outsider is granted the status of a friend. Non-Indians who are respected by the rural Oglalas are often honored with Indian names. And for those whites who are willing to share the social obligations and harsh living conditions of the hosts rather than meeting them with admonishment, "adoption" may result. This pattern of acceptance has been noted as one general form of Indian-white interpersonal relations (Hallowell 1963). Whites who are so adopted are referred to as *wašičuŋ* only for the purposes of secondary clarification, for they are, in fact, "allies" and not "doers."

The concept of human nature which typifies American culture needs be stated only briefly. Individuals are seen as capable of determining their own characters and their destinies. Individuals are capable of *developing* their natural abilities. Everyone is, in a sense, a "self-made man" and is ultimately responsible to himself. Children are taught "to be someone when they grow up," "to do something with their lives." Individual opportunity, the chance to develop one's talents, is thus a crucial concept, and the establishment and protection of opportunities is a basic goal of government. This position, in a one-dimensional simplification, typifies many of the BIA programs, including education, presented to the Oglalas. Few Oglala individuals who have passed childhood are able to secure a comfortable adjustment to both systems. The very few cases I have observed have reached such idiosyncratic resolutions that they are unable to pass them on to the next generation faced with the same basic conflicts.

The problem is further complicated for those Oglalas who choose a basically white orientation toward the proper life. The white concept of human nature as capable of self-development conflicts with the attitudes held about the Indian "race," that they lack the natural abilities and/or self discipline to actually "amount to anything." The Oglala individual who chooses this path often finds that he is headed for disappointment, bitterness, hatred of whites, and hatred of his own "Indianness." As James has observed for the "deculturated" Chippewas of Lac Court Oreilles, Wisconsin:

> The racial element of the negative stereotype is enormously important because it anchors such "inferiority" in the biology of the individual, beyond his control. It thereby blocks adjustment to the very forces that generate the desire to escape subcultural status. [1961, p. 721]

The crises that develop within families and within individuals because of the contradictory perceptions of reservation life have been a major area of study, perhaps most notably in Erikson's formulation of modern Oglala personality (1950), and will not be discussed in detail here. Suffice it to say that problems of identity often overshadow the considerable problems of finding food, clothing, and shelter in a difficult environment.

V. OGLALA IDENTITY AND SIOUX NATIONALISM

The Current Challenge

A review of Sioux history would show that the challenges of today, and the resources being used to answer them, are far distant from the conflicts with guns and the struggles over treaties. The Oglalas today are faced with a dwindling land base, growing population, serious problems of unemployment, glaring inadequacies in the educational programs (in both the on-reservation school system and the off-reservation relocation and on-the-job training programs), threats to certain special legal rights as Indians, and even the powerful threat of "termination," that is, being "deserted by the Bureau of Indian Affairs." Despite the constant complaints about the Bureau, the Oglalas fear that the total removal of the Pine Ridge Agency could only mean fewer beneficial programs, handled even more poorly. Beyond any consideration of governmental efficiency, however, is the realization that the presence of the agency in large measure contributes to the special qualities and hence "Indianness" of the current situation. Most

Oglalas would prefer to stay under the wing (or the heel, depending on the point of view) of the Bureau rather than run the risk of losing this distinct position. Their relationship with the Bureau has been characterized by the term "hostile dependency" (Hagen and Schaw 1960, pp. 6–8). Although termination may be a remote possibility at this date, and hence is not a daily threat in their lives, neither is it an empty one.

Adding to the challenge is a growing awareness that American society is independently experiencing major changes in the realm of group boundaries. Many Oglalas are deeply concerned, and poorly informed, about the current social movements. In 1963 different individuals asked me quite spontaneously, "Is it true the Kennedys are going to pass a law that says everyone has to be Catholic?" "Is the country going to lose the individual freedoms?" and "They don't let the Negroes in Chicago go to school, do they?" Some people were worried about the implications of the Supreme Court decision on prayers in the schools (there is close cooperation between the federal and parochial schools on the reservation). One political activist, busy accumulating affidavits on the mistreatment of Indians in South Dakota county jails, was shocked by the idea of Negro public demonstrations: "I hope the Indian people never march in the street." For the Oglalas, the pressures for the exclusion of race and religion as valid discerning factors in American society were a baffling and unwanted phenomenon. They are baffling because such changes seem to contradict the basic assumptions of blood descent on which the federal agency operates. They are unwanted because although the categorizations of blood descent may fit Oglala concepts rather poorly (and often serve as the basis of policies they consider unjust), current developments offer a scheme which would apparently take even less notice of the Oglala claims for special distinctions.

In this uncertain position the Oglalas are threatened with disintegration, not only individually, but collectively. The history of Oglala-white contact has been marked by social divisions among the Oglalas. The current lines these divisions have taken has been discussed above. Although there are now deep splits in the "Indian" population of the reservation, the majority of the Oglalas have maintained a sense of society, strained at times and generally unable to support sustained group action, but nonetheless real in the lives of the people who feel this common bond. Two basic patterns emerge in the expression of a sense of unity, and as one might suspect from the above discussion, unity in this case is not always defined to include everyone who in some way qualifies as being an Oglala. Both patterns are characterized by concern with demonstrating the distinct position of an Oglala social unit *within* the larger sphere of American society. Both are developments (still in process) in response to the greater society, and neither can be dismissed as merely a retention of former customs. This is rather obvious in a discussion of the first pattern and it can be dealt with, for the purposes of this paper, rather briefly.

The Activist Approach

In 1963 the reservation was buzzing with talk of statewide petitions and referendums, of affidavits and hearings on civil rights. A tribal leader appeared on local television to argue against the impending transfer of police jurisdiction on Indian lands from federal to state authorities; the tribal council sponsored a meeting to encourage the people of the rural communities to speak their minds to the federal educators. The tribal council saw the Pine Ridge housing projects and the Felix Cohen Memorial Home for the Aged (financed by the Federal Housing Authority and the sale of tribal bonds) near completion. They debated applying for systematic development of public wells under a new Public Health Service program. In September of 1964 two former presidents of the council discussed the national political campaign in terms of the possible benefits for the Oglalas from the war on poverty.

Realizing that the Oglalas are inextricably involved in American society and politics, some individuals have entered political affairs as private citizens and in a few cases as professional politicians. In trying to develop the beneficial aspects of this involvement, they have based their arguments on their rights as citizens of the United States and of South Dakota. Likewise the arguments presented by these activists for the continuation of a distinct Indian identity are increasingly based on the federal and state constitutions rather than on special treaty rights. They speak of their activities as a "fight for our Indian people."

The shift in the civil rights movement from an emphasis on integration to an emphasis on Black Power and the legitimation of a distinct black position within American culture can only be more welcome to the Sioux. Many Indian activists around the country have adopted a similar style with "Indian Power" buttons, "liberation newspapers," and the like. The influence of these new developments on the people of Pine Ridge Reservation has not yet been investigated.

Only a few Oglalas engage in political activities in a full-time capacity. Many more take up the arguments as individual issues arise; some problems arouse the majority of the reservation population. The distinctly activist approach, however, may be characterized as atypical. To the average "country Indian" it is a mixed-blood approach, both in its perceptions of the problems and in its methods. The country Indians assert the rights of the Oglalas to a distinct place within American society by a totally different pattern of behavior on a different level of perception and justification.

The Oglalas in American History

The majority of the reservation population (the country Indians, conservatives, full-bloods, sociological full-bloods, real Indians, backward Indians, or whatever one wishes to call them) demonstrate their common position in a largely symbolic manner. The Lakotas find that their major significance in American life lies in history. Lakota views of their history are similar in pattern to the folk histories of other peoples overrun by the expansion of Western society (cf. Barnes 1951): (1) it remains primarily an oral history among a people who are generally literate or semiliterate; (2) the events of the past have been simplified and condensed so that the Oglalas speak of three main events—the Battle of the Little Big Horn, the Treaty (actually a long series of treaties), and the Wounded Knee Massacre; (3) references are made to a golden age when all was right in the world; and (4) the events of the past are used variously to justify the current social divisions and to assert the bonds among the Lakotas and with their conquerors.

For the purposes of maintaining distinctions between the "real Indians" and the "mixed-bloods" the Oglala full-bloods speak of their past as having been polarized by two leaders, Red Cloud and Crazy Horse. While the reservation is advertised as "the Land of Red Cloud" (he personally picked the location for the Pine Ridge Agency), most people prefer to think of themselves as the people of Crazy Horse. Crazy Horse is the symbol of Sioux resistance and is considered to have been truly *wakaŋ* (spiritually powerful). His death at Fort Robinson resulted from the treachery of the whites and the collaborators in Red Cloud's "loafer camp" around the fort. Red Cloud, on the other hand, is now considered to have "sold out." He signed away the holy ground of the Black Hills with "a bunch of drunken teen-agers" acting as his basis for authority. He wanted to teach the Oglalas "civilization" (a word spoken with great scorn). Such accusations are still heard on the reservation; at a discussion among the old men (the "chiefs") in 1963, one bold man presented similar charges to Red Cloud's great-grandson. The polarization of Oglala history as personified by these two leaders often leads to historical reconstructions approaching fantasy. For example, I was told that Crazy Horse resisted intermarriage with whites while Red Cloud encouraged it at every turn (with implications of immoral unions as well). To continue this corruption of Indian blood, "Red Cloud and his mixed-bloods" were forced to assassinate Crazy Horse. "If he had lived there would be no breeds today."

The general image of Red Cloud conveniently forgets that he was reported to have held over one hundred coups, that he was a major figure in several military conflicts with the United States Army before the Little Big Horn fight, and that his actions as first leader of Pine Ridge Reservation amounted to a "cold war" against the agency superintendents (McGillycuddy 1941). He was described to me as "a nobody who was called chief because he did a lot of talking with the whites." [21] For most of the Oglalas the era of armed resistance is

[21] The exact nature of Red Cloud's chieftaincy has apparently been a source of debate ever since his ascendancy. The arguments in great measure stem from the complicated series of political offices among the prereservation Oglalas: a "chiefs' society" composed of the majority of able men over forty years of age, including seven "chiefs" (*wičaša itačaŋ* or "headmen") who appointed four *other* men as councilors ("shirt wearers") for life or until resignation. All of the above also annually elected four officers, or "chiefs" (*wakičuŋ*), with anyone but the "shirt wearers" being eligible. The *wakičuŋ* in turn appointed two orderlies and a camp herald to serve them and selected two "head policemen" (*akitčita itačaŋ*), who in turn picked two assistants. The four *akitčita* leaders then selected one of the men's societies, or eight to ten men from different societies, to serve as the policemen for the yearly encampment and mass buffalo hunt (Wissler 1912, pp. 7–10). It is doubtful that the agents of the federal government took notice of these complications, or that they proved efficient in the reservation situation. Mekeel (1932a) recorded several departures from this pattern in 1930, and considering the great flexibility shown in Lakota organizations, it is reasonable to presume earlier changes. In support of the "full-blood" view of Red Cloud as a "talker," Wissler reports:

> The last men to serve as *wakičuŋ* were, according to Running Hawk, Afraid-of-horse, American-horse, Crazy-horse, and George Sword. Red-cloud never held this office but was for many years a special official, or minister, to look after the dealings of the Indians and the white people. [1912, p. 8 n]

However, Wissler also notes that after the establishment of Pine Ridge Reservation, Red Cloud started a rival "chiefs' society" in order to justify his adoption of the idealized as the Battle of the Little Big Horn. Crazy Horse was there; Red Cloud was not.

Yet while Crazy Horse is thus a figure of Oglala separatism, he is also a major feature of American frontier history. His name is known to millions of American schoolchildren. His statue is now being carved into a mountainside in the Black Hills in proportions that will dwarf Mount Rushmore. With such men as Crazy Horse and the Hunkpapa Sitting Bull the Lakotas claim an important place in American history, and in a sense, the side they were on does not detract from this significance.

It is not easy, however, to rest on one's laurels when discussing contributions to the formation of America. This is particularly true for the Oglalas, who feel an estrangement from Crazy Horse and his contemporaries. Legitimation of a minority-group position in America is expressed in terms of "earning one's place." What, then, do the Oglalas have which can be viewed as a continuing contribution to the nation by both themselves and white America? What are their grounds for claiming a place in the nation?

The problem reduces itself quickly to two commodities possessed by the Oglalas and useful to the nation: land and people. By the nature of the cultural contact situation, land was never defined as a gift received by the whites. The question of land has always stood between the Sioux peoples and white society. But in the case of people, of human lives, the traditional cultural patterns of the Oglalas and of general America are compatible. Oglala attitudes toward warriors have found accommodation in American attitudes toward the war dead. It is in this narrow realm, the sacrifice of Indian men in the nation's wars, that the sentiment of Sioux Nationalism finds expression meaningful to all. The Oglalas are still bitter that part of their reservation was taken for a bombing range in World War II; they are proud that they joined the defense in human terms.

The Sioux National Anthem

The Lakotas' conception of America and their continuing contributions to it are expressed in a behavioral complex here called Sioux Nationalism. While the term may suggest something quite different from the actual sentiments involved, I have used it to *stress* these

---

symbols of leadership (ceremonial pipe bag, hair-trimmed shirt, etc.). At the same time Agent McGillycuddy was organizing the federal Indian police in order to undercut the power of the traditional *akitčita* structure, then controlled by Red Cloud.

differences. The Oglala themselves speak proudly of the "Sioux National Anthem." It was the first Sioux song I heard, the one I heard most frequently, and the one most often called to my attention. Among a people who so regularly blame the federal government for the destruction of all that was good in their past and for all that is bad in their present situation, the words are particularly significant:

> *Tuŋkašilayapi tawapaha kin,*
> President's flag the
>
> *ɔwihaŋko šni henajiŋ kte lo.*
> end without stands will
>
> *Iyohalateya oyate kiŋ haŋ, wičičagiŋ kta*
> Underneath people the is will continue to grow
>
> *ča lecamun welo.*
> therefore I have done that

The flag of the President of the United States will stand forever. Underneath it, the people will continue to flourish, now and in future generations. For this purpose have I done this.[22]

This song, in the Lakota dialect, was composed by Ellis Clisp of Wanblee, and was first sung in public at the conclusion of the sun dance celebration at Pine Ridge in 1955 (Feraca, personal communication). It is a song sung by a soldier going off to war (and, by implication, to die in the defense of his country). As was explained to me repeatedly, "It's not one particular soldier, but *all* soldiers." The nation referred to in the title is *both* the Sioux nation and the United States. The word *oyate* ("the people") is *not* restricted in meaning to just Indians. It is an expression of Sioux involvement as Americans. It is particularly interesting to note that the idealized motives of the

---

[22] The Lakota text and a rough translation were supplied by Matthew Two Bulls with the comment "This wording is full of meanings—I'll just give one." Word breaks were not included in the original and I have supplied them and attempted an interlineal translation as best as possible, using two inadequate dictionaries of the Dakota dialect (Riggs 1852; Williamson 1902). I have in a few places changed the orthography to be consistent with the other Lakota words appearing in this paper. There are several disagreements with the dictionaries concerning spelling, especially of vowels. This might be due to dialectal differences not fully noted in the dictionaries, to Matthew's incomplete control of the orthography, or to linguistic changes in this century. The first word, *tuŋkašilayapi*, means literally "everyone's grandfather" and is the term commonly used for the President of the United States. (Similarly, the superintendent of the reservation is referred to as *ateyapi*, from *ate:* "father.") The utterances *lo*, *welo*, and *yeeelo* are, I believe, indicators of the male oratorical style and add a sense of emphasis to the statements.

hypothetical singer are totally foreign to the motives of personal aggrandizement generally held to have inspired the Sioux warriors of former days. The words of this anthem refer to the main symbols of Sioux Nationalism, and its usage is closely correlated with other acts in this behavioral complex.

The Flag

The use of the American flag and its significance to the Oglalas have undergone a transition from its adoption as a trophy of war (as is so often depicted in paintings of "Custer's Massacre" and other battles). Although the exact changes in its significance cannot be dated, the continuity of its presence in Lakota ceremonial life is clearly demonstrated. An American flag appears painted on a tipi in a photograph dated about 1890 (Hassrick 1964, pp. 100 f.). It is clearly in evidence at celebrations in 1902 (Malan 1957) and a few years later (Densmore 1918, plate 78). Postcards of Oglala gatherings in the 1920s show the flag prominently displayed and painted on canvas tipis. It is likewise in evidence in many more recent photographs. Today the American flag is flown at every major outdoor dance. Along with other nationalistic symbols such as the eagle in Federalist style, it is a common design motif in the beadwork decorations of dance costumes. Today the flag is directly linked to the main theme of Sioux Nationalism: the war dead. During World War II the government presented a large American flag to each family which lost a man in the armed forces. These flags are, in a sense, symbolically equated with the lost man. At social dances there are often honorary songs to the dead servicemen, and their flags are re-presented to their families throughout the years. This brief ceremonial usually takes place during a pause in the regular dancing. It may, however, be combined with the lowering of the main flag at dusk. At this time the "Sioux National Anthem" is sung. After it is repeated a few times, the dancing starts again, and as the singers pick up the drum and walk toward the exit, continuing to sing, the dancers swarm out around them. Such "dance outs" mark the close of every afternoon and evening dance at the major celebration of the year, the sun dance powwow. In 1963 one of the largest sessions was ended with a tribute to Vincent Fast Horse, a sailor who died in the Pacific at the very close of World War II. The singers chosen for the honorary song and the anthem carried a drum painted "In memory of Vincent Fast Horse" with a large anchor in the middle. The flag was lowered (his flag had flown that day as a special tribute) and was presented by a pair of Oglala servicemen home on leave to the father and brothers of the deceased. None of the several hundred adults present was left unmoved.

While the American flag has taken on a very special significance for the Lakotas, they apparently have not made similar changes in attitude toward other flags. At the Pine Ridge sun dance parade of 1963, some visitors were shocked to see a truck filled with dancers and draped with an enormous Nazi swastika. It was a trophy.

The Fourth of July and the Sun Dance

The continuity of use and gradual shift in significance of the flag is part of a larger process in which the Lakotas have adopted the Fourth of July as a major ceremonial occasion of Sioux Nationalism. It is difficult to date the first Indian-organized celebrations of the Fourth, but they probably started after 1881, the year of the last Lakota sun dance for several decades (Densmore 1918, p. 4). Being forbidden to hold further sun dances, the Lakotas evidently started observing the Fourth as a time for great secular dances (though even these were occasionally prevented). Several writers have noticed the continuities with the earlier sun dance:

> There were few celebrations which [Pine Ridge and Rosebud Reservations] united in observing, one exception to this rule being the fourth of July—Ahn-páy-too wah-káhn táhn-ka, the Great Holy Day. This celebration [in 1900 at White River, Rosebud Reservation] lasted a full week and culminated in a sham battle commemorating the Custer Massacre.[23] [Kneale 1950, p. 63]
>
> An illustration of the continuity of the hospitality pattern is the annual Fourth of July celebration, which in some measure replaced the Sun Dance as a time to get together. [Malan 1956, p. 39]
>
> The greatest power was acknowledged them [the "committee," or functional replacements of the earlier *akitčita*] at the Fourth of July celebration held in the district itself. This is the only time the traditional camp circle is now used. This affair comes near the time of the former Sun Dance and arouses much talk of "old times." [Mekeel 1932a, p. 281]

Interestingly enough, Memorial Day, with its similar idealization of the casualties of war and its celebrations of social unity (Warner 1958) parallel to those of the great summer dances, is not celebrated extensively by the Oglalas. The adoption of the Fourth of July and not Memorial Day for celebrations may be explained by the fact that

---

[23] A present-day parallel is mentioned below, page 241.

the latter holiday originated in memory of the losses of the Grand Army of the Republic in 1868 and was not recognized as an official holiday in New York until 1873 and in Ohio until 1881 (Douglas 1937, p. 310). The memorial to the Union Army was not a very pertinent occasion in civilian life on the frontier, and in Dakota Territory (North and South Dakota achieved statehood in 1889) Memorial Day celebrations were probably not available to the Lakotas as an alternative to the sun dance.

The current Fourth of July celebrations consist of great secular dances (the Omaha or grass dances), which draw hundreds of people. As at smaller dances held throughout the summer, the symbols of Sioux Nationalism are everywhere in evidence, as are loudspeakers, pop bottles, tribal policemen, etc. The major celebration of the Fourth is marked by a series of brief flag ceremonies and honorary songs and dances.

Today the Fourth is not, however, the major event of the year. The ban on the sun dance was removed in the 1930s and the religious ceremony has been revived (Feraca 1963). The sun dance among the Oglalas is now celebrated each year in early August. The religious ceremony takes place on Thursday, Friday, and Saturday mornings, and draws a crowd of a few hundred onlookers including some whites: tourists, visitors to the reservation, interested government employees, and anthropologists. The real attraction of the encampment, however, is the powwow, or social dancing held in the afternoons and evenings, Thursday through Sunday. Hundreds of families camp around the dance area, creating a scene reminiscent of the great encampments of the nineteenth century.[24] Thousands more come in the afternoons and evenings by car. On Saturday and Sunday nights the crowds are enormous; as many as five hundred costumed male dancers may be in the arena at one time with hundreds of women and girls joining in.

---

[24] The tents are arranged in small groups of related and interacting households, each being placed in the same position each year. These groupings are generally similar to the local groupings or communities of the rural residences, but not exactly so. The communities were originally settled by bands (*tiyošpayepi*), but the allotment act requiring that families live on their own land holdings has scattered many of these *tiyošpayepi* over large areas. Further, the complexities of land inheritance have caused people to move geographically, while the social ties have not always shifted. I suspect, therefore, that the households clustered together at the sun dance encampment more closely approximate the former *tiyošpayepi* in sociological pattern than do the year-round local residence groupings. Unfortunately, no one has done a tent-by-tent survey during a major encampment.

Indians from other Sioux reservations and from other Plains tribes come hundreds of miles to take part. There are special events throughout the celebration: the parade, solo dances, dance contests, the selection of Miss Pine Ridge (including costume judging and "old" and "new" style dance contests and a give-away the next day by the winner's family), buffalo feasts for all who come (hundreds), incessant visiting, and much more. A full night's sleep on the camp grounds is unheard of.

Although the more assimilated "mixed-bloods" look upon such celebrations as backward and are accordingly neither present nor missed, the great celebration is ostensibly open to all who wish to take part. Friction may develop between the "true believers" (who participate in the religious observance) and the tribal council committeemen (who have advertised it as a "reenactment") during the morning, but at the social dancing all internal disagreements and invidious distinctions are put aside. The sun dance powwow is the demonstrable proof that an Oglala society continues to exist. And at this time the sentiments of Sioux Nationalism are given their fullest expression: the Oglalas are fully American while continuing to be distinct.

The American Legion

To further stress the balance between the unique (Indian) and the national (American) aspects of Sioux Nationalism, I will turn to a discussion of the organization which is in some sense the curator of the symbols: the Sam White Bear Post of the American Legion. The contrasts with the Legion post in the nearby farm town of Martin are striking.

The Pine Ridge Legion hall burned down in 1959 or 1960 but the charred rubble was cleared away only several years later. The farm community post operates in a large brick building which dominates their town's main street. It is the social center for the county's permanent residents. Its parties are the only "night life" acceptable to its middle-class membership, which includes the prominent people of the county. The members are frequently involved in Legion activities on a greater geographic and social scale. They receive the Legion magazine containing commentary on national and international issues.

The Sam White Bear Post deals not in greater social interaction but in the symbols of greater Oglala identification. The post maintains honor rolls of veterans in each of the reservation towns. It provides leadership in flag ceremonies at dances. It turns out for funerals of veterans. It is not a political force; membership is not a sign of economic position; it is not a "fun" organization. The closest it came to holding a recreational outing was the staging of the capture of a Japanese flag, complete with the firing of blank ammunition, prior to a community dance. The flag was then flown over one of the victors' wall tents much like a scalp on a tipi pole of old. The mock battle was quite enjoyable, but apparently was staged to impress as well as to amuse the crowd.

At the end of the summer of 1963 I had the unpleasant opportunity to witness two burials. Both were Episcopal services, but at one the Legion was dominant; it was the burial of a veteran. The Legion provided a color guard and a four-man rifle squad (who also acted as gravediggers and pallbearers), a bugler, and about a dozen boy scouts (Indian). American flags were flown at the deceased's house and at the chapel. They were carried by the honor guard and by the boy scouts. A flag was draped over the coffin. Throughout the day, from the gathering of friends at the home to the end of the graveside service, the Legion members made great efforts to observe proper military style. The fact that the khaki uniforms did not match, that two of the rifles were actually hunting guns, and that the responses to the drill commands were bumbling did not matter. The post had obviously gone to the limit of its resources. The Legion's finest moment came when it folded the flag over the coffin and presented it to the widow (who once again broke into sobbing and wailing) with the words "The Sam White Bear Post of the American Legion proudly presents you with the flag which our comrade John served under." Yet for all the attempts at a correct military funeral, there were elements of the ceremony, including those involving the Legion, which were common to the funeral of the nonveteran and cannot be dismissed as either Christian or general American influences. At the end of the grave side service, the veterans lowered the coffin into a pine box and put the lid in place. One legionnaire then stood on the box and nailed it closed. The grave was then filled in as rapidly as possible, with the legionnaires replacing each other at the shovels as soon as one of them showed signs of slowing up. When this was completed, the deceased's thirteen-year-old son, now the man of the household, paid each of the diggers twenty-five cents, just as the brother of the nonveteran had paid his friends who had done the same. The ceremony was then over.

Sioux Nationalism is a symbolic, group behavior pattern. I did not see any of its symbols in domestic contexts. At John's funeral it was not relevant that his large family had been supported by his father's old age checks or that his death resulted from a drunken brawl among Indians in a white farm town. Similarly, there is a disparity (as in America generally) between the image of war portrayed by the symbols and the accounts of the individual veterans. The veterans I had talked with had told the usual stories of how much they drank, of the blondes in Paris, and the fears they felt in combat in Italy or in some remote Pacific jungle. There were stories of their friends in the army, of how everyone called them "chief," and of Indians from other tribes in their barracks. There was no mention of why they were at war, no mention of fascism or democracy. There were stories of personal wounds but no mention of overall victory or defeat. The personal realities and the group symbolism are two distinct realms. The Oglala Legion Post and the sentiments of Sioux Nationalism are explicitly involved only in the latter.

The above description pertains to events in 1961 and 1963. A brief visit to Pine Ridge for the Fourth of July celebration in 1969 indicates that some of the attitudes associated with Sioux Nationalism are changing. The reason for the differences is the nature of the war in Viet Nam. Today, Sioux warriors are again returning home in government-issued pine boxes. New flags are being presented to bereaved relatives. The flag ceremonies, the speeches and prayers, the give-away ceremonies, and the words of the "Sioux National Anthem" have an immediacy which heightens their meaning. But many Sioux, for much the same reasons as other Americans, feel deeply discontent with the war: several young men from Pine Ridge have been killed, while appropriations for local programs started as part of the war on poverty have now been cut off. People on Pine Ridge Reservation were reluctant to discuss their feelings at length, and it was difficult to gauge the extent of such discontent. But perhaps the contradictions many find in trying to confirm one's identity through Sioux Nationalism in the present situation were well expressed by one woman while watching a new flag presentation: "Most of the people here don't like the war at all, (pause) but they don't like those Indian boys who are draft dodgers either."

VI. Concluding Remarks

This paper has tried to describe how various labels of the cultural identity of American Indians are applied on one reservation, starting with the overt use of concrete words and ending with the expression of implicit general symbols. An understanding of the more general terms is possible only in light of the very elusive usage of the more restricted terms. A study of current conditions on Pine Ridge and similar reservations must deal simultaneously with the tensions between exclusion and inclusion both in social structure and in the evaluation of cultural traits. An approach which places observable behavioral data within the conceptual context makes it possible to analyze many of the *apparent* contradictions in the actions of this heterogeneous population. Seen from this point of view, the Pine Ridge situation is neither static nor one in which one cultural system slowly but inexorably undoes and partially replaces another. Instead, this approach reveals a situation in which people are experiencing both change and continuity by seeking their identities in both narrower and broader terms, often at the same time. Contradiction in both thought and action is a very real aspect of reservation life. The data presently available allow only a limited view of the complexities which lie behind even the seemingly simple facts of daily life. Yet it is clear that if a neat answer cannot be furnished here to the perennial question, What is an Indian? it is in part due to the fact that the answer is still a struggle for the Oglalas themselves.

REFERENCES

BARNES, J. A. 1951. History in a changing society. In *Human problems in British Africa*, vol. 3, pp. 1–9. Lusaka, Northern Rhodesia (Zambia): Rhodes-Livingstone Institute. Reprinted in *Cultures and societies of Africa*, ed. Simon and Phoebe Ottenberg, pp. 318–27. New York: Random House.

DENSMORE, FRANCES. 1918. *Teton Sioux music*. Bulletin of the Bureau of American Ethnology no. 61. Washington, D.C.: G.P.O.

DOUGLAS, GEORGE W. 1937. *The American book of days*. New York: H. W. Wilson Co. Revised by Helen Douglas Compton, 1948.

ERIKSON, E. 1950. Childhood and society. New York: Norton.

FERACA, STEPHEN E. 1963. *Wakinyan: Contemporary Teton Dakota religion*. Browning, Mont.: Bureau of Indian Affairs, Blackfeet Agency.

FERACA, STEPHEN E., AND HOWARD, JAMES H. 1963. The identity and demography of the Dakota or Sioux tribes. *Plains Anthropologist* 8: 80–84.

HAGAN, EVERETT, AND SCHAW, LOUIS C. 1960. The Sioux on the reservation. Mimeo. Massachusetts Institute of Technology Center for International Studies.

HALLOWELL, A. IRVING. 1963. American Indians, white and black: The phenomenon of transculturation. *Current Anthropology* 4: 519–30.

HASSRICK, ROYAL B. 1964. *The Sioux*. Norman: University of Oklahoma Press.

Home of the Oglala Sioux. 1963. Mimeo. Pine Ridge, S. Dak.: Bureau of Indian Affairs.

HOWARD, JAMES H. 1960. The cultural position of the Dakota: A reassessment. In *Essays in the science of culture*, ed. G. E. Dole and R. L. Carneiro. New York: Thomas Y. Crowell Co.

JAMES, BERNARD J. 1961. Social-psychological dimensions of Ojibwa acculturation. *American Anthropologist* 63: 721–46.

KNEALE, ALBERT H. 1950. *Indian agent*. Caldwell, Ida.: Caxton Printers.

McGILLYCUDDY, JULIA B. 1941. *McGillycuddy, agent*. Palo Alto, Calif.: Stanford University Press.

MALAN, VERNON D. 1957. A changing Dakota Indian culture—comparison of the 1902 and 1956 Fourth of July celebrations reveals some changes. *South Dakota Farm and Home Research* 8: 11–15.

MEKEEL, H. SCUDDER. 1932. A discussion of culture change as illustrated by material from a Teton-Dakota community. *American Anthropologist* 34: 274–85.

———. 1936. *The economy of a modern Teton Dakota community*. Yale University Publication in Anthropology no. 6.

———. 1943. A short history of the Teton-Dakota. *North Dakota Historical Quarterly* 10: 137–205.

NEIHARDT, JOHN G. 1932. *Black Elk speaks*. New York: William Morrow and Co. Reprinted Lincoln: University of Nebraska Press, 1961.

RIGGS, STEPHEN R. 1852. *Grammar and dictionary of the Dakota language*. Smithsonian Contributions to Knowledge, vol. 4. Washington, D.C.: G.P.O.

———. 1893. *Dakota grammar, tests and ethnography*. Contributions to American Ethnology, vol. 9. Washington, D.C.: G.P.O.

SCHUSKY, ERNEST. 1960. The Lower Brule Sioux. Ph.D. dissertation, University of Chicago.

TAX, SOL. 1961. What the Indians want. *Chicago Sun-Times*, June 11, 1961.

USEEM, RUTH HILL. 1947. The aftermath of defeat: A study of acculturation among the Rosebud Sioux of South Dakota. Ph.D. dissertation, University of Wisconsin.

WALKER, J. R. 1917. *The sun dance and other ceremonies of the Oglala division of the Teton Sioux*. Anthropological Papers of the American Museum of Natural History, vol. 16, part 2. New York.

WARNER, W. LLOYD. 1958. An American sacred ceremony. In *Reader in comparative religion*, ed. William A. Lessa and Evon Z. Vogt. Evanston, Ill.: Row, Peterson and Co.

WAX, MURRAY, WAX, ROSALIE H., AND DUMONT, ROBERT V. 1964. Formal education in an American Indian community. *Social problems* (Supplement) 11, no. 4.

WILCOX, LLOYD. 1942. Group structure and personality types among the Sioux Indians of North Dakota. Ph.D. dissertation, University of Wisconsin.

WILLIAMSON, JOHN P. 1902. *An English-Dakota dictionary.* New York: American Tract Society.

WISSLER, CLARK. 1912. *Societies and ceremonial associations in the Oglala division of the Teton-Dakota.* Anthropological Papers of the American Museum of Natural History, vol. 11, part 1. New York.

Familial and Extra-Familial Socialization in Urban Dakota Adolescents[1]

L. S. Kemnitzer

I

FOR A LONG TIME American Indians have been trickling into the San Francisco Bay Area as part of the polyglot population. Indian population in the city was insignificant before 1955, when an office of the Voluntary Relocation Program of the Bureau of Indian Affairs opened in Oakland, across the bay from San Francisco. A second office opened in San Francisco the next year, and a third a year later in San Jose, seventy miles south but still in the metropolitan area. In 1961 the Indian population was estimated at ten thousand, and public agencies were taking notice of their presence.

Continuing poverty, increasing population, and few immediately practical economic programs for many reservations were some of the reasons for the Voluntary Relocation Program, which, essentially, presented to individuals and families the opportunity of removal to

[1] This paper is based on data gathered as part of a larger study of American Indian Urban Integration, J. A. Hirabayashi, Director, at San Francisco State College. The investigation was supported by a P.H.S. research grant (MH 05628) from the National Institute of Mental Health. Part of this paper was part of a presentation in a seminar in social organization with Dr. D. Gamble, San Francisco State College. Thanks are due the above and Dr. I. Kopytoff, Dr. E. Nurge, and Dr. R. H. Useem for reading and criticizing earlier versions of this paper.

industrial areas. This program paid the costs of transportation to the city, subsistence and medical care for a limited time, and some counseling services. Later the Area Vocational Training Act augmented this program by providing support to study at selected trade schools. The more or less explicit assumption behind these programs was that Indians who moved to the city would become in effect part of the dominant society and no longer be part of the "Indian problem." In spite of economic, psychological and moral hardships, many relocated Indians have become economically self-sufficient. However, very few of them have disappeared as Indians.

This paper is based on data gathered as part of a two-and-a-half-year study of American Indian urban integration, directed by Dr. James Hirabayashi, San Francisco State College, and supported by a research grant from the National Institute of Mental Health. While the overall study focused on the structure of the adult community, another interesting question had to do with the permanence of this community and raised these more general questions: Are Indian communities becoming continuous, viable, self-sustaining communities comparable to those of other national and language groups, or are they transitional enclaves? Further, are there forces which can be identified as operating in one or the other direction? It was hoped that an examination of the position of Indian children after extended residence in the city and exposure to the influence of the urban environment as contrasted to the traditional family environment not only would throw light on these questions but would also contribute to an understanding of the differentiation of cross-generational and intra-generational socialization.

The overall study was an investigation of urbanization processes in all the major tribes relocating in the Bay Area; these included Navajo, Kiowa, Pueblo tribes, Oklahoma tribes, Northwest Coast tribes, Eskimos, and California Indians, as well as Sioux. A demographic questionnaire, administered by a staff of workers, was the core of this study; but during the field period, I worked especially with the Sioux and conducted unstructured interviews, observed and participated in picnics, formal and informal meetings of organizations, visits, drinking parties, and religious observances, and made two field trips to the Rosebud and Pine Ridge Reservations in South Dakota for the same kind of observation among returned migrants and among relatives of relocated Sioux. Supplementary and supporting data were provided by official and unofficial agencies, among them the Bureau of Indian

Affairs Relocation Offices on the Pine Ridge and Rosebud Reservations and in Oakland, San Francisco, and San Jose; the Alameda
County Health Department; the American Friends Service Committee Intertribal Friendship House; the Indian Affairs Committee
of the Episcopal Church, San Francisco; and the American Indian
Council of the Bay Area.

Official records alone do not adequately describe the size or location
of the Dakota population in the Bay Area. A provisional list made
from these records and from information provided by formal and
informal Dakota leaders was shown to all persons interviewed and the
information crosschecked and augmented. Information concerning
kinship and friendship ties was also collected at this time. About
three hundred units were located, half of which were contacted in
one way or another. Eighty-six of these units—families or single
people—were selected for more extended interviewing, and they form
the sample. Investigation focused on processes of group formation, and
a questionnaire was developed to explore sources, kinds, and objects
of aid; standards for admitting or excluding people to aid circles; and
reasons for respecting people. Adolescents and young adults who had
spent a major part of their adolescence in the Bay Area were also
interviewed concerning their experiences growing up in the city.

The general hypothesis to be examined in this paper is as follows:
The self-identity and the identification of Dakota children in the city
is a resultant of (1) the family membership and economic ties of the
parents in the home culture; (2) the relevance to urban living of social
and cultural skills transmitted by the parents; and (3) the degree of
acceptance in, and satisfaction from, preadolescent and adolescent
peer groups. A unitary approach to the Dakota population in the
San Francisco Bay Area, as well as the sample under consideration,
is complicated by the fact that the Sioux have undergone a complex
acculturation process over the last hundred years.

Characteristics of the Dakota population in the Bay Area will be
described first, followed by a description of the sample of adolescents
and their families in terms of the variables mentioned above, and
finally this evidence will be discussed and some further hypotheses
suggested.

II. The Population in the Bay Area

Dakota occupations run the gamut from veterinarian or psychologist
to tree-trimmer or casual laborer, but are predominantly semiskilled

or skilled. Less than a fifth of Dakota migrants are unskilled or unemployed, in contrast to the three-fourths who were unskilled upon arrival. Almost all migrants are woven into a network that reaches throughout the Sioux and Indian population. Various needs are met and services exchanged by members of overlapping kinship and visiting groups and formal and informal associations. This allows, for example, an individual who possesses traditionally valued skills but who is poorly adapted to city life by Euro-American industrial standards, to be protected and aided in city living by kin and associates who are more knowing in "white ways." Prestige accrues to both parties from being known as one who "helps people."

Thus although separated geographically, the Dakota residents have a high rate of visiting and mutual aid in the Bay Area which contributes to a fairly cohesive community. Different modes of adjustment to demands of urban living and different kinds and amounts of traditionally valued skills contribute to an interdependent system. This system is selectively open to the larger, urban system, on the one hand, and to the reservation system on the other hand.

Dakota social life revolves around informal but often ritualized visiting, patronizing "Indian bars" and attendance at celebrations. Celebrations are held intermittently. The bars are open every day and are regularly attended with varying frequency by a large proportion of the Indian community, new arrivals and old settlers alike. The Indian bar serves as a communication center; a place to borrow money, a car, or tools; a place to find someone to repair a car, or to get advice about city life; and in general to keep in contact with friends and associates. One's presence in a bar does not necessarily imply heavy drinking. Nondrinkers patronize bars for the sociability and consume soft drinks, and one pitcher of beer can serve a couple for an evening of entertainment.

Since the clientele of the Indian bars is neither exclusively Sioux nor exclusively Indian, and some patrons tend to move from bar to bar in an evening of drinking, the bars also serve as a door to a sector of the dominant urban white society. While two bars are managed by Indians, other bars are owned or managed by whites who hire Indian bartenders. One white owner of two bars serves as a bank for regular patrons and hires Indians as maintenance men in his real estate business, and another hires Indians as drivers in his hauling business. Thus the Indian bartender or barmaid becomes a focal person in the pan-Indian network.

At least one celebration per month throughout the year seems to be the pattern in the Bay Area (as of 1965), although they are held more often in the winter and early spring because summer is the time for traveling the powwow circuit in the Middle West and high Plains. Celebrations are sponsored by formal organizations, informal groups, and individuals, on the occasion of a birthday or the arrival or departure of a relative. The most prominent private sponsor of celebrations in the Bay Area has been a Kiowa, although music is provided by a group that includes Sioux, and Sioux attend to dance or watch.

Formal organizations include non-Indian organizations such as the Intertribal Friendship House sponsored by the American Friends Service Committee, the Four Winds Club sponsored by the YWCA, an Indian Alcoholics Anonymous club, and an Episcopal American Indian Committee. Autochthonous organizations include the Santa Clara American Indian Council, the American Indian Council of the Bay Area, and athletic teams. Other organizations exist, but are of minimal importance to Sioux life, for example, two missions to the American Indians of the Southern Baptist Church, a Muskogee church, tribal organizations, and more or less specialized activities by other churches.

These organizations serve a number of functions: as gathering places for Indians of different tribes; to aid in communication with urban social services (the Intertribal Friendship House and the Episcopal American Indian Committee each employ a full-time social worker); to provide intertribal organizational experience; to provide services and the exchange of services within the population; and as foci for tribal organizations and specialized groups such as ladies' clubs, dance clubs, or young adult clubs. Sioux have been prominent in pan-Indian formal organizations, either taking visible active leadership and communicating roles, or playing less noticeable but supportive roles of visiting and behind-the-scenes communication. Nevertheless, although other tribes are reasonably successful in forming tribal organizations, formal Sioux clubs have never lasted beyond the first meeting.

Although visiting rates are generally higher within socio-economic classes, the intermittently employed working-class Sioux and those on welfare are regular visitors with steady working-class and upward-aspiring Sioux. The former are thus part-time employees, semidependents, and providers of news and tradition. One comment that has been made a significant number of times by steadily employed working-class and upward-aspiring Sioux is "My rule is to help a person out two times. If he can't take care of himself after that it's his problem." However, in practice, the same respondent is apt to help out the same person time after time, with the loan of a truck to perform a casual hauling job, a short painting contract, emergency food, baby-sitting jobs, or rides to celebrations or social gatherings. People of all classes may provide temporary shelter to visiting or migrating kinsmen, who may include cousins of the third or fourth degree, or schoolmates or relatives of schoolmates. The social and mutual-aid groups tend to reinforce attention on reservation affairs. Many respondents make regular trips to either the husband's or the wife's home reservation, or both.

The general mobility of the Sioux is epitomized in the remark of a self-relocated machinist, a conservative who returned after a year's residence:

> In the old days we used to go to Nebraska, to Rapid City, to earn money, and come home. Nowadays it doesn't take much longer to come out to the coast. That's what the Indians are doing. San Francisco now is just like Rapid City was in the old days.

Although the main reason for relocation is economic, others may relocate to make a fresh start after trouble with the law or the family, to escape boredom, or to escape discrimination in the white-dominated towns on and near the reservation. No matter what the reason for migration, migrants had traveled widely before moving to the Bay Area, and their parents had traveled widely before them. New relocatees, people returning to the reservation, visitors to and from the reservation, and perennial travelers between the reservations and one or more cities, all are the personnel in a continuing urban-reservation Dakota system.

"It seems like we've gotten more Indian since we came out here" is a common remark of Dakotas living in the city, many of whom are characterized by more traditional Sioux as "not hardly Indian at all." In the city they become involved in Indian organizations and discover that being an Indian is an asset, in contrast to the liability that it is in towns near the reservation. Some aspects of culture have to be relearned; some aspects have to be learned for the first time; and children tend to get interested one way or another in either pan-Indian affairs or reservation affairs, or both. The daughter of one family shocked her aunt on the reservation when she wanted to go to a celebration. "We never go to Indian dances here; they're just for the full-bloods," said her aunt. The tensions between factions tend to become reduced in the city, where the two meet more or less on equal terms, but the mistrust and condescension are under the surface, to reappear upon the Indians' return to the reservation. Pan-Indianism is also evident in the fact that while 11 percent of known Sioux marriages are cross-tribal, better than half of them were contracted on relocation, in one city or another. Still, the majority of couples are both Sioux.

Leadership in Indian activities in the city entails an interest in reservation affairs to the extent that urban leaders apparently feel that their leadership must be validated by traditional reservation symbols. An example of this kind of behavior is provided by a prominent dancer in the Pine Ridge sun dance, who has been living for a number of years in Southern California, where he moved under the relocation program. He visits his son in the Bay Area regularly—and incidentally visits prominent Sioux and intertribal gatherings. One of the prominent Bay Area pan-Indian leaders intended to dance in the sun dance in 1964, but was torn by doubts based on religious conflict.

Although a majority of Sioux interviewed reported that half or more of their friends were non-Indians, most of them said they "feel more comfortable" with other Indians, some respondents restricting their contacts only to other Sioux and a few seeing only relatives. The same is not true for the children. While adults tend to socialize with other Indians, whites, or nonwhite non-Negro minorities, children tend to orient toward "nonwhite other" as a result of isolation from other Indians, discrimination on the part of teachers and students, and a dissonance in interaction patterns between whites, Indians, and Negroes. This problem will be examined in detail in the following section.

III. Description of the Sample

The Parents

Tables 1 to 3 demonstrate the orientation of Dakota children in relation to class and relocation status of parents, traditional or non-traditional background of parents, and occupation of parents. In these tables numbers refer to households, and numbers in parentheses refer to number of children. "White," "Indian," and "Mexican" refer to the primary orientation of the children in terms of friends,

TABLE 1

CLASS AND RELOCATION STATUS OF PARENTS AND ORIENTATION OF
CHILDREN

Type of Relocation and Class	Orientation of children			
	White	*Indian*	*Mexican*	*Mixed*
Self-Relocated				
Middle-class	4 (5)	0	0	0
Working-class	1 (3)	1 (2)	0	2 (4)
Government-Relocated				
Middle-class	0	0	0	0
Working-class	0	2 (7)	3 (8)	1 (3)

language, and self-identification, without regard to class subculture. "Mixed" means that the children are involved in groups of Indians and non-Indians, or that some of the children in a family are white-oriented and some are Indian-oriented.

Explored in this way, neither the family background nor the relevance of the skills of the parents to urban living can give an explicit picture of the processes involved in adolescent socialization. Instead, we shall focus on the context of the transmission of these skills and examine the attitudes of parents toward the relevance of their tradition to modern life. It is assumed that if the parents reject Dakota tradition they will not try to expose their children to it, or at least will discourage Indian association. Acceptance or rejection of Indian culture is generally expressed in two ways: in behavior and precept, and in friendships and associations. Accordingly, five logical categories can be set up: (1) parents who teach aspects of Sioux heritage by precept and example and who actively associate with other Indians, (2) parents who associate with other Indians but do not try to transmit

TABLE 2

TRADITION OF PARENTS AND ORIENTATION OF CHILDREN

Orientation of Parents	Orientation of Children			
	White	*Indian*	*Mexican*	*Mixed*
Traditional	0	1 (3)	1 (5)	2 (5)
Nontraditional	2 (3)	2 (6)	0	0
Mo traditional	3 (6)	0	0	0
Fa traditional	1 (4)	0	1 (2)	2 (5)
Unknown	1 (1)	0	1 (1)	0

TABLE 3

OCCUPATION OF PARENT AND ORIENTATION OF CHILDREN

Occupation of Parents	Orientation of Children			
	White	*Indian*	*Mexican*	*Mixed*
Semiprofessional	4 (5)	0	0	0
Skilled	1 (3)	2 (6)	0	2 (5)
Steady semiskilled	2 (6)	1 (3)	0	0
Unskilled	0	0	2 (7)	0
Unemployed	0	0	1 (1)	1 (3)

native traditions or values, (3) parents who teach aspects of tradition but do not associate with other Indians, (4) parents who reject Indian associations and values, and (5) parents who differ. Table 4 summarizes the relation of these categories to the orientation of the children.

Apparently the association pattern of the parents is important in the development of white orientation in the offspring, but is not as determinant in the development of Indian orientation. This will be examined in more detail.

Three of the four families in the first category will be discussed in the following section, but here we can note that both parents in the fourth family came from families associated with a Protestant proselytizing church. The father's family was more traditional, and included a prominent churchman and active seekers after tradition. The family visits the home reservation regularly, and one daughter is in a religious school for Indian girls. The parents are both involved in Indian oganizations in the Bay Area, including formal and informal organizations and an Indian Alcoholics Anonymous club. The two sons divide their interests and associations between Indian and non-Indian friends. The older son, a skilled worker in the same trade as his

TABLE 4

TRANSMISSION OF TRADITION AND ORIENTATION OF CHILDREN

Transmission of Tradition	Orientation of Children			
	White	*Indian*	*Mexican*	*Mixed*
Association plus tradition	0	2 (7)	0	2 (5)
Association only	0	1 (2)	3 (8)	1 (3)
Tradition only	3 (7)	0	0	0
Rejectors	2 (2)	0	0	0
Divided	2 (5)	0	0	0

father, is actively integrated in the "sporting" section of the Indian community, and is married to a non-Indian. He lives near his father and rides to work with him. The younger son has attended one year of college, during which time he was active in sports and student organizations, and he plans to return to college after a tour of Europe. He lives with his family and helps with household chores, but goes elsewhere for recreation and social contact. He has also been active at one time or another in the autochthonous pan-Indian organizations previously mentioned, and he tried unsuccessfully to start a youth group. The mother's father, a retired minister, lives with the family, and the mother, father, and mother's father are respected in the Indian and the white community. The mother complains that she has lost control over her sons since the move to the Bay Area and says the older son will have to work out his drinking problem himself.

Association with other Indians (primarily Sioux, but also including Chippewas, Nez Percés, Salishans, Winnebagos, Choctaws, and Apaches) but without active transmission of tradition characterize the people in category two. In two of the five families the father is absent. One of the Mexican-oriented families is discussed in more detail in the next section. The oldest daughter of one family dropped out of school at the age of fifteen and has six siblings under twelve, not included in this study. Her father has not been in the household for two years, since he became a traveler between South Dakota and the Bay Area, and in that period the family has depended on relief for subsistence. The mother denied Indian association in an interview, but her close neighbor is a Dakota woman in the same position, and other Dakota respondents relate much visiting with her. The second family is one of the earliest arrivals under the government relocation program. Both parents are traditional, and the father, who is disabled as a result of a war injury and a recent automobile accident, does not work regularly. The father spends most of his time with Indians (Dakotas, California Indians, and Southwestern tribes), and the few contacts outside the immediate family that the mother maintains are with other Sioux. There are five children in the family: the two sons, twenty-two and seventeen, are steady industrial workers, the older married to a Mexican-American, the younger leaving high school in the last year; the oldest daughter married a Mexican after she had attended a city college trade course and worked briefly; the youngest two daughters are still in high school, with their primary orientation toward Mexicans. The younger son still lives with the parents, and the married children visit often. Friends of the children visit them at the parents' apartment, and every interview was accompanied by music and interaction with these friends. The father speaks Lakota more fluently than the mother; and when asked about the children's language, the mother said they should learn Spanish.

The parents of the two Indian-oriented boys are government workers who raised the boys in the Bay Area and returned to South Dakota with them after a long period in California. The boys came to San Francisco on the government vocational training program and quickly became involved in the "sporting set" of the Indian young adult community. Most of the members of this group are young single trainees, living in boarding houses or rooming houses and focusing their social life around the ten all-Indian athletic teams, the San Francisco Indian Center (formerly sponsored by St. Vincent de Paul Society, now sponsored by the autochthonous American Indian Council of the Bay Area), and some of the Indian bars. Although Navajos are underrepresented, all tribes, from Eskimo to Eastern Cherokee, are represented in this group, which is also the source of most of the cross-tribal marriages in the city.

After a short marriage to a non-Indian, the older brother was active for a time in the sporting set, and left the area for another city. The younger brother had taken an accounting course but claimed that the course of instruction sponsored by the training program did not leave him qualified for a job. He has become active in a politically oriented pan-Indian organization, is marrying a girl from another tribe, and is looking for a job as an office worker, meanwhile working as a strike-breaker. He has learned to "dance Indian" since his return to the Bay Area and says he is learning the language also.

The three "mixed" young men are in the service and were not available for interview; however, their mother and associates say that when they visit, they divide their time between Indian and non-Indian associates. Their parents are separated, the mother living in the city, the father traveling between the Bay Area and South Dakota. The mother is a respected, if peripheral, member of a cross-tribal informal association focusing around two bars frequented almost exclusively by Indians. Although the parents of all these families are actively involved in the Indian community in one way or another, the parents in three families have said explicitly that "Indian ways" have no relevance for modern times.

Fathers in two families in category three are skilled workers with minimal contact with the Indian community; the father of the third family is a high-level civil service employee. One of the mothers, herself a skilled worker, says, "It's funny, but I just don't want to be around my own people." Her children, still in high school, are planning to go to college. The parents do not systematically transmit their tradition and do not speak Lakota, although they know the language; but since they experienced discrimination in South Dakota, they say they teach their children to stand up for themselves and to be proud they are Indians. The father in this family has been in a wheelchair for nine years and the activities of the family have been organized around his rehabilitation. Both the children are involved in their high school, which is in a suburban community; there are other Indians going to the school, but they don't know them. The family makes yearly visits to the reservation, but the children are not interested beyond the pleasant country experience and abstract history.

The oldest son of the next family is taking college courses while in his last year of high school, and his younger sisters are interested in college, one of them wanting to be a surgical nurse. The father is an orphan; the mother is connected to a politically prominent family on the reservation, also wealthy in land, and the family makes yearly visits. The father is a skilled worker, and the early years of the marriage were spent in sending the father to school to learn his trade and in subsequent apprenticeship, at the same time supporting two of the wife's cousins through school. The mother is a skilled office worker but was not working at the time. The children attend high school in a primarily middle-class residential community, although they live in a government housing project. Both parents speak Lakota and the children know "a few words." The children have no Indian associations in the city, although they look forward to the yearly visits to the home reservation and the son has become interested in tribal affairs. Although the parents say they are proud of their heritage and try to tell their children to be proud, the mother is concerned about the heavy drinking and disorganization evident on the reservation and in the Indian community in the city; and as a result, the parents' only contact with Indians in the city beyond infrequent attendance at public affairs is the weekly visit with the wife's cousin, who lives in another housing project five miles away.

A college senior majoring in social science has never seen her parents' reservations, and she has had only one Indian friend, from another tribe, in the time she was growing up. Her mother made sure that she read books about Indians "instead of the usual fairy tales," and she says she knows she is genetically Indian but feels no emotional ties with other Indians. However, she has a formal association with a pan-Indian service organization and has intensified Indian contacts since the end of the research period.

The fourth category contains two middle-class families, in one of which the father is absent. The parents disparage their Indian background and maintain that they have been successful according to white middle-class standards in spite of their ancestry and heritage. The offspring are going to college, or have graduated, and have no affiliation with the Indian community or Indian tradition. Their lack of visibility, either as Indians or as "nonwhite other," aids in their integration into the dominant society.

In both families in the last category, the father is interested in Indian culture and his people, while the mother disparages her past. The children in both families are white-oriented, and four have married Anglos: the daughter of the professional is married to a businessman, the children of the industrial worker to working-class spouses; one is a serviceman. The daughter of the professional doesn't understand why her father dresses in costume and goes to Indian dances and still associates with nonprofessional Indians and relatives who just depend on him. Both parents in the second family work in industrial jobs, the mother as a machine operator, the father as shift foreman in a chemical plant. Following the example of the mother, the children do not hesitate to chide the father about his "Indianness." This family has lived off the reservation since marriage, first when the father was working in another state, and later following the father's army moves. Now the only Indian contacts the family has are with the mother's relatives, who live two hours' drive away, and the rare visits to the reservation are unsatisfactory for the mother and the children. Of four adolescents in the family, three did not finish high school, and the youngest, who is thirteen, is moving toward taking an adult role, working at his mother's place of employment.

The Children

So far, I have looked at some of the characteristics of families of teen-agers. Now the focus shifts to the offspring and their social environment. Since the offspring have not been interviewed as extensively as their parents, a few representatives will be discussed in relation to the hypotheses in the introduction. Some general characteristics of this sample can be seen in Table 5.

TABLE 5

AGE OF CHILD WHEN FAMILY LEFT RESERVATION ACCORDING TO
EDUCATION STATUS OF CHILD

Education	Age Group		
	0–6	7–12	Over 12
College	2	0	4
High School Graduate	6	2	6
Student	3	11	0
Dropout	1	4	0

J., a college student, spent most of his life on or near his mother's home reservation in a state near his father's home reservation (his father is a Sioux, his mother enrolled in another tribe, and he is legally enrolled in his mother's tribe). He went to public schools near the reservation and graduated from high school in San Francisco. His mother belongs to a wealthy and influential family on her home reservation, and his father's family is also wealthy in land that is successfully grazed and in employment. The father has been a steadily employed skilled worker, both before and after relocation. J. doesn't say much about his high school experiences. During the time he was in San Francisco in high school, and especially in the two years he was attending a local college, he followed his parents' example in being active in pan-Indian organizations for youth. He was one of the organizing circle of a youth organization, and he attended adult white-sponsored conferences. But now, two years later, he thinks they were ineffectual. He says pan-Indianism works to some extent in the city but not on the reservation, which is where the main problems of the Indians lie: although the material culture and externals may be smoothed out, the Indians will still stay tribal "inside." He criticized non-Sioux who wanted to "run the organization" and is also critical of his own earlier ideas and behavior. He wanted to "make it" in white society and found out he couldn't; he became hostile to whites, and romantically nationalistic. He didn't want to associate with anyone but Indians. During this period he entered a seminary, and during his one year of attendance he found that he didn't want, or need, to be accepted by whites and that he could accept himself and be proud of his Indian heritage and still live with whites. He decided to major in community development at a secular college and return to the reservation to work with his people. While at college now he associates with Indians almost exclusively and is learning the languages of his mother and father. Since his appearance is not especially Indian, he was questioned about acceptance by Indians. His answer was that language is most important, along with sincerity, and he doesn't anticipate any trouble in this respect. He says his parents have become more Indian since moving to the city and he thinks he has a less detached interest in reservation affairs than do his parents.

J. is the fourth child in a family of seven. His two younger brothers married Indians from different tribes, one of them returning to the reservation to a semiskilled job, the other remaining in the Bay Area unemployed; his sister returned to the reservation after graduating from high school, and won a scholarship to college. The parents have talked of returning and actively planned their return all the time they have lived in the city and have been active in Indian affairs on and off the reservation during this time.

W., the second daughter of three, was born in Oakland after the family relocated without Bureau assistance. For the first five years the family was very poor and the father worked only sporadically. The mother remembers feeding W. chocolate pudding mix and flour because that was all they had in the house and how she had developed an allergic reaction. Since then the father has become a journeyman craftsman and has been making payments on a house in a lower-middle-class area for the last twelve years. The parents have always been conscious of prejudice and say that is one of the reasons they moved from South Dakota. They have taken pains to tell their children that they are Indians and to take pride in their heritage. The children remember being teased about their "Indianness" and being taught to fight back if provoked, but not to seek a fight. The parents found relatives in the area and have built up an extensive network of visiting and mutual aid over the years, to the extent that about five years ago they started organizing annual Sioux picnics. At the same time they have been getting more and more involved organizationally in pan-Indian groups, most often involving the daughters. The oldest daughter dropped out of high school to marry a semiskilled non-Indian, and W. also dropped out in her last year and lived with her mother's mother in South Dakota. While living there she became involved in the social life of the Indian community in the off-reservation city where her grandmother lives. This took place during and after a period of heavy drinking on the part of her father when her mother also returned to South Dakota. When the family was reunited W. also returned to

Oakland, finished high school, and took a trade course. Shortly after finishing the trade course, and while her parents were becoming more active politically in Indian organizations, she said that she would like to become a social worker among Indians in the city. But while she was making plans for this she married a non-Indian professional. In this she followed the example of her sister only too well. While her sister had moved a short distance away when she married so that she could spend the major part of the day with her mother, W. never moved out of the maternal house—although her husband is still living fifty miles away.

This family has been interviewed and visited extensively over a two-year period and each visit has been an occasion marked by much conviviality. Indian and non-Indian friends of parents and children come and go; the whole scene is one of happy confusion. The parents, successful in economic adjustment, are hospitable and generous to Indian and non-Indian, relatives and friends, although both have said that "some kind of barrier" still exists between them and non-Indians, that friendships with whites are more superficial than friendships with Indians.

W. contrasts the kinds of intergroup behavior in the Bay Area and in South Dakota: White children are "meaner" in elementary school and more polite in junior college in San Francisco; and while the teachers are "mean" in South Dakota, the Bay Area teachers are more polite and thoughtful of Indians, but there is continual pressure from white high school children. In the Bay Area there is freedom to make a choice of friends, but in South Dakota "you had to be all Indian or all white—there isn't any in-between." She maintains one friendship she made in high school—a non-Indian minority group member—and says she and her friend stayed aloof from the general social life in high school, in contrast to W.'s younger sister, who is active in social life and much concerned with peer activities and values. The parents say that their children get along well with other nationalities. However, the children have had unhappy experiences. W. spent much time with her grandmother during her childhood, and says she has an advantage over her sisters in this respect: she learned more about her Indian heritage and developed a habit of church attendance which her sisters never learned. Furthermore, she feels that she is not as belligerent as her younger sister.

G. and T. achieved high scores on school-administered intelligence tests a year ago when they were living in a World War II housing project. At the time the tester commented that both girls lacked confidence and seemed withdrawn. The parents, while demonstrably solicitous for their children, led an erratic life before relocating. The father was an itinerant construction worker and farm laborer, and after relocating he went from job to job and the family moved from adequate to inadequate housing and back again and from one school to another. The family has been off and on relief three times in the last two years and the father has held three jobs for periods of two weeks to one month. At the same time, the household is a center of communication for a large group of Indians and non-Indians in the same social and economic status and a stopping place for traveling Sioux. The mother and father are known and respected throughout this community as generous and honorable people, although none of this respect is reflected in economic well-being. A year ago, when the family was living in a school district that included upper-class neighborhoods, G. became close friends with a wealthy non-Indian girl. After the girl moved to the suburbs, G. visited her overnight two or three times, but since then the friendship has not been kept up.

The family has moved twice since then, first to a housing project, and later to a basement apartment. Their earliest lodging, in an auto court, consisted of two small one-room shacks for the family of eight, although one shack was used for storage and for the father's privacy more often than for lodging. The lodging in the housing project was a two-bedroom upstairs apartment in a multiracial compound. Since the parents were afraid of other races, the girls were kept inside as much as possible and their friends apparently were other Indian girls in the project. The parents didn't like the project and said that since the move the girls had become more "mouthy" and did not do as well in school. However, after an episode when G. stayed away from school, was punished, and ran away from home, both girls were placed in accelerated classes and became interested in school. The girls resented the last family move, to a depressed area, and resented attending a predominantly Negro school, with no accelerated classes and much friction between Negroes and non-Negroes. The girls have retreated into themselves again and feel as if they are being attacked by Negroes and non-Negroes, as well as by adults. The mother says she wants the girls to go to college, but she doesn't think they are going to make it with their school record the way it is. Since they are so poor the children will have to depend on scholarships, and the mother is aware of the difficulties involved in this. G. says she feels alone in the world now.

The girls' closest friends are Mexican-American girls; the Anglo girls "talk too loud." The father speaks Lakota and now and then the girls ask their father the meaning of a Lakota word, but they have not followed the advice of a family friend that they take advantage of the opportunity to learn the language. The father has taught them not to let anyone push them around and to hit back if somebody hits them. G. feels that this has resulted in conflict at school. She "won't take anything off of anybody," and as a result she is suspended from school for fighting. Like W.'s younger sister, she feels that this is the only way she can gain respect at school.

Finally, I will consider dropouts, people who left school before graduating. Two of these are girls who left to marry non-Indians. One young man had a summer job he didn't want to leave to return to school; he lost the job after school started but shortly got a better one. Another "just got tired of school" in the ninth grade, made abortive attempts to work or attend night school, got into a few scrapes, including a joy-riding charge, and finally went back to live with his father's mother on the reservation, saying he would go back to school there. He hadn't done so six months after the move and was last heard from working as a wrangler with a traveling rodeo stock outfit.

Neither L., this last subject, nor his sisters feel at home in the city, although they have been here since 1955, when L. was eight years old. The family has lived in a housing project with a reputation for disorganization ever since they arrived, and although the father had had the same well-paying job for the last eight years, he started drinking soon after arrival and only recently stopped after nearly dying from ulcers. The mother "used to cry all the time" from loneliness when they first moved. She said she didn't know what to do about her husband's drinking problem and feels the same inadequacy about her children's problems. When talking about their delinquency she often intersperses, "I don't know where I went wrong," and says that both she and her husband have been strict about time and house-hold chores with the children, hoping to provide good examples.

Before L. went home he said he would like to get away from the continual fighting in the project, and he told about the many times he had had to protect his honor, and about his reputation as a fighter. He belonged to an interracial gang that he described as being violent and committing petty theft. When his grandmother came out to live with his father's brother, L. moved in with them, but his stay was short-lived since his uncle was "always yapping" at him (his mother said his uncle "tried to talk to him"; this is a traditional form of control). After the grandmother went home, L. was despondent and ran away, was picked up on his way to the grandmother's, worked off the fare, and then tried again, this time successfully. Visited the day after he arrived at his grandmother's, in a small, isolated, conservative community, he displayed much affection toward his grandmother and again talked about the peace and quiet on the reservation in contrast to the friction in the city. Within two weeks he had stabbed a man in a fight in an off-reservation town and had gotten into a fight at a celebration on the reservation. He had quickly drifted into the work pattern common to the reservation—casual and intermittent farm labor—and had forgotten his promise to parents and grandparents to finish school on the reservation. While his parents visited the grandmother L. stayed away all the time they were there.

The family has been plagued by illness, drinking, and disorganization during its stay in the city, and L. makes reference to discrimination as well as to friction in his experiences. His solution, he thinks, has been to accept the values of his peers and to try to show them he can do as well as they in their activities. His parents visited regularly with relatives whose children are approximately the same age and who are college-oriented. L. would not discuss these children, and said only that he had never had anything to do with them. A few months after the field research for this study had been completed, L. called me and showed up in cowboy hat and boots, on his way through the city as an employee of a rodeo outfit. He talked of friction with his paternal uncles over their shiftlessness and inability to provide for the grandmother and claimed that he was contributing to the support of the reservation household. Asked if he was going to look up his old city friends during his visit, he said, "Those punks!"—a pause, and then, "I thought I was pretty big."

IV. Discussion

Certain themes recur in the stories of urban adolescent Sioux, as well as in those of their parents and their contemporaries who have recently arrived.

(1) *The conflict in attraction of reference groups:* The reference group of the extended family and tribe is an ascribed group. It maintains norms and provides satisfactions that are not found in the reference groups of the dominant society. In fact, these norms and satisfactions are in

many ways inimical to and disparaged by the dominant group. Status in one group does not necessarily bring status in the other. Although status in the dominant group is achieved, the amount and kind of achieved status is ascribed on the basis of physical appearance and group membership.

(2) *Conflict in self-characterization of the individual's in-group:* Individuals tend to evaluate their in-group by the standards of the dominant out-group and to identify with the devalued section of the group as part of their identification with the in-group as a whole, that is they apply the dominant out-group's stereotype to themselves (cf. Lewin 1948, pp. 169–200; Kerckhoff and McCormick 1955).

(3) *Indeterminacy of behavior in others, especially members of the dominant society:* Patterns of behavior that signify acceptance and friendliness, for example, mock hostility, physical contact, and loud or fast talking, are taken as insults by Indian children, and patterns of behavior that signify respect and gravity, for example, averted eyes, reserved speech, and diffidence, are taken as signs of unfriendliness by white and Negro children. At the same time, the concept of friendship and sociability is interpreted differently by members of the different groups. On the one hand, a cautious and patient approach is followed by an interdependent and intimate relationship; on the other hand, a less intimate acquaintance follows an open, quick approach (see Wax and Thomas 1961; also Lewin's comparison of German and American friendships, 1948, pp. 3–33).

Older adolescents and young adults who come to the city under the government relocation and vocational training program are thrown into contact with other Indians at the field relocation office, boarding houses, vocational schools, and Indian gathering places. They have some control over the choice of Indian or non-Indian contacts. Adolescents growing up in the city are still under at least minimal parental and geographical control in choice of associations. By far the most important socializing influence is in the school environment: adolescents' friends are nearly all chosen from among schoolmates, and few friendships are continued when the individual changes schools. Accordingly, the conflicts and indeterminacy referred to above take place at the time when the individual is facing his developmental problems of social identity and finding the group that will accord him status, and reinforce, modify, or conflict with his earlier training and orientation. Since Indian families do not live in such close concentration that either a Sioux or a cross-tribal Indian reference group is readily available for the developing individual, he is faced with a choice of peers from groups of Anglo children of different social and economic classes, Negroes, or other national groups that may have the same relationship with the dominant society as Indians have.

Kerckhoff and McCormick (1955) studied the relationship of group status, group identification, and rejection to "marginal personality" in Chippewa children near a reservation, and concluded that while the tendency of a member of a subordinate group to identify with the dominant group increases with the possibility of acceptance, the differences in "permeability of the barrier" or possibilities of acceptance within the dominant group are less important if the individual identifies with the subordinate in-group. In the case of the Dakota adolescent, the lack of a concentrated population necessitates identification with other subordinate in-groups, such as working-class Anglo and Mexican-American groups. As Pope (1953), Coleman (1961), and others have shown, values and behavior in these groups tend to influence the behavior and at least to reinforce the values of their members.

The research reported in this paper was primarily an exploratory study of urban Dakota adolescents. I have attempted to determine their position in the urban social structure and to delineate variables relating them to familial and extra-familial socialization. Because the sample was small and the investigation not as systematic as might be desired, the results are suggestive for future corroboratory or amending work. One quality seems to be common to all the subjects in this sample, that is, their marginal status in relation to the dominant society and the core Dakota reservation society. Those who have oriented to non-Dakota reference groups associate with subordinate status groups or, as in college, tend to associate with marginal student groups. Although many of the parents say that they have moved to the Bay Area to escape subordinate status in their home state, and say they and their children do not experience the effects of this status as much in the city, the children report hostile behavior on the part of teachers and peers based on their status as Indians or dark-skinned people. Nevertheless, the children grow up within the social structure of the dominant society in which a large amount of socialization is left to the peer group rather than to the parents or parent-surrogate, and thus their educational, class, and occupational aspirations tend to reflect those of their associates. Therefore some hypotheses can be adapted from hypotheses concerning social structure and socialization of urban adolescents in general.

(1) Class, occupational, and educational aspirations of Dakota children will reflect the aspirations and background of the dominant class of students in the school the children attend (cf. Wilson, n.d.)

(2) Children of parents who maintain kinship and associational ties with Dakota or pan-Indian culture will choose minority-group and lower-status Anglo groups as peer groups.

(3) Although membership in low-status groups is in large part by ascription, behavior expectations and modes of interaction of the lower-status out-group are more congruent with the traditional Dakota modes of interaction than those of higher-status out-groups.

(4) Those Dakota children who drop out of school in the upper grades will leave for the purpose of assuming adult roles, which they perceive as unattainable as students.

These hypotheses are provisional, and reflect the limits of field work with the adolescent subjects. More rigorous testing of these hypotheses is necessary, within the group reported here, and also against reservation-trained young adults who come to the city on the vocational training program, and with comparable groups of adolescents and young adults from other tribal and cultural backgrounds.

REFERENCES

COLEMAN, J. S. 1961. *The adolescent society.* Glencoe, Ill.: Free Press.

KERCKHOFF, A. C., AND McCORMICK, T. C. 1955. Marginal status and marginal personality. *Social Forces* 34: 48–55.

LEWIN, K. 1948. *Resolving social conflicts.* New York: Harper.

POPE, B. 1953. Prestige values in contrasting socioeconomic groups of children. *Psychiatry* 16: 381–85.

WAX, ROSALIE, AND THOMAS, ROBERT K. 1961. American Indians and white people. *Phylon* 23: 305–17.

WILSON, A. B. N.d. Some effects of social stratification upon the academic achievement of elementary school students. Mimeo. University of California, School of Education.

Contemporary Oglala Music and Dance: Pan-Indianism versus Pan-Tetonism

William K. Powers

INTRODUCTION

DURING THE PAST twenty years I have observed and recorded American Indian music and dance in Oklahoma, South Dakota, and many urban Indian centers.[1] I have watched the evolution of the powwow, and am convinced that pan-Indianism, by any definition, has sustained a vital American Indian practice. At times this practice has seemed homogeneous across many tribes. At other times a conglomerate of traits has served to revive an individual tribal past. But whether tribalistic or pan-Indianistic, the complex is irrefutably "Indian."

Today we are witnessing a cultural metamorphosis which may nationalize the American Indian, but the degree to which nationalization can replace tribal identity is little known. In the past, what has been suggested as typical pan-Indian has been basically an aggregate of pan-Plains cultural elements. Thomas (1965, p. 77) states:

> It is on the Plains that we find the historic roots of modern Pan-Indianism. The horse not only enabled Plains Indians to become extremely mobile in hunting and "warfare," but also increased inter-tribal contacts. Even a sign language developed in the area to provide communication across linguistic

[1] I have made eighteen field trips to Oklahoma and South Dakota, and have attended approximately two hundred powwows. My last field trip, made possible by

boundaries. By the 1800's not only had intensive "warfare" and very mobile hunting developed, but tribes were beginning to ally with one another, camp with one another and inter-marry with one another. Most significant for the later development of Pan-Indianism, the Plains style of life was extremely attractive to tribes on the edges of the Plains area. Plains traits and institutions were spreading to other areas even at the time that Plains Indians were becoming pacified and settled on reservations. Indeed, the Plains style of life was very attractive to American Indians completely outside of the Plains area. This is one of the historic sources and causes of what is generally referred to as "Pan-Indianism" which I am suggesting now is in some degree an extension of the Plains culture area.

Not only have the music and dance aspects of pan-Indianism been treated as an extension of the Plains culture, but most anthropologists have tended to investigate the complex as it flourishes in Oklahoma (Howard 1955) and in urban America wherever there are American Indian centers (Lurie 1965). In Oklahoma and in a number of cities Indians representing a multitude of tribes congregate but are not always conscious of the nature of their unification.

Previous definitions of pan-Indianism tend to focus on pan-Indianism in its aggregate form without taking into consideration the many ramifications of its elements (tribal or non-Indian) which comprise the total complex. Yet each element of pan-Indianism can be traced to either tribal or non-Indian origins. In treating pan-Indianism as an aggregate, only the results of pan-Indianism become apparent, and the causative elements are neglected. Hence, the individuals directly involved in pan-Indian events seem to be the recipients of what might be termed incongruous tribal innovations.

Three questions may be raised: What are the prominent elements in Oklahoma pan-Indianism which are alien to and incompatible with well-rooted tribalistic patterns? What form does pan-Indianism take in a tribe or division of tribes which are closely related by a common language and sense of tribal heritage? Where tribal identity is still strong, particularly on reservations, what elements do a tribe contribute to pan-Indianism outside their boundaries? It is the purpose of this paper to discuss the various elements of pan-Indianism as they appear among a Teton division, the Oglalas, and to analyze to what extent typical Oklahoma pan-Indianism affects what might be called

---

the American Philosophical Society, was in 1966 to Pine Ridge, and in speaking of what is happening today, I am referring to 1966. This paper was first published, in slightly different form, in *Ethnomusicology* 7 (September 1968): 352–72.

the "pan-Teton" complex as it is manifest in North and South Dakota.

THE PAN-TETON COMPLEX

Pan-Tetonism,[2] as used here, is the complex whole shared by seven Teton tribes with similarities in language, historical relationship, interpretation of various Plains traits such as the sun dance, vision quest, warrior and chief societies, etc. The seven tribes designate themselves as (1) Oglala, "they scatter their own"; (2) Sicangu, "burned thighs," also known as Brule; (3) Mniconwoju, "they plant near the water," also called Miniconjou; (4) Hunkpapa, "end of the horn"; (5) Sihasapa, "black foot"; (6) Itazipcola, "without bows," also called Sans Arc; and (7) Oohe nunpa, "two boilings," also called Two Kettle. Historically the Oglalas and Sicangus are referred to as the southern Tetons, while the remaining five are known collectively as the Saones, an anglicized spelling of *canona* (Nakota dialect). The origin of this word has been lost, but it refers in some way to woods. Although linguistically and historically related, the tribes do not have identical traits; in fact, there are differences in Lakota dialect from reservation to reservation, and some disagreement from tribe to tribe as to which individuals were most important historically, etc.

[2] In using the term "pan-Tetonism," I also suggest a larger categorization which is comprised of all divisions of Sioux: Lakota, Nakota, and Dakota. The title "pan-Dakota" as opposed to "pan-Teton" may seem more appropriate to some students; however, from an ethnosemantical point of view, the Tetons do not speak Dakota, but rather Lakota (likewise, the middle group speaks Nakota). I realize that the Teton division, with which this paper is primarily concerned, traditionally has been referred to in anthropological literature as Teton-Dakota, but, again, from a linguistic standpoint, the two terms are ambiguous. Unfortunately, "pan-Siouan" cannot be used because the term conflicts with the larger Hokan-Siouan language stock.

I also realize that in this paper I make reference to a "North Dakota" style, which, in fact, is traceable to true Dakota as well as non-Teton tribes. However, the North Dakota style is diffused into South Dakota through the Hunkpapas at Standing Rock, who are Teton. In addition, much of the North Dakota style is influenced by the Canadian Prairie tribes, including the remnants of Sitting Bull's band in Saskatchewan, again a Teton group.

Likewise, the title suggests other "pan" groups, such as pan-Blackfeet; these occur wherever there are strong tribal confederacies supported by a common language. Not only is there a connection between pan-Tetonism and pan-Indianism, but between other "pan" groups, for example, pan-Tetonism and pan-Plains, or, hypothetically, pan-Tetonism and pan-Blackfeet.

Within pan-Tetonism there are two forces: One is tradition, which all members of the complex refer to as "Sioux." The other is rooted in North Dakota and is referred to by the tribes living in South Dakota as "North Dakota." Both forces have been influenced by Oklahoma pan-Indianism, especially in the mid-1950s, and it is my contention that recently the strongest influences on the Teton tribes have come from within the pan-Teton complex itself. Hence, the South Dakotans are more directly influenced by that which is "North Dakota" than that which is generally accepted as pan-Indian. The greatest significance is that today more than ever the pan-Teton group is influencing the larger pan-Indian complex, even in some instances proving more significant than Oklahoma pan-Indianism.

To illustrate the connections between Oklahoma pan-Indianism and pan-Tetonism, we shall investigate: (1) characteristic elements of Oklahoma pan-Indianism, (2) characteristic elements of pan-Tetonism, (3) Oklahoma elements found in pan-Tetonism, (4) pan-Teton elements found in Oklahoma pan-Indianism, and (5) the Oglalas: survival versus revival.

The Oglalas will serve to illustrate pan-Tetonism, keeping in mind that criteria would change somewhat if a North Dakota tribe were substituted. The specific media for analysis are music and dance, including those customs and paraphernalia which are employed in the performance of music and dance.

CHARACTERISTIC ELEMENTS OF OKLAHOMA PAN-INDIANISM

Following are brief descriptions of those elements which are most constant at Oklahoma powwows.

Powwow. The powwow is the main pan-Indian celebration. It is a secular event featuring group singing and social dancing by men, women, and children. The elements of the powwow originate from both tribal functions and non-Indian influences. Today's powwow is a vestige of the grass dance complex described by Howard (1951) that spread across the Great Plains during the mid-nineteenth century. The powwow in Oklahoma is sponsored by almost all Plains tribes, and may take place on patriotic holidays such as the Kiowa Veterans' Day celebration. Sometimes smaller powwows are held spontaneously. In larger cities at the local Indian centers many are held on a weekly or monthly basis. The powwow affords the Indian an opportunity to put on his costume and "be Indian" whether he is conservative or acculturated.

War dance. The most prominent dance at the powwow is the war dance. While performed by men, women, and children, it is designed primarily for men. The dance is free-style and individualistic, although there are common steps and a variety of accepted body movements. The male dancers improvise on a theme; the women perform one basic walking step. In Oklahoma, the dance has two forms: the fancy war dance, a fast and lively style which is also used for contest dancing; and the straight dance, a slow, conservative dance which is particular to the lower Siouan-speaking tribes and their Pawnee neighbors. The fancy war dance has influenced non-Oklahoma Indians across the nation, while the straight dance (with many customs observed in the original grass dance) is not popular outside Oklahoma, and, to some extent, Kansas and Nebraska.

During the course of a powwow, which may last from one evening to a weekend, the war dance is danced more than any other. In Oklahoma the songs are usually sung in series of four, each song being sung progressively faster, with only a slight pause between them to keep the dancers on the floor.

War dance song. This song is sung for the war dance accompaniment. While there are literally hundreds of war dance songs, they all conform to one basic structure. In Oklahoma, they are often sung without words, only vocables. Many of today's songs have diffused from the north, and there is some indication that Oklahoma musical creativity is diminishing.[3]

The Procession. This is a paradelike dance which usually brings the dancers onto the dance area. One of the most popular songs used is adapted from a Comanche religious song sung without its original words. The procession concept is non-Indian in origin.

The Round Dance. This is the second most popular dance at powwows, and is performed in a circle by men, women, and children moving clockwise. Sometimes the dancers hold hands or lock arms, but this is not mandatory. The round dance is different from any other and must not be confused with other dances performed in a circle. When

---

[3] In a personal interview, the lack of creativity in Oklahoma was suggested by Tony Isaacs, an ethnomusicologist specializing in Southern Plains music. I have personally observed that many new Oklahoma songs have a northern influence. They are usually called Winnebago songs by the Oklahomans. The Winnebagos identify them as Sioux songs, thus tracing their diffusion.

there is no processional, the round dance is performed first. The name "welcome dance" is often applied to it in urban centers. Its origin is most often attributed to the Plains scalp dance or other societal dances performed in a circle.

Round dance songs. Round dance songs are sung exclusively for the round dance; and although there are hundreds of them, they, like the war dance songs, conform to a singular pattern easily recognizable by the dancers.

The Forty-nine. The forty-nine is a social dance for young men and women performed in concentric circles around a group of male singers who beat on a drum or other resonator. Always performed in the nighttime, in mufti, usually in total darkness and accompanied by heavy drinking by the participants, it is sometimes followed by drunken brawls. Local authorities attempt to prevent forty-nines whenever possible. The origin of this dance was in Oklahoma and has been described by Feder (1964).

Forty-nine songs. These songs are sung exclusively for forty-nines, often without words, although many contain English phrases. They are played faster than round dance songs but have a similar structure, one having its origin in Kiowa war travel songs.

Stomp dance. This dance, one of the few non-Plains elements in Oklahoma pan-Indianism, is Creek-Seminole in origin, but it has become an integral part of the powwow. The dance is serpentine, like follow-the-leader; its songs are antiphonal and vary depending on the repertory of the leader. Both men and women participate. The women wear turtle-shell or milk can "shakers" strapped below their knees. This provides the only accompaniment. The Creek-Seminole stomp dance has been described by Howard (1965a); the Iroquois version by Kurath (1964). It fits in well as a competitor of the forty-nine. At some powwows both dances occur simultaneously a few yards apart. The young people run back and forth from one dance to another, forming concentric circles at the forty-nine drum or attaching themselves to the tail of the stomp dance line.

Contests. The most popular is the fancy war dance contest, which is divided into age groups—junior and senior. The rules of the contest generally state that the dancers (who are judged on an individual, or "championship," basis) must keep in time with the music, stop on precisely the last beat of the drum, and not drop any article of costuming. The songs for the fancy war dance contest are extremely fast and are normally sung through twice without a coda. There are also contests in straight dancing and miscellaneous specialty dances. Contests of these types are non-Indian in origin.

Powwow Princess. At each of the larger pan-Indian powwows, a powwow Princess representing her tribe and/or the celebration itself is chosen. Prerequisites match those of most non-Indian beauty contests, but she must (1) have a certain percentage of Indian blood and (2) be dressed in the traditional costume of her tribe. Upon being invested as Powwow Princess, she usually leads the round dance and two-step with the head dancer.

Head dancer. A head dancer is usually a young fancy dancer and championship war dancer whose duty it is to lead (be the first to dance) each war dance. No other dancer may begin until the head dancer is on the floor. At larger celebrations more than one may be chosen.

Tail dancer. Tail dancers are found only in conjunction with straight dance rules and are a vestige of a grass dance custom.

Whip dancer. Whip dancers are only used in conjunction with straight dancing or secular societal functions. The whip is symbolically used to command someone to dance and is a vestige of the original grass dance.

Female war dancers. There are a handful of young women who dress in the manner of young men and dance the war dances with equally virile movements. This practice appears to have originated in Oklahoma.

Give-away. The custom of giving away blankets, shawls, food, or money to friends or in honor of someone, usually a deceased relative, is observed in Oklahoma and usually takes place between war dances and other parts of the program. This custom is observed by all Plains tribes, but the formality of the give-away has its genesis in the grass dance complex.

Feast. At some powwows, food is given away to anybody who attends. This is also a standard pan-Plains trait.

Committee. Each powwow has a powwow committee which oversees all arrangements, including the selection of the head dancers, singers, master of ceremonies, and other miscellaneous details. The announcements at Oklahoma powwows are made in English; however, upon occasion an old man may be asked to give an invocation in his tribal language. The committee is a vestige of the various men's societies which alternated as sponsors.

Flag song. Most tribes have their own flag songs which supplant the national anthem at powwow functions. Most good singers know the flag songs of other tribes. They are usually sung with vocables only; however, each song has a set of words which are sung at purely tribal functions. The flag song is of non-Indian origin and became one of the patriotic elements initiated by Indian participation in World War I.

Specials. There are a number of dances called "specials" performed in conjunction with pan-Indian powwows. They are usually show numbers, although some are purely social dances in which all participate. Normally the dances listed below are performed only once a day (or evening), whereas the dances mentioned above are performed in succession throughout the day and night. The most frequent dances are:

(1) Two-step. A partner dance in which men and women clasp hands in skater's position and shuffle forward. Its origin is non-Indian, in a simulated waltz first observed at army posts.

(2) Snake and buffalo. A group dance for men and women. Actually, they are two dances performed in succession as if they were one. The snake dance is a follow-the-leader dance. The first man in line is the head of the snake, while the last man is the tail. Although the name indicates a Southwest origin, the choreography more closely resembles that of Southeastern serpentine dances. The buffalo dance originated as a Plains dance—probably Comanche—in which the dancers imitate the movements of the buffalo.

(3) Spear and shield dance. A typical show dance in which two men or several groups of two carrying spears and shields pretend to fight each other. It originated purely for show.

(4) The hoop dance. Another spectacular show dance in which a solo dancer manipulates one or more hoops over and about his body. Sometimes there are hoop dance contests. The origin of the hoop dance is debatable. The greatest exponents are the Pueblos; however, dancers on the Northern Plains carried similar hoops in dream society functions.

Each of the above specials except the hoop dance have their own particular songs which are not interchangeable with any other. The hoop dance is usually accompanied by a standard war dance song.

Men's costumes. Howard (1965b) has described the fancy war dance costume of the Oklahoma male. The style of this costume is found nearly everywhere pan-Indian dancers celebrate. There are no tribal differences in costumes. It basically consists of a porcupine and deer tail headdress, beaded aprons, cuffs, armbands, belt, galluses, moccasins, choker, and characteristic neck and tail feathers called bustles.

The Oklahoma costume is highly tailored by non-Indian standards, featuring matched beadwork and featherwork.

Women's costumes. Unlike the men, there is no typical pan-Indian costume among the Oklahoma women; each costume represents the woman's tribal clothing. At some functions, however, women wear clothing of non-Indian manufacture augmented with a shawl or blanket over her shoulders if she is not in costume, but she carries it folded over one arm if in costume.

Peyote paraphernalia. Even though the Oklahoma pan-Indian powwows are of a secular nature, certain religious items connected with peyoteism are carried by male and female dancers. These include for the most part fans, silverwork accessories, blankets, and sashes. Wearing peyote paraphernalia does not necessarily indicate that the dancer is a peyoteist.

Patriotic organizations. A highlight of many pan-Indian powwows is the presence of various Indian patriotic organizations such as the War Mothers' Club, Veterans of Foreign Wars, and American Legion. Occasionally dances are either sponsored by them or given in their behalf.

Characteristic Elements of Pan-Tetonism

The elements of Oklahoma pan-Indianism described above have infiltrated Pine Ridge, but the Oglalas have not completely forsaken tribal customs for the "new" Indianism. There are elements which parallel each other, but, in the main, pan-Indianism simply provides a framework for specific tribal celebrations, in which the dances and songs are generally related to earlier tribal functions.

To illustrate, let us compare typical Oglala elements with those found in Oklahoma.

Powwow. This term is new to the Oglalas. However, today it is used commonly to denote what was originally called *wowaci,* or *wacipi,* both nouns signifying "dance." In speaking Lakota, the traditional term is used in preference to "powwow." This is not true in other instances when a common English word replaces a Lakota equivalent. The term "powwow" probably became popular in the mid-1950s.

War dance. These words are becoming popular. However, in Lakota the general term is "Omaha *wacipi,*" or "Omaha dance," thus called because the Oglalas received the older grass dance from the Omaha tribe. The traditional Omaha dance of the Oglalas closely resembles the Oklahoma straight dance but is less conservative in movement. In the mid-1950s the Oklahoma style of war dancing became popular on the Pine Ridge Reservation, along with the Oklahoma fancy dance costumes; however, since then the Oglalas have been adapting the North Dakota style, in both dance and costume.

To fully appreciate the nuances of war dancing, it is necessary to discuss just what is meant by "style" and what constitutes "popular styles."

In all pan-Indian war dancing, whether in Oklahoma, urban areas, or on reservations, there are primary styles of war dancing, each primary style having one or more sub-styles discernible to the trained eye.

Style in dancing does not apply only to certain accepted dance patterns, choreographies, or standardized steps, postures, and directional movements. It also reveals a certain attitude. Ultimately, the "good" dancer is judged by other dancers and the general viewing public on his ability to combine an accepted style with his personal attitude, which ultimately becomes *his* style, *his* individuality expressed through the medium of dance. Thus there are an infinite variety of sub-styles, but for sake of taxonomy, we will discuss only three— (1) the traditional style, (2) Oklahoma style, and (3) Northern style— because these three predominate on the Plains.

The traditional style. This is the original grass dance style which was popular during the mid-nineteenth century and which still survives through performance by some of the older conservatives. It was also the typical "show" dancing of the Buffalo Bill tours. The characteristic features are the concentrated use of the head and shoulders; the full exposure of the face and chest, suggesting a sense of arrogance or pride; and little concern with footwork other than keeping time to the music. The entire upper torso dances; the face is alive with expression, an explicit awareness of enjoying the dance. Traditional-style dancers are similar through all tribes. There is some vestige of traditional style in Oklahoma, but for the most part it survives on reservations. The younger generation looks upon traditional style as old-fashioned, but the older generation looks with admiration at the few exponents of this style and agree that this is "*ikcewacipi*," "real dancing," or "*ikce-Lakota*," "old-time Ind'*an*."

The Oklahoma style. This style is the style most often reported as *the* pan-Indian style which originated in Oklahoma sometime after World War I. It was disseminated in urban areas by relocated Indians, eventually reaching all over the nation. The major differences betweeen Oklahoma style and traditional style are the former's faster tempo and emphasis on fancy footwork with little regard to head and shoulder movements. There are abrupt changes in posture with quick spins and dips. It has become the accepted contest and show dance at intertribal gatherings in Oklahoma and urban areas, and in the mid-1950s was popular at Pine Ridge for possibly five years.

The Northern style. Like the Oklahoma fancy war dance, the Northern style seems to have originated at the time of World War I. Its greatest exponents are the Crees, the Three Affiliated Tribes, the Plains Ojibwas, and the Canadian Sioux as well as the Sioux of Standing Rock, Cheyenne River, and recently Rosebud and Pine Ridge reservations (in the order of diffusion). The Northern style took root in Pine Ridge about 1960, although Northern dancers had always participated in the sun dance secular events to some degree.

It differs from both traditional and Oklahoma style in its footwork and body movements, although it employs more traditional style elements than does Oklahoma style. Characteristically, Northern dancers shake their shoulders, sway their torso (from the hips) from side to side, dart suddenly, changing their direction of dance, and employ a series of trick steps, giving the appearance that they are off balance, but they always gracefully retrieve themselves.

What is most significant is the attitude of the younger Northern dancers—"cool," "hip" (many wear dark glasses); they convey a feeling that they are dancing for themselves, within themselves, but spasmodically and furiously as if suddenly shaken from a deep narcosis. Unlike Oklahoma-style dancers, the Northern dancer is not committed to the viewing public, only to himself; yet periodically in the song he becomes alive with enthusiasm in his movements.

In 1960, the Oglalas were somewhat skeptical, if not derisive, about the North Dakota influence. While the North Dakota Sioux simply called their particular style *"peji waci,"* "grass dance," the Oglalas called it *"galala waci,"* or "ribbon dance," because the Northern dancers wore long fringes from their back aprons. The conservative Oglalas described the most significant part of the dance *iglucancan,* a verb meaning "to shake oneself," and explained that the dancers wore "raggy" costumes (instead of chainette, some dancers cut fringe from cotton cloth). Even today, conservative Oglalas prefer that which is "Sioux" to that which is "North Dakota," but the Northern style, it would appear, has found acceptance at Pine Ridge.

War dance songs. It is unquestionably in the music that the pan-Teton group makes its greatest contribution to pan-Indianism. Music composed at Pine Ridge is finding its way into the repertory of singers outside the pan-Teton complex. First, this is possible since war dance music of all Plains tribes is interchangeable. Second, Oglala music is particularly vital; new pieces are composed every year. The Oglalas today also draw heavily from the North and become prime instruments in diffusing Northern music to Oklahoma as well as urban areas.

The war dance song is generically described by the Oglalas as "Omaha *olowan*," "Omaha song." Certain songs have words, while others have only vocables (Powers 1961). This is one of the major links in the pan-Teton structure: that every word-song is mutually intelligible by the seven tribes. As a consequence word-songs diffuse rapidly within the pan-Teton structure.

But just as there are primary dance styles, there are also related song styles, and at Pine Ridge the traditional song, although still vital at tribal events, is being popularly replaced by Northern-style songs, that is, songs diffusing from "North Dakota,"[4] at larger celebrations such as the sun dance. However, the Oglalas have never included Oklahoma songs in their war dance repertories.

Traditional songs. The majority of Omaha songs of this category have words and many can be traced to World War I. Densmore (1918) recorded similar songs among the Hunkpapas at Standing Rock. The peculiarities of the traditional songs, however, are more closely related by their structure and the style in which they are sung. All traditional songs begin with a particular kind of introductory phrase containing vocal ornamentation—sometimes resembling animal cries. They are sung three or four times through and end with a brief coda called "*sinte*," or "tail." The music is accompanied by drumming—a steady pulsating beat periodically emphasized with accented duple beats. Some traditional songs end without drum accompaniment. Like other song styles typical of the Plains, the melodic lines are constructed on a descending, or cascading, scale.

Oklahoma songs. Songs composed in Oklahoma have not diffused to the Oglalas, although the reverse is true. Basically the Oklahoma song style is closely related to the Oglala traditional style, but the songs are sung in a lower register. Oklahoma Indians agree that the Sioux sing

---

[4] There are song-makers at Pine Ridge, especially around Potato Creek, who compose simulated Northern songs.

"really high." When Oglala songs diffuse to Oklahoma, their register
is lowered and phonetics are altered to conform to Oklahoma vocables.

Northern songs. All three styles conform to a basic song structure;
however, Northern songs have several characteristics which make them
unique. They are, first of all, sung in a much higher register than
either of the two previous styles. Many traditional singers are unable
to reproduce this vocal technique. The introductory phrase of the
songs are sung soprano (the Oglalas refer to these voices as tenors) in
elongated, sustained, clear tones. The coda is repeated, often more
times than the theme proper of the song. Often the drumming decreases
in volume at the end of the song until it is inaudible; the last beat
is accented. Most of the "new powwow" songs on the Teton reservations are Northern, not traditional. Their origin may be traced to the
Plains Ojibwas and Plains Crees of the Rocky Boy Reservation in Montana, Canadian Prairie tribes, and North Dakota Sioux.

Procession. There are no processions as such in Pine Ridge. Recently,
however, the Oglalas have invented a "snake" dance which usually
takes place at least once during each day of the celebration in order to
count the dancers.[5] The length of the dance depends on how quickly
the committee tallies them. The step is the common war dance step;
the movement is follow-the-leader in a counterclockwise direction.
This is obviously a copy of the snake and buffalo dances of Oklahoma.
Any Omaha song may be used as accompaniment.

The Round dance. This has never been a popular dance at Pine Ridge.
The Sioux have several circle dances, most of which are related to
former war societies and the women's victory dance, in which female
relatives of warriors carried trophies of war. The round dance is
most conspicuous at other pan-Indian functions, especially in Oklahoma. At Pine Ridge the round dance is called *"naslohan wacipi,"*
"dragging feet dance," so called because of its particular side-stepping
movement. It was commonly referred to in the late 1940s and early
1950s as the *"kangi wacipi,"* "crow dance," which was originally a
dance of the *Kangi yuha Okolakiciye,* or Crow-owners society, and
appropriate Crow-owner songs were used for its accompaniment.
Another circle dance, *tokala wacipi,* or fox dance, a remnant of the
Tokala Okolakiciye, Fox, of Kit-fox society, was also popular during the
late 1940s and early 1950s. Both societies have been described by
Wissler (1912).

5 The success of any powwow is largely determined by the number of dancers and
groups of singers in attendance.

Round dance songs. While there is a class of songs specifically sung for *naslohan wacipi*, some with patriotic themes, other of vocables or English lyrics, they are not as popular as Omaha songs. Between the Oklahoma and Oglala songs, tribes outside the pan-Teton complex consider Oklahoma round dance songs more melodic ("prettier").

The Forty-nine. The forty-nine has never received a strong reception at Pine Ridge, although there was some attempt to perform the dance in the late 1930s or early 1940s. The Oglalas performed it indoors, dancing in mixed partners under blankets. It was allegedly suppressed by the government superintendent because of licentiousness.

Forty-nine songs. Forty-nine songs composed on the Teton reservations resemble Oklahoma songs rhythmically, but are unrelated melodically. The Tetons prefer word-songs sung part in Lakota and partly in English.

Stomp dance. The Creek-Seminole style of stomp has not yet reached the Oglalas. There is, however, a dance called "*nasto wacipi*," "stomp dance," in which the dancers prance to the accompaniment of a slow, steady beat of the drum, which changes to a fast Omaha dance. There are many stomp dance songs identical in structure. The stomp dance as performed at Pine Ridge and Rosebud is part of the North Dakota influence, and is also popular at Cheyenne River and Standing Rock. It reached the Oglalas in the early 1960s.

Contests. While the Oklahoma groups seem to thrive on contests, there are relatively few in Pine Ridge. In fact, the idea of a contest only reached Pine Ridge in the past three or four years. Up to that time, one heard many dancers brag of their "championships," but these were usually won off the reservation. There are now war dance contests at most of the smaller powwows and at the annual sun dance. The contest rules are officiated (as the Oglalas say) "Oklahoma style." The Oglalas admit that stopping on the last beat of the drum was never considered important until they heard of it in Oklahoma. The typical characteristic of the Oglala contest is that of endurance. The war dance songs, unlike the twice-through version in Oklahoma, may be sung through eight or nine times. The dancers must keep in time, and loss of an article of costuming means immediate disqualification. Most war dance champions at Pine Ridge and Rosebud are in their late teens.

Powwow Princess. Like the contest, the selection of the Powwow Princess is new—within the past three or four years. At the 1966 sun dance there was a Powwow Princess selected from candidates from each of the reservation districts—similar to the Oklahoma method of selecting from candidates of representative Oklahoma tribes. The Powwow Princess at Pine Ridge does not play a particularly important role at the sun dance, in contrast to the Oklahoma Princess, who with the head dancer leads the round dance and two-step.

Head dancer. There are no head dancer roles at Pine Ridge.

Tail dancer. There are no tail dancer roles at Pine Ridge, although they were common up through the 1940s.

Whip Dancer. Whip dancers, originally members of the *Omaha Okolakiciye,* or Omaha society, described by Wissler (1912), were common through the late 1940s but have not been witnessed since.

Whistle bearers. According to Howard,[6] certain dancers may prolong the dance by blowing their whistles over the heads of the singers. This is a Northern influence popular at Pine Ridge in recent years.

Female dancers. These have never been popular at Pine Ridge; however, in 1965 at least one war dance contest in Rapid City, South Dakota, was won by a young lady dressed as a man. It might be well to note that Oglala singers were impressed by a group of women war dance singers from the Crow Agency, Montana, who performed at many of the North Dakota powwows.

Give-away. The *otuȟ'anpi,* or give-away, has always been a popular custom at Pine Ridge and still survives at smaller powwows and other functions of a religious or secular nature. In the give-away ceremony, one gives money or something of value to another, usually in honor of a deceased relative. At Pine Ridge there are appropriate give-away songs in which the singers mention the name of the deceased. All transactions are handled through the *eyapaha,* or announcer, who announces the intentions of the donor. The singers are also recipients of donations. The give-away was always popular at all events, but has decreased at the sun dance powwows because it interrupts dancing time.

Feast. The *wohanpi,* or feast, takes place at all Oglala functions. Buffalo meat is normally served at the sun dance, beef at smaller functions. Dog meat is still served to the older men.

Committee. The committee, called *mazaša yuha,* or "has the penny (money)," is the sponsor of the powwow. The Oglala tribal council elects a committee to organize the sun dance, but all other, smaller functions are run by committees chosen from within the district in

[6] Personal correspondence with James H. Howard, 1964.

which the powwow takes place. The committee has always been an Oglala institution, dating back to war and chief societies.

Flag songs. For about ten years the Oglalas have had a flag song, which they called the national anthem, and which serves the same purpose at most tribal events. It is sung by an individual over a public address system or by a group with drum accompaniment during the raising and lowering of the American flag. The words are:

> Tunkašilayapi tawapaha kin oihankešni he najin kte lo.
> Iyoȟlate kin oyate kin cana wicicagin kte ca lecamon welo.

Free translation:

> The flag of the United States will stand forever.
> Beneath it the people will live on.
> That is why I do this (honor the flag).

The flag song is sung on all Teton reservations; however, each reservation has its own set of words, which are similar but not identical. During the flag song, the people rise and men remove their hats.

Specials. As in Oklahoma, there are a number of specialty dances. Most are specifically pan-Teton in nature and have not been diffused to other reservations or urban areas. The dances most often performed are:

(1) The *maštincala wacipi*, or rabbit dance (Powers 1962a), which is choreographically similar to the Oklahoma two-step. There is a class of rabbit dance songs which are used exclusively as accompaniment. The rabbit dance is called the owl dance in North Dakota, although the latter is sometimes performed differently.

(2) The *tonweya wacipi*, or "sneak-up" (literally, "scout dance"), is probably related to a warrior society. It is danced by a line of men who simulate the actions of warriors. There is only one sneak-up dance song (Powers 1962b).

(3) The kettle dance. *Ceȟomni wacipi*, or "they dance around the kettle" dance, sometimes called the "pot dance," is a custom originally observed in the grass dance. It is danced prior to the feast. The dancers, two or four of whom are armed with forked sticks, pass around the kettle, finally spearing prime pieces of dog meat contained within. This dance has been routinized in the past ten years for use as a show dance at the Intertribal Ceremonial at Gallup, New Mexico, as well as other public performances. There are five separate kettle dance songs which are sung in specific order.

(4) The hoop dance. The *cangleška wacipi*, "hoop dance," is occasionally seen as a show dance.

(5) Miscellaneous. There are a number of dances related to former societies which are occasionally performed in conjunction with smaller powwows.

Men's costumes. The traditional Sioux costume circa 1900 consisted of a porcupine and deer-tail headdress, beaded or porcupine-quilled moccasins, cuffs, armbands, bone chokers and breastplates, and beaded and sequined aprons. The basic body attire was either dyed long underwear or shirts and trousers of non-Indian manufacture. The bustles were clusters of predatory-bird feathers arranged rather haphazardly, thus leading some observers to call them "mess bustles." The earlier "crow belt" was also popular. There was no particular attempt to match the beadwork and featherwork. Many old timers wore traditional "chief suits," consisting of a warbonnet and matching buckskin shirts and leggings. In the late 1940s and early 1950s there was a gradual decline in traditional costumes, until in the mid-fifties the typical dance costume was replaced by a poorly simulated Oklahoma fancy dance costume. For about five years there seemed to be no direction to Oglala costume styles; outlandish substitutes for costumes were used. Then in the 1960s the North Dakota fringed costume began to appear. Although the Northern costume featured the common hair roach, decorated "choke springs" were inserted in place of eagle feathers. There was a marked absence of bustles. The outstanding characteristic of the costume was the ribbonwork back apron and matching shirts and pants (usually black) which had V-shaped designs outlined in long chainette fringe. The costume was replete with heavy matching beadwork: the galluses were much longer than those worn in Oklahoma, sometimes reaching to the ankles. Belts were wider, cuffs larger. Many dancers wore tennis sneakers instead of moccasins. Accessories for this costume were not limited to beadwork. Sequins, rhinestones, and miscellaneous items from the local dry goods stores were used as decoration. Individual ornamentation was highly creative, yet all the costumes were definitely discernible as Northern.

Today the Oglalas and Sicangus at Rosebud have somewhat modified the North Dakota costume into what they call the "real Sioux" outfit. It is necessarily a combination of the Oklahoma and North Dakota styles, retaining the tailored bustles of the South and the fringe and heavy beadwork of the North.

Occasionally one sees some of the old-time costumes. While many of the older conservatives have costumes from the 1900 period, few of them wear them at powwows.

Women's costumes. While many of the women still own traditional Sioux dresses with characteristic full beaded yokes, most of them wear homemade cotton dresses or dresses of non-Indian manufacture. All, however, wear hand-fringed shawls or substitutes when they dance. This has lead the announcer to refer to the women as "shawl dancers."

Peyote paraphernalia. For all practical purposes peyote paraphernalia does not exist as a dancer's costume accessory.

Patriotic organizations. As in Oklahoma, various Indian patriotic organizations are active at powwows.

Oklahoma Elements Found in Pan-Tetonism

By comparing elements found in Oklahoma pan-Indianism with those in pan-Tetonism, it becomes clear which Oklahoma, or non-Indian, elements have infiltrated the pan-Teton complex. The most outstanding (in the order of their frequency) are: (1) the fancy war dance style, with its related costume; (2) the contest, which is becoming more and more popular; (3) the Powwow Princess; (4) the procession, which is represented at Pine Ridge by the snake dance; and (5) female war dancers.

Compared to the total number of elements comprising pan-Tetonism,[7] the above elements represent about twenty percent of the pan-Teton aggregate, or, in other words, Oklahoma pan-Indian elements seem to comprise about one-fifth of pan-Tetonism. The round dance, the forty-nine, the stomp dance, the Oklahoma "specials" (with the exception of the hoop dance), the various positions of head and tail dancers, and the wearing of peyote paraphernalia do not exist at all in pan-Tetonism. This accounts for approximately fifty percent of Oklahoma elements which *do not* manifest themselves in pan-Tetonism. The remaining thirty percent represents common Plains elements similar in both Oklahoma pan-Indianism and pan-Tetonism.

On the other hand, of the twenty percent of Oklahoma elements found in pan-Tetonism, half have been influenced by the North Dakota style (war dance, contest, and whistle bearer), so that essentially very little of Oklahoma pan-Indianism exists in pan-Tetonism.

[7] I realize that not all elements are equally important. This is simply an illustrative approximation.

PAN-TETON ELEMENTS FOUND IN OKLAHOMA PAN-INDIANISM

The pan-Teton complex also contributes certain elements to the pan-Indian aggregate. The most important is music, but Teton music is not supplanting Oklahoma music; it merely influences it. It appears that in time more and more Teton, or at least Northern, songs will influence pan-Indian singers off the Sioux reservations.

The only other contributory elements influencing the pan-Indian aggregate are (1) the Northern style of war dance and (2) men's costuming. These influences are being strongly felt in urban areas. Only a few Northern dancers have appeared in Oklahoma, and at this time the Oklahomans are skeptical of the intrusion. It is difficult to predict how popular Northern style will ever be in Oklahoma, but its influence is certainly a major factor among the Oglalas, and it would appear that by accepting the Northern complex, which is basically pan-Teton, the Oglalas are essentially striving to adhere to that which is "Sioux," rather than that which is "Indian."

THE OGLALAS: SURVIVAL VERSUS REVIVAL

The connotation of pan-Indianism is not only nationalization, but survival. But in what direction is pan-Indianism leading the American Indian? Will he ever reach the point where tribal identity is lost in a potpourri of "Indianness?" Will Oglala tribalism be submerged in a pan-Teton complex, to be later lost in a true pan-Indian aggregate? The answers, of course, require far more data than are currently available, but one important question is, Might not pan-Indianism lead its members into a stronger appreciation of tribalism? Let us briefly examine recent Oglala history, as well as some significant movements in Oklahoma.

Authorities do not agree in which direction pan-Indianism is leading American Indians. While there is a definite trend toward similarity of religious, economic, and political thought, the trends of dance and dance costumes are less predictable. One should assume a priori that there is a trend toward the disintegration of tribalism. Even in Oklahoma, which is considered the cradle of pan-Indianism, several tribal functions have been revived in the prime of the pan-Indian movement. Among these have been the Ponca rejuvenation of the Heduška, the Kiowa Black Legging Society, and the Kiowa-Apache Black Foot Society. While these survivals may not be based entirely on distinctively tribal functions of the last century, they nevertheless are an indication that active tribes need something more than the homogeneity of pan-Indianism to fulfill their identity as Indians (Powers 1966).

The Oglalas had at least one significant revival in 1959 when the sun dance, including its self-torture, was performed. Before that time the United States government had prohibited the torture. Since 1959 the sun dance has been performed every summer, each year with more and more dancers participating in the "piercing." However, the sun dance, under the sponsorship of the Oglala tribal council, which presents it as a tourist attraction, has deteriorated to the point where it is little more than an unsuccessful side show—a flesh carnival, if you will—in which the audience is invited to watch the spectacular of self-inflicted pain. The conservatives consider this a mockery of the earlier religious practice and want to band together to direct the sun dance themselves and to eliminate the tribal council's authority. Like the Arapahos, whom the Oglalas respect for their religious ceremonies, the Oglala conservatives want to keep the sun dance separate from the powwow.[8] The problem has been in the talking stage for eight years, and if they do separate the sun dance from the powwow, it will be a major achievement.

There are some other revivals of lesser importance. The kettle dance has been performed more frequently on the reservation in the past eight or nine years; earlier it survived only as a show dance performed off the reservation. A change in the character of the dance has occurred: there is today more religious symbolism involved than was true when I first witnessed the traditional form in 1949. In general, an attitude prevails today that whatever is old-time is similarly religious. Because of this attitude, revived secular events may assume a new, religious significance.

Some women, at least at the smaller functions, are dancing "old-time," that is, simply bobbing in place around the outer perimeter of the dance area. This was the old Oglala style of dance until the mid-1950s, when under the Oklahoma influence women began to dance in the same area as the men. Another change is that, at the larger functions, the Oglala women dance clockwise around the men, performing

[8] The Wind River Arapahos have two dance arbors, one for the sun dance, the other for powwows. Powwow dancers are not permitted to dance in the sun dance arbor.

the "walking" step of the Oklahoma women. However, they dance on the inside of the circle near the center pole, in contrast to the Oklahoma women, who dance among the men in the same direction.

Further, women do not wear traditional costuming to the extent they did before the mid-1950s; they simply wear shawls over cotton dresses. They still own traditional costumes but, like the men, now consider them antiques and hesitate to risk damaging them by usage. There was a great deal of men's costuming reminiscent of the 1940s and early fifties worn at the 1966 sun dance celebration. Such costuming was not prevalent in the late fifties and early sixties.

While announcements are bilingual at the larger celebrations, at the small functions they are in Lakota. Many public signs are written in Lakota (the instruction sign at the Pine Ridge laundromat is written in Lakota and English!).

Another subject which is not reported on here but is worth investigating is the retention of religious practices. The nativistic religion, Yuwipi, as well as the sweat lodge and vision quest are still popular, even among the younger generation.

It would appear that if the aspects of behavior which are pan-Indian do not lead directly to tribalism, they at least give tribal members an opportunity to reconsider the revival of important ceremonies and customs.

It also appears that with the strong North Dakota influence, which is characteristically more conservative than pan-Indianism, what appears as new to the Oglalas is really a revival. A case in point is the custom of begging from tent to tent by a group of singers. This custom, called in English the "doorway," or "they dance in front of the doorway," was introduced at the 1962 sun dance as a North Dakota custom. Upon investigation, however, I discovered that the custom was also observed at Pine Ridge "a long time ago," and is related to what Densmore (1918) calls the "Begging dance."

SUMMARY

Pan-Indianism has been treated as an aggregate which has not been sufficiently investigated. It is comprised of elements which may be traced either to tribal or non-Indian origin and which in turn evolve and change. Within pan-Indianism there is a smaller but equally vital complex which may be called pan-Tetonism. Pan-Tetonism, as it affects the Oglalas, may be divided into two groups, the traditional, and the North Dakota style. Among the Oglalas there are three prevalent styles of music and dance, as well as related customs and material culture: (1) traditional, (2) Oklahoma, and (3) Northern.

By comparing the elements of Oklahoma pan-Indianism with pan-Tetonism we find that fewer Oklahoma than North Dakota traits influence the Oglalas. Although there was a strengthening of Oklahoma pan-Indianism in the mid-1950s, the prominent features are being replaced by Northern traits. This gives the impression that the Oglalas still maintain a stronger allegiance to that which is "Sioux" than to that which is "Indian."

While more data are needed, there is some indication that pan-Indianism may be directing American Indians to a greater appreciation of tribal traits. The Oglalas, as well as some Oklahoma tribes, have brought about such revivals within the past eight years. There is also some indication that forgotten customs may reappear under the guise of modern innovations.

REFERENCES

DENSMORE, FRANCES. 1918. *Teton Sioux music.* Bureau of American Ethnology bulletin no. 6. Washington, D.C.: G.P.O.

FEDER, NORMAN. 1964. Origin of the Oklahoma forty-nine dance. *Journal of the Society for Ethnomusicology* 3, no. 3: 290–94.

HOWARD, JAMES H. 1951. Notes on the Dakota grass dance. *Southwestern Journal of Anthropology* 7, no. 1: 82–85.

———. 1955. The pan Indian culture of Oklahoma. *Scientific Monthly* 18, no. 5: 215–20.

———. 1965a. The compleat stomp dancer. University of South Dakota *Museum News* 26, nos. 5–6: 1–23.

———. 1965b. *The Ponca tribe.* Bureau of American Ethnology bulletin no. 195. Washington, D.C.: G.P.O.

KURATH, GERTRUDE P. 1964. *Iroquois music and dance.* Bureau of American Ethnology bulletin no. 187. Washington, D.C.: G.P.O.

LURIE, NANCY OESTREICH. 1965. An American Indian renascence? *Midcontinent American Studies Journal* 6, no. 2: 25–50.

POWERS, WILLIAM K. 1961. The Sioux Omaha dance. *American Indian Tradition* 8, no. 1: 24–33.

———. 1962a. The rabbit dance. *American Indian Tradition* 8, no. 3: 113–18.

Powers, William, K. 1962b. Sneak-up dance, drum dance, and flag dance. *American Indian Tradition* 8, no. 4: 166–71.

———. 1966. Feathers' costume. *Powwow Trails* 3, nos. 7–8: 4–19.

Thomas, Robert K. 1965. Pan-Indianism. *Midcontinental American Studies Journal* 6, no. 2: 75–83.

Wissler, Clark. 1912. Societies and ceremonial associations in the Oglala division of Teton-Dakota. In *Anthropological Papers*, vol. 11, part 1. New York: American Museum of Natural History.

Bibliography

Prepared by Ruth Hill Useem and Ethel Nurge.

ABLON, JOAN. 1964. Relocated American Indians in the San Francisco Bay Area: Social interaction and Indian identity. *Human Organization* 24: 296–304.

ADAMS, EVELYN C. 1946. *American Indian education.* New York: King's Crown Press.

ARTICHOKER, JOHN, AND PALMER, NEIL M. 1959. *The Sioux Indian goes to college.* Institute of Indian Studies and South Dakota State Department of Public Instruction.

BATESON, GREGORY. 1935. Culture contact and schismogenesis. *Man* 35: 178–83.

BEALS, RALPH L. 1951. Urbanism, urbanization and acculturation. *American Anthropologist* 53: 1–10.

———. 1953. Acculturation. In *Anthropology Today*, ed. A. L. Kroeber, pp. 621–41. Chicago: University of Chicago Press.

BEATTY, WILLARD W. 1956. Twenty years of Indian education. In *The Indian in modern America*, ed. David A. Baerris. Madison: State Historical Society of Wisconsin.

BROPHY, WILLIAM. 1953. The federal government and the Indian. In *Ethnic relations in the United States*, ed. E. C. McDonagh, pp. 211–19. New York: Appleton-Century Co.

BROWN, JOSEPH L. 1953. *The sacred pipe.* Norman: University of Oklahoma Press.

BURDICK, USHER L. 1941. *The last days of Sitting Bull, Sioux medicine chief.* Baltimore: Wirth Brothers.

COOMBS, MADISON L., KRON, RALPH E., COLLISTER, GORDON E., AND ANDERSON, KENNETH E. 1958. *The Indian child goes to school: A study of interracial differences.* U.S. Department of the Interior, Bureau of Indian Affairs, Lawrence, Kansas: Haskell Institute.

DALE, GEORGE A. 1955. *Education for better living*. Washington, D.C.: U.S. Dept. of Interior, Bureau of Indian Affairs.

DANIELS, WALTER. 1957. *American Indians*. New York: H. W. Wilson Co.

DELORIA, ELLA C. 1944. Dakota treatment of murderers. *Proceedings of the American Philosophical Society* 88: 368–71.

———. 1944. *Speaking of Indians*. New York: Friendship Press.

DEVEREUX, GEORGE. 1951. *Reality and dream*. New York: International Universities Press.

DEVEREUX, GEORGE, AND LOEB, EDWIN M. Antagonistic acculturation. *American Sociological Review* 8: 133–47.

DORNER, PETER. 1959. The economic position of the American Indian: Their resources and potential for development. Ph.D. dissertation, Harvard University.

DURATSCHEK, MARY C. 1943. The beginnings of Catholicism in South Dakota. Ph.D. dissertation, Catholic University of America.

———. 1947. *Crusading along Sioux trails: A history of the Catholic Indian missions of South Dakota*. New York: Grail Publishers.

EGGAN, FRED R., ED. 1937. *Social anthropology of North American tribes*. Chicago: University of Chicago Press.

EICHER, CARL K. 1961–62. An approach to income improvement on the Rosebud Sioux Indian Reservation. *Human Organization* 20: 191–96.

Family income and related characteristics among low-income counties and states. Welfare Research Report 1. U.S. Dept. of Health, Education, and Welfare.

FARBER, W. O. 1957. *Indians, law enforcement and local government*. Report no. 37. Governmental Research Bureau, University of South Dakota.

Federal Indian legislation and policies. 1956. Prepared by the Workshop on American Indian Affairs, sponsored by the University of Chicago Dept. of Anthropology.

FERACA, STEPHEN E. 1957. The contemporary Teton Sioux sun dance. Master's thesis, Columbia University.

———. 1961. The Yuwipi cult of the Oglala and Sicangu Teton Sioux. *Plains Anthropologist* 6: 155–63.

FEY, HAROLD E., AND McNICKLE, D'ARCY. 1959. *Indians and other Americans*. New York: Harper.

GLADWIN, THOMAS. 1957. Personality structure in the Plains. *Anthropology Quarterly* 30: 111–24.

GORDON, MILTON M. 1963. Recent trends in the study of minority and race relations. *Annals of the American Academy of Political and Social Science* 350: 148–56.

———. 1964. *Assimilation in American Life*. New York: Oxford University Press.

GRINNELL, IRA H. 1959. The tribal government of the Oglala Sioux of Pine Ridge, South Dakota. Master's thesis, State University of South Dakota.

HAGAN, WILLIAM T. 1961. *American Indians.* Chicago: University of Chicago Press.

HANNA, JOHN A. 1961. Civil rights—a national challenge. *South Dakota Law Review* 6: 1–30.

HARMON, GEORGE D. 1941. *Sixty years of Indian affairs.* Chapel Hill: University of North Carolina Press.

HASSRICK, ROYAL B. 1944. Teton Dakota kinship system. *American Anthropologist* 46: 338–48.

HAVIGHURST, ROBERT J., AND NEUGARTEN, BERNICE L. 1955. *American Indian and white children.* Chicago: University of Chicago Press.

HOWARD, JAMES H. 1951. Two Dakota dream headdresses. *University of South Dakota Museum News* 12: 1–3.

———. 1954a. The Dakota Heyoka cult. *Scientific Monthly* 78: 254–58.

———. 1954b. Plains Indian feather bonnets. *Plains Anthropologist* 2: 23–26.

———. 1960. The northern style grass dance costume. *American Indian Hobbyist* 7: 18–27.

———. 1962. Peyote jokes. *Journal of American Folklore* 75: 10–14.

———. 1963. News report number 18, Institute of Indian Studies. *State University of South Dakota Bulletin*, ser. 63, bull. no. 28.

———. 1966. *The Dakota or Sioux Indians: A study in human ecology.* Dakota Museum, University of South Dakota, Anthropological Papers, no. 2. Vermillion, South Dakota.

———, ED. 1969. *The warrior who killed Custer: The personal narrative of Chief Joseph White Bull.* Lincoln: University of Nebraska Press.

HURT, WESLEY R. 1960a. Factors in the persistence of peyote in the Northern Plains. *Plains Anthropologist* 5: 16–27.

———. 1960b. The Yankton Dakota church. In *Essays in the science of culture,* ed. G. E. Dole and R. L. Carneiro, pp. 269–87. New York: Thomas Y. Crowell Co.

———. 1960c. A Yuwipi ceremony at Pine Ridge. *Plains Anthropologist* 5: 48–52.

HURT, WESLEY R., AND HOWARD, JAMES H. 1952. A Dakota conjuring ceremony. *Southwestern Journal of Anthropology* 8: 28–29.

HYDE, G. E. 1937. *Red Cloud's folk.* Norman: University of Oklahoma Press.

Institute of Indian Studies occasional papers. 1959. No. 1. State University of South Dakota, Vermillion, South Dakota.

JESSER, CLINTON J. 1958. The changing traditional value system of the Dakota Indians. Master's thesis, South Dakota State College.

JOHNSON, CHARLES. 1957. Fort Thompson, South Dakota, an American non-self governing community. Master's thesis, Columbia University.

KEHOE, ALICE B. 1968. The ghost dance religion in Saskatchewan, Canada. *Plains Anthropologist*, 296–304.

KELSEY, F. E. *The pharmacology of peyote.* Scientific paper, State University of South Dakota, Vermillion.

KRAENZEL, CARL. 1955. *The Great Plains in transition.* Norman: University of Oklahoma Press.

LA BARRE, WESTON. 1964. The diabolic root. *New York Times Magazine,* Nov. 1, 1964, pp. 96–98.

LADD, ANDERSON. 1953. *The educational achievement of Indian children.* Bureau of Indian Affairs.

LANDES, RUTH. 1968. *The Mystic Lake Sioux: Sociology of the Mdewakantonwan Santee.* Madison: University of Wisconsin Press.

LOVRICH, FRANK. 1952. The assimilation of the Indian in Rapid City. Master's thesis, University of South Dakota.

MCALLISTER, GILBERT J. 1955. Kiowa-Apache social organization. In *Social anthropology of North American tribes,* ed. Fred Eggan, pp. 99–169. Chicago: University of Chicago Press.

MCCONE, CLYDE R. Time and tide: A study of the conflicting concepts of time of the Dakota Indians and Western Civilization. Master's thesis, South Dakota State College

MCGILLYCUDDY, JULIA B. 1941. *McGillycuddy, agent.* Palo Alto, Calif.: Stanford University Press.

MACGREGOR, GORDON. 1942. Indian education in relation to the social and economic background of the reservation. In *The changing Indian,* ed. Oliver LaFarge. Norman: University of Oklahoma Press.

————. 1963. *Plains Indian personality and social adaptation.* U.S. Dept. of Health, Education, and Welfare, 1963.

MACK, RAYMOND. 1964. The components of social conflict. Remarks before the plenary session on "Perspectives and Strategies" of the Society for the Study of Social Problems, Montreal, P.Q., Canada, August 29.

MALAN, VERNON D. 1956. Tuberculosis among the South Dakota Indians. *South Dakota Farm and Home Research* 7: 112–15.

————. 1959a. *An annotated bibliography of culture change for the Teton Dakota Indians.* Pamphlet no. 120, Rural Sociology Department. South Dakota State College, Brookings.

————. 1959b. Indian college students plan for the future. *South Dakota Farm and Home Research* 10: 10–15.

————. 1961. Theories of culture change relevant to the study of the Dakota Indians. *Plains Anthropologist* 6: 13–20.

————. 1962a. *The social system of the Dakota Indians.* Extension circular 606, Cooperative Extension Service. South Dakota State College, Brookings.

————. 1962b. To change a culture. *South Dakota Farm and Home Research* 13: 12–14.

————. 1963a. *The Dakota Indian economy: Factors associated with success or failure in ranching.* South Dakota Experiment Station Bulletin no. 509. South Dakota State College. Brookings, South Dakota.

————. 1963b. The value system of the Dakota Indians. *Journal of American Indian Education* 3: 21–25.

MALAN, VERNON D., AND JESSER, CLINTON J. 1959. *The Dakota Indian religion.* South Dakota Experiment Station Bulletin no. 473. South Dakota State College, Brookings.

MALAN, VERNON D., AND McCONE, CLYDE. 1960. Time concept, perspective, and premise in the socio-cultural order of the Dakota Indians. *Plains Anthropologist* 5: 12–15.

MALAN, VERNON D., AND POWERS, JOSEPH F. 1960. *The Crow Creek Indian family.* South Dakota Experiment Station Bulletin no. 487. South Dakota State College, Brookings.

MALAN, VERNON D., AND SCHUSKY, ERNEST L. 1962. *The Dakota Indian community.* South Dakota Experiment Station Bulletin no. 505. South Dakota State College, Brookings.

MARTIN, HARRY W. 1964. Correlates of adjustment among American Indians in an urban environment. *Human Organization* 23: 290–95.

MATTES, MERRIL J. 1960. The enigma of Wounded Knee. *Plains Anthropologist* 5: 1–11.

MEKEEL, H. SCUDDER. 1936. An anthropologist's observations on Indian education. *Progressive Education* 13: 151–59.

———. 1943. A short history of the Teton-Dakota. *North Dakota Historical Quarterly* 10: 137–205.

MISHKIN, BERNARD. 1940. *Rank and warfare among the Plains Indians.* American Ethnological Society Monograph 3. Seattle: University of Washington Press.

NADER, RALPH. 1956. American Indians: People without a future. *Harvard Law Record,* May 10, 1956.

NEWCOMBE, W. W., JR. 1950. A re-examination of the causes of Plains Indian warfare. *American Anthropologist* 52: 317–30.

NURGE, ETHEL. 1966. The Sioux sun dance in 1962. *Proceedings of the XXXVI Congreso Internacional de Americanistas,* vol. 3. Seville, Spain.

OLIVER, SYMNES C. 1962. *Ecology and cultural continuity as contributing factors in the social organization of the Plains Indians.* Berkeley and Los Angeles: University of California Press.

OVER, WILLIAM H. 1950. *Life of Sitting Bull.* Vermillion: University of South Dakota Museum.

A program for Indian citizens: A summary report. 1961. Albuquerque, New Mexico: Commission on the Rights, Liberties, and Responsibilities of the American Indian.

Program and proceedings of First Annual Conference for Tribal Judges, Vermillion, South Dakota, March 2–6, 1959.

PROVINSE, JOHN J. 1937. The underlying sanctions of Plains Indian culture. In *Social Anthropology of North American Tribes,* ed. Fred Eggan, pp. 341–74. Chicago: University of Chicago Press.

Report on preliminary survey of civil rights problems of American Indians. May 9, 1960. Commission on Civil Rights.

RICHARDSON, JANE. 1940. *Law and status among the Kiowa Indians.* American Ethnological Society, Monograph 1. Seattle: University of Washington Press.

ROBERTS, FRANK H., JR., ED. 1964. *River basin surveys paper.* Washington, D.C.: Agency Archeological Salvage Program.

ROBERTS, WILLIAM O. 1943. Dakota Indians: Successful agriculture within the reservation framework. *Applied Anthropology* 11: 37–44.

SCHUSKY, ERNEST. 1959. *Politics and planning in a Dakota Indian community.* Institute of Indian Studies, State University of South Dakota.

———. 1962. Contemporary migration and culture change on two Dakota Indian reservations. *Plains Anthropologist* 7: 178–83.

SCHUSKY, ERNEST, AND MALAN, VERNON. 1962. *Social and economic factors in the development of Pine Ridge Reservation.* Agricultural Experiment Station, South Dakota State College.

SECOY, FRANK RAYMOND. 1953. *Changing military patterns on the Great Plains.* American Ethnological Society, Monograph 21. Seattle: University of Washington Press.

SKINNER, THOMAS. 1885. *United States Congressional Record,* 40th Congress, 2d Session, vol. 17, pt. 2.

SLOTKIN, JAMES S. 1956. *The peyote religion.* Glencoe, Ill.: Free Press.

South Dakota State Planning Board. 1937. *Indians of South Dakota.* Brookings, South Dakota, Central Office.

SPINDLER, GEORGE AND LOUISE. 1957. American Indian personality types and their socio-cultural roots. *Annals of the American Academy of Political and Social Science* 311: 147–57.

STERNER, ARMIN H., AND MACGREGOR, GORDON. 1939. The Pine Ridge vocational survey. *Indian Education* 31: 2–8; 32: 2–7.

THOMPSON, LAURA. 1948. Attitudes and acculturation. *American Anthropologist* 50: 200–15.

———. 1951. Personality and government: Findings and recommendations of the Indian Administration Research. *Ediciones Del Instituto Indigenista Interamericano,* Mexico, D.F.

TYLER, LYMAN S. 1964. *Indian affairs: A study of the changes in policy of the United States toward Indians.* Institute of American Indian Studies at Brigham Young University, Provo, Utah.

UNDERHILL, RUTH MURRAY. 1953. *Red man's America.* Chicago: University of Chicago Press.

USEEM, RUTH HILL. 1954. Statement by Ruth Hill Useem. *American Anthropologist* 56: 393–94.

VOGET, FRED. 1958. The American Indian in transition: Reformation and status innovation. *American Journal of Sociology* 62: 369–78.

WAX, MURRAY. 1962. The notions of nature, man, and time of a hunting people. *Southern Folklore Quarterly* 26: 175–86.

WAX, MURRAY, AND WAX, ROSALIE. 1964. Cultural deprivation as an educational ideology. *Journal of American Indian Education* 3: 15–18.

WAX, ROSALIE. 1961. *A brief history and analysis of the workshops on American Indian affairs conducted for American Indian college students, 1956–1960, together with A study of current attitudes and activities of those students.* Department of Anthropology, University of Miami, Coral Gables, Florida.

WEDEL, WALDO R. 1953. Some aspects of human ecology in the Central Plains. *American Anthropologist* 55: 499–514.

Appendix I: Compilation of Maps and Population Figures

THE COMPILATION of useful population statistics is no small task. Officials in the United States Census Bureau are cognizant of the problems and, particularly, some of the associated scientists are concerned with the need for the identification of the tribal affiliation of Indians, whether such Indians dwell on their own or on another reservation, in a city, or elsewhere. It is hoped that an item making tribal identification possible will appear in the 1970 census questionnaire. Other desiderata would include information on education, income, and occupation, the triad on which so many social-class studies are based. Meanwhile, one of the difficulties of working with published population figures is that the sums are often given in terms of a geographical or political unit rather than in terms of ethnic composition. While it was not within the scope of our project and we had neither funds nor personnel to undertake a full study, an effort was made (1) to find out how many residents each Dakota reservation had, and (2) to prepare a map showing the reservations (or reserves, as they are called in Canada) where the Sioux lived. Neither task was simple and I am not satisfied with the results, but the maps printed in this volume do present data graphically and economically.

The maps on the following pages were prepared by Mr. C. E. Heidenreich, a graduate student at McMaster University in the Department of Geography, and were based on material and instructions provided by me. The sources are:

1. *Sioux Territory, 1680–1963.* This map was modified slightly from one prepared by Royal B. Hassrick for his *The Sioux: Life and Customs of a Warrior Society* (University of Oklahoma Press, 1964). Both the author and the Press have granted permission for its reproduction.

2. *Sioux and Neighboring Reservations in the Western United States and Canada.* This map was drawn from the following maps: (1) *Indian Land Areas* (United States Department of Interior, Bureau of Indian Affairs, Washington, D.C., 1961); and (2) *Prairie Provinces* (Canada Department of Mines and Technical Surveys, Ottawa, 1962).

3. *Population of Sioux Reservations in the Western United States and Canada* is based on *Indian Land Areas, Prairie Provinces,* and the following:

S. Feraca, Sketch map of *The Sioux and Their Indian Neighbors in 1965.* With population information extracted from the *Bureau of Indian Affairs U.S. Indian Population and Land Report, 1962.* Canadian population figures for Saskatchewan came from Indian Affairs Branch Report of December, 1963.

C. I. Fairholm, Secretariate, Indian Affairs Branch, Ottawa, Ontario, information supplied on the location of Sioux Reserves in Canada (letter to Nurge dated May 21, 1965).

W. M. Hlady, Regional Liaison Officer, Department of Citizenship and Immigration, Winnipeg, Manitoba, information supplied on population and location of Sioux Reserves in Manitoba for 1958 and 1964 (letter to Nurge dated June 15, 1965).

A. B. Kehoe, Regina, Saskatchewan, information supplied on the location and size of Sioux Reserves in Saskatchewan (letter to Nurge dated June 13, 1965).

T. E. Kemnitzer, Philadelphia, Pennsylvania, information supplied on population figures for Sioux Reservations in Nebraska, North Dakota, and South Dakota in 1960, abstracted from U.S. Public Health Service, *Indians on Federal Reservations in the U.S., Aberdeen Area, 1959;* information supplied on *Dakota and Related Groups, Indian Population and Land by State, Agency, Reservations, and Tribe,* abstracted from U.S. Department of Interior, Bureau of Indian Affairs, *United States Indian Population and Land, 1962* (Washington, 1963).

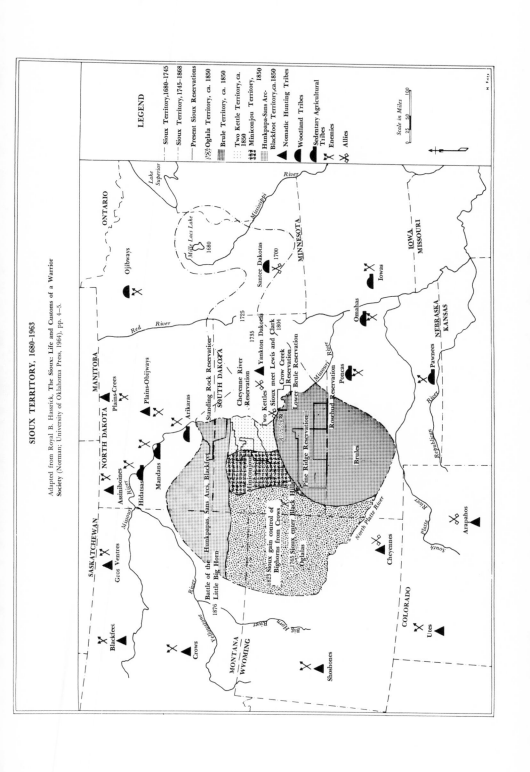

SIOUX TERRITORY, 1680-1963

Adapted from Royal B. Hassrick, The Sioux: Life and Customs of a Warrior Society (Norman; University of Oklahoma Press, 1964), pp. 4-5.

LEGEND

- Sioux Territory, 1680-1745
- Sioux Territory, 1745-1868
- Present Sioux Reservations
- Oglala Territory, ca. 1850
- Brule Territory, ca. 1850
- Two Kettle Territory, ca. 1850
- Minikonjou Territory, 1850
- Hunkpapa-Sans Arc-Blackfoot Territory, ca. 1850
- Nomadic Hunting Tribes
- Woodland Tribes
- Sedentary Agricultural Tribes
- Enemies
- Allies

Scale in Miles
0 25 50 100

SIOUX AND NEIGHBORING RESERVATIONS IN THE WESTERN UNITED STATES AND CANADA

Compiled from Indian Land Areas (Washington, D.C.: U.S. Dept. of the Interior,
Bureau of Indian Affairs, 1961) and Prairie Provinces (Ottawa, Canada: Dept.
of Mines and Tech. Surveys, 1962).

ROUND PLAINS 94A
WAHPATON 94B

MOOSE WOODS 94

STANDING BUFFALO 78

Regina

BIRDTAIL 57
OAK LAKE 58
Winnipeg
OAK LAKE 59   LONG PLAIN 6A

ALBERTA   SASKATCHEWAN   WOOD MOUNTAIN 160   MANITOBA   ONTARIO

TURTLE
MOUNTAIN

FORT PECK   RED LAKE   NETT
LAKE   GREATER
FORT BELKNAP   DEVILS   LEECH LAKE   Lake
FORT   LAKE   WHITE   Superior
BERTHOLD   EARTH   FOND DU LAC   Duluth

MILLE
LACS   LAC COURTE
CROW   STANDING ROCK   NORTH DAKOTA   ST. CROIX   OREILLE
TONGUE   SOUTH DAKOTA
RIVER   CHEYENNE RIVER   SISSETON   Minneapolis   St. Paul
MONTANA   PRAIRIE ISLAND
WYOMING   LOWER   UPPER   PRIOR
SIOUX   SIOUX   LAKE
LOWER   CROW   Flandreau   MINNESOTA
BRULE   CREEK
WIND RIVER   PINE RIDGE   ROSEBUD   YANKTON
PONCA
SANTEE
WINNEBAGO
OMAHA   Des Moines

COLORADO   Omaha   IOWA
Lincoln   MISSOURI

NEBRASKA
Denver   KANSAS
Topeka   Kansas City

LEGEND

Sioux Reservations ▨   Other Reservations ⣿   Scale in Miles

71 ━━ Interstate Highways   0 25 50   100   200   300

Note: Fort Peck Reservation includes some Sioux. The number opposite
Canadian reserves denotes the federal reserve number.

POPULATION OF SIOUX RESERVATIONS IN THE WESTERN UNITED STATES AND CANADA, 1962

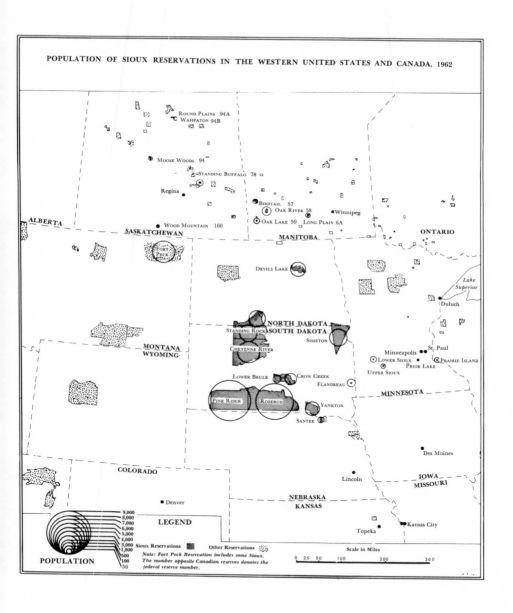

Sol Tax, map, *The North American Indians* (Department of Anthropology, University of Chicago, 1950). A 1960 revision of this map was consulted, but the population figures were identical to the 1950 figures.

In the course of preparing the maps, the table below was compiled to show precisely what population figures were available for what dates. It is reprinted to show both the spotty nature of the data and the changes in totals over a period of time. The reader is cautioned that what is depicted must be interpreted with care:

TABLE OF AVAILABLE POPULATION FIGURES

	1950	1958	1960	1962	1963	1964
MANITOBA						
Birdtail (# 57)	103	137				175
Long Plain (# 6A)	446	159				191
Oak Lake (# 59)	451	172				220
Oak River (# 58)	124	611				718
MINNESOTA						
Lower Sioux				192		
Prairie Island	582			86		
Prior Lake				22		
Upper Sioux				97		
MONTANA						
Fort Peck	3,285			3,071		
NEBRASKA						
Santee	1,372		317	300		
NORTH DAKOTA						
Fort Totten	1,300		1,463	1,476		
Standing Rock	4,500		3,751	2,300		
SASKATCHEWAN						
Standing Buffalo (# 78)	258				396	
Wahpaton (# 94A)					81	
White Cap (# 94)	81				121	
Wood Mountain (# 160)	38				50	
SOUTH DAKOTA						
Cheyenne River	4,307		3,493	3,734		
Crow Creek	1,132		1,183	1,058		
Flandreau	289		264	283		
Lower Brule	705		596	509		
Pine Ridge	10,648		8,200	8,780		
Rosebud	8,183		6,512	7,201		
Sisseton	3,542		2,315	2,271		
Yankton	2,391		1,426	1,533		

Appendix II: Unpublished Source Materials

FOLLOWING IS a summary of unpublished and other miscellaneous materials which were listed in the responses to the questionnaire sent to people who had worked among the Dakotas. Published material is listed in the Bibliography. The departmental affiliation or the partial addresses given are those of the respondents at the time they answered the questionnaire (1965), and in some instances, this information was corrected in response to an invitation in 1967 to update and correct the information about their work and their whereabouts.

Daniel Beveridge of the Department of Sociology, University of Saskatchewan, Saskatoon, Saskatchewan, wrote that he had a thesis or dissertation (which, is not specified) called "The Socio-ecological Correlates of Economic Dependence in Four Dakota (Sioux) Communities in Saskatchewan." The four communities are not designated. He has in his possession journals for 1962 and 1963, including field notes of visits to the four Dakota communities in Saskatchewan and 85 interview schedules for households in which someone was questioned about the age, sex, educational level, birthplace, ethnicity, and language of inhabitants; level of living; households visited and frequency; communities visited and frequency; social participation; income sources and amounts for 1962; and parentage. In addition, he has some genealogies and miscellaneous agricultural statistics from 1890 to 1963.

Robert E. Daniels, presently at the Department of Anthropology, University of North Carolina, who has contributed to this volume, first wrote about his thesis, written at the University of Chicago, as follows:

> I am currently writing my M.A. thesis on "The Symbols of Cultural Identity among the Oglala Sioux." It is a structural analysis of the readily discernible, and often rather trivial aspects of reservation life which serve as diagnostic symbols of group identity. Included is a discussion of family names, clothing styles, house types, and most importantly, terms in English and Lakota used by people on the reservation to identify themselves, and to classify (and thus judge and influence) others, e.g., *wasicun*, *eyeska*, *lakota*, *hasapa*, full-blood, mixed-blood, and half-breed, white, Negro, etc. By discussing these terms in the contexts in which they are used, I hope to arrive at statements about the rules or criteria involved, the contrasts between different sets of criteria used by whites and various "types" of Indians, and perhaps some changes in the sets of criteria (cognitive system) of the Oglala when compared with data from the pre-reservation and early reservation period.
>
> I am also interested in discussing the symbolic behavior of the Oglala with respect to "America," i.e., patriotism to the U.S., the significance of the Sioux National Anthem (national meaning U.S.), the patterns of honoring the flag, the war dead, etc. I am relating this to a general discussion of the Oglala perceptions of themselves as a group both within and apart from American society. I have not yet decided if the latter will be a separate manuscript.
>
> In the analysis of these matters I was led first to abandon a discussion of what is today "Indian" according to a strictly descriptive, historical-origins approach and, second, the contrast the cognitive reality of "groups" with the sociological definition of groups in terms of interaction. I feel this is necessary to deal with the vexing problem of "group" boundaries among the reservation population.

He also has sixty single-spaced pages of field notes in rough sentence form, organized as a journal or diary for the period June 14–August 12, 1963. He was particularly interested in the Wright-McGill fishhook factories on the reservation and their employees. His notes also contain descriptions of unrelated observations and interviews. He named the informants for a series of key interviews, but their names are deleted here; their statuses are given when known. The subjects were (1) local politics and a fight over the transfer of reservation jurisdiction to state level; (2) discrimination by "mixed-bloods" from the point of view of a "full-blood"; (3) the organization and history of the local factories, given by the Wright-McGill reservation supervisor; (4) wages and working conditions, by assorted employees; (5) the impact of the factory, by the relocation officer; and (6) general topics volunteered by the Episcopal missionary and his family.

Dr. Daniels also has a few pages of observations of the 1963 sun dance at Pine Ridge, some on local social dances in Manderson and Wounded Knee, and a few on the American Jewish Society for Service work camp in Pine Ridge town and Oglala. There is also a summary table of the number of employees on the Kyle factory payroll, weekly through June 28, 1963. Besides the journal, he has approximately three minutes of tape recording of grass dance songs, and approximately six minutes of 8mm film of the 1963 sun dance, both the religious service and the afternoon grass dancing, and the parade in Pine Ridge town following the completion of the religious dance; and he possesses a six-inch reel of tape, recorded at $1\frac{7}{8}$ rpm at Crow Creek Reservation in the summer of 1961 by another investigator and including the singing of both grass dance songs and Episcopal hymns in Lakota.

Dr. William O. Farber reports that he has been making studies of the planning process with special reference to the Indian reservations in South Dakota and recently supervised an M.A. thesis by Richard E. Brown, "The Planning Process of the Pine Ridge and Rosebud Sioux Indian Reservations in South Dakota: A Comparative Analysis" (University of South Dakota, June, 1967, 124 pp.). In addition, he has been preparing materials on the duties of tribal officers.

Mr. Stephen E. Feraca, community development officer at the Seminole Indian Agency, Bureau of Indian Affairs, Hollywood, Florida, has been studying Teton religion, economics, political development, and, to a lesser extent, education, since the summer of 1954. He spent five summers on the Pine Ridge and Rosebud reservations. Mr. Feraca was involved in the establishment of the Wright–McGill fishhook and snelling industry during the period 1959–1962 and in a number of community development projects, including the establishment of village sites. While in the employ of the Office of Tribal Operations, Bureau of Indian Affairs, Washington, D.C., from 1962 to 1966, he wrote a report, "The History and Development of Oglala Sioux Tribal Government" (100 pp., Bureau of Indian Affairs, Washington, D.C.), which is on file at that office.

Dr. Virginia Ford has written a dissertation, "Cultural Criteria and Determinants for Acceptance of Modern Medical Theory and Practice among the Teton Dakota of the Rosebud Indian Reservation, South Dakota," at Catholic University, Washington, D.C., 1967. This is available on microfilm at Microfilm Inc., University of Michigan, Ann Arbor, Michigan.

Mrs. Beatrice Medicine Garner, a graduate student in the Department of Anthropology, Michigan State University, East Lansing, Michigan, had impressionistic notes on Rosebud and Pine Ridge for an unspecified date, and, for 1964, tapes, songs, and conversations from two Dakota reserves in Canada.

Dr. James H. Howard has in his possession many field notes, derived largely from the Tetons and Yanktonais of Standing Rock Reservation, North Dakota and South Dakota, and several tapes of Santee, Yankton, and Teton music.

Dr. Alice B. Kehoe wrote a Ph.D. dissertation (Harvard University, 1964) on "The Ghost Dance Religion in Saskatchewan: A Functional Analysis," and has field notes on Saskatchewan Dakota (Santee) history, religion, medicine, and contemporary living conditions.

Dr. Luis S. Kemnitzer of the Department of Anthropology at San Francisco State College has about three hundred pages of interview and field notes covering the period from December 1961 to June 1964. The topics covered are kinship, reservation and city associations, life style, formal and informal associations, attitudes toward city and reservation life, tradition and change, relocation, and race relations.

Dr. Vernon D. Malan of the Department of Sociology and Anthropology at Oregon State University reported that he had the following manuscripts:

1. "Dakota Indian Health," an analysis of food practices, diet, and nutrition, and the role of incapacitating illness on the Pine Ridge Indian Reservation. The first part of the manuscript is a baseline study of traditional food practices and a systematic approach to the investigation of contemporary health situations in rural communities on Pine Ridge. The second part statistically summarizes the dietary beliefs, values, and practices which are specifically associated with the sick role.

2. "Systematic Analysis of the Social System of the Dakota Indians," a comprehensive analysis of social organization and changes using the conceptual model of the social system.

3. "Value Orientation and Alcoholism on the Pine Ridge Indian Reservation" is the title for a proposed report. Data have been

collected and analyzed on the association between social participation, attitudes toward the law and uses of intoxicants, value
orientation, and arrests for public intoxication.

Mr. R. Clyde McCone has a manuscript titled "The Implications
of Time Perspective in the Behavior of Present-Day Dakota Indian
Adolescents."

Dr. Ethel Nurge's field notes consist of about one hundred pages
(three hundred to four hundred words typed to a page) written during
the summer of 1964. The data are heavily concentrated on present-day
diet, including the sources, costs, and social factors related thereto.

Besides the published materials listed in the Bibliography and his
contributions to this book, Dr. Ernest Schusky wrote a dissertation,
"The Lower Brule Sioux: The Description of a Distinct Community
and the Processes Which Keep It Distinct." He has a mimeographed
manuscript, "Dakota Indians in Today's World," and field notes from
Lower Brule made in March to August, 1958. Schusky also has Bureau
of Indian Affairs data on family organization, number in family,
relation to head, and occupation and income of head—data which
would be useful in the study of change over a period of time as well as
for comparison of reservation vs. nonreservation residents.

Mr. Robert K. Thomas has in his possession fifty-one questionnaires
from Calico Community (total residents) on the Pine Ridge Reservation, 1958. The data cover social, economic, and educational aspects.
He also has field notes made in 1957 and 1958 in an unspecified
quantity oriented toward the community study.

Mr. Kenneth Tiedke has data on IBM cards which are not run but
which are in storage. His project was designed to illuminate personality
differences in relation to cultural change. He viewed as controlling
variables age, education, degree of Indian blood, outside experiences,
and religion. His techniques of investigation were historical analysis
and intensive interviews plus small-scale TATs and Rorschachs.

Drs. Wilson D. and Ruth S. Wallis have much unpublished material
on the Manitoba (Eastern) Dakotas and the Minnesota Dakotas which
falls into two categories: (a) folklore consisting of beliefs, rites, and
tales, and (b) material on women and children. As to the folklore, the
Wallises are preparing a manuscript of perhaps three hundred pages
with the first third devoted to history and ethnography and the last
two-thirds to tales. The Wallises have 125 pages of closely typed
interviews with women between the ages of seventeen and eighty
(including the last medicine woman).

Drs. Murray and Rosalie Wax, together with their research assistant, Robert V. Dumont, Jr., conducted field work in Pine Ridge, 1962–63, and briefly again in 1965, and M. Wax again in 1966. The geographic focus of their work tended to be the Oglala community and adjacent areas served by the Loneman School. However, they also interviewed and collected data elsewhere throughout the reservation. Much of the data has been utilized in their publications, but for those interested in examining them, there are field notes, classroom observations, and interviews with parents, youngsters, and teachers. In addition, Roselyn Holyrock conducted surveys in 1964 of the Indian populations of the towns adjacent to the reservation, including Gordon, Hay Springs, Chadron, and Rushville; while these interviews were modest in scope and are likely to be of little value in themselves, they would be of interest for anyone who wanted to begin the study of the proletarian off-reservation Indian communities.

As of summer, 1967, the Waxes were planning to develop some of their field diaries from Pine Ridge in the context of a book that R. Wax is writing on anthropological field methods.

From the years 1957 and 1958, the Rev. Robert A. White, S.J., has personal field notes of interviews with 150 families in Rapid City. In addition, he wrote a master's thesis, "The Urbanization of the Dakota Indians," at St. Louis University in 1959. From 1962–63 he has approximately three hundred hours of tape-recorded interviews focusing on the family histories of fifteen Sioux families in Rapid City and data on the Sioux pentecostal movement viewed as a nativistic movement. From 1963 he has approximately five hundred schedules of a complete census of the Indian community in Rapid City. Also from 1963 he has data on perception and attitudes toward Indians from one thousand non-Indian families randomly selected in Rapid City; brief case histories of job records of approximately three-fourths of the Sioux employees in Rapid City; and data from social workers, police, and other official agencies working with the urban Indians.

From 1964 he has an unpublished seventy-page report summarizing the Rapid City research up to and including 1963. From 1965 there are approximately forty hours of transcribed tape-recorded interviews with families in the lower-class culture of poverty. There are also about twenty additional hours of transcribed tape-recorded interviews with informants in Rapid City and on the Pine Ridge Reservation on the life and institutions of the Sioux reservations from 1900 to 1940.

The foregoing is the extent of the information volunteered in response to questionnaires. In addition, in 1965, Professor Useem and I wrote to Mr. Martin Holm of the Bureau of Indian Affairs at Aberdeen, South Dakota, telling him that we were interested in assembling recent documents on the Dakotas, particularly those which were reports prepared by superintendents of the Sioux reservations and which are public property and could therefore be cited and referred to. Another body of data which we thought would be most useful was statistics on land status, resident and enrolled population, number of children in school, mortality and morbidity rates, etc. Mr. Holm replied carefully and at length. He said that there were not too many documents prepared for public use. Some such are feasibility studies and the economic development plans. He also reported that there were a few documents of the nature of "The Land of Red Cloud." In addition, the following records exist and, if clearance is individually and personally arranged, may be made available to an investigator for study in the Aberdeen office or at the central office of the United States Department of the Interior Bureau of Indian Affairs, Washington, D.C.: annual school reports giving grade breakdowns; annual education reports on the summer school programs and on adult education activities; annual reports of those in higher education; monthly reports on the Office of Economic Opportunity progress; South Dakota State Johnson-O'Malley education assistance reports; special reports on dropouts; agency welfare narrative reports; employment assistance statistics, including relocation and adult vocational training; land status statistics; land use statistics, particularly for range land; land sales statistics; loan statistics and credit reports; reports on housing developments, particularly low-rent; agency monthly projects development reports and area quarterly reports; industrial development materials; tribal council minutes; monthly tribal operations reports; population figures as of March, 1965, giving employment and unemployment, age breakdown, etc.; family income estimate as of December, 1964; mortality and morbidity rates; sanitation and housing reports; reservation ten-year goals, 1964; and withdrawal reports, August, 1953, giving much statistical information.

Other data, which are confidential and therefore probably not available for citation or reference, are: welfare statistical reports, case-load and child welfare data, etc., and law and order statistics.

Appendix III: A Partial Bibliography of Archival Manuscript Material Relating to the Dakota Indians

Raymond J. DeMallie, Jr.

At the Conference on the Modern Dakota in 1965, the need for a bibliography of Dakota manuscript material was quite evident. Each of the conferees knew of some archival material which would be of value to others, but because of the time-consuming nature of the work of preparing such a bibliography, no one had undertaken the project. During the spring of 1967, when Dr. Nurge learned that I would be working during the summer at the Smithsonian Office of Anthropology Archives (now the National Anthropological Archives), she asked me to prepare for this volume a listing of the Dakota manuscripts deposited there. Mrs. Margaret C. Blaker, Archivist of the NAA, for whom I was working under a National Science Foundation research participation grant, supported the project; during the course of the summer, I recatalogued all the Dakota manuscripts. However, because of space limitations and the probable interests of the users of this volume, references to manuscripts of primarily linguistic interest have been omitted here.

In order to gain some idea of the nature of the manuscript material in other repositories, I wrote to a number of institutions during the summer of 1967. Most replied, giving some kind of listing of their Dakota manuscripts. These lists, in edited form, are presented as an appendix to the NAA list, and the name of the person supplying the information is placed directly after the address of the institution.

I plan to continue and expand this bibliographic survey in the future and would be grateful for any suggestions or manuscript listings. They may be sent to me at the Department of Anthropology, University of Chicago, 1126 East 59th Street, Chicago, Illinois 60637. The completed "Guide to Dakota Manuscript Collections" will be a valuable research tool to anthropologists, linguists, and historians working with the Dakotas.

I extend sincere thanks to all who helped in this project, but particularly to Margaret Blaker, who acted as steadfast advisor and editor, and to Jill C. Rhodes, who did the typing.

Abbreviations used

A.	autograph
AA	*American Anthropologist*
AMNH-AP	*Anthropological Papers of the American Museum of Natural History*
approx.	approximately
BAE	Bureau of American Ethnology
BAE-AR	Bureau of American Ethnology *Annual Report*
BAE-B	Bureau of American Ethnology *Bulletin*
c.	copy
ca.	circa (dates only)
c.c.	carbon copy
CNAE	*Contributions to North American Ethnology*
D.	document
JAFL	*Journal of American Folklore*
L.	letter(s)
L. (after a no.)	leaves
MS (MSS)	handwritten or manuscript(s)
n.d.	no date
no.	number
o.s.	old series
p., pp.	inscribed page(s)
PAAAS	*Proceedings*, American Association for the Advancement of Science
S.	signed

SCK	*Smithsonian Contributions to Knowledge*
slips	inscribed sides of half sheets or less
SMC	*Smithsonian Miscellaneous Collections*
SOA	Smithsonian Office of Anthropology
T.	typed
USNM	United States National Museum
v., vol.	volume
[ ]	supplied information

NATIONAL ANTHROPOLOGICAL ARCHIVES, SMITHSONIAN INSTITUTION. Washington, D.C. 20560.

The NAA contains the MS collections of the former Bureau of American Ethnology. Much of this material is linguistic in nature. In addition to the MS collection, the Archives houses the correspondence files of the BAE, which contain some material concerning the Dakotas, but which are not indexed by subject.

The following is a list of the Dakota MS material which is not entirely linguistic in nature:

Allison, E. H. "The Stone Boy and the Spider." June 1, 1899. A. D. S. 28 pp.

A myth, in Lakota, with interlinear and free English translations.

MS no. 945

Allison, E. H. Myth of how the Spider married his mother-in-law. [1899?]. A. D. S. 33 pp.

Lakota text with interlinear and free English translations. Myth related by Log, a Two Kettle Dakota.

MS no. 3738

Allison, E. H. Letter to W. J. McGee, BAE, Washington, D.C., Sept. 22, 1897. A. L. S. 1 p.

Transmits small stone "idol" given to Allison in 1881 by the Hunkpapa chief Black Moon.

MS no. 1387

Allison, E. H. Miscellaneous writings on the Dakotas. [1903].

"Games played by Indian children," A. D. S. 3 pp. with one sketch; "How Sioux Indians receive their names," A. D. S. 12 pp.; "Thunder's Slaughter," a myth, A. D. S. 5 pp.; "One good Indian and one bad one," A. D. S. (dated 1903) 11 pp.; "Maternity and

Midwifery among the Sioux," A. D. S. 15 pp.; "Gall, Battle Chief," T. D. 13 pp. Copies of "One Good Indian and One Bad One," T. D. 7 pp., and "Gall, Battle Chief," T. D. 14 pp.

MS no. 1754

Allison, E. H. Material on Sitting Bull. [1897?]. 94 pp.

"Surrender of Sitting Bull," A. D. S. 47 pp.; copy of "Surrender of Sitting Bull" with extensive notes by John G. Carter, 1933, T. D. 40 pp.; letter from Arthur W. Tarbell, editor of the *National Magazine*, Boston, to Allison, Oct. 6, 1897, T. L. S. 1 p.; note by Allison on the meaning of the name "Sitting Bull," A. D. S., 1 p. with critical note by Stanley Vestal, A. D. S. 1 p.; article by Allison on Custer Battle, from *Washington Evening Times*, July 3, 1897, 1 p.

MS no. 1755

Anonymous. Ninety-two colored drawings by Indians. [1873–76]. 65 L.

Letter from James Mooney to W. H. Holmes, Chief, BAE, identifying the drawings as "Western Sioux, of date about 30 years ago." Cantonment, Oklahoma. April 19, 1906. A. L. S. 1 p.

Part 1. 83 Teton Dakota drawings in pencil and crayon on 55 ledger sheets ($11\frac{3}{4}'' \times 7\frac{1}{4}''$), bearing storekeeper's [?] accounts in the names of several Indians. Dates on the sheets range 1873–July 1876. On one sheet the words "Pine Ridge, D.T." are written in pencil, now faded, followed by other writing in the Dakota language. The drawings depict war exploits, horse stealing, dance scenes, and mounted men and women.

Part 2. 9 drawings on 10 sheets of various sizes ($10\frac{1}{2}'' \times 8''$ to $12\frac{1}{4}'' \times 15''$), executed in ink, pencil, water color, and crayon. They seem to be Cheyenne: two are marked with the Cheyenne names O kum Ka'h^u Kit ['Little Wolf'] and Iss Ko Wits ['Porcupine'].

MS no. 39-d

Anonymous. Oglala Dakota winter count, 1759–1919. n.d. c.c. T. D. 5 pp.

An identical winter count for the years 1759–1896 has been published with notes by William K. Powers. See "A Winter Count of the Oglala," *American Indian Tradition*, v. 9, no. 1, 1963, pp. 27–37.

MS no. 2261

Anonymous. Notes on the meaning of the name "Oglala." n.d. A. D. 6 pp.

Critical notes on an unnamed paper on Dakota games. n.d. A. D.
5 pp.

MS no. 4017

Burkholder, D. F. "Anug Ite, or Both-Sides-Face." n.d. T. D. 8 pp.

MS no. 1168

Culbertson, Thaddeus A. "Journal of an expedition up the Missouri
River." March 21, 1850–April 25, 1850. A. D. 48 pp.

Tables showing the tribes of the Upper Missouri River. June 1850.
A. D. S. 9 pp.

Letter from Culbertson, Fort Pierre, Dakota Terr., to Spencer F.
Baird. May 30, 1850. A. L. S. 12 pp.

All printed in "Journal of an Expedition to the Mauvaises Terres
and the Upper Missouri in 1850," by Culbertson, edited by John
Francis McDermott, BAE-B 147, Washington, D.C., 1952.

MS no. 1426-a

Densmore, Frances. Transcriptions of Teton Dakota music published
in "Teton Sioux Music," BAE-B 61, Washington, D.C., 1918. n.d.
Approx. 155 pp.

Includes approx. 55 pp. "corrected copy" of transcriptions and
approx. 100 pp. of transcriptions which are not arranged in numerical sequence.

MS no. 3370

Dorsey, James Owen [translator]. Lakota texts by George Bushotter.
Washington, D.C. 1887–88. MS. D. Approx. 3,500 pp.

259 texts; nos. 189 and 253, as well as parts of 223 and 224, are
by John Bruyier, 1888. Interlinear translations by Dorsey, aided by
Bushotter and Bruyier. Some notes in pencil in the handwriting of
John R. Swanton, 1899–1900.

A free translation of these texts, made by Ella C. Deloria, is in the
Library of the American Philosophical Society, Philadelphia,
Pennsylvania.

Lakota texts by George Bushotter:

1. Sword Keeper and his brother. The latter meets Two Faces, a
   mythic giant. [The myth of Miwaka^n Yuhala.] 8 pp. and 3 pp.
   (notes) and 1 p. (partial translation).
2. The Mythic Buffalo. 10 pp.
3. Two Faces. Explains the origin of arrows, pipes, axes, knife-
   sharpeners, beads, etc. 14 pp.

4. Three brothers who had a witch sister. 17 pp. (incomplete).
5. Children, a bad old woman cannibal, and Spider (the mythic Trickster). 12 pp.
6. Spider, animals, and women. 15 pp. and 6 pp.
7. A man and his ghost wife. 9 pp. and 5 pp.
8. Two against one: a ghost story with a song. 10 pp.
9. A man, a female ghost, and a male ghost who wrestled with the man. 15 pp.
10. Ghost on the hill, who could not be hit by arrows. 8 pp.
11. Treatment of the sick, burial customs. 22 pp., 4 pp. notes, 2 pp. and 1 sketch.
12. The man who came to life again. 14 pp. and 2 pp. translation. Note by Bruyier at end.
13. The man and woman in the moon. 6 pp.
14. Man, two in the lodge, female ghost, and the friendly wolf. 8 pp.
15. The man who spared the wolf cubs. 11 pp.
16. The Thunder Being and the Unkcegila (a mastodon?) 12 pp.
17. Waziya, the northern giant who brings snow. 4 pp.
18. Buffalo people who attacked the Indian people. 10 pp.
19. Spider and the land turtle. 29 pp.
20. The man and his two sons. 18 pp. and 2 pp. notes.
21. The turtle who wished to fly. 10 pp.
22. The man who could become a grizzly bear. 6 pp.
23. How the Indians cured the sun. 3 pp.
24. Spider and the horned water monster. 7 pp.
25. The strange lake with large subaquatic animals. 6 pp.
26. The warrior surrounded by a serpent. 4 pp.
27. The one-eyed serpent with short legs and large body. 3 pp.
28. Why they pray to stones, the sun, etc. 9 pp.
29. The mountain in which was a large serpent. 6 pp.
30. Adventures of a man and his wife. 8 pp.
31. Spider and the Prairie Chicken. 6 pp.
32. Adventure of Rabbit Carrier. 6 pp.
33. The woman who turned to a fish from her waist down. 22 pp.
34. Spider and the Rabbit; how the latter made snow. 5 pp.
35. The male ghost and his living wife. 8 pp.
36. The man with the magic sword, and the one with the powerful breath. 6 pp.
37. Swift runner (he who tied stones to his legs). 10 pp.

38. The man who was rescued by eaglets. 10 pp.
39. The Double-woman. 5 pp.
40. Spider and the mice. 14 pp.
41. Spider and the ducks—how they got red eyes. 13 pp. and 1 sketch.
42. Spider and the Rabbit; how the latter lost his long tail. 11 pp.
43. The man who resembled the man in the moon. 11 pp.
44. The young lover who was rescued by the girl. 12 pp.
45. The warriors who met Heyoka (Sunflower) who was singing and dancing. 2 pp.
46. The flying Santee (a ghoul). 8 pp.
47. How the Santees first saw buffalo. 8 pp.
48. How the Lakotas went against the Rees. 5 pp.
49. Adventures of the Short Man. 8 pp.
50. Smoke Maker's adventures: a war story. 7 pp.
51. Fight between the Lakota and the Blackfeet. 4 pp. (incomplete).
52. Fight between two unarmed men and a grizzly bear. 8 pp.
53. Treatment of an Omaha spy caught by the Lakotas. 6 pp.
54. The wide man, a nude cannibal. 4 pp.
55. He who uses the earth as an ear. 7 pp.
56. Why horses are called, in Lakota, "mysterious dogs." 7 pp.
57. The man who could understand ravens. 5 pp.
58. Of the two small stones that were servants of the people. 6 pp. (Brief note at end appears to be in Swanton's hand writing.)
59. The Wahankśica, a strange animal. 3 pp.
60. The animal in the Missouri River which breaks up the ice in the spring of the year. 4 pp.
61. How the wind brought sickness to Medicine Butte Creek. 6 pp.
62. Beliefs about day and night. 6 pp.
63. The man in the forest and his contest with ghosts. 8 pp.
64. The feast in honor of the Anti-Natural God. 18 pp.
65. Of the Heyoka man who dreamed of his death by lightning. 13 pp.
66. Fight between the Lakota and the Blackfeet. 6 pp.
67. Of the mysterious man who knew about the distant Omaha war party. 5 pp.
68. Of the wise man who caught his eloping wife. 8 pp.
69. How the Rees or Blackfeet came against the Lakotas. 5 pp.
70. Origin of the buffalo. 5 pp.

71. The Sun Dance. 148 pp. and 6 sketches.
72. The man who could lengthen his arm at will. 7 pp.
73. What a young man must do before he can marry. 11 pp.
74. How the Crows surrounded some Lakotas. 12 pp.
75. A raid on a Lakota camp. 4 pp.
76. Story of a warrior who was not wounded. 9 pp.
77. Fight between the Lakota and white soldiers. 20 pp.
78. Of the Santees, and their fondness for certain foods. 4 pp.
79. What the Lakota thought of the first white people whom they saw. 13 pp.
80. Belief respecting lakes. 6 pp.
81. Belief about this world. 7 pp.
82. The calumet dance. 39 pp. and 2 diagrams.
83. How they honor the dead (the Ghost Feast). 15 pp., 2 pp. and 18 pp.
84. Men who are arrow and bullet proof. 8 pp.
85. Of love potions, etc. 5 pp.
86. The acts of a wounded warrior. 7 pp.
87. Actors clothed in buffalo robes with the hair out detect wrongdoers. 11 pp.
88. Those who imitate the elk. 14 pp.
89. Why a man may not speak to his mother-in-law. 11 pp.
90. Rules for feasting, smoking, and visiting. 11 pp.
91. Of certain boyish customs. 8 pp.
92. A ghost story. 7 pp.
93. Origin of the white people. 10 pp.
94. Games and their seasons. 10 pp.
95. Education of a boy. 10 pp.
96. Of a youth killed in battle, and of his faithful horse. 12 pp.
97. The people who lived in the north. 7 pp. and 2 sketches.
98. The ghost woman and the robin. 9 pp. Note at end by Bruyier.
99. The flying serpent whose touch was fatal. 5 pp.
100. Origin of twins. 5 pp.
101. George Bushotter's autobiography. 117 pp.
102. Belief concerning a loved one who has been called by a ghost. 7 pp.
103. Fight between two gamblers near Chamberlain, Dakota. 7 pp.
104. The singing elk. 7 pp.
105. Belief about Spider. 9 pp.
106. War of the Lakota against the Omaha. 7 pp.
107. Narrow escape of Bark Bird's Tail (a Lakota). 5 pp.

108. Bushotter's cousin's war adventure. 11 pp.
109. How certain men (doctors, priests, etc.) have become mysterious. 16 pp.
110. How the Lakota fought the Cheyennes and Black Men (Comanches?). 22 pp.
111. Rules of etiquette for brothers, sisters, cousins. 21 pp.
112. Ghost story. 5 pp.
113. The habits of beavers. 8 pp.
114. Spider and the old woman who fed all the animals. 24 pp.
115. The handsome man who was rescued from a pit by a wolf. 32 pp.
116. Trick of a myth-teller. 9 pp.
117. Of thistles. 4 pp.
118. How Indians regard the past and their ancestors. 22 pp.
119. The grass dance. 12 pp.
120. The Big Belly Society. 6 pp.
121. The Mandan Society. 10 pp.
122. "Following one another," a Lakota game. 7 pp.
123. "They make it run by pushing," a Lakota game. 46 pp. and 2 colored sketches.
124. Horse racing. 5 pp.
125. Hitting the moccasin, a game. 9 pp.
126. Shooting at the cactus, a game. 5 pp.
127. Hitting the bow, a game. 5 pp.
128. Shooting at bunches of grass, a game. 5 pp.
129. Shooting at the lights of an animal, a game. 6 pp.
130. Taking captives from one another, a game. 9 pp.
131. Trampling on the beaver, a game. 6 pp.
132. "Howi! Howi!" a ring game for boys or youths. 12 pp.
133. "They touch not one another," a game. 6 pp.
134. Game with a long grass which has a long, sharp beard. 6 pp.
135. "The old woman accuses them," a game. 8 pp.
136. A game with slings. 5 pp.
137. "Goose and her children," a game. 10 pp.
138. Buffalo horn game. 7 pp. and 1 p.
139. A stick which is hurled. 5 pp., 1 p. and 2 sketches.
140. "Making the wood dance by hitting it," a game. 8 pp.
141. "Making the wood jump by hitting it," a game. 8 pp.
142. "Making the bow glide by throwing," a game. 6 pp.
143. Coasting. 8 pp.

144. Game of ball. 12 pp.
145. "Shooting at an arrow set up," a game. 7 pp.
146. Grizzly bear game. 12 pp.
147. Deer game. 10 pp.
148. "Running towards one another," a game. 9 pp.
149. "They cause one another to carry packs on their backs," a game. 10 pp.
150. "They hit one another with mud," a game. 10 pp.
151. Hitting the ball, a game. 11 pp.
152. A game with a rawhide hoop. 43 pp. and 2 sketches.
153. Game of earthen horses. 8 pp.
154. "They slide by pushing," a game. 14 pp.
155. "They kick at one another," a game. 14 pp.
156. "The hoop is made to roll by the wind," a game. 9 pp.
157. [Popgun game. Text missing.] 1 p. sketch.
158. Wrestling. 8 pp.
159. Courting the girls. 9 pp.
160. Game with bow and small wood-pointed arrows. 10 pp.
161. Swinging. 10 pp.
162. "Taking places from one another," a game. 9 pp.
163. "Playing with small things," a game. 18 pp.
164. Pinching the backs of hands, a game. 11 pp.
165. "Scattering them," a game. 9 pp.
166. "Who shall get there first," a game. 10 pp.
167. Hopping. 9 pp.
168. Throwing arrows, by hand, at a target. 6 pp.
169. Ghost game. 21 pp.
170. Hide and seek. 13 pp.
171. Jumping down from a high object. 12 pp.
172. Plumstone game. 18 pp.
173. Odd or even? A game with sticks. 12 pp.
174. Throwing chewed leaves into the eyes, a game. 7 pp.
175. Game with the ankle-bones of a deer. 12 pp.
176. Native wooden harmonicon, played by boys. 14 pp. and 5 sketches.
177. Mysterious game. 17 pp.
178. Playing doctor. 10 pp.
179. Pretending to be dead, a game. 10 pp.
180. Hunting young birds in summer. 12 pp.
181. Hunting eggs in spring. 10 pp.

182. Going to make a grass lodge. 11 pp.
183. Scrambling for presents. 11 pp.
184. Sitting on wooden horses, a game. 8 pp.
185. Making a bone turn and hum by twisting a cord. 15 pp. and 2 sketches.
186. "String twisted in and out among the fingers." 8 pp.
187. Tumbling and somersaults. 7 pp.
188. "Game with large things." 17 pp.
189. About two young men who were friends. 51 pp. By Bruyier.
190. A bird that foretells cold weather. 14 pp.
191. Cause of scrofulous sore on the neck. 10 pp.
192. Meaning of ringing sounds in the ears. 10 pp.
193. The Brave and Fox societies. 18 pp. and 4 sketches.
194. Dog Society. 31 pp., 2 sketches and 1 p. drawing.
195. "Killing by Hitting," or "Taking the Buffalo Paunch," a society of women. 12 pp.
196. Scalp dance society. 16 pp. and 1 sketch.
197. Night dance. 18 pp.
198. Mysterious society. 16 pp.
199. Grizzly Bear dance. 19 pp.
200. Belief about the Kildeer. 13 pp.
201. The acts of a leader. 17 pp.
202. Return of the night hawk in the spring. 7 pp.
203. Belief concerning the Ski-bi-bi-la, a small grey bird which says "Gli Hunwo?" ("Coming home?"). 16 pp. Also earlier version of the same, with mistakes. 10 pp.
204. About hanging the "tablo" ("shoulder blade") at the door of the lodge. 7 pp.
205. Trying to excell others. 12 pp.
206. Scolding or whipping a woman. 12 pp.
207. How Indian paints are made. 18 pp.
208. Acting like the buffalo bull. 9 pp. and 1 p. drawing.
209. Law about bowls. 9 pp.
210. Meaning of a rooster's crowing. 8 pp.
211. The taking apart of fetishes. 24 pp.
212. How one man drowned another. 21 pp.
213. Concerning warts. 8 pp.
214. Of a woman who was killed by mosquitoes. 32 pp.
215. Concerning hermaphrodites. 22 pp.
216. Belief concerning the grebe or dabchick. 10 pp.

217. Rules for eating dogs. 8 pp.
218. Bushotter's recollections of a certain famine. 19 pp.
219. Why Lakota men should not wear women's moccasins. 16 pp.
220. Customs relating to bowls. 10 pp.
221. Meanings of various kinds of twitchings. 10 pp.
222. "Kicking out his elder brother's teeth." 10 pp.
223. How a boy wounded his grandfather in the scrotum. 13 pp. Bruyier's revision of the same. 13 pp.
224. Legend of the nude Spider woman. 12 pp. About the woman who was deceived by the grizzly bear, with an account of the prairie hen. 20 pp. By Bruyier.
225. "Punishment of the prairie." 19 pp.
226. Part of the punishment of a murderer. 12 pp.
227. About a foolish wife. 42 pp.
228. How a ghost stunned Bushotter's father. 21 pp.
229. Occasions for scolding wives. 12 pp. Half-page corrected sentence at end by Bruyier.
230. Setting out food, etc., for ghosts. 16 pp.
231. Concerning widows and widowers. 30 pp.
232. About a newborn child. 9 pp.
233. Tatala, a humorist. 6 pp.
234. Vegetal lore. 16 pp.
235. About the year when the stars fell (1833). 18 pp.
236. Concerning shells used as necklaces. 8 pp. and 2 sketches.
237. Game with a ball of mud. 8 pp.
238. "Throwing fire at one another." 11 pp.
239. Punishment of a liar. 8 pp.
240. Invocation of the Thunder. 13 pp.
241. About spiders. 15 pp.
242. The mysterious imitation of ghosts. 14 pp.
243. What they carry when they migrate. 20 pp.
244. What happened when the Lower Brules went to a mountain. 24 pp.
245. Concerning guardian spirits. 16 pp.
246. About the Thunderers (People dwelling in the clouds). 25 pp.
247. About lizards, frogs, etc., rained from the sky. 11 pp.
248. Deer Women. 28 pp.
249. Bird Societies. 31 pp.
250. Ways of dancing. 26 pp.
251. About gashing the limbs when mourning. 7 pp.

252. On Fellowhood. 16 pp.
253. Ceremonies at birth. 8 pp. Bruyier's revision. 5 pp.
254. Bushotter's step-father's prophetic gifts. 15 pp.
255. The recovery of Bushotter's younger brother. 14 pp.
256. Why a son or daughter acts in a childish manner. 9 pp.
257. Giving birth to one child while still nursing another. 13 pp.
258. Courting. 48 pp., 3-page color folding drawing and 1 p. drawing.
259. Heyoka woman. 8 pp.
    (Note: most titles of texts were composed by Dorsey.)

MS no. 4800

Dorsey, James Owen. George Bushotter's first Lakota text, "The Myth of Miwaka^n yuhala, ['Sword Keeper']." [1888?]. T. and A. D. 14 pp.

T. Lakota text with A. interlinear translation by Dorsey. Includes 4 pp. notes by Dorsey, and 2 pp. incomplete translation.

MS no. 4800

Dorsey, James Owen [collector]. Colored drawings by George Bushotter. 1887. 10 drawings on 9 pp.

Drawn to illustrate various stories by Bushotter, but withdrawn by Dorsey from the accompanying texts for publication in his "A Study of Siouan Cults," BAE-AR 11, Washington, D.C., 1894.

Illustrations of the sun dance, ghost lodge, ghosts, heyoka dancers.

MS no. 4800

Dorsey, James Owen. "Teton Folk-lore." [1887?]. T. D. 41 pp.

Concerning ghosts; extracted from the George Bushotter Lakota texts. Printed in AA, o.s., v. II, 1888, pp. 143–58.

MS no. 4800

Dorsey, James Owen. Letter from Joseph W. Cook. Greenwood, Dakota Terr. Oct. 8, 1887. A. L. S. 2 pp. enclosing A. D. 1 p. and T. D. 1 p.

Letter returns 1 p. T. c. of George Bushotter's 17th text (the myth of Waziya) as rewritten by Bushotter in the Yankton Dakota dialect, with 1 p. critical note. Cook states: "I see nothing special to criticize except the spelling in some cases. . . ."

MS no. 4800

Dorsey, James Owen [collector]. Letters in Yankton Dakota from Walking Elk and Running Bull to Two Bears. Omaha Agency,

Nebraska Terr. Oct. 7, 1878. A. L. S. 4 pp. with 2 pp. partial copy in handwriting of J. O. Dorsey.

MS no. 4800

Fletcher, Alice C., and Francis LaFlesche. Personal papers and ethnographic notes. Ca. 1881–98. 34 boxes.

Includes the following material on the Dakotas:

Item 100:

1. Notebook by Fletcher on Pine Ridge sun dance, elk mystery ceremony, and miscellaneous. Summer 1882. A. D. 243 pp. 12 drawings of sun dance and elk mystery ceremony.
2. Miscellaneous notes by Fletcher, mostly on sun dance. n.d. A. and T. D. 55 pp.
3. "The Sun Dance," by Fletcher. 1882. A. D. S. 5 drafts. Approx. 160 pp. Printed in PAAAS, 1882, pp. 580–84.
4. "The Sun Dance of the Sioux," by Frederick Schwatka, from *Century Magazine*, Vol. XXXIX, 1890, pp. 753–59. Draft of article written in reply by Fletcher. n.d. A. D. S. 5 pp.
5. Notes on the sun dance and Dakota religion. 1882, 1896. A. and T. D. 18 pp. Letter from Alfred L. Riggs, Santee Agency, Nebraska, to Fletcher, concerning the Eastern Dakota sun dance. Aug. 14, 1882. A. L. S. 5 pp. Newsclipping on 1882 sun dance at Cheyenne River Agency.
6. Two newsclippings from the *New York Herald*, Sept. 28 and 29, 1877, concerning the Dakota delegation in Washington, D.C.
7. "Sioux Story." n.d. A. D. 40 pp. Apparently fictitious.
8. "Oglalla Tradition of the Tribal Pipe," by Hollow Horn Bear. Feb. 4, 1898. T. D. 2 pp.
9. "Making Soldiers," among the Dakota on Rosebud Agency, told by Yellow Bull, a Ponka. 1896. T. D. 2 pp.
10. Words of some Dakota, Omaha and Ponka songs. T. D. 4 pp.
11. "William Garnett's story of the death of Crazy Horse, Oglala Sioux, May [*sic:* September], 1877." c.c. T. D. S. by Garnett, 21 pp.

Item 101:

1. Notebook #1, by Fletcher. Sept. 16–Oct. 14, 1881. A. D. Approx. 200 pp. and 27 loose drawings cut from notebook. 3 drafts of letters by Fletcher. A. D. 10 pp.
2. Notebook #2, by Fletcher. Oct. 15–Nov. 2, 1881. A. D. Approx. 150 pp. and 5 loose drawings cut from notebook.

3. Transcript by LaFlesche of greater portions of notebooks 1 and 2, to Oct. 25, 1881. A. D. 175 pp. Miscellaneous notes. A. D. 11 pp.
4. Copy of LaFlesche's transcript, excluding pp. 111–13 and 115–18. T. D. 108 pp.
5. "Life among the Indians, Part I, Camping with the Sioux," by Fletcher. 1887. MS. D. S. by Fletcher with A. annotations. 157 pp.

MS no. 4558

Galbraith, Thomas J. Letter introducing "Tate-iyo-pas[?]-mani," a Sisseton Dakota chief. Sioux Agency, Yellow Medicine, Minn. July 17, 1861. A. D. S. 1 p.

Requests "all persons ... to respect this man and treat him kindly." The name is perhaps Tate iyopta mani ['Wind moves on (forward) as a cloud'].

MS no. 4777

Gardner, W. H. "Ethnology of the Region about the Valley of the Red River of the North, near Fort Abercrombie, D. T." Dec. 31, 1868. A. D. S. 8 pp.

Enclosed as "Report F" in a letter (now missing) to the Military Division of the Missouri. Gardner was Assistant Surgeon and Bvt. Major, U.S. Army, at Fort Abercrombie.

MS no. 4776

Harries, George H. "The Omaha Dance." Wounded Knee, South Dakota. June 27, 1891. 1 p.

Newsclipping from the *Evening Star*, Washington, D.C., July 11, 1891. Describes the dance in camp of Young Man Afraid of His Horses at Pine Ridge Agency. 3½ columns, with 6 line drawings.

MS no. 4753

Herman, Eddie and Vera. Material on the Dakotas. 1922–50. 25 pp. and 1 photograph.

Biographical data on Yellow Horse, Northern Oglala, and the murder of John Richard, Jr., A. D. S. 7 pp. "A Prayer of the Lakota" (poem), T. D. 1 p. "Tepee Creek Legend," c.c. 1 p. Ten letters from Valentine T. McGillycuddy to William Garnett, one from Garnett to McGillycuddy, c.c. 17 pp. [published in mimeographed form in pamphlet entitled "Odds and Ends" by Fred

Hackett, Chicago, Illinois, ca. 1950?]. Photograph captioned "Yellow Horse, Northern Oglala."

MS no. 4685

Higgins, Eli L. "Surrender of Rain in the Face, the Reported Slayer of Gen[eral] Custer." n.d. T. D. S. 5 pp.

MS no. 2107

Hinman, Samuel D. Dakota myths. n.d. A. D. 10 pp.
"The rabbit and the well," "The Rabbit and the buffalo-boy," in Dakota, with free English translations.

MS no. 2353

Jones, Henry. List of Dakota families at Santee Agency, on the Santee Reservation, Nebraska. n.d. A. D. S. 24 pp.
Lists 187 families, giving Dakota and English names of each individual. Possibly a complete census of the Santees at Santee Agency. Blue *x*'s next to certain names seem to have been made by James Owen Dorsey; cf. his "Indian Personal Names," AA, o.s., v. IV, 1890, pp. 263–68.

MS no. 3167

Lightfoot, Virginia Dorsey. Biographical data pertaining to George Bushotter. 1945. T. D. S. 2 pp.
Mrs. Lightfoot (1880–1963) was the daughter of James Owen Dorsey.

MS no. 4395

McChesney, Charles E. "Red Horse's Account of the Battle of the Little Big Horn, Montana, June 25, 1876, in Gesture-Signs, to Illustrate the Syntax of the Sign-Language of the North American Indians." 1881. A. D. S., with diagrams, 60 pp. and T. c., without diagrams, 76 pp.
Literal translation of sign text, free translation, and detailed description, with diagrams, of all signs in the order of their appearance in the text. 594 signs. English translation printed in Garrick Mallery, "Picture Writing of the American Indians," BAE-AR 10, Washington, D.C., 1893, pp. 563–66.

MS no. 2367-b

Mallery, Garrick. Material relating to sign language and pictography. Ca. 1875–85. 12 boxes.
Most of this material was published in Mallery's "Pictographs of the North American Indians—A Preliminary Paper," BAE-AR 4,

Washington, D.C., 1886, pp. 13–256, and in his "Picture-Writing of
the American Indians," BAE-AR 10, Washington, D.C., 1893, pp.
3–822. The collection includes the following material specifically
concerning the Dakotas:

Box 3, "Plains" folder:
Letter from Charles E. McChesney to Mallery, concerning the
Dakota sign language. Fort Bennett, Dakota Terr. Jan. 12, 1880.
A. L. S. 7 pp.
Letter from Hugh L. Scott to Mallery, concerning the Dakota
sign language. Fort Totten, Dakota Terr. Jan. 5, 1880. A. L. S. 3 pp.

Box 6, "Dakota" folder:
Three copies of Mallery's "A Collection of Gesture Signs . . .
Distributed only to collaborators." Washington, D.C., 1880. 329 pp.
Annotated for signs used by the Dakotas:
By C. E. McChesney. Fort Bennett, Dakota Terr., 1880.
By Bland D. Taylor. Governor's Island, New York Harbor.
March 10, 1880, with letter of transmittal. A. L. S. 4 pp.
By W. H. Corbusier, annotated for Dakotas and Arapahos. n.d.

Box 7, "Siouan" folder:
One copy of Mallery's "A Collection of Gesture Signs . . ."
annotated by F. F. Gerard for signs used by the Blackfeet, Crows,
Arikaras, Hidatsas, Dakotas, and Mandans. Letter from Gerard to
C. E. McChesney. Fort A. Lincoln, Dakota Terr. Feb. 28, 1880.
A. L. S. 6 pp. with note of transmittal from McChesney to Mallery,
dated Fort Bennett, Dakota Terr., March 28, 1881.

Box 11:
Drawings by Little Big Man, Oglala, in pencil, crayon, and water
colors, depicting Little Big Man and Lone Bear in a fight with
Crow Indians. 4 pp. With transmittal letter from Willard D.
Johnson to Mallery. Worcester, Mass. April 13, 1885. A. L. S.
2 pp.
Letter from V. T. McGillycuddy to Mallery. Pine Ridge Agency,
Dakota Terr. Aug. 17, 1884. A. L. 1 p. (incomplete). Same. Sept. 15,
1884. 1 p. Both letters are in regard to the pictographic "census."
Pictorial census of heads of families of Big Road's band of Oglalas,
drawn by Big Road in pencil, crayon, and water colors. 1 p. Printed
in BAE-AR 4, Plates LII–LVIII.
Pictorial census of Red Cloud's band. Reproductions of originals
lent by T. A. Bland for copying. 22 pp. (some duplicates). Printed in
BAE-AR 10, Figures 583–637.

"Red Cloud Agency. Names of Indians with Bland-Dorsey[?] collection of illustrations." MS D. 9 pp. Signed on last page, "William Garnett, Pine Ridge Agency, D. T." Lists names of individuals pictured in census, above.

Blank book with nine drawings of the war exploits of Red Dog, Oglala Dakota. Executed in pencil and crayon. 9 pp.

J. H. Trumbull to Mallery, concerning Dakota "clans or 'totemic' families." Hartford, Conn. Jan. 19, 1877. A. L. S. 3 pp.

J. P. Williamson to Mallery, concerning Dakota "totemic families" and bands. Greenwood, Dakota Terr. April 10, 1877. A. L. S. 2 pp.

"Key to the Picture Writing of 'Sitting Bull' [the Oglala]." n.d. Xerox c. of MS D. 4 pp. Original in USNM, acc. no 4515. The drawings, said to be made at Cheyenne River Agency in 1869, have not been located.

Miscellaneous notes on Dakotas. 13 pp., various authors.

Box 12, Folder 1 :

Full-size tracing of painted buffalo robe belonging to Black Crow, Yanktonai Dakota. Also photographic reproductions [part printed in BAE-AR 10, fig. 683]. Description of pictographs by P. W. Morris, A. D. S. 15 pp. (also partial copy, MS D. 5 pp.). Letter from A. L. Riggs to Morris, regarding the meaning of the pictographs. Santee Agency, Neb., Feb. 26, 1878. A. L. S. 7 pp.

Flame's winter count. 1 tracing on muslin, 4 pictographic reproductions, 1 partial copy on 2 pp., keys to the pictographs, MS D. 13 pp. (three copies).

Lone Dog's winter count. 4″ × 5″ color transparency of winter count (BAE-AR 10, Plate 6) and two photographic reproductions. Key to pictographs by H. T. Reed. Fort Rice, Dakota Terr. Nov. 5, 1876. A. D. S. 4 pp. Key by Jean Premau. Cheyenne [River] Agency, Dakota Terr. 1868. MS D. 5 pp. Key by James C. Robb. Cheyenne [River] Agency, Dakota Terr. 1870. MS D. 5 pp.

Correspondence regarding the winter count: S. D. Hinman to Mallery. Santee Agency, Neb. April 26, 1877. A. L. S. 2 pp. H. T. Reed to Mallery. On board steamer Fauchon, Yellowstone River. May 18, 1877. A. L. S. 4 pp. H. T. Reed to Mallery. Richmond, Indiana. Jan. 18, 1878. A. L. S. 8 pp. and T. c. 4 pp. Joseph Bush to Mallery, Fort Wayne, Michigan, Feb. 22, 1878. A. L. S. 5 pp. Bush to Mallery. Mackinac, Michigan. April 28, 1877. A. L. S. 1 p. Luther S. Kelly to Director, BAE. Parachute, Colorado. June 21, 1891. A. L. S. 3 pp.

Box 12, Folder 2:

Little Swan's winter count. Facsimile on tracing cloth by W. H. Hoffman of a copy in possession of Dr. John R. Patrick. Ca. 1872. Also 3 photographic reproductions. See BAE-AR 4, p. 93, and BAE-AR 10, p. 266. Key to the pictographs, xerox c. of MS D. 7 pp. Original in USNM, acc. no. 4515.

Box 12, Folder 3:

Winter count of Battiste Good, Brule, facsimile in sketch book, drawn by himself. [1880s]. 19 pp. Executed in pencil and water colors. Collected by Dr. William H. Corbusier. Cf. BAE-AR 10, p. 287.

Winter count of Cloud Shield, facsimile in sketch book, drawn by himself. [1880s]. 34 pp. Executed in ink and water colors. Collected by Corbusier.

"Dakota Winter Counts," by Corbusier. [1880s]. A. D. S. 71 pp.

Correspondence relating to Dakota winter counts: Corbusier to Mallery. Fort Mackinac, Michigan. Nov. 6, 1883. A. Postcard S. Same. Sept. 8, 1884. A. L. S. 4 pp. Same. Fort Grant, Arizona. May 11, 1887. A. L. S. 4 pp. Same. Fort Wayne, Detroit, Michigan. Feb. 12, 1891. A. L. S. 2 pp. Anonymous to Mallery. Camp Bidwell, California. Dec. 18, 1878. A. L. (fragment). 2 pp. [Possibly from F. V. Hayden?]

Mallery, "A Calendar of the Dakota Nation," Bulletin, U.S. Geological Survey, pp. 1–25. Each page pasted on single sheet, with many MS additions and deletions by Mallery. n.d. Approx. 55 pp. Apparently printer's copy for BAE-AR 4, pp. 89–127.

Letter from J. K. Homish [?] to W. W. Belknap. Keokuk, Iowa. March 8, 1877. A. L. S. 12 pp. Claims that the "Dakota Calendar" published by Mallery is really "A numerical exposition of the great doctrines of the sun religion."

4 pp. miscellaneous fragmentary notes on Dakota winter counts.

                                                        MS no. 2372

Manger, Alfred. "Fantasie on Sioux Indian Melodies." n.d. Photostat. 15 pp.

Manuscript musical score, with words of various Dakota songs (e.g., "Song of the Strong Heart Society" sung by Grey Hawk; theme song of a social dance, recorded by Bear).

Location of original unknown.

                                                        MS no. 4305

Michelson, Truman. Anthropometric measurements of a half-Dakota, half-Arapaho woman. [1927?]. A. D. 1 p.

MS no. 3353

Michelson, Truman. Anthropometric measurements of a half-Dakota, half-Cree woman. [1920s?]. A. D. 1 p.

MS no. 2081

Mooney, James. "The Indian Messiah and the Ghost Dance, with a Sketch of the Sioux Outbreak of 1890." 1894. T. and A. D. 866 pp. and 2 original drawings.

Published as "The Ghost Dance Religion and the Sioux Outbreak of 1890," BAE-AR 14 (Part II), Washington, D.C., 1896. Original drawings of Fig. 61, Kanakuk's heaven ($5\frac{1}{4}'' \times 3\frac{7}{8}''$) and Fig. 64, Smohalla's flag ($8'' \times 12''$).

MS no. 3249

Neave, James L. Letter to Major John W. Powell, BAE. Fort Berthold Agency, Dakota Terr. Oct. 29, 1881. A. L. S. 4 pp.

Reports on self-mutilation as a form of mourning for a deceased relative. Neave was agency physician at Fort Berthold Agency. Letter was written at the request of Dr. W. J. Hoffman.

MS no. 1521

Red Horse. Pictographic account of the Battle of the Little Big Horn, drawn by Red Horse, a Miniconjou Dakota. Cheyenne River Agency, Dakota Terr. 1881.

42 sheets, numbered 0–41 (no. 27 missing), approx. $24'' \times 36''$, drawn in pen, pencil, and colored pencil on paper resembling newsprint. 1 p. MS in Charles E. McChesney's handwriting summarizing subjects as follows: Sheet 0, Map of battleground; 1–5, Soldiers approaching village; 6–10, Indian village; 11–15, Indians charging soldiers; 16–20, Custer's column fighting; 21–25, Dead cavalry horses—Custer's; 26–30, Dead Sioux killed by Custer's column; 31–35, Dead Cavalry—Custer's column; 36–41, Indians leaving the battleground.

Collected by Charles E. McChesney, M.D., Acting Asst. Surgeon, U.S. Army, and forwarded with No. 2367-b (see McChesney, above) to Garrick Mallery. Sheets 0, 5, 8, 12, 16, 27 (now missing), 30, 32, 39, and 41 published by Mallery in "Picture Writing of the American Indians," BAE-AR 10, Washington, D.C., 1893, Plates 39–48.

MS no. 2367-a

Riggs, Alfred L. "Religion of the Dakotas." [1880s?]. A. D. S. 13 pp.

Discusses the sun dance, the "Wotahway," the Society of the Sacred Dance, and the "Toonkan."

MS no. 3453

Riggs, Stephen R. and Thomas L. Notes on Dakota culture. [1880s]. A. D. 20 slips and 3 newsclippings.

Siouan tribal divisions and migrations, 19 slips by Stephen R. Riggs, and one slip on Dakota linguistics by Thomas L. Riggs [utilized by J. Owen Dorsey in editing CNAE IX, S. R. Riggs' "Dakota Grammar, Texts, and Ethnography," Washington, D.C., 1893]. Clippings: 1880 Pine Ridge sun dance [printed with revisions in CNAE IX, pp. 229–32], myth of the dog, the old woman, and the pack [printed in BAE-AR 1, p. 589], "Are the Indians Wasting Away?" [printed with revisions in CNAE IX, p. 168].

MS no. 925

Roman Nose [?]. Ledger book filled with native Dakota drawings in pencil, ink, crayon, and water colors. [1866?]. 87 drawings on 74 L. ($12\frac{1}{2}'' \times 7\frac{3}{4}''$).

The drawings depict mainly war exploits, including fights with U.S. soldiers. They seem to be the work of more than one artist.

Inscription in the volume, by Samuel E. Strong, M.D., Desloge, St. Francis County, Missouri, Sept. 5, 1900, states that the drawings are the work of "Roman Nose, half brother of Red Cloud," and that after Roman Nose's capture in 1866 [?] he gave the book to Augustus Griffith of St. Genevieve County, Missouri, who in turn gave it to Strong. Captions under the drawings were made from the explanations of Charles C. White, or Fast Horse, Dakota interpreter at Pine Ridge but then (Dec. 21, 1889) employed with the Kickapoo Indian Medicine Co., Ironton, Iron County, Missouri.

MS no. 1303

Scott, Hugh Lenox. Notes on sign language and miscellaneous ethnographic notes. 4 boxes.

Much of this material is relevant to the Dakotas. Includes: miscellaneous notes on Dakota history, bands, and sign for "Dakota," A. D. approx. 100 pp. (Box 2); account of the Battle of the Little Big Horn by He Dog, Red Feather, and Whirling, A. D. 7 pp. (Box 3); The Custer Battle with the Sioux, A. D. 10 pp. (Box 3); notes on sign language in general, its history and distribution, A. and T. D. 1 box (Box 4).

MS no. 2932

Scott, Hugh Lenox. Papers accumulated while serving on the Board of Indian Commissioners, 1919–33. 5 boxes.

Includes reports from agencies: Cheyenne River Agency (1928) 5 pp., Fort Peck (1919–33) approx. 60 pp., Fort Totten (1924–26) 9 pp., Pine Ridge Agency (1924–32) approx. 45 pp., Standing Rock Agency (1919–32) approx. 70 pp. with album of photographs of Agency, and descriptive text, approx. 55 pp.; material on Dakota wars with U.S. Army, particularly the Custer battle, approx. 75 pp. with copy of William A. Graham's "Abstract of Record of the Proceedings of a Court of Inquiry in the Case of Major Marcus A. Reno, 7th Cavalry, Chicago, 1879," 1921, 145 pp.; signed statement of William Garnett regarding the death of Crazy Horse n.d. 21 pp. [published in mimeograph form by Fred Hackett, Chicago, Illinois ca. 1950?]; miscellaneous notes on "Sioux ethnography," approx. 20 pp.

MS no. 4525

Sitting Bull. Pictographic autobiographies of Sitting Bull and Jumping Bull ("The Kimball Record"). Drawn by Four Horns, 1870. 55 drawings on 54 L. Executed in ink and water colors. For history, description, and reproductions, see M. W. Stirling, "Three Pictographic Autobiographies of Sitting Bull," SMC v. 97, no. 5, Washington, D.C., 1938, pp. 3–34.

Letters from John P. Williamson. Fort Randall, Dakota Terr. Dec. 12, 1881. A. L. S. 2 pp. and 7 pp. "Index" describing each drawing. Also T. c.c. 5 pp. Miscellaneous T. notes by Stirling. 3 pp.

The drawings were originally mounted on sheets of paper. No. 54, thought missing in 1938 (cf. Stirling, p. 70), was discovered on the reverse of no. 53 when the whole series was unmounted and laminated in 1952.

MS no. 1929-a

Sitting Bull. Pictographic autobiography of Sitting Bull ("The Smith Record"), drawn by Sitting Bull. 1882. 22 drawings on 22 L. (8¼″ × 13¼″).

Executed in pencil, ink, crayon, and water colors, each sheet autographed. For history, description, and reproductions, see M. W. Stirling, "Three Pictographic Autobiographies of Sitting Bull," SMC v. 97, no. 5, Washington, D.C., 1938, pp. 25–48.

Letters from W. Tear. Fort Randall, Dakota Terr. Aug. 10 and Aug. 16, 1882. A. L. S. 2 pp. and A. L. S. 2 pp. enclosing 9 pp.

explanation of each drawing, as dictated by Sitting Bull. Also T. c.c. 8 pp. Mounted newsclippings about Sitting Bull, 15 pp.

MS no. 1929-b

Sitting Bull. Extracts from newsclippings about Sitting Bull. 20 pp.

From *Harper's Weekly*, July 29, 1876 (T. D. 10 pp. and c.c. 10 pp.), and the *St. Louis Globe-Democrat*, July 10, 1876 (MS D. 4 pp. and T. C. 1 p.), both regarding the "Kimball Record" (MS no. 1929-a).

Printed in M. W. Stirling, "Three Pictographic Autobiographies of Sitting Bull," SMC v. 97, no. 5, 1938, pp. 4–6.

"Relics of Sitting Bull," *Detroit Free Press*, ca. 1900. T. D. 3 pp.

"Sitting Bull's Pictures," *Daily Graphic*, N.Y., July 13, 1876. Photostat. 1 p.

MS no. 1929-c

Snider, G. L. "A Maker of Shavings," the life of Edward Forte, formerly 1st Sergeant, Troop "D", 7th Cavalry, U.S. Army, stationed at Standing Rock Agency, North Dakota; also miscellaneous notes and correspondence. 47 pp. and 4 photographs.

"A Maker of Shavings," by Snider, A. and T. D. S. 13 pp. with 2 pp. synopsis; statement by Forte, mainly regarding Sitting Bull, A. D. 4 pp.; letter from Forte to Frank B. Fiske, Oct. 25, 1932, A. L. S. 8 pp., regarding murder of Sitting Bull; miscellaneous notes by Snider, 10 pp.; miscellaneous correspondence, mainly regarding possible publication of Snider's MS, 1936, 10 pp.; two photographs of Edward Forte, 1931, 1932; one photograph each of Red Tomahawk and Mad Bear [1890s?] (both copyrighted by Fiske).

MS no. 4437

Sword, George. "Wanaǵi wacipi toranpi owicakiyakapi kin lee" ['This is what they say happens in the Ghost Dance']. Pine Ridge Agency, S. D. Dec. 7, 1891. T. D. 9 pp.

Copy of the original MS by Sword. Text in Lakota with diacritical marks and English title supplied in the handwriting of James Mooney. Printed in English in Mooney, "The Ghost Dance Religion," BAE-AR 14 (Part II), Washington, D.C., 1896, pp. 797–98.

Collected by Miss Emma C. Sickels, and copy obtained from her.

MS no. 936

Take-Way-from-Crow. Letter in Lakota to his sister-in-law, White Cow, Pine Ridge Agency, South Dakota. Stacyville, Iowa. March 1, 1890. A. L. S. 2 pp. and photostat copy 2 pp.

English translation 1 p. and miscellaneous correspondence 3 pp.
Letter collected by Edgar A. Mearns and given to Walter Hough.
Miscellaneous correspondence: Frederick W. Hodge to Truman
Michelson, Oct. 4, 1915, A. note; Michelson to Hodge, Nov. 2, 1915,
A. note S.; Hodge to Francis LaFlesche, Nov. 2, 1915, A. note S.;
LaFlesche to Hodge, Feb. 11, 1916, T. L. S., 1 p., enclosing 1 p.
free English translation of Take-Way-from-Crow's letter, made by
Joseph Black Spotted Horse and Louis Bordeaux.

MS no. 1748

Webb, H. G. "The Ghost lodge" and "Healing a Sick Woman."
June 6, 1894. Salt Lake City, Utah. A. D. 10 pp.
Note in J. Owen Dorsey's handwriting shows that these manu-
scripts were used in the preparation of his "A Study of Siouan
Cults," BAE-AR 11, Washington, D.C., 1894.

MS no. 1395

Webb, H. G. "The Dakota Sun Dance." Salt Lake City, Utah. June 6,
1894. A. D. 20 pp.
Description of the Oglala sun dance of 1883, obtained from
members of Little Wound's band of Oglalas.

MS no. 1394-a

Webb, H. G. "The Omaha Dance of the Oglalas." Salt Lake City,
Utah. Oct. 2, 1894. A. D. 7 pp.
Description of dance in Little Wound's band of Oglalas.

MS no. 1394-b

Witthoft, John. Description of Dakota [?] buffalo robe painted in
"border and box" design. 1954. c.c. T. D. 2 pp. and 1 photographic
print of line drawing of robe.
Tribal identification uncertain. Robe dates from first half of
nineteenth century and is the property of Robert E. Coppock,
Lancaster, Penn., on loan (1954) to the Pennsylvania State Museum.

MS no. 4424

AMERICAN MUSEUM OF NATURAL HISTORY. Department of Anthro-
pology. Central Park West at 79th St., New York, New York 10024.
R. DeMallie, July, 1968.
List of Dakota MS material in the Department of Anthropology:

Blish, Helen Heather. The Amos Bad Heart Buffalo Manuscript. A Native Pictographic Historical Record of the Oglala Dakota. 1934. T. D. 3 vols. with numerous photographs of original drawings.

Mekeel, H. Scudder. Dakota field notes, summer, 1930, and summer, 1931. White Clay District, Pine Ridge Reservation, South Dakota. T. D. 34 pp. and 72 pp.

Nines, Richard. Notes on the Dakota Indians, primarily on warrior and dancing societies. Pine Ridge Reservation, South Dakota. [Ca. 1900–1910]. T. D.

> Includes: introductory note, 2 pp.; notes on conversation with Woman's Dress, 9 pp.; Euptala or Miwatani, 5 pp.; Akitcita societies, 6 pp.; Tokala society, 5 pp.; notes from Iron Tail, 2 pp.; Blotaunka, 7 pp.; Tokala society, 4 pp.; notes from Thunder Bear, 2 pp.; notes from High Bear, 7 pp.; Bear Cult, 3 pp.; Elk Cult, 3 pp.; Omaha society, 4 pp.; Witcheska, 6 pp.; Omaha, Big Belly societies, 2 pp.; Witcheska, 2 pp.; Turnip digger, 1 p.; The Tanners, 1 p.; Silent Eaters, 1 p.; Night Dance, 1 p.; societies, 1 p.; Big Bellies, 2 pp.; Crow Owners, 2 pp.; Braves, 2 pp.; White Horse Owners, 4 pp.; Sun Dance notes from High Bear, 4 pp.; copies of Short Man's winter count, 1827–1913, and Iron Crow's winter count, 1785–1902, one envelope.
>
> This material forms the basis for the account of societies given in Clark Wissler, "Societies and Ceremonial Associations in the Oglala Division of the Teton-Dakota," AMNH-AP v. 11, no. 1, New York, 1912.

Walker, James R. "Dakota Texts and Translations." 1903–1916. 1 box.
> Main contents: "Mato Ihanblapi Oyakapi," 'Bear Visions Told,' by George Sword. Lakota text, T. D. 14 pp.; Lakota text with interlinear translation, T. D. 9 pp.
>
> "Ikce wicaśa Wakinyan oyakapi," 'Ordinary Men / Winged One / Relate They, [i.e., Lakota account of Wakinyan, the Winged God].' Lakota text, T. D. 5 pp.; Lakota text with interlinear English translation, T. D. 5 pp.
>
> List of Lakota names for animals. T. D. 2 pp.
>
> Lakota songs. T. D. 3 pp.
>
> "Mastincala Huśte" ['Lame Rabbit']. A. D. by Walker. 6 pp.
>
> Lakota text by George Sword concerning the sun dance. Revision by Charles Nines. A. D. 140 pp. with interlinear translation. Free

translation, A. D. by Walker, 22 pp. Introduction in English, T. D. 2 pp.

"Itazipa wakan tawicahan oyakapi," by Sword. Lakota text, A. D. 30 pp.; two free translations "The Revealing of the Mystical Healing Power to the People by the Medicine Man as Seen by Him. The Holy Bow," MS D. 15 pp., T. D. 11 pp.

"The Story of How to Make Indian Soldiers," by Sword. Lakota text, A. D. 12 pp.; two translations, MS D. 6 pp., T. D. 5 pp.

"During War, How the Wounded Were Healed with Medicines," by Sword. Lakota text, A. D. 14 pp.; two free translations, A. D. by Walker, 7 pp. and T. D. 6 pp. Note by Walker, T. D. S. 1 p. States that Sword was paid $2.00 for writing the original, and Clarence Three Stars was paid 15 cents per page for rewriting and translating it (total $2.10).

"Iktomi," by Sword [?]. Lakota text, MS D. 13 pp. and note, T. D. 1 p.

Walker, James R. "Notes on the Dakota Indians, Pine Ridge, S. D." [Ca. 1898–1916.] Main contents:

Notes on Oglala customs and ceremonies from Sword, Tyon, Little Wound, and Short Bull. T. D. 13 pp.

Notes on mythology and religious beliefs, from Tyon, Garnett, Thunderbear, Sword, and Blunt Horn. T. D. 18 pp. numbered 56–74.

Hunka Lowam [*sic:* Hunka Lowan]. Lakota text. T. D. 34 pp.

Notes on Sioux from published sources, checked with Indians. T. D. 7 pp.

Wakan, told by Little Wound. T. D. 3 pp.

Tatanka Lowanpi, a Ceremony. T. D. 19 pp.

Interview with Finger, concerning Calf Pipe. T. D. 4 pp. numbered 7–10.

Calf Pipe. T. D. 5 pp. numbered 75–79.

Hanbleceya, by Thunder Bear. T. D. 9 pp. numbered 80–88.

Diagram of Hunka lodge with explanation by Antoine Herman. MS D. 2 pp.

Letter from Walker to Clark Wissler. Feb. 7, 1912. T. L. S. 3 pp. Concerns Teton Dakota religion.

Order of camping of various bands. T. D. 2 pp. numbered 6–7.

Notes on religion, sacred pipe. T. D. 6 pp. numbered 2–7.

Iktomi. T. D. 2 pp.

The Four Winds, told by Red Rabbit. T. D. 4 pp. numbered 48–51.

Notes on religion from Short Feather. June 6, 1898. T. D. 3 pp.

Wakan tanka, told by Good-seat. T. D. 3 pp. numbered 8–11.

Associations among the Oglala Sioux, told by Tyon and John Blunt Horn. T. D. 7 pp. numbered 89–95.

Dakota pipes. T. D. 22 pp. numbered 37–58.

Hunka ceremony, by Sword. T. D. 29 pp. numbered 159–87.

MS on Hunka by Walker. Three drafts, T. D. 33 pp., 24 pp. and 58 pp.

Letter from Walker to Wissler. March 21, 1912, enclosing Hunka MS. T. L. S. and T. D. 34 pp.

Walker, James R. "The Sun Dance and Other Ceremonies of the Pine Ridge Indians," by Thomas Tyon. Ca. 1912.

Lakota text, with interlinear translation by Walker. 23 pp.

Notes by Charles Nines concerning warrior societies and ceremonies. 15 pp.

Walker, James R. Notes on the Oglala Dakotas. 1 envelope.

Main contents: Tokala society, by George Sword. T. D. 11 pp. and 1 p. note.

Bear songs, by Sword. Mimeographed, 3 pp. and 1 p. note.

Associations among the Oglalas, told by Tyon and Blunt Horn. T. D. 4 pp.

The wizard and his wife. T. D. 13 pp.

Wakan Tanka, told by Good-seat. 4 pp.

Hanbleceya. 9 pp. numbered 80–88.

Spirit Pipe, by Sword. T. D. 6 pp.

Wissler, Clark. Notes on the Dakota Indians. [1903]. 1 box.

"Field Notes on the Dakota Indians. Collected on Museum Expedition of 1902." c.c. T. D. 198 pp.

Notes on the Hunka ceremony. c.c. T. D. 13 pp.

2 colored drawings by Thunder Bear, Oglala. 1903.

24 colored drawings by Thunder Bear and George Sword of body paints and costumes of sun dance and various ceremonies and warrior societies. 1903.

Letter from Mrs. Elliot L. Bow (née Pfanner) to Wissler. June 17, 1932. Encloses two Dakota stories: Iktomi, prairie chickens and wolf; and Woman who lived with the wolves, an anecdote. One story dated Feb. 11, 1909. MS D. 15 pp., T. c. 7 pp.

AMERICAN PHILOSOPHICAL SOCIETY. 105 South Fifth Street, Philadelphia, Pennsylvania 19106.

The MS material relating to the Dakotas in the Society's Library is listed in detail in *A Guide to Manuscripts Relating to the American Indian in the Library of the American Philosophical Society* by John F. Freeman and Murphy D. Smith, Philadelphia, 1966. Most of the Dakota MSS in the APS are the work of Ella C. Deloria, ca. 1920s–1930s.

ASSUMPTION COLLEGE. Richardton, North Dakota. Rev. Louis Pfaller, O.S.B., Archivist.

The College archives include the following MS collection pertaining to the Dakotas:

McLaughlin, James. Personal papers. Ca. 1870s–1920s[?]. Approx. 20,000 pp.

A large portion of the collection relates to McLaughlin's activities as Indian Agent at Devil's Lake and Standing Rock reservations. It will be supplemented by microfilm copies of McLaughlin material in other repositories.

Rev. Pfaller plans to have the whole collection microfilmed and to publish a descriptive guide.

STATE HISTORICAL SOCIETY OF COLORADO. Colorado State Museum, E. 14th Avenue and Sherman, Denver, Colorado, 80203. Mrs. Enid T. Thompson.

List of Dakota MS material in the Society's Library:

Spencer, Lebbeus Foster. Papers collected while serving as U.S. Indian Agent. Rosebud Agency, South Dakota. Sept., 1886–Sept., 1889. Approx. 1,200 pp.

Includes originals and copies of correspondence relating to administrative affairs at Rosebud Agency; will of Spotted Tail, Jr.; a winter count; miscellaneous newspaper clippings; 76 original photographs, by various photographers.

Walker, James R. Papers relating to researches among the Dakotas while serving as agency physician. Pine Ridge Reservation, South Dakota. Ca. 1895–1915. Over 1,000 pp.

Includes copy of No Ears's winter count; ethnological notes from Seven Rabbits, Thunder Bear, George Sword, and others; several incomplete drafts of a collection of Dakota myths; material on the sun dance; autobiography and miscellaneous texts written in Lakota by George Sword, some with translations; text in Lakota on the sun dance by Thomas Tyon, with interlinear and free translations; several vocabularies and lists of personal names; anthropometric and vital statistics on Oglala and mixed-blood individuals.

Much of the collection consists of repetitive partial copies, and duplicates other copies in the American Museum of Natural History, New York (q.v.).

ROBERT H. LOWIE MUSEUM OF ANTHROPOLOGY. Kroeber Hall, University of California, Berkeley, California 94720. Frank A. Norick, Museum Anthropologist.

The Museum possesses no MS material relevant to the Dakota, but does have the following pertinent material:

Films:

The Calumet: The Pipe of Peace. 821'. Time: 23 min. Copyright 1964. Includes material on Dakota pipe manufacturing.

Pounding choke cherries. 400'.

Sound tapes:

Blackfoot and Sioux sign languages. 2,400'.

Sioux and Ojibway Songs. 1,200'.

Sioux and Ojibway Ceremonies. 600'.

Sioux Sign Language. 1,200'.

Pipe Ceremony. 600'.

Brule Sioux Songs. 600'.

Story of the First Pipe. 500'.

MINNESOTA HISTORICAL SOCIETY. St. Paul, Minnesota.

The society's extensive manuscript holdings relating to the Dakotas are listed in *Chippewa and Dakota Indians: A Subject Catalog of Books, Pamphlets, Periodical Articles, and Manuscripts in the Minnesota Historical Society*, published by the Minnesota Historical Society, 1969.

MUSEUM OF THE AMERICAN INDIAN. Heye Foundation, Broadway at 155th Street, New York, New York 10032. Dr. Frederick J. Dockstader, Director.

List of Dakota MS material in the Museum Archives:

Densmore, Frances. Data pertaining to her collection of Dakota artifacts.

Published in part in *Indian Notes and Monographs*, v. XI, no. 3, New York, 1948.

Gilmore, Melvin. Notes on Siouan ethnobotany. 1910–11.

Harrington, M. R. Data on Dakota collections. 1909–15.

McGillycuddy, Valentine T. Letter to W. T. Sherman. 1884.

Skinner, Alanson. Data on collections gathered from several Dakota tribes. Ca. 1915.

Smith, DeCost. Lakota vocabularies. Standing Rock Reservation, North Dakota. Ca. 1884.

Wildschut, William. Data on Dakota collections. 1910–12.

In addition the Museum also possesses many specimen catalogues, some of which include brief data (occasionally with Dakota names of items).

NEBRASKA STATE HISTORICAL SOCIETY. 1500 R Street, Lincoln, Nebraska 68508. Douglas A. Bakken, Archivist.

The Archives of the Society contain a large volume of material relating to the Dakotas, particularly to the Indian wars, and Indian-white contact during the last half of the nineteenth century. An on-going series of *Bulletins* entitled "A Guide to the Archives and Manuscripts of the Nebraska State Historical Society" describes the collection. To date three numbers have been published: no. 1, 1965, and no. 2, 1966, edited by William F. Schmidt, and no. 3, 1967, edited by Douglas Bakken.

STATE HISTORICAL SOCIETY OF NORTH DAKOTA. Liberty Memorial Building. Bismarck, North Dakota 58501. Craig A. Gannon, Librarian.

A partial listing of the MS material in the Library of the Historical Society was printed in *North Dakota History*, v. 30, no. 1, Jan. 1963, pp. 17–61.

The Society's holdings concern mostly local history; material on the Dakotas relates mainly to Standing Rock Reservation.

The MS collection is at present being recatalogued more accurately and fully, much material having previously been uncatalogued.

SIOUX INDIAN MUSEUM AND CRAFT CENTER. P. O. Box 1504, Rapid City, South Dakota 57701. Miss Ella C. Lebow, Director.

The Museum possesses the following MS relating to the Dakotas:

Deloria, Ella C. "Study, Sioux Indian Exhibit and Crafts Center. Commissioned by the Indian Arts and Crafts Board." June 20, 1960.

Part 1. Written Dakota.

Part 2. Alphabetical listing of types of artifacts in the Sioux Indian Museum. In book form and on index cards. 260 entries.

Part 3. Informal commentary. Dakota tribal organization and dialects; discussion of various artifacts listed in Part 2.

SOUTH DAKOTA STATE HISTORICAL SOCIETY. Pierre, South Dakota 57501. Will G. Robinson, Secretary.

Partial listing of Dakota MS material in the Society's library:

Collins, Mary C. Several manuscripts, including: "Practical Suggestions on Indian Affairs," "Sioux Church and Missionary, Brown Earth Church," "Notes on Origin of Rain in the Face and Sitting Bull," and "Little Eagle's Death."

Hare, William H. Correspondence and miscellaneous MS material pertaining to Bishop Hare.

Riggs, Thomas L. "Stories about Rev. T. L. Riggs."

Shoots Walking. Affidavit on the death of Sitting Bull.

The foregoing is to indicate the nature of the Society's holdings; a complete list of MS material pertaining to the Dakotas is in preparation.

UNITED STATES NATIONAL ARCHIVES. Washington, D.C. 20408.

MS material relating to the Dakotas will be found largely in the following Record Groups: 48, Department of the Interior; 75, Office of Indian Affairs; 94, Adjutant General's Office; 98, United States Army Commands; 111, Office of the Chief Signal Officer (photographs).

The following publications of the Government Printing Office will be of use in locating material:

Guide to the Records in the National Archives. 1948.

List of National Archives Microfilm Publications. 1966.

Cartographic Records of the Office of the Secretary of the Interior. Preliminary Inventory Number 81. Compiled by Laura E. Kelsay. 1955.

Records of the Bureau of Indian Affairs. Preliminary Inventory Number *163*. 2 vols. Compiled by Edward E. Hill. 1965.

List of Documents Concerning the Negotiation of Ratified Indian Treaties *1801–1869*. Special List No. 6. Compiled by John H. Martin. 1949.

List of Cartographic Records of the Bureau of Indian Affairs. Special List Number 13. Compiled by Laura E. Kelsay. 1954.

Records of the Office of the Chief Signal Officer. Preliminary Inventory Number *155*. Compiled by Mabel E. Deutrich. 1963.

UNIVERSITY OF MISSOURI LIBRARY. Joint Collection Western Historical Manuscript Collection, State Historical Manuscript Collection, State Historical Society Manuscripts. Columbia, Missouri. Mrs. Nancy C. Prewitt, Assistant Director.

The University Library possesses one MS collection relevant to the Dakotas:

Neihardt, John G. Papers, 1893–1959.

Includes: Family correspondence, 1896–1958, 52 folders; general correspondence, 1896–1959, 57 folders; MSS 1905–50, 121 folders; notes and references, 34 folders; miscellaneous, 28 folders; pictures, 20 folders; tape recordings of *Cycle of the West*, 50 reels; video tape of "Song of the Indian Wars."

Of particular interest are correspondence and interview notes from Black Elk, an Oglala Dakota shaman, which form the basis of Neihardt's *Black Elk Speaks*, New York, 1932.

Written permission from Dr. Neihardt is required for the use of these papers.

UNIVERSITY OF NEBRASKA LIBRARY. Lincoln, Nebraska 68508. Frederic S. La Croix, Assistant Librarian.

The Social Studies Division of the University Library possesses the following MS material on the Dakotas:

Blish, Helen Heather. The Amos Bad Heart Bull manuscript; a native pictographic historical record of the Oglala Dakota. M.A. thesis, University of Nebraska. 1928. Cat. no. 378.782 UOb111.

Holmgren, Philip S. Sioux and white relations. Ph.D. dissertation, University of Nebraska. 1950. Uncatalogued.

Marley, Everett Leslie. History of Pine Ridge Indian Reservation. M.A. thesis, University of Nebraska. 1935. Uncatalogued.

Index

345